THE MEDICO-LEGAL LIBRARY FROM WILEY LAW PUBLICATIONS

AIDS and the Law
William H.L. Dornette

Emergency Medicine Malpractice
Scott M. Lewis

Handling Birth Trauma Cases (two volumes)
Stanley S. Schwartz and Norman D. Tucker

OB/GYN Malpractice
Scott M. Lewis

Plastic Surgery Malpractice and Damages
Jeffrey D. Robertson and William T. Keavy

Psychiatric Malpractice
Jeffrey D. Robertson

The Right to Die
Alan Meisel

PLASTIC SURGERY MALPRACTICE AND DAMAGES

PLASTIC SURGERY MALPRACTICE AND DAMAGES

JEFFREY D. ROBERTSON, Esquire

Member of the Bar
of the State of New York

Partner
in the national law firm of
Wilson, Elser, Moskowitz, Edelman & Dicker

WILLIAM T. KEAVY, M.D., J.D.

WILEY

Wiley Law Publications

JOHN WILEY & SONS

New York • Chichester • Brisbane • Toronto • Singapore

ISBN 0-471-60831-9

Printed in the United States of America

10 9 8 7 6 5 4 3 2 1

To my mother, Irene Keavy,
Whose wit and wisdom,
Candor and caring,
Have made all the difference.

W.T.K.

This book is lovingly dedicated to my father,
Arnold Robertson, who has always tried so hard.

J.D.R.

PREFACE

> Please Time, not now
> Don't lay your clammy hand
> Upon my brow
> Don't wither my fair skin
> Don't streak my hair with gray
> I'll give you all I own
> If you go away
> And come to claim my youth
> Another day
>
> Agnes Robertson, "Time Not Now"
> The Me Inside of Me (Gull Books, 1987)

Americans in record numbers have been giving "all they own" to postpone that day of reckoning. Plastic surgery, both reconstructive and cosmetic, has become the fastest growing medical specialty in the United States during this decade. Well over one million operations are performed every year with such exotic sounding names as rhinoplasty, liposuction, blepharoplasty, and rhytidectomy. From 1981 to 1984 there was a 61 percent increase in plastic surgery procedures according to the American Society of Plastic and Reconstructive Surgeons. But this relentless search for the fountain of youth is no longer the domain of only the rich and famous. Patients from all walks and economic levels of life are searching for that beauty which only God can bestow or Hollywood create. For example, according to the American Society of Plastic and Reconstructive Surgeons only 19 percent of the patients having cosmetic surgery in 1982 had incomes that exceeded $50,000. In fact 39 percent had incomes between $15,000 and $20,000 and 29 percent had incomes that range between $25,000 and $50,000. Men in increasing numbers have now challenged the old axiom that "vanity thy name is woman." In 1984 men accounted for 25 percent of the rhinoplasties performed, 14 percent of the blepharoplasties and 10 percent of the face-lifts.

A myriad of factors has contributed to this trend including vanity, self-esteem, career advancement, peer acceptance, employment pressures, and of course the media's promotion of perfection. Plastic surgery has become an option that is within the reach of almost all Americans. In many cities, clinics provide the quid pro quo of experience for their young residents in exchange for cosmetic procedures for the poor.

But the insatiable desire to look younger has been fueled more by advertising than by vanity in recent years. One plastic surgeon recently took out a full page ad in the New York Times to explain "a few reasons why plastic surgeons are the most popular doctors in America." He answered his own question by displaying pictures of beautiful models with captions such as "prettier noses, fuller breasts, flatter stomachs." The physician-entrepreneur even offered a free booklet "Everything you always wanted to know about plastic surgery."[1]

But with this democratization of plastic surgery has also come a proliferation in malpractice lawsuits. A decade ago, the chance for a plaintiff to succeed in a vanity or cosmetic suit might have seemed slim. But today juries are much more sophisticated and sympathetic. They will hold the doctors to the same standard of care as for an operation prompted by a medical necessity. Verdicts have escalated dramatically especially for misplaced anatomical parts, loss of sexual function and sensation, and psychological overlay.

An example of the escalation of damages can be seen in this 1989 newspaper caption reporting that "Actor's $10 million suit says Doc wiped dimples from his face." The plaintiff was a New York actor who brought a $10 million suit against a plastic surgeon claiming that the defendant went too far in nipping and tucking more than he wanted. He claimed that his face meant dimples to people who cast TV commercials and that his employment provided him with a substantial income until the defendant caused him to lose his left dimple following a mini face-lift to tighten jowls he was developing. He allegedly told the surgeon how important the dimples were and was assured they would be safe. However, the surgery caused him to lose his all-American look and he could no longer find employment. In his lawsuit he sued for breach of contract, lack of informed consent, and negligence, but the defendant said that he gave the plaintiff no guarantees and fully advised him of the risks of plastic surgery.[2]

This book discusses the fascinating history of this specialty in the context of understanding both the physician and the patient. The book is divided into sections addressing both the legal and medical aspects of plastic and reconstructive surgery in both malpractice and personal injury litigation. Dr. William Keavy, a Board Certified Plastic and Reconstructive Surgeon with a law degree, addresses the medical aspects of the most common types of cosmetic procedures such as rhinoplasty, blepharoplasty, breast reduction and augmentation, and rhytidectomy. Dr. Frederick Lukash, a Board Certified Plastic Surgeon, has written a concise but comprehensive chapter on the medical aspects of reconstructive surgery such as cleft lip, ear deformities, burns, and scars.

---

[1] N.Y. Times, Sept. 11, 1989, at B7.

[2] N.Y. Post, Aug. 30, 1989, at 7.

The book is designed both for the plaintiff and defense bar as well as for physicians who seek to practice good risk management or who survive the turmoil of litigation directed against them.

An in-depth profile is drawn of the typical vanity patient who brings a lawsuit. Understanding this special type of plaintiff is essential for the physician who treats her or him and the lawyer who represents or defends against her or him. Social issues that may affect jury selection, such as advertising and the inherent competitiveness between various specialties that characterize the practitioners of this unique art, are presented. Has the profession become too crass and commercial? Will the ubiquitous advertising become its Achilles Heel? Is this sculpture of the living or seduction of the gullible? A complete analysis of the trial techniques necessary to master the plastic surgery case is presented together with trial transcripts annotated with comments and suggestions. Model depositions of other plastic surgery cases are also provided to assist both the novice and the experienced trial lawyer. The overriding theme of the book is to present a practical guide for the trial lawyer or physician who finds herself involved in litigation involving plastic surgery as an issue of damages or liability. A glossary of key medical terms is provided as well as an appendix of sample interrogatories and complaints. Many medical illustrations are presented in the medical chapters.

The plastic surgery case will become one of the most common malpractice trials of the future thanks in part to the advertising frenzy of the medical profession and the increasing expectations of the public. Not only will the juries be awarding dollars for the physical scars and unfavorable results of surgery but will be compensating the psychological scars as well. Both the plaintiff and defense attorney must understand this potential for large verdicts since the public as well as the patient seeks to recapture lost youth or self confidence. As we tend to live longer thanks to today's medicine, we will also empathize more with the poet who wrote:

> There are two of me
> And I am afraid . . .
> I don't know the other me . . .
> I know the young and eager girl
> Just reaching out to life
> But there is the other
> She is looking at me
> From the glass
> In the windows that I pass
> Who is this creature with graying hair
> And skin no longer young and fair?
> I cry out! . . . I am not she! . . . I am Me

I want to hide . . . I want to run
But the creature that I fear
Ever close and ever near
Just follows . . . and
Lies in wait
To swallow me.

Fanny Gersten, There are Two of Me

For the lawyer who doesn't prepare carefully, the jury will also be the one to fear and the creature "ever close and ever near . . ."

We hope that our book will help you in your quest for perfection in the presentation of your case.

New York, New York
November, 1989

JEFFREY D. ROBERTSON
WILLIAM T. KEAVY, M.D.

ACKNOWLEDGMENTS

This book would never have been possible without the help of many people who have assisted us in its preparation. Coauthor Robertson acknowledges the love, nurturing, and endless hours of work of Debra DeMarchena. Without her attention to detail and unspoken support, both as a lawyer and a friend, especially when times were tough, the manuscript never would have been complete.

We also wish to thank our editor, Mary Hope, for her expertise and support. Coauthor Robertson thanks his partners Tom Wilson, John Elser, Harold Moskowitz, Tom Hyland, and of course Herbert Dicker. Without Mr. Dicker's support and encouragement this project never could have been realized.

Coauthor Keavy would like to express his special thanks and appreciation to Hilda Frutig, who assists him unfailingly in his daily endeavors, and to Christine Gagnon, whose help in assembling and typing these chapters was indispensable. He also acknowledges the talent and creativity of John De Amicis in his illustrations and thanks him for always meeting an impossible deadline.

We also wish to thank Dr. Lukash for his contribution on reconstructive surgery.

J.D.R.
W.T.K.

ABOUT THE AUTHORS

Jeffrey D. Robertson is a partner in the national law firm of Wilson, Elser, Moskowitz, Edelman & Dicker and is a recognized specialist and trial lawyer in all phases of medical malpractice and health law.

Mr. Robertson is the author of *Psychiatric Malpractice,* published by Wiley Law Publications and co-author of *The Psychiatric Malpractice Manual* and *The Medical Malpractice Manual,* both published by Federal Publications; and *Direct and Cross Examination of the Orthopedic Expert* by Professional Education Systems Inc. He is currently the editor-in-chief of *Medical Malpractice: Law and Strategy,* a national monthly publication of the New York and National Law Journal, which carries his monthly column, "Off the Record." He is also co-editor of *Risk Management for Nurse Practitioners,* a national newsletter by Cotterell, Mitchell, and is a contributing editor to the *Annual Review of Clinical Psychiatry & The Law,* published by the American Psychiatric Press.

Mr. Robertson, who is a member of the bars of the State of New York, the United States District Court, and who is admitted to practice before the United States Court of Appeals, is a member of numerous bar associations, an extensive lecturer, seminar faculty member, and network television and radio guest in the area of medical malpractice.

Dr. William T. Keavy has been practicing plastic and reconstructive surgery in New York City and Stamford, Connecticut, for 15 years. He has received his bachelor of arts degree at Fairfield University, majoring in English and philosophy. He went on to his premedical studies at Georgetown University and received an M.D. degree from Marquette University School of Medicine.

After internship and a general surgery residency in New York, he specialized in plastic surgery. Having done his formal training with Dr. D. McCullagh Mayer at the Medical College of New Jersey, he did preceptor fellowships with Dr. John Converse at New York University School of Medicine; the Plastic Surgery Center and Burn Unit at East Grinstead, Sussex, England, and in Rio de Janeiro with Dr. Ivo Pitanguy.

He has traveled throughout the world lecturing and demonstrating surgical techniques. In addition to his practice in the United States, he operates in Rome, Italy, and is consultant to the Soviet Union for his specialty.

Dr. Keavy is conversant in six foreign languages. He was recently graduated from the Fordham University School of Law with a J.D. degree. His interest in law is academic, and he plans to continue his practice in plastic and reconstructive surgery.

ABOUT THE CONTRIBUTOR

Dr. Frederick Lukash is a plastic and reconstructive surgeon certified by the American Board of Plastic Surgery and the American Board of General Surgery. He is a Fellow in the American College of Surgeons. He is an active member in the American Society of Plastic and Reconstructive Surgery, the American Society of Maxillofacial Surgery, the American Society of Head and Neck Surgery, the International Microsurgical Society, the American Association of Hand Surgery, and the prestigious Plastic Surgery Research Council. Dr. Lukash has multiple publications to his credit including a landmark article on lower extremity reconstruction in the *New England Journal of Medicine* and an article on functional jaw reconstruction in the *American Journal of Plastic and Reconstructive Surgery.* Dr. Lukash also holds a patent for a device that monitors blood flow in microsurgical operations. In addition to his large cosmetic surgery practice, Dr. Lukash enjoys a special interest and expertise in pediatric plastic surgery.

Dr. Lukash is an assistant clinical professor of surgery at the State University of New York Stony Brook and is in private practice in Manhasset, New York.

SUMMARY CONTENTS

DETAILED CONTENTS

PART I

LEGAL ISSUES

CHAPTER 1

INTRODUCTION

§ 1.1 An Overview

It has been said that "a plastic surgeon does not simply alter a man's face. He alters the man's inner self. The incisions he makes are more than skin deep. They frequently cut deep into the psyche as well."[1] It is this element of psychic as well as physical damages that gives the plastic surgery malpractice case great potential monetary value. Million dollar verdicts are not uncommon in both reconstructive and cosmetic surgery cases. Whether a malpractice case or one arising out of a personal injury, jurors are often deeply touched by the psychological scars that even time cannot erase.

Plastic surgery has become the fastest growing medical specialty of this decade. From 1981 through 1984 cosmetic procedures increased by more than 50 percent. In 1985, over half a million patients went under the plastic surgeon's scalpel. No one foresaw this extraordinary growth in plastic surgery when surgeons pioneered reconstructive surgery during the First and Second World Wars. Today, cosmetic surgery is a booming market with some three million Americans having their tummies tucked, chins trimmed, and faces lifted each year.[2]

For the lawyer who is either prosecuting or defending a plastic surgery case, a thorough knowledge of both cosmetic and reconstructive surgical procedures is essential. The dichotomy between the malpractice case and the personal injury lawsuit must also be appreciated. In the former, the surgeon is the plaintiff's antagonist. In the latter, she is the ally. In the cosmetic malpractice case, plaintiffs have a more difficult burden of proof

[1] M. Maltz, *Psycho-Cybernetics* in *Beauty by Whose Standards?*, F. Simon (ed.), Chocolate Singles, May 1987, at page 11.

[2] *Cosmetic Surgery: Is it for you?*, Readers Digest, July 1987, at page 67. *See also* Hughes, *Body Not Perfect*, The Wall Street Journal, August 2, 1988, at page 1, col. 3.

than that required by law because the jury is skeptical of the motives for surgery and the damages claimed. However, in personal injury cases involving reconstructive surgery, there is a natural residual sympathy that inures to the plaintiff.

The danger for the plaintiff in the cosmetic case is that she or he may be seen as an egotistical patient who is seeking a beauty that only God can bestow or Hollywood create. But in the last decade many different social segments of our society have come to accept the idea of improving one's looks. Vanity has fueled the cosmetic surgery revolution as patients unabashedly ask their surgeons to repeal the years or correct what they see as nature's flaws. On the other hand, some surgeons, in a frenzy of competitive zeal, often seduce patients with unrealistic promises. Some surgeons may even lack the necessary skill or experience. One need not be board-certified or even eligible in order to practice plastic surgery. Many different specialists such as dermatologists, otolaryngologists, and opthalmologists, and general surgeons perform plastic surgery.

Damages in personal injury cases involving plastic surgery have escalated dramatically over the past two decades. Twenty years ago, for example, a jury awarded little Brent Wicker only $10,000 for very serious facial injuries sustained in an auto accident. His nose and upper lip were so lacerated that "a side of his nose flapped and turned up towards his forehead and over the other eye."[3] His plastic surgeon testified that, even if he had Z-plasty surgery to minimize scarring, he would always have a permanent injury. Today such a case would probably be worth several hundred thousand dollars. In a 1985 case, the court awarded $5 million to a 4-year-old girl who suffered extensive burns over her body when her flannel pajama shirt ignited.[4]

Other personal injury cases involving plastic surgery damages are summarized in the *Personal Injury Verdict Reporter.* These include burns caused by household products, farm utensils, butane lighters, gas explosions, surgical equipment, and hairdresser negligence; auto accident lacerations; and dog bite lacerations.

§ 1.2 History of Plastic Surgery

The history of plastic surgery can be traced to ancient times. The first accounts of skin grafting appear in the sacred book of the Hindus. Cheek and forehead flaps were used in nasal reconstruction in Egyptian and Indian civilizations. According to one historian,

> [i]t has been said that every human being has the divine right to look human . . . [but] many people believe it is their human right to look divine.

---

[3] Wicker v. U.S. Fidelity, 211 So. 2d 420 (La. 1968).

[4] Nelson v. F.W. Woolworth, Madison, WI, U.S. Dist. Ct. No. 81-6-643-5 (1984).

> No wonder that the history of plastic surgery is almost as old as the story of mankind!
> It's a far cry from the kohl pots of old Egypt to modern plastic surgery; but the thousands of years in between represent an unbroken search for physical perfection.[5]

The Greeks were well known for performing surgery on many congenital anomalies. Galen, in the second century, wrote of techniques for restoring lost portions of the lips, ears, and nostrils. In the sixteenth century the Italian physician Tagliacozzi performed a procedure in which he would take skin from the arm to build a new nose and lip in what became known as the "Italian method." In 1597 he published perhaps the oldest book on plastic surgery entitled *De Churigia Curtorum per Institunem.* Thereafter, plastic surgery lagged until Carpue, an Englishman, revived Indian reconstructive methods in the eighteenth century. But Europe and America were slow to pioneer plastic surgery procedures. Ericksen, the leading surgeon of his day, wrote in the 1860s that plastic surgery was only a reconstructive process by which "mutilations are repaired and loss of structure replaced."[6] The major procedures described were blepharoplasty and nose and lip flap. No elective cosmetic or vanity surgery was even contemplated. In fact, the most common calling for the European plastic surgeon was as an official dueling surgeon, perhaps similar to today's football team physician. According to Ericksen,

> The most remarkable instances of this kind are those related by Dr. Hoffacher. Dr. Hoffacher was officially appointed to attend as surgeon at the duels which were at one time frequent amongst the students at Heidelberg, and, as at these encounters broad-swords were used, he had an opportunity of seeing a considerable number of incised wounds, and has related no less than 16 cases in which portions of the nose, lips, or chin, had been sliced off, and being put on again, contracted adhesions. Amongst the most remarkable of these, is a case in which the end of the nose was sliced off by a cut with the broad-sword, and fell under a chest of drawers; it was not found for some time, but on being recovered and washed, was stitched on, when it became firmly attached. In another instance, a dog that was in the room snapped up the detached portion of the organ as it fell to the ground, but the nose being immediately taken out of the animal's mouth and put on again, became firmly fixed![7]

The emergence of plastic surgery in the United States can be traced back to the efforts to repair the traumatic war injuries of World War I. But few surgeons centered their practice on plastic surgery. As one physician historian noted:

---

[5] J.W. Maliniak, Sculpture in the Living 21 (1934).

[6] Ericksen, The Science & Art of Surgery 692 (1860).

[7] *Id.* at 692–93.

In the years after the war, the practice of plastic surgery was different from what it is today. Very few qualified plastic surgeons practiced in the United States and patients were referred from many miles away for treatment. Most surgery was reconstructive, although treating head and neck cancer and correcting congenital deformities formed a considerable portion of plastic surgeons' endeavors. The most frequent cosmetic operation was rhinoplasty; face lifts were rare. Reduction mammoplasty was not done. An occasional augmentation with fat grafts was reported but long-lasting results were usually disappointing. Occasionally, these early plastic surgeons saw a patient who had received paraffin injections to smooth out wrinkles or possibly to build up a depressed nasal bridge, with devastating results. Then as now, as in all fields of medicine and surgery, charlatans and quacks attempted to exploit the public.

* * *

The training period usually lasted three to five years. When the new plastic surgeon established an individual practice in a new city, other physicians often had to be educated about this new specialty and what it offered. To become known, plastic surgeons tried to get on the programs of city, county, or state medical societies, sometimes putting up exhibits to show what they could do. Early referrals were usually patients the referring physician wanted to get rid of, or those who were too poor to pay a professional fee, or were unable to get admitted to a hospital. Plastic surgeons faced problems they had not encountered during training and often had no one to call on for consultation or advice.[8]

§ 1.3 Conclusion

Today Americans accept cosmetic surgery as a means to improve the quality of life. The medical fraternity proudly views elective cosmetic surgery as a legitimate way to heal people. In our narcissistic culture, procedures with such exotic sounding names as rhinoplasty, rhytidectomy, blepharoplasty, mammoplasty, and lipectomy have become household words.

In **Chapters 2** and **3** the psychology, strategy, and techniques of trying the cosmetic case are explored. In **Part II** a medical primer on the most common types of cosmetic surgical procedures is presented. In **Part III** a medical survey of the major reconstructive surgical cases is provided for the attorney. The trials and depositions in a reconstructive surgical case are analyzed in **Part IV**.

For the lawyer who is going to undertake a cosmetic vanity suit, the next two chapters provide an introduction and insight into the patient and the physician who will confront each other in the courtroom.

---

[8] W.G. Hamm, M.D., *The Development of Plastic Surgery During the Past Sixty Years,* 12 Annals of Plastic Surgery, at 102–04 (Feb. 1984).

CHAPTER 2

COSMETIC SURGERY

§ 2.1 Dichotomy of Expectations

Elective cosmetic surgery is unique among all medical specialties. It is sculpture of the living. It is magic. It is mysterious. It is also unnecessary. No one needs a face-lift or an aquiline nose or a buxom bosom to survive. Unlike reconstructive plastic surgery, which is performed to restore a measure of normality, cosmetic surgery has been called a frivolous luxury. According to one expert commentator,

> [i]t is elective, expensive indulgence in self-approval. What's more, it is subject to misuse, disappointment and disaster. Follow-up operations to correct the errors of previous surgery are prevalent enough to occupy a two volume 1,134 page reference work entitled "The Unfavorable Result in Plastic Surgery."[1]

As the number of plastic procedures has increased, so have malpractice lawsuits. Patients claim breasts don't match, eyes won't close, noses aren't straight, and faces they can't face. Are these suits frivolous? Are they the result of the patients' vanity? Or do they exist because of negligent surgery done by doctors who are overextended and underprepared?

To successfully litigate plastic surgery suits, one must understand that the procedure is more art than science. Cosmetic surgery is unique because of this artistic dimension.[2] The plastic surgeon has been deified. But human flesh is not marble or clay. Errors can leave scars that are much

---

[1] Linden, *Cosmetic Surgery,* Town & Country, May 1987, at 112.

[2] J. Malnick, The Sculpture of the Living 31 (1934).

more than skin deep. Although either malpractice or false vanity can fuel a lawsuit, the cause is most often a misunderstanding between doctor and patient.

There is a dichotomy of expectations between the surgeon and the patient. Because beauty is in the eye of the beholder, the surgeon's concept of success is often different from the patient's. The surgeon's training is concerned with reconstruction that is the anatomic ideal. She may be contemplating *Gray's Anatomy* while the patient is contemplating *Cosmopolitan* or *GQ*. It is because of this dichotomy that the courtroom often becomes the ill-suited crucible in which these misunderstandings are resolved.

The American Board of Plastic Surgery has reported an increase in the number of plastic surgeons at the rate of 10 percent per year. Of these, 40 percent devote the majority of their time to cosmetic surgery. Surgical techniques continue to proliferate, with office surgery and microsurgery becoming the more acceptable. There is a new trend toward computerized imaging and digitalized impressions. Surgeons can now use a technique in which a computer takes a photograph of a patient and stores 250,000 measurements. This data can be used to simulate an image and to assess the effect of the planned surgery. Many surgeons feature the use of this computer-imaging in their advertising. But these high-tech gadgets are not without their liability problems. According to one critic,

> Some offices have an added wrinkle: computerized imagery, an $18,500 gadget advertised in professional journals as a sales tool for surgeons. You get the picture from the hard-sell pitch: "Help alleviate . . . uncertainty." "Graphically demonstrate additional surgical procedures." "Increased consultation fees and surgical revenues." The fact is, while imagers are fun to play with and can help illustrate how weird you would look with a perfectly symmetrical face or Lee Radziwill's nose, they are only two-dimensional, the same as the photos surgeons customarily sketch on. They cannot show what lies beneath the skin, what will happen to the tip of your nose if the bridge is reduced, how you will heal or actually look. Even the 3-D imagers that help surgeons preplan operations are not sophisticated enough to show final results.[3]

These high-tech procedures and Madison Avenue techniques can cause false expectations and increase the potential for litigation. Are patients seduced into unnecessary surgery by slick ads? Do they demean the profession? Do they promise more than they can possibly deliver? **Section 2.2** examines the advertisements themselves for the answers to these questions.

---

[3] Linden, *Cosmetic Surgery,* Town & Country, May 1987, at 116.

§ 2.2 Competitive Advertising

The boom in advertising has led to cutthroat competition among many plastic surgeons, particularly in California and New York. Aside from the obvious ethical issues involved in advertising, one must also contemplate its legal implications. Does the surgeon subject herself to a breach of contract action? Does she guarantee a result or standard of care beyond what the law requires? Will the ad become a major trial exhibit to inflame the passions of the jury? Will the surgeon be accused of seducing an unsuspecting patient? Note in the following recent advertisements the obvious appeal to vanity and short cut methods to achieve a lean and healthy look.

Bumps and Bulges

> After a month of strict dieting and faithful exercising you still can't harden up the bumps and bulges of fat that have settled in your thighs, buttocks, abdomen and chin. But you don't have to live with it. We can do it for you. Just call . . . .[4]

The Look

One surgeon advertised in the local newspapers for patients and in the legal journals for attorneys.

> Free Consultation . . .
> Just Call 1-800-THE-LOOK[5]

and

> Need Expert Testimony?
>
> —Noted Plastic Surgeon—Distinguished 20-year history of Expert Testimony available for review of Malpractice Liability and third party actions
>
> Scars
> Burns
> Cosmetic
> Face
> Congenital
>
> CV & Publication on request: Call 800-THE-LOOK.[6]

---

[4] 1987, in several New York City Newspapers.

[5] The New York Post, Aug. 9, 1988, at 9.

[6] New York Law Journal, Mar. 24, 1988, at 1.

One surgeon showed the public a photo of his beautiful new office suite and boasted: "Why our New Face Lift makes us such a good place to have yours."[7] Another, who specializes in rhinoplasty, advertised by using his patients' before and after photographs in a collage he called "Winning by a Nose."[8] A San Francisco dermatologist shocked the public with a gross picture of a fat backside replete with saddle bags and implored the readers to "Kiss It Goodbye."[9]

The Ferrari. One of the most recent controversial ads was on the West coast. Magazine readers saw a photo of a beautiful model sprawled over a bright red Ferrari.

> The photo is a stunner: In an eight-page fold-out magazine ad, a brunette bombshell in a white bathing suit and silver spike-heels stands, chest thrust forward, next to a bright red sports car. Above them the copy reads: "Automobile by Ferrari. Body by Forshan."
>
> Body by Forshan? The woman is an android, maybe? A robot?
>
> Neither. Forshan, readers learn, is Vincent R. Forshan, a Rancho Mirage, Calif., cosmetic surgeon. Never mind that he hadn't laid a scalpel on the bombshell. "It didn't say '*this* body by Forshan'," explains the doctor . . . .
>
> "Let's be honest. What are cosmetic surgeons? We are superstars. If I were a family practitioner, who would [care] about Vince Forshan? Nobody!"[10]

The Natural Look. In 1987, the New York clinic Profiles & Contours asked patients: "Your thighs—Do they have a mind of their Own? Profiles & Contours—When you have done all you can." In 1988, the clinic used the "all-natural" concept: "Introducing plastic surgery that doesn't leave you looking plastic—Natural Beauty—that's what great plastic surgery should look like."[11]

The plastic surgery market is so competitive and potentially lucrative that some doctors have resorted to hiring publicity agents, marketing advisers, and ad agencies. In 1988, the California attorney general's office began investigating whether their ads are truthful as well as whether doctors give patients enough information about the risks involved in cosmetic surgery. Much of the hype comes from a new breed of practitioner: the specialist in dermatology, gynecology, or some other field who has begun doing cosmetic surgery in the office to cash in on a trend.[12]

---

[7] Washington Post, Mar. 29, 1988, at 2.

[8] Washington Post, Nov. 24, 1987, at 23.

[9] California Magazine, June 1987, at 97.

[10] Hughes, *Body Not Perfect,* The Wall Street Journal, Aug. 2, 1988, at 1.

[11] New York Post, Oct. 11, 1988, at 19.

[12] Hughes, *Body Not Perfect,* The Wall Street Journal, Aug. 2, 1988, at 1.

> The upshot of the newly flooded marketplace is a panicky competition for consumer dollars. Many of the young surgeons—and some older doctors beset by ailing practices, overextended bank accounts or boundless egos and avarice, tackle the situation aggressively. Faced with high rent for chic addresses to entice the carriage trade, staff salaries, costly equipment and payments of $50,000 to $100,000 a year and up for malpractice insurance, the fledglings rush to bypass the five years' hard work it takes to earn valid reputations and referrals from colleagues and patients. The classic process is arduous: a compilation of extensive experience, consistently good results, and peer recognition for contributions to reputable national journals where acceptance is subject to peer review. The hungry use a speedier substitute: media exposure. . . . They hire advertising agents to place ads selling people on surgery as if it were a trip to the Bahamas. They pay publicists thousands of dollars a month to hector editors into plugging their names in newspaper, magazine and television features. In the interviews their publicity agents drum up, they cannily focus on intriguing, newsworthy-sounding techniques: some real, some fantasy, some harmful or untested by time . . . .[13]

§ 2.3 Regulation of the Profession

Who are the surgical sorcerers to whom thousands of people each year entrust their bodies? Despite popular belief to the contrary, cosmetic surgery can be performed by any licensed physician. There is a lot of panicky competition for the plastic surgeon dollar among dermatologists, general surgeons, otolaryngologists, ophthalmologists, and other physicians.

The first national organization for plastic surgeons, the American Association of Oral Surgeons, was organized in 1921. This was changed to the American Society of Oral and Plastic Surgeons in 1927. Finally in 1931 the Society of Plastic and Reconstructive Surgery was organized, which in 1941 became the present day American Society of Plastic and Reconstructive Surgeons. In 1937 the American Board of Plastic Surgery was established and standardized training programs for surgeons desiring to specialize in plastic surgery.

In this country, a cosmetic surgeon's basic knowledge, experience, and continuing education are certified by the American Board of Medical Specialties. Although the exact number of Board-certified cosmetic surgeons is not known because some plastic surgeons concentrate exclusively on reconstructive surgery, the best estimate is 5,000 to 6,000. Most are fellows of either of two organizations whose criteria for acceptance demand certification: the American Society of Plastic and Reconstructive Surgeons (ASPRS), whose 2,800 members perform surgery of the face and

---

[13] *Cosmetic Surgery: Is It For You?* Reader's Digest, July 1987, at 67.

body, and the American Academy of Facial Plastic and Reconstructive Surgery (AAFPRS), whose 2,700 members specialize in surgery above the collarbone. About half the AAFPRS members are otolaryngologists who do eyelids, face-lifts, and especially noses. The rest are dermatologists, who treat problems of the skin and hair, and ophthalmologists, whose field is eyelid surgery.[14]

To be certified as a plastic surgeon a physician must complete a three-year general surgical residency or residency in one of several recognized surgical specialties. This must then be followed by a two- or three-year plastic surgery residency. The plastic surgery resident learns both aesthetic techniques as well as reconstructive procedures. The American Society of Plastic Surgery is a member of the American Board of Medical Specialties (ABMS), which is affiliated with the American Medical Association. The competition between the American Board and the otolaryngologists and other specialties has been called a surgery turf war in California.

> The conflict of which speciality should receive a referral for plastic surgery from the local Medical Society recently spawned a suit in California. Until recently, if you called the Orange County Medical Assn. and asked to be referred to someone who does face lifts or nose jobs, you would have been put in touch with a plastic surgeon certified by the American Board of Plastic Surgery Inc.
>
> Today if you call the Association, you are as likely or more likely to be referred to a doctor certified by the American Board of Otolaryngology or the American Board of Cosmetic Surgery. This seemingly subtle change of policy is the result of an $8.6 million lawsuit filed by three Orange County physicians against the Orange County Medical Assn. in May of 1985 and quietly settled out of court for considerably less last summer.[15]

There are also several other boards that are related to the performance of cosmetic surgery. One is the American Board of Cosmetic Surgery, which is not related to the American Medical Association and which is self-monitored. To qualify for this board's exam, a surgeon must be certified by another ABMS recognized board, must have practiced cosmetic surgery for five years, and must have performed 1000 cosmetic procedures within the past five years, including 200 within the last year. This board is not limited to plastic surgeons, but also includes a large number of otolaryngologists. The American Academy of Facial Plastic and Reconstructive Surgeons draws members from otolaryngologists, dermatologists, and opthalmologists, in addition to the plastic surgeons. To qualify for this organization a physician must be board-certified by an ABMS-recognized

---

[14] Linden, *Cosmetic Surgery,* Town & Country, May 1987, at 114.

[15] B. Spichen, *Battle Over Beauty: In Changing Face of a Turf War, Cosmetic Surgeons Gain Ground,* Los Angeles Times, Orange County Edition Nov. 4, 1986, at 1, col. 3.

board and also must be a fellow of the American College of Surgeons. In the past 10 years these various boards have battled with each other over the qualifications and acceptability of the board members. But according to one commentator there are also "outsiders" whose training in cosmetic surgery is minimal or questionable.

> General surgeons, general practitioners, obstetrician/gynecologists faced with rocketing malpractice insurance costs, even chiropractors have added lucrative cosmetic procedures to their repertoires. The array is bewildering to patients who must make a choice . . . .
>
> The ranks are burgeoning. In fact, in recent years, so many medical school graduates have chosen to specialize in plastic surgery that nearly half the current members of ASPRS and AAFPRS are under age 40, which means they have been in practice five years or less.[16]

Two leading surgeons are very critical of some of their peers:

> "The danger," says Dr. John Little, director of the Division of Plastic and Reconstructive Surgery at Georgetown University Medical Center, "is that it is a trap for the untrained. The trouble with plastic surgery is that it looks easy. It appears simple to anybody who's had some training with a scalpel."
>
> Another prominent plastic surgeon, Dr. Jeffrey R. Fischman, assistant clinical professor of plastic surgery at the Mount Sinai School of Medicine in New York, says people are "being bombarded" by ads that are persuasive and seductive but give no information about the qualifications of the surgeons. But most of all, Fischman says, he is seeing more and more patients "who were operated on by unqualified people" who come to him to undo mistakes that a fully trained plastic surgeon would never have made in the first place.[17]

The American Association for the Accreditation of Ambulatory Plastic Surgery Facilities (AAAAPSF) guarantees at least that a private cosmetic surgery suite has met "minimal guidelines for safety," including maintenance of proper sterility, and staff members trained in cardiopulmonary resuscitation with proper equipment, among other things.

The standard of care of the plastic surgeon may vary from other specialties. This is largely dependent upon the types of surgical procedures used rather than the differences of the specialties. For example, otolaryngologists are more involved in the functional aspects of surgery with little emphasis on the cosmetic nature.

---

[16] Linden, *Cosmetic Surgery,* Town & Country, May 1987, at 114.

[17] S. Rovner, *One Word About Plastic Surgeons: Caution,* Washington Post, Apr. 17, 1985, at 15.

The courts often permit specialists in one field to testify against specialists in another field if they have some experience. The use of a non-plastic surgeon in a plastic surgery case provides great opportunities for cross-examination.

§ 2.4 Conclusion

The lawyer trying a plastic surgery suit should be familiar with the profile of the surgeon and the craft. The advertising phenomenon may be a key theme in either prosecuting or defending a case. Some patients are so indoctrinated by the ads that they may be seduced into surgery without the opportunity to reflect upon the procedure's potential risks. But others, like the "scalpel slaves" or "plastic junkies," will have very little credibility before the jury.

CHAPTER 3

THE VANITY PATIENT

§ 3.1 Psychological Profile of the Vanity Patient

"Darling," an aging Tallulah Bankhead once ruefully observed, "they're not making mirrors the way they used to."[1] The mirror may well be the motivation for the increasing popularity of plastic surgery.

Plastic surgery malpractice can distort the face, impair breathing, mutilate the breasts, and leave unnecessary and devastating scars. But the focus of this chapter is on the patient who, out of vanity, is often the only one who believes that the result is unfavorable. A great number of these vanity cases are filed and the practitioner should carefully consider each case's merits before accepting a retainer. Are the complications common risks that were explained? Is the result, if not perfect, a reasonable one? Will jurors resent the vanity, personality, wealth, or social status of the plaintiff? Is the plaintiff a plastic surgery junkie, addict, or regular? Will false vanity lead to exaggeration or even alteration of records (see **§ 3.3**)?

Cosmetic surgery cases are sometimes referred to as vanity suits to distinguish them from reconstructive surgical procedures to repair congenital defects or treat trauma patients. In reconstructive surgery there is a natural residue of sympathy for the patient and the surgeon. But in a vanity suit, the plaintiff may be seen as frivolous or egotistical because

[1] Linden, *Cosmetic Surgery*, Town & Country, May 1987, at 111–16.

there has been no serious or obvious injury. If the jury perceives that the plaintiff is a scalpel slave or plastic surgery junkie, the case stands little chance of success. Counsel must recognize the peculiar qualities that characterize the vanity lawsuit in order to successfully represent the prospective client. Several recent psychological studies suggest that there is a distinct profile of the vanity patient. In one study, Lavell and Lewis[2] surveyed 55 patients undergoing cosmetic facial surgery and asked them to complete a questionnaire containing demographic data and items to gauge self-perception. The findings indicated that the patients who were overly anxious, excessively concerned with detail, or had perceived themselves as being unattractive were least likely to be satisfied with cosmetic facial surgery. As a result, Dr. Lewis set forth the following recommendations when performing a psychological evaluation of the cosmetic patient:

1. Assess anxiety, note nervous habits, inquire into depression
2. Evaluate the patient's perception of attractiveness
3. Observe the patient for compulsive characteristics and/or excessive involvement with detail
4. Assess unrealistic expectations.

Another study assesses certain factors that predict the success of a mammoplasty.[3] Mammoplasty patients who experienced complications were found to have characteristics distinct from the general population. For example, 28 percent of the patients in a noncontrol group were divorced, compared to only 11 percent of the control group. There was also an increased incidence of suicide attempts and poor sexual relations in the noncontrol group. These emotional predicates for surgery have implications for the medical and legal profession. To the surgeon, it might suggest that these patients are unstable and will be prone to litigation. Counsel should carefully assess a patient's prior medical history and demeanor and record of prior litigation.

A third study on patients undergoing rhinoplasties found that a major motive for undergoing a rhinoplasty was to change the patient's life situation in general.[4] This motive is often subconscious and not explicitly revealed to the physician. Candidates who expressed internal motives, such

---

[2] Lavell & Lewis, *SAFE: A Practical Guide to Psychological Factors in Selecting Patients for Facial Cosmetic Surgery,* 12 Annals of Plastic Surgery, Mar. 1984, at 256–59.

[3] Beule, Lisper, Ohlsin, & Palm, *Augmentation Mammoplasty: The Surgical and Psychological Effects of Operation and Prediction of Results,* 14 Annals of Plastic Surgery, June 1985, at 473–93.

[4] Meyer & Jacobson, *The Predictive Validity of Psychosocial Factors for Patient's Acceptance of Rhinoplasty,* 17 Annals of Plastic Surgery, Nov. 1984, at 513–20.

as wanting to improve self-esteem or body image, were found to be better candidates than those who had external motivation for undergoing surgery, such as concern for the opinions of friends and/or spouses. **Section 3.2** summarizes the personal trial experiences of patients who fit this profile in whole or in part.

§ 3.2 An Example of a Vanity Patient

An affluent Park Avenue septuagenarian sued her surgeon for negligence in the performance of a blepharoplasty (removal of excessive fat from the eyelids). She claimed it resulted in a permanent failure of the eyelids to close (ectropion), which in turn caused a chronic infection (keritites). However, she was a plastic surgery addict and had undergone no less than 10 elective cosmetic surgical procedures in the past 15 years, including face-lifts, eye-lifts, chemical peels, and a tummy tuck. Her own attorney neglected to elicit this medical history on direct examination. Yet it was probative to the informed consent issue and branded her as a frivolous vanity case.

When the patient first met the defendant, she severely criticized her last surgeon. This was a telltale sign of a suit in the making. In his records the defendant noted her fanaticism about her prior surgeons. She was termed "combative" in nature and "unstable" in personality. But, perhaps being a victim of vanity himself, the surgeon accepted her as a patient anyway.

At trial the patient displayed a demeanor that made her appear very vain, antagonistic, and condescending to the blue-collar jury. Cross-examination revealed her to be a peripatetic professional patient wandering from doctor to doctor in a relentless search for the fountain of youth. She also alienated at least one member of the jury when, as part of the mitigation of damages defense, she was asked why she would not agree to undergo a simple corrective procedure. She replied that she would rather go on suffering than risk the chance that the corrective procedure might leave her looking like an Oriental. Not only was this answer of most dubious medical authenticity, but it certainly alienated the Japanese member of the jury.

The defense counsel called her treating ophthalmologist to the stand to testify that she did not have the ectropion. His diagnosis was conjunctivitis (pink eye) due to soaking her contact lenses in Perrier with lime. However, upon cross-examination, her counsel proudly produced an apparently authentic copy of the doctor's medical office record, which had a check mark and underline next to the words "Ectropion of the lower lids." However, the diagnosis on the report was conjunctivitis, not ectropion. There was also no reference to ectropion in the corresponding insurance form or in the billing records. On redirect this form was found to be "doctored." The office carbon copy was blown up to reveal no check marks. It appeared that even the plaintiff's attorney was deceived. The patient had altered the record to give herself an ectropion. She was called to the stand to testify about the alterations and then took the fifth amendment. The effect upon the jury was devastating to her case. The trial judge referred the matter to the district attorney's office. The original doctored document served as dramatic demonstrative evidence and a constant reminder of this fraud throughout the trial. An excerpt from the trial record appears in **§ 3.3**. After the defense verdict, the defendant sued the patient and her counsel for fraud.

§ 3.3 —Excerpt from a Vanity Trial

Comment. After presenting evidence to prove that the plaintiff may have altered her own medical record to prove her allegation of ectropion of the eye, the defense wanted to call her as a witness to confront her with the accusation. Her lawyer objected, citing her fifth amendment right against incrimination. He argued that such questioning in front of the jury would obviously prejudice her case, and claimed she could not be forced to take the stand. However, this was not a criminal trial, and the defense counsel argued that she had to take the stand. The district attorney was present during this phase of the case to monitor and investigate any criminal evidence of perjury or spoilation of evidence. Plaintiff's counsel tried to withdraw the altered record to avoid having her called back to the stand, but to no avail. See **Chapter 7** for an analysis of the trial transcript of the plaintiff and her expert.

PLAINTIFF'S LAWYER: Now, I must say, your Honor, in all my experience as an attorney, I have never witnessed what is going on. There is an assistant district attorney sitting here right now; I must say that I have been chilled by the fact that detectives and district attorneys have been present in this courtroom, and the fact that I have found it necessary to advise my client, on the record, that she should obtain criminal counsel in order to protect herself. It has impeded the freedom with which I might have my client testify, because I have had to put worry about conflicts of interest, about privilege against self-incrimination, and about her criminal rights into the picture.

There has been such a chill in this courtroom towards the proper presentation of the plaintiff's rights.

Furthermore, I note your Honor has informed me that you yourself obtained the presence of the district attorney who has been here since Wednesday, I believe, last. There has been, as your Honor told me, an attempt to preserve a chain of possession of evidence in a criminal case.

I think that on Wednesday afternoon your Honor took a piece of paper, went over to the district attorney's office and obtained the presence of a district attorney in this courtroom.

THE COURT: That is slightly in error.

PLAINTIFF'S LAWYER: If that is wrong, please correct me, your Honor.

THE COURT: What I did was, I called my law clerk and asked my law clerk to call Mr. Benitez of the district attorney's office, advise him of the testimony in the case, and request the presence of a representative from the district attorney's office in the courtroom.

PLAINTIFF'S LAWYER: On Wednesday afternoon there was a great stir in the courtroom in the presence of the jury when the district attorney and one or two detectives came in. Since that time the district attorney has been present. I have no criticism of him. I am sure he was assigned here and is following his orders.

Since that time he has been provided with copies of the transcript.

At one time the court officer was directed by your Honor to take possession of the exhibits. It was every morning or every evening, and it was delivered, I think, to the district attorney's detectives, although this was a marked court exhibit.

THE COURT: That is not accurate, sir. It was delivered to the detectives on one occasion. Thereafter, it has been in custody of court officers.

PLAINTIFF'S LAWYER: Now, it has been in the custody of court officers, and on one occasion the court officer took it and delivered it to the detective in the presence of the jury, while the jury was in the courtroom.

THE COURT: No, sir.

PLAINTIFF'S LAWYER: At least that is my recollection.

THE COURT: The court officer did not deliver it to the detective until after the jury had left, and he made a record with the court reporter of transferring custody to the detective investigator.

PLAINTIFF'S LAWYER: Well, at any rate, if your Honor pleases, I must say that this has presented a burden to me emotionally, and an emotional burden to my client. She has had . . . I have consulted with at least two other lawyers on her behalf, I made a record of advising her on the record that there might exist a conflict of interest here between herself and myself, and that she should obtain legal counsel, which she did.

I consulted with two other lawyers on her behalf and I just wish to memorialize the atmosphere which has obtained during the course of this trial.

THE COURT: On the subject of the district attorney's presence and the presence of the detective investigators from his office, that was not the action of the defendant, or defendant's attorney, or his law firm, it was my action. It was my action consistent with my obligation as a public official. It is my obligation as a citizen. I think it is a breach of obligation of a public official, particularly the judge, to see false sworn testimony which is a crime and to see it unreported. I accept full responsibility for reporting the matter to the district attorney. I feel it was a proper thing to do in the circumstances, and if faced with a similar situation again in another case, I would not for a moment hesitate to do it again. That is consistent with my obligation to hear such testimony, and then to be shown such evidence as was produced by Dr. Bloom and to do nothing about it would, in my view, be a clear breach of an implicit obligation and an explicit obligation. It is not a matter of subtlety, sir, it is a matter of direct obligation, one which I do not hesitate to carry out.

THE COURT: Where do we go next, gentlemen?

DEFENDANT'S LAWYER: I have several minutes of questioning for the plaintiff and then I will rest.

PLAINTIFF'S LAWYER: Now that creates a problem, Judge.

DEFENDANT'S LAWYER: I guess we are not ready to proceed?

PLAINTIFF'S LAWYER: That creates another problem, Judge. The plaintiff has been cast under a criminal cloud in this case. She has been called by me as a witness. She has been called by my adversary as a witness. Every question that could have been asked has been asked. The only thing that [the defendant's counsel] could ask her about is the document in question. [Concerning] everything else he has closed his examination.

DEFENDANT'S LAWYER: I won't concede that.

PLAINTIFF'S LAWYER: Just a minute, let me finish. If he has anything else, I respectfully say to your Honor he should have asked it on cross, which took three days of cross-examination, it didn't take three full days, but it extended over three days.

On top of that he called her as a witness and he had her on for a portion of a fourth day. Every question which he could have asked has been asked.

During an informal conversation on Friday before your Honor he informed me he wants to call her again. I say to your Honor, the only thing he could ask her about now, which he didn't have an opportunity to ask her about then, is this document. At best it is a collateral matter, a collateral matter that he has made his point with. To require the plaintiff to take the stand now would be a breach of her privilege—it would be improper, in my opinion, an improper trial procedure because the defendant has had every opportunity to question her over the course of four days. He has made a blackboard with all the names, and I respectfully ask that a photograph of this blackboard, which was taken by defendant's counsel, be produced and marked in evidence.

THE COURT: Yes, it should be.

PLAINTIFF'S LAWYER: Because an appellate court would want to probably look at that.

Now, if any question is asked about that event—about that document—the plaintiff has been advised by me and her other counsel to immediately take the fifth amendment because the presence of the district attorney and detectives indicates that there is an active investigation, criminal investigation going on. Any such event in front of the jury would have a highly prejudicial effect. And, therefore, I would say, your Honor, that the defendant should not have the opportunity to call the plaintiff to the stand. I think whatever point he is going to make with regard to that document has been made, because Dr. Bloom was recalled to the stand and after he produced his records in the afternoon—which he didn't have in the morning under my cross-examination when he first came—he produced his records and, at best, I consider the accuracy of the document which I used to impeach him with and which he accepted originally and then changed his mind on, and which I then moved on the record to withdraw as an exhibit in view of the doubts which have been raised with regard to it, I think that is all in front of the jury, nothing further need be said, and I don't think—if there is anything else counsel wishes to ask, he had his opportunity, he can't go on forever.

I think he should be denied the opportunity of placing the plaintiff on the stand.

And, of course, if the plaintiff were to take the stand, I would tell her with regard to every question that is asked of her, she should say the following words: "I refuse to answer upon the grounds that it may incriminate me." And that every question which will be put to her she must answer in this way. And that this would be highly prejudicial.

DEFENDANT'S LAWYER: Your Honor, I will address myself to those issues in reverse order.

The privileges plaintiff's lawyer referred to, the fifth amendment, can't, of course, be taken in a civil case, but that is no prohibition in a criminal case in placing a witness on a stand and asking her a question. This is new matter which did not exist before; I was unable to question the plaintiff about this apparently questionable document when I had her on cross-examination. In fact, it is evidence that she has put forward affirmatively, vouching as it was for its authenticity, for its accuracy and it is far from a collateral matter in the case, it goes on to the very heart of the substance, as well as the issue of credibility, which is a key in this question of informed consent.

I say it goes to the heart because the plaintiff and counsel, as her counsel, offered this document to impeach the testimony of Dr. Bloom, her treating physician, and to establish the fact that this woman had a permanent ectropion, even today, in October of 1981. What could be more substantial, relevant, and material to the issue in this case as to whether or not she has this injury which she has claimed for the past seven years? If this document were accepted by the jury, it would, in fact, make out a prima facie case for the plaintiff, and I would dare say that I would probably lose it considering the manner in which it was introduced. It is probably the only evidence whatsoever ever proffered by this plaintiff to establish any of the prima facie elements of her alleged damages since all the treating physicians that I have called, and the records that have gone into evidence, bear clearly in the conclusion that she has never suffered any permanent ectropion whatsoever.

Even the records and testimony to date indicate that it was, at best, a temporary condition that lasted perhaps for three or four weeks. She now seeks dramatically to introduce this document signed by Dr. Bloom on September 15, 1981, in which it appears that he has checked off the disorder of ectropion, and he goes further by underlining the words "lower lid." What could more clearly impeach my witness in my case and establish their case than this purported authenticated document?

Now we had an opportunity to hear from Dr. Bloom when he got his original records. He testified that "someone has doctored my records," and I can use that openly. There is no jury here. "Someone has altered my records," he said. "It certainly wasn't me or my secretary." And he proved by overwhelming evidence that if a patient ever had such a disorder it is never indicated by putting a check mark next to the box with an underline, but rather his records revealed he would put a price next to that disorder for the treatment rendered, and that he would then write at the bottom of the form the diagnosis of ectropion.

However, in this questionable document the only diagnosis was conjunctivitis. I think Dr. Bloom's testimony in the afternoon was so compelling and so manifest that he had been shown a doctored report, an altered document, that, for the plaintiff to seek to withdraw it or to prevent me from asking questions when he seeks to establish his case by it, would be highly prejudicial to my case.

He may not wish to call the plaintiff, but having been the party to introduce the evidence, apparently for the facts contained therein, she has no right whatsoever to refuse to answer questions about it.

THE COURT: She certainly has a right to refuse to answer questions. But she has no lesser Constitutional privilege than anyone else.

DEFENDANT'S LAWYER: I don't question her Constitutional right to assert the privilege, I merely say she has no right to refuse to ascend that witness stand having made this the key issue in the case.

THE COURT: You are aware that the only thing which would result from her testimony would be a claim of privilege as opposed to a portion of testimony where the witness does testify as to some matters and claims privileges to others. But where you have a situation where nothing will happen other than the claim of privilege, do you have any authority that suggests that that is appropriate?

DEFENDANT'S LAWYER: Yes, there is authority, your Honor. It is a civil case. A witness can be called and asked the questions. Inference, perhaps, can be drawn.

THE COURT: If you will give me the authority I will read the case, or if you have a copy of the case with you. If you will cite me the cases, I will certainly consult them before I make a ruling, but giving you my impression, apparently you feel that the cases hold otherwise, and hold that you should be able to call her for the purpose—and I will read the cases before I rule.

My impression is that she cannot be called solely for that purpose where you know she will answer no questions.

DEFENDANT'S LAWYER: I don't know that, your Honor, until she takes the stand.

THE COURT: Counsel has told you that, and you can assume that that is what will happen. But if you will get me the cases, I will read them before ruling on whether or not you may recall the plaintiff.

DEFENDANT'S LAWYER: Your Honor, without reference to any cases, I don't believe counsel can preclude the question by advising us in advance the answer is no, "therefore, don't bother."

THE COURT: He cannot. That is true. There is a procedure to be followed, and when we get to the point where I must rule on it after consulting with the cases, I will follow that procedure and that procedure normally is that the witness is asked, out of the presence of the jury, concerning certain actions which she might take if she were to testify.

DEFENDANT'S LAWYER: I think a jury—particularly this one—since the document was circulated, to use counsel's word, when he waived it triumphally last week, they have every right to hear her take that approach.

THE COURT: I am willing to be guided by the cases which deal with the question.

PLAINTIFF'S LAWYER: May I be heard?

THE COURT: Why don't we get the cases first and see what the cases say, and there may be no need to hear you on the issues, depending on what the cases say and the circumstances are.

[A short recess was had, after which the trial continued.]

THE COURT: Is this on the subject of calling the plaintiff with knowledge that she would invoke her privilege against self-incrimination?

DEFENDANT'S LAWYER: Your Honor, with respect to this question as to whether I have the right to call the plaintiff and ask her questions of a criminal nature that she is indicating she will plead the fifth amendment in a civil action, I will cite the authority of Levine v. Bornstin, 174 N.Y. Supp. 2d, 574, which held that despite the fact that the plaintiff had a right to claim the privilege against self-incrimination when questions were propounded at an EBT, no less, the defendant also had a right to develop an affirmative defense that might destroy the plaintiff's right to maintain that action. And the plaintiff's claiming of the privilege would, in fact, be improper, could even result in a motion to strike the case if they refused to take the stand.

THE COURT: But that is as to an examination before trial, and a refusal to testify at all. Here the witness has testified, so that case is somewhat different.

DEFENDANT'S LAWYER: Your Honor, as the court well knows, in an examination before trial, the purpose is to develop testimony that may become necessary for the trial itself. Here we are faced with a jury, not an examination before trial where there is no trier of facts. I must face the task of overcoming this apparently altered document which impeaches my case. Now I am not permitted the chance to prove that it is an altered document or that it has been made by persons unknown. Perhaps the plaintiff can provide some testimony in that effect.

I will be totally prejudiced.

THE COURT: Except that Dr. Bloom has testified that the document was not as he prepared it. He has supplied his office copy, which is on paper, which might be described as carbon or duplicated paper, which does not show the markings, and upon the suggestion that his secretary may have had access to the original, his secretary also testified to the effect that she did not make those marks on that paper and they were not there when it left her hand.

DEFENDANT'S LAWYER: The court's concern might have some application in a case that was not in the nature of simple negligence or even medical malpractice or contract. Yet, by own admission, by his opening statement and by the pleadings before the court and the testimony before this jury, this case now turns on one issue, and that is the credibility of the plaintiff as opposed to the defendant.

This jury has been told, since jury selection, that this poor woman underwent an unauthorized operation, an assault, in effect, because as she has testified the defendant never advised her that he was going to perform surgery on her lower lids, that he never advised her of any risks that were inherent to the procedure.

I think the case is at a juncture now where we can almost concede there is no medical malpractice case proven, and the only issue that is going to go to this jury is, who is telling the truth. Did the defendant tell her about the procedure? Or is she telling the truth when she said, "I was never told. I was assaulted. It is an unauthorized operation, and these are the results."

Counsel has used these words before the court and to me, and therefore, credibility on an informed consent issue is the total question for the jury.

Because of this, as well as the question [of whether] she [has] a permanent ectropion, if it turns out that the plaintiff had checked off that disorder, that is certainly something the jury has a right to know as to credibility, and the ultimate facts to be determined. If she refused to answer by taking the privilege against self-incrimination, that is something else they are permitted to draw inferences from.

There is another case, your Honor—

THE COURT: Can they not as well draw the inference from the fact that she has not denied it after it had been put into evidence in her presence in the courtroom?

DEFENDANT'S LAWYER: No, I don't believe so.

I am permitted to ask them to draw the strongest inference, how can I ask them anything if I don't question her myself? We have a similar situation herein, a court of appeals case, which I think should be somewhat controlling in Laverne v. Incorporated Village of Laurel Hollow. This is a court of appeals in July, 1966, the citation is 18 N.Y.2d 635. The case stands for the proposition that the Constitutional privilege against self-incrimination was intended to be used solely as a shield. Thus, the plaintiff could not use privilege as a sword to harass a defendant and to thwart effectively any attempt by defendant. This was a pretrial discovery also to obtain information relevant to causes of action alleged—and that is important—and possible defenses.

I submit to you what could be more relevant to my defense of the cause of action than to show that the defendant's credibility should be accepted over the plaintiff's, than asking her questions that might expose that she has not told the truth, or at least taking part in an alteration of a document? Nothing could be more relevant or salient, your Honor. I submit these cases to your Honor as to authority, as well as a common sense approach, that a witness should not be permitted to show an altered document, and there is testimony that it is altered to impeach a defendant's case and to establish her own, and then to seek to withdraw to the gallery of the spectator section, and be permitted not to avoid the jury.

I think that is highly unfair. I did not introduce the document, [the defense counsel] did through his client.

So, I would submit, respectfully, sir, I should at least be permitted to put the question in front of the jury.

THE COURT: May I see the cases, please?

[Handed to the Court.]

THE COURT: I need one more case which deals with the matter, which is the Marine Midland case against John E. Russo Produce Co., at 50 N.Y.2d 31.

I am sending for this case and I will read it before I rule.

However, in order to know whether we are dealing with a matter of Constitutionality, or a matter which is speculative, now in the absence of the jury, in order that the record may be complete, I will ask the plaintiff, who is present in court:

Plaintiff, if I permitted counsel to recall you to the witness stand and to ask you certain questions, particularly questions concerning your visits with Dr. Bloom and any diagnosis of Dr. Bloom, and any documents, receipts, claim forms or papers, or anything of that nature provided by Dr. Bloom, or any insurance forms or anything else of that nature, if I were to permit [the defense counsel] to ask you questions about those things, and you have heard here that he has asked me to ask you questions about those, would you testify before the jury and answer such questions?

PLAINTIFF: I would refuse to answer on the grounds it might incriminate me.

THE COURT: Thank you. The record is clear now. The question is only whether that can be done before the jury. There was no question that the plaintiff had been so advised by counsel, but the decision ultimately would be hers to make, and she has now made clear on the record what her decision is after consultation with counsel.

The question remains only when or whether or not she may be recalled to the stand with the knowledge that that would be her response.

DEFENDANT'S LAWYER: Your Honor, may I also ask if the witness were to assert the privilege concerning questions about what manner this photostated document was produced—who produced it, where it came from, and its origin.

THE COURT: I take it that all of that was included in my question when I said any questions concerning any such documents.

PLAINTIFF'S LAWYER: It was, Judge.

THE COURT: As soon as the captain returns with that Marine Midland case, I will make the volume available to both counsel and we will then proceed.

[The case was produced.]

THE COURT: Gentlemen, I have read what appears to be the most recent case on the matter which I have found, which is Marine Midland Bank v. John E. Russo Produce Co., decided by the court of appeals in 1980. The citation is 50 N.Y.2d 31; parallel citation is 427 N.Y. Supp. 2d 961.

Apparently the court has come through with a different conclusion than I have, and I am bound by their ruling.

Judge Fuchsberg holds that it is appropriate in a civil case to have the refusal to testify before the jury. And he differentiates it from criminal cases and other cases where it's prohibited by saying: "For here the parties are in an equal footing; the only disadvantage threatened is liability to compensate an adversary for damages.

"We therefore decline to extend to civil cases a rule originally designed as a safe ground in criminal prosecutions."

And further, they suggest an appropriate charge to the jury in cases in which a party has refused to give evidence on a point.

PLAINTIFF'S LAWYER: I haven't read the case, Judge, but I only want to point out to your Honor that we have gone way beyond a civil case in this situation. We have had a district attorney—

THE COURT: That is not different. In that case it involved an action, a civil action, but with clear, criminal implications involving fraud, et cetera, so that it also was a case that had gone well beyond the usual bounds of a civil case.

PLAINTIFF'S LAWYER: Your Honor felt the criminal matter, the implication serious enough in this case to summon the district attorney to be present in this courtroom for the past three days, as he is at the present moment.

THE COURT: Sir, I find any evidence which indicates to me, at least reasonable cause, to believe a felony has been committed to be serious enough to summon the appropriate law enforcement authorities. I do not make those balancing tests when there is evidence that a crime may have been committed. That is a matter to be invested by the appropriate public officials.

PLAINTIFF'S LAWYER: Of course. But your Honor felt it was so serious in this matter that you didn't wait until the end of the case, you summoned him during the course of the trial.

THE COURT: Of course, that is because of the rules regarding the chain of custody of matters of physical evidence which were involved.

The plaintiff had to take the stand. The defense counsel asked her if she knew who altered the medical record. She took the fifth. She was asked whether she did it. She took the fifth. "I refuse to answer on the grounds it may put me in jail . . . is that the right way Mr. [plaintiff's lawyer]?" The jury returned with a verdict for the defense.

THE COURT: You are aware that the jury may be charged that if they find that a party has altered evidence, they may take that as an admission of the weakness of the party's case?

PLAINTIFF'S LAWYER: Your Honor has told me that you intend to charge that and I understand that. And, of course, that goes for both sides of the case.

THE COURT: Of course.

PLAINTIFF'S LAWYER: I have no quarrel with your Honor charging that.

THE COURT: And in making that determination, they have a right to have an inquiry as to what the cause of the alteration is. I will permit the witness to be called. Thereafter, I will reserve decision on the motions. I am aware of what the motions will be. I will reserve decisions on the motions, and we will go into summations.

PLAINTIFF'S LAWYER: In other words, you are going to allow [the plaintiff] to take the stand?

THE COURT: Yes.

PLAINTIFF'S LAWYER: And she will then assert her privilege to every question?

THE COURT: Yes. She will assert her privilege to a couple of questions and once it becomes clear that she intends to persist on that, I may ask her if her answers to other questions will be the same, if that then is the result, there is no need to detain her longer on the stand.

PLAINTIFF'S LAWYER: Now, I object to that and I think it is highly prejudicial.

THE COURT: Now, there is no waiver of your position which has been made abundantly clear, that is, that you object to it. My ruling is over your objection, and I do not take anything which is said now as being an acquiescence by you in my ruling.

PLAINTIFF'S LAWYER: And I wish, in view of the strangeness of the circumstances to again advise plaintiff on the record. [Plaintiff], if you are called on the stand in this case, as his Honor intends to do so, I advise you that every question which is asked of you, you should answer and you will be best advised to answer, "I cannot answer that question upon the ground that it may incriminate me."

Comment. This example should not suggest that all vanity patients will go to such extremes, but it does indicate the great caution that must be exercised by the practitioner in accepting a vanity case.

§ 3.4 Another Example

In another action, an affluent 70-year-old socialite claimed that her occipital nerve was severed during a routine face-lift, even though this nerve is not even involved in the operation. She insisted that she lived every day with a "toothache in [her] head" and could no longer function normally. She also claimed a lack of informed consent because she was doped and coerced into signing the consent form. (She was given sedatives just prior to signing because she kept changing her mind about the operation and the doctor had finally given her a Valium to calm her down.)

There was no evidence in the record of a laceration or severance of a nerve. The woman's neurotic nature had preceded her surgery. She also had a history of many cosmetic procedures. A neurological and psychiatric examination conducted by the defense revealed that her problems were of psychological or unrelated neurologic etiology. Although she believed that the cosmetic results were unflattering, to the objective eye she looked wonderful.

§ 3.5 Scalpel Slaves

The following excerpt from a recent national magazine study provides a good profile of the vanity patient:

> When Barbara first made an appointment with Dallas plastic surgeon Dr. Frank Dunton in 1980, she had no particularly compelling reason to seek cosmetic surgery. Since then the 55-year-old housewife and student has gone under Dunton's knife at least a half dozen times. She started with a full face-lift. Two years later she had a temple-lift, and an eyebrow lift the year after that. Then she had a rerun of the temple-lift. In between operations, she's had numerous collagen injection treatments. Dunton expects to keep up the remodeling work.[5]

Are scalpel slaves more prone to sue? Yes, because they are at greater risk of complications and more likely to sue the last surgeon seen out of anger or frustration. Doctor-hopping scalpel slaves run a much higher risk of getting into trouble. After being turned away by several doctors because of personal problems, they soon learn the ropes and can provide just the answers that doctors want to hear. Turned down for a third or fourth face-lift by a reputable surgeon, they seek out any doctor who will do what they want. Once the damage is done, it isn't easy to repair. According to one author, after multiple procedures some patients start to look very artificial, with tilted noses, no foreheads, and paper-thin skin. Reputable plastic surgeons are leery of fixing botched jobs because they worry about getting tangled up in malpractice suits.[6] Dissatisfied patients often wind up suing the last surgeon to operate.

Who are the scalpel slaves today? How do they differ from patients a generation ago? According to one study,

> These days, it's not just wealthy socialites and surreptitious celebrities who purchase eyes to sigh for, baton-sleek thighs, perfect bosoms and chinlines as crisp as a teenager's; the multitudes are leaping onto the bandwagon as well. Egged on by a torrent of ads and articles, waitresses, secretaries and bank tellers save up for operations as they do for fur coats.[7]

---

[5] *Scalpel Slaves Just Can't Quit,* Newsweek, Jan. 11, 1988, at 58.

[6] *Id.*

[7] Linden, *Cosmetic Surgery,* Town & Country, May 1987, at 111–16.

> And what of the male patients? Ten years ago, perhaps five or six percent of cosmetic surgery patients were men: a few hair transplants here, an eyelidplasty there. Today, men account for somewhere between ten and twenty percent; not a stupendous rise, but part of the tide . . . . The men are executives fending off replacement by younger comers in the latest corporate takeover; board chairmen who have everything and want more; politicians, doctors and lawyers who don't want to look like has-beens; pilots away from home a lot; and men whose wives or lovers convince them that they look as if their warranty periods have expired.[8]

§ 3.6 Guidelines for the Surgeon

It is the plastic surgeon's responsibility to realistically prepare and inform her patients of the potential benefits, risks, and detriments of the cosmetic procedure. However, some patients are so intent on the end result that they selectively screen out the discussion of the risks. In many cases the patient cannot or will not accept the results of cosmetic surgery, even when performed flawlessly. The surgeon should explore the psychological motivations and makeup of the potential patient. She should screen out those whose temperament and psychological profile indicate that they are not suitable candidates. Not every litigious patient should be rejected, but the surgeon must realize that today's infatuated patient may become tomorrow's embittered enemy.

The following suggestions are based on forensic guidelines—defensive medicine if you will—rather than usual medical standards of care. These suggestions may go beyond the usual medical standards of care but they should be consulted and considered by the surgeon to avoid unnecessary litigation in the first place.

§ 3.7 —First Consultation

It is essential that the physician establish a satisfactory rapport with the patient at their very first meeting. To be sure, not all patients seeking surgery to reduce a slightly bulbous nose, straighten a slightly deviated septum, or erase an unwanted wrinkle are litigious or psychologically impaired. However, the patient's personality, motivations, and expectations for the surgery must be realistically assessed and documented. A psychological screening might be considered. Because these are elective procedures, a refusal to operate cannot be construed as abandonment.

---

[8] *Id.* at 113.

Good communication is of the utmost importance. There must be a solid foundation between patient and physician. The patient who is condescending or rude is often egocentric, overbearing, and difficult to communicate with and should be avoided. At the very least, any outbursts or scenes caused by the patient should be carefully documented.

The surgeon should begin by determining if there are deep-seated psychological problems such as depression, neuroses, or inferiority complexes that may spawn future litigation. If such problems are observed, the clinician should document them, together with all of her attempts to ameliorate the situation. Although many patients are adept at hiding their emotional problems, the written record, if complete, is still the best defense to any lawsuit. However, the physician should make a special effort to empathize with the vanity patient. If tender loving care and sensitivity are applied as part of the doctor's bedside manner, the risk of unnecessary and frivolous litigation may be minimized. Indeed, the chances for a successful emotional outcome for the patient are also enhanced.

The physician must ask the patient the specific reason for the operation. How long has the patient considered it? Have friends or family pressured him? If so, the doctor should advise the patient against the procedure. Of course, the physician herself should never pressure the patient to undergo the operation under any circumstances. She should avoid falling prey to the Pygmalion complex of attempting to beautify the world by suggesting cosmetic improvements to patients. Otherwise, she may be accused of unprofessionally soliciting patients.

Does the patient have an unrealistic expectation that after the operation he will live happily ever after or find his fantasy lover? Does he believe he will be perfect afterwards? Is there any question of the mental competence to give an informed consent? If so, or if there is any serious underlying psychological problem, referral to a psychiatrist may be appropriate. Indeed, in elective procedures involving sex change operations, long-term psychological counseling is mandatory before any procedure is performed.

§ 3.8 —The Ten Commandments

Nothing can guarantee protection from a lawsuit, but the following defensive legal medical commandments should be practiced by any physician trying to reduce the risk of being sued, even if they are all not medically necessary.

1. Assess Appearance. Appearance can sometimes provide definite symptoms of a disturbed or disoriented patient. Psychiatrists have long recognized that a disheveled appearance can be a sign of psychological impairment. On the other hand, patients who are immaculately attired or obsessive-compulsive about their appearance may be neurotic perfectionists. They are not good risks for cosmetic surgery because no one can live up to their expectations. Surgeons should also beware the seductive patient. Vanity patients who exaggerate extremely minor defects are also unrealistic and difficult to please.

2. **Beware the Emotional Crises.** Patients who are going through emotional crises in their lives should have surgery postponed. This includes patients in the midst of a divorce or grief following the death of a loved one. Other patients to avoid are those who bring pictures of famous people or models they would like to look like.

3. **Take Detailed Prior Plastic Surgery History.** The physician should take a detailed and probing history with particular emphasis on the patient's psychological motivation and all prior elective procedures.

4. **Note Biographical and Cultural Data.** The physician should take note of the patient's age as well as her social, religious, and cultural background because these factors may influence a patient's view and expectation of cosmetic surgery. Ultimately, it may also affect a jury's perception of the operation. For example, in one case a Colombian woman of Mayan Indian background sued because of the appearance of her nose following surgery. The defense claimed that the shape of her nose and the limitation of the surgery were governed by genetic racial factors. See **Chapters 16–19**.

5. **Consider Psychological Referral.** If the patient's psychological history and assessment reveals underlying pathology, the physician should consider referral to a psychiatrist. The surgeon should not play the role of psychiatrist himself but instead should screen all patients psychologically as well as medically and reject those who are unstable or poor candidates for the proposed surgery.

6. **Record Animosity to Prior Surgeons.** The doctor should document any underlying psychological problems, particularly any history of dissatisfaction with other surgeons or unrealistic expectations and disappointments following prior surgery.

7. **Give a Detailed and Timely Informed Consent Discussion.** The clinician should take particular pains to explain the risks, complications, and period of recovery involved with the elective procedure to prevent any claim of lack of informed consent, confusion, or disappointment. Following plastic surgery, the face is temporarily swollen and discolored, and complications may occur. The patient should be told that this should not be a cause for undue concern. Some physicians are now videotaping the

informed consent discussion or showing their patients professionally produced informed consent videos. Although this may become the state-of-the-art standard, it weakens the all-important doctor-patient relationship.

8. Take Before and After Photos. The doctor should take standard before and after photographs, particularly because they can demonstrate to a jury that there has been an improvement in the patient despite the patient's own negative view of the results.

9. Never Promise Too Much. The physician should engage in a comprehensive informed consent discussion listing all the possible serious complications. A nurse should be present if possible and serve as a witness to the signing of an informed consent document. If possible, the best practice is to allow a two- or three-day minimum grace period between the signing and the surgery.

10. Beware Insurance Forms. A physician should not guarantee that cosmetic procedures will be covered by the patient's insurance. He should not accommodate a patient by fudging insurance or medical reports in order to help procure insurance coverage. Such conduct—however well-intentioned—may subject the doctor and the patient to civil or criminal liability. It also allows the plaintiff to attack the physician's credibility before the jury.

CHAPTER 4

PREPARING THE PLAINTIFF'S CASE

§ 4.1 Evaluating the Plaintiff

When contemplating taking an elective plastic surgery case, you must evaluate the potential plaintiff from several points of view. Interview the plaintiff to determine the motivation for bringing suit. Does the patient have legitimate complaints or is she merely dissatisfied with a less than perfect result that is not indicative of negligence? Discuss in detail the factors that brought the plaintiff to the surgeon initially and the vital details of all communications that were held. Be especially wary of any claims or details that seem particularly outlandish, or of the plaintiff who has a documented history of litigation.

The plaintiff's present demeanor, appearance, articulation, and sincerity must be assessed. What is the potential jury appeal? If negative, are the siblings or family members potentially good witnesses? Are they reliable sources of information? In this investigative stage, all the facts must be taken into consideration before undertaking this costly and time-consuming litigation.

Because of the possible unstable nature of some vanity clients, have a retainer agreement drawn that specifically reserves your right to withdraw or delegate authority after an investigation of the facts. Explain any anticipated difficulties and attendant expenses. Outline the chronology of the lawsuit. Do not ever make guarantees or promise a speedy trial.

If you accept the case, discuss all settlement offers and reduce them to writing. If there is any question as to your client's competence to understand a settlement offer, consider obtaining permission to consult with a relative or close friend. In open court, make a record of your conversations with the plaintiff and procure her informed consent under oath to any settlement offer.

§ 4.2 Evaluating Medical Records

In any medical malpractice case the evaluation of the medical record is a crucial determinant of the validity of a claim. A plastic surgery case is one in which the medical records should be particularly scrutinized, as they should provide substantiation for the plaintiff's claims.

The following data should be extrapolated from the records in order to ascertain whether there is a basis for a valid action.

1. Operative Report
   - **a.** Does the operative note contain pertinent details of incisions, findings, and length of procedures or is it devoid of crucial factors?
   - **b.** Is the operative report simply a boilerplate form containing standardized language with no individualization for the particular patient? Such a report potentially exposes a defendant to attack.
   - **c.** Were any complications noted during the procedure such as excessive bleeding, problems with tension, or neurological injury?
   - **d.** Who signed the operative report? Was it the surgeon or a resident?
   - **e.** When was the report dictated and typed? A report dictated long after the procedure implies the possibility of alteration or of an "ideal" report not reflective of true events.
2. Preoperative Notes
   - **a.** Was an adequate history recorded?
   - **b.** Were there obvious contraindications to surgery?

c. What is the documentation concerning informed consent?
d. Were preoperative photos taken?
e. How long before surgery was the patient first evaluated? Did it allow the patient enough time to make an informed decision?
f. Did the physician call in appropriate consultation—medical and/or psychiatric—if indicated?

3. Postoperative Notes
   a. What conversations are documented? Did the plaintiff voice complaints? What were the defendant's responses?
   b. When were sutures and bandages removed?
   c. What instructions were given by the defendant to the plaintiff?
   d. What activities did the patient resume? If a patient failed to adhere to restrictions, she may have been responsible for the result or at least contributorily negligent.
4. Laboratory Results
   a. Were there abnormalities in laboratory values that should have alerted the surgeon to the potential for complications?
5. Nurses Notes
   a. Often these provide indications of a patient's complaints, the care rendered, and the conversations held. Are these consistent with the progress notes or do they reflect discrepancies that enhance the possibility of malpractice?
6. Informed Consent Form
   a. When was this signed? Who were the witnesses?
   b. Did the plaintiff sign it with all items completed or was it blank?

§ 4.3 Assessing Plastic Surgery, Psychiatric, and Litigation History

You must discover the plaintiff's past medical, legal, and surgical history before the defense does. Be alert for signs of the surgical junkie or the habitual litigator. You may discover a history of prior psychiatric problems.

A thorough history must be ascertained regarding pending or prior claims. Has this client made similar claims and suffered similar injuries? Has he been represented by other attorneys in this claim or any prior ones? In prior personal injury actions, emotional damages such as depression and anxiety may have been pleaded. If you do not claim aggravation of these conditions, the client's credibility will be severely impeached and the value of the case diminished.

In many states the prior litigation history of the plaintiff can be determined through a central index bureau, which for a nominal fee will provide a listing of all cases brought by the plaintiff. In addition, attorneys can review the index books of their local jurisdictions to ascertain if there is any pending or prior litigation brought by the plaintiff.

§ 4.4 Parties to Suit

Plaintiff

The plaintiff's counsel should join all parties as plaintiffs who have a right to recover. In a plastic surgery case this would generally include the plaintiff's spouse, who may have a cause of action for loss of consortium.

Defendants

Generally, the defense counsel should join all individuals who have potential liability. However, caution must be taken that a suit is not brought without substantiation, as this may result in the imposition of sanctions for bringing a frivolous suit. See Fed. R. Civ. Proc. 11.

Individuals you may want to consider joining are:

1. Referring physicians
2. Anesthesiologists
3. Nurses
4. Manufacturers of products.

§ 4.5 Causes of Action

The plaintiff's attorney should assert alternate causes of action (if permitted in her jurisdiction). The potential claims in a plastic surgery case may include:

1. Negligence
2. Breach of warranty of contract
3. Breach of confidentiality
4. Assault and battery
5. Lack of informed consent.

An astute attorney should investigate all of these potential claims and plead appropriately.

Alternative causes of action may be even more significant when statutes of limitations differ. For example, an action may still be viable under a breach of contract theory but barred by the malpractice statute, which is generally shorter.

The statute of limitations must be evaluated during this initial period. Even if the statute apparently bars an action, explore whether exceptions exist. In some states a discovery rule may toll a statute until the time a deformity is discovered.

§ 4.6 The Surgeon's Office Records

Surgeons often keep incomplete notes. However, the failure to document creates an unfavorable impression on a jury and may be contrary to accepted standards. You must demand copies of the original dictated records. Never assent to a mere summary report. Insist on original notes and impressions.

Medical records are designed to chronicle the history of a patient's treatment. They also provide a forum of communication for all those who have treated or will treat the patient.

Sometimes when the surgeon suspects that a malpractice suit may be commenced, he may record follow-up notes to protect himself. For example, where there is a bad result, the surgeon might write up subsequent conversations with the family, hospital personnel, or other treating doctors. The defense counsel may argue that these are privileged and not discoverable, because they do not relate to treatment. The plaintiff's counsel should depose the defendant on these subjects and move to compel production, because (1) it is unlikely that these notes were actually prepared for litigation, (2) they cannot be independently duplicated, (3) they may have been used to refresh the witness's recollection, and (4) they are medical records kept in the ordinary course of business.

Some key questions concerning recent events that should be asked include:

History

1. Has the doctor documented his rationale for treatment? Good practice dictates that he should and that a treatment plan be prepared.
2. Did he consult prior treating physicians and surgeons? Did he speak with family members, particularly if the patient is a poor or unreliable historian?
3. Did the surgeon ever obtain prior treatment records such as those of a hospital, clinic, or private physician?

Side Effects of Medication

1. Did the doctor monitor side effects of medication or perform any physical examination? It is poor practice not to inquire into the adverse effects set forth in the *Physicians' Desk Reference.* Did the doctor check blood pressure and pulse or check potential side effects such as dizziness, headaches, and blurred vision? Did he bother to ascertain whether the patient was on other medications that might be contraindicated?
2. Did he refer the patient to another doctor because of any physical side effects of medication? For example, did blurred vision cause him to refer the patient to an opthalmologist or neurologist?
3. Did the surgeon make a differential diagnosis? Did he consider other treatments?

Failure to fully document the medication prescribed is another Achilles' heel for many psychiatrists. Sometimes free samples of drugs obtained from the pharmaceutical company's detail man are dispensed without any record. Very often, the surgeon does not document any informed consent conversations concerning the administration of the drug. Considering the wide range of adverse side effects associated with psychotropic medications, this can be devastating evidence at trial. The absence of documentation does not mean, however, that such conversations did not take place.

The records, no matter how well documented, should be kept in an extremely confidential and secure environment. If they are obtained by a third party because they were not secured, liability can be imposed for breach of confidentiality.

§ 4.7 Hospital Records

Hospital records, as distinguished from those of physicians, must adhere to the standards of the Joint Commission of Accreditation of Hospitals if the institution is accredited or receives Medicare reimbursement. These records are the results of interactions between the members of the surgical team. Typically, these professionals include a surgeon, several resident interns, nurses, aides, technicians, and other ancillary therapists. Each specialist records observations, opinions, and findings through the medium of the hospital chart. But there are many records that often are not maintained with the official chart. They must therefore be demanded during discovery, before taking the deposition. They may include the following:

1. The Kardex. Index cards are used by the nursing staff to make notations regarding a patient's care, medication, and treatment and are used as a quick reference for orders or treatment. Notes are usually made in pencil and discarded upon the patient's discharge. These notes usually duplicate the official record but may have additional information that never gets recorded in the chart.

2. **The incident report.** Hospitals require a report of any unusual event (for example, a fall from bed, suicide attempt, or violent episodes). This report is not always considered part of the regular record but is maintained in the regular course of business and filed separately. It is generally discoverable but usually will not be produced voluntarily. Sometimes its existence can be determined by a specifically colored sticker dot on the chart folder, even though the report is not kept with the chart. The incident report often comments on negligence factors and remedial measures suggested to avoid repetitions. In some states, it may be shielded as a work product or as an educational document prepared to further medical knowledge.

3. **The log books.** These may detail problems with equipment, doctors, or patients. These records are not permanently maintained but may contain information that, in retrospect, is important, such as the length of a procedure or a shortage in the staff complement. If an incident or injury later arises out of this situation, the log book description may be more complete and incriminating than the subsequent hospital record.

4. **Psychological test results.** These are often included in the hospital records and are especially significant in plastic surgery procedures.

If any of these records are missing, it does not necessarily mean that the hospital is intentionally withholding information. If the log book or Kardex no longer exists, depose the nurses who were on duty. It is amazing how many attorneys will forgo nurses' depositions and rely instead on the deposition of an administrator or head nurse.

§ 4.8 Plaintiff's Discovery

The plaintiff's counsel must plan discovery with care and complete it before conducting the deposition of the defendants. A timetable should be set and meticulously adhered to. Defendants have been known to delay because of the press of other business. All hospitals' and physicians' records must be obtained and reviewed carefully before the deposition. The deposition is not the time to first discover and digest records or answers to interrogatories. Time is needed to review materials to frame proper penetrating questions and obtain binding answers. The defendant should be confronted with the authoritative texts at the deposition.

§ 4.9 Reversing Priority of Discovery

In most jurisdictions, the defendants have priority of discovery. However, a vigilant and resourceful plaintiff's counsel may be able literally to steal that priority away. This can be done with:

1. A motion for discovery prior to filing the action to frame a complaint
2. Laches, if the defendant fails to serve discovery notices promptly or sleeps on his rights
3. Special circumstances that entitle the plaintiff to reverse priority and obtain expedited discovery.

The general criteria for priority to be granted are that:

1. The complaint alleges a breach of fiduciary duty
2. The information relevant to the action is in the custody, knowledge, or possession of the defendants, or
3. The evidence sought will be submitted in anticipation and support of a motion for injunctive relief.

In New York, if special circumstances warrant the plaintiff's examining first, or some other plan appears desirable in an individual case, the Court has ample authority under New York Civil Practice Law and Rules 3103(a) to vary priorities.

§ 4.10 Expert Witnesses

The expert witness will, of course, be a crucial factor in the potential success of any lawsuit. Thus, a plaintiff's attorney must take particular care to choose one who will facilitate the proof of her case. The following guidelines should be used by counsel for either side when an expert is sought.

1. Board certification: Most plastic surgeons are members of the American Board of Plastic Surgery. The highest qualification is a Diplomate and preference should be given to choosing someone with this qualification. Experts may also be chosen from other fields such as otolaryngology or dermatology but it must be demonstrated at trial that the expert is familiar with the standards that a plastic surgeon would use.
2. Academic credentials: Ideally, experts should have excellent academic qualifications. The plastic surgeon who has an appointment as a professor often impresses the average juror.

3. Publications: An expert who has published articles and/or books also may be impressive to a jury. However, the attorney must be familiar with any publication that has any implication for the particular case as a contradiction could prove to be most embarrassing at trial.
4. Experience in court: A potential expert should not be known as a professional witness. Ideally, the expert should have some experience both as a plaintiff's and as a defendant's expert to avoid claims of bias. However, be cautious of an expert who derives a substantial portion of his income from litigation. Also, the expert who advertises should be avoided.
5. Experience with the procedure in question: The expert used should be well versed with the procedure used. Nothing can be more embarrassing than having an expert admit she hasn't performed a procedure in years.

§ 4.11 Avoiding the Professional Witness

Another important consideration is the extent to which an expert has previously testified. Has he become a "professional witness"? If so, does the defense have transcripts of his testimony? Has he appeared too often for one side or the other? Does he advertise in the legal trade papers in any way that will demean him and discredit your case? See **Chapter 2** for examples of recent expert advertisements found in national law magazines and the dangers therein.

§ 4.12 Choosing the Best Expert

Often the best liability experts can be chosen from among the very highest ranks of their professions. Professors and other academicians often are the most critical of their peers. However, an otherwise highly qualified but very pedantic expert witness should be used in conjunction with a psychologist or therapist endowed with the "common touch." A combination of disciplines may be your best approach. Other potential experts can be social workers, nurses, occupational, physical, music, or art therapists. If this combination approach is not possible, the next wisest course is to offer testimony by an expert who practices the same specific speciality as the defendant. There is no such thing as the perfect expert, but you should seek a witness who:

1. Is not overly identified as a plaintiff's expert
2. Is board-certified, but do not assume that board certification in forensic psychiatry is always an advantage. It may be that such an

expert treats very few patients, testifies constantly, or has written extensively on such topics as "how to testify and dress successfully" for trial and charges more per hour for court cases than for treating patients.

3. Has written applicable professional articles
4. Has some prior courtroom experience
5. Has a teaching affiliation with a major university
6. Is not overly pedantic, but charming and able to communicate well to the jury
7. Conveys an aura of trustworthiness, sincerity, and reasonableness
8. Has the time and patience to meet with you and review the records.

CHAPTER 5

PREPARING THE DEFENDANT'S CASE[1]

§ 5.1 Receiving the Summons

> The unfolded paper in her hand was a summons with an attached complaint that accused her of being a negligent doctor, of being a careless and indifferent physician who had done grievous harm to Terry Walker. She was being sued for $10 million . . . . The psychiatrist stared down at the summons, at the title that had so suddenly been given to her. For unrelieved months and years to come she would be known as the defendant.[2]

These words were written by Dr. Sarah Charles, a psychiatrist who was sued for malpractice in a suicide case. Even though she was ultimately

[1] This chapter is adapted from *Preparing the Defendant's Case* in J. Robertson, Psychiatric Malpractice 45–64 (John Wiley & Sons 1988). Used with permission.

[2] S. Charles & E. Kennedy, Defendant: A Psychiatrist on Trial for Medical Malpractice 6–7 (1985). *See also* T. Gutheil & J. Applebaum, Clinical Handbook of Psychiatry and the Law 201–02 (1982).

exonerated, the experience moved her to publish a research paper[3] and a best-selling book on the psychological effects of litigation on physicians.

Dr. Charles conducted a survey of 500 physicians to assess the impact of medical malpractice litigation on their professional practices and personal lives. The subjects were a sample of physicians in Cook County, Illinois, who had been sued between 1977 and 1981. Although this study cannot be used to generalize the total physician population, it does provide a fascinating and sobering insight for physicians, patients, and their counsel.[4]

Most respondents felt that the plaintiff's suit was unjustified. Many resented efforts of insurance and legal counsel to settle the case, and 60.4 percent felt that settling the case was tantamount to an admission of guilt. However, more than half (54.5 percent) felt that litigation is part of practicing medicine in today's world and not an affront to one's competence.

As a result of being sued, most respondents (69.1 percent) kept more meticulous records, but many (25.3 percent) recorded less pertinent information. Most (61.8 percent) ordered diagnostic tests for protection, even when clinical judgment indicated that these were not necessary. A total of 41.8 percent stopped treating certain kinds of patients, and 28.2 percent stopped performing certain high-risk procedures.

Many of these physicians (18.8 percent) admitted to indecisiveness and an inability to concentrate as well as a repetitive loss of nerve in some clinical situations. Even if symptoms lasted only a few weeks (some admitted that symptoms lasted for years), there was an undeniable impact on the physician's ability to practice.

More than half (56.6 percent) of the respondents said they and their families had suffered as a result, and 19.4 percent felt that their medical practices had suffered. More than one-third had thoughts of retiring early. Another 8.1 percent noted the onset of physical illnesses; three of these experienced a coronary during the time of litigation. Ten of 136 physicians (7.4 percent) who responded acknowledged an exacerbation of a previously diagnosed condition (for example, angina, duodenal ulcer, spastic colon, and hypertension).

More than a quarter of the doctors surveyed mentioned feelings of aloneness in their efforts to vindicate themselves, but only about 10 percent sought moral support from their peers. Another 20.3 percent reported pervasive anger accompanied by changes in mood, inner tension, frustration, irritability, insomnia, fatigue, gastrointestinal symptoms, or headaches. Interestingly, none of the respondents to this survey had actually suffered an adverse trial verdict.

---

[3] S. Charles, J. Wilbard, & E. Kennedy, *Physician's Self-reports of Reactions to Malpractice Litigation,* 141 Am. J. Psychiatry 563–65 (1984).

[4] S. Charles & E. Kennedy, Defendant: A Psychiatrist on Trial for Medical Malpractice, viii–ix, 7 (1985).

In her book, Dr. Charles summarized her reactions during the course of her own malpractice case:

> My first feelings after being charged with medical malpractice were of being utterly alone. Suddenly I felt isolated from my colleagues and patients. Since then I have learned, in the course of my own suit and trial and in the research I have conducted, that this feeling of aloneness is not at all unusual, that almost every physician accused of being negligent has a similar reaction. I also understand that what I experienced during the five year span of my own case—that it swallowed up my life completely, demanded constant attention and study, multiplied tension and strain, generated a pattern of broken sleep and anxiety because . . . my integrity as a person and as a physician had been damaged and might be permanently lost—became the common reactions of most doctors accused of negligence.[5]

Upon service of the summons, the defendant undoubtedly undergoes a trauma unique to an accused. She experiences a roller coaster ride of emotions including fear, rejection, and anger. She feels as if she has been indelibly branded as a defendant for all time. Plastic surgeons, among other physicians, seem to be severely affected by a malpractice suit. This may be in part because of the intimate nature of their relationship with many of their patients. In vanity cases there is also a touch of the artistic temperament aroused in the surgeon.

This initial trauma may cause the doctor to withdraw to such an extent that cooperation in her own defense becomes impossible. The sensitive defense attorney must understand this. You must explain that this is not a criminal proceeding but a civil one. Loss of license is not usually involved. The accusations are not to be taken personally but, rather, professionally. An objective approach assures that the doctor will be neither apologetic and obsequious nor hostile and condescending.

After the initial shock subsides, some defendants retreat into rage and resistance. However, their ardor often turns to apathy as time and discovery drag on.

When the suit involves death or serious personal injury, a doctor may become overwhelmed by feelings of guilt. He may internalize the lawsuit and blame himself out of all proportion to the magnitude of the suit. This is the time that unwitting admissions are made or written records changed or supplemented. Most often the words or the writings do little to help his position at trial. If hauled before a jury at this stage of the proceeding, this mea culpa attitude practically guarantees an adverse verdict. Despite the fact that a valid legal defense may exist, punishment appears to be his only salvation. Neither anger nor guilt is an appropriate

---

[5] *Id.* at xiii. Even more extreme reactions have been reported. *See Worried about Malpractice Suit, Physician is an Apparent Suicide,* N.Y. Times, Nov. 2, 1986, at B8.

emotional predicate for preparation of the defense. Many physicians become so incapacitated by their emotions that they subconsciously suppress important facts. If these facts come to light as surprises during a deposition or trial, it will be too late to counteract them.

As defense counsel, you should help to restore personal and professional confidence and self-image to the doctor. Not only will this improve the attorney-client relationship, but it will enable counsel to better implement the defense strategy. The plastic surgeon must go through this cathartic experience before he can properly assist in preparation of the defense. These emotions of anger, anguish, and guilt must be expeditiously expunged. The physician should be advised that the Draconian window dressing of the complaint is little more than boilerplate allegations used interchangeably from one lawsuit to another.

Be sensitive to the effects of the trauma of the summons on your client. Whether the doctor wins or loses the case may be much less important than the ultimate emotional damage suffered.

§ 5.2 Choice of Counsel and Other Insurance Issues

Although initially the insurer almost invariably selects defense counsel, there can be many exceptions. If there is a reservation of rights with respect to coverage of any of the claims in the complaint, the physician may have an absolute right to choose her own independent counsel at the expense of the insurance company. For example, in sexual misconduct cases, the carrier often defends and indemnifies on the negligence allegations but not on any claim of an intentional sexual liaison between the doctor and patient. Theoretically, counsel selected by the insurer may not defend the noninsured allegations as vigorously as those that are covered by the insurance policy. The plastic surgeon can, in most jurisdictions, demand her own counsel because of a potential conflict of interest between the doctor and counsel selected by the insurer. Because the insurer and the defense counsel have probably enjoyed an ongoing business relationship, courts have held that this creates the appearance of a conflict, which entitles the insured to select counsel of her own choice.[6]

[6] Schwartz v. Sar Corp., 19 Misc. 2d 660, 195 N.Y.S.2d 496, *rev'd on other grounds,* 9 A.D.2d 910, 195 N.Y.S.2d 819 (1959) (it is duty of insurer to act impeccably and in good faith and in a careful and prudent manner, giving to the insured its undivided support); Trader's & Gen. Ins. Co. v. Rudco Oil & Gas Co., 129 F.2d 621 (10th Cir. 1942) (it is insurer's duty to conduct the whole defense and to protect the insured, as well as itself, against liability at all stages of litigation); Smoot v. State Farm Mut. Auto. Ins. Co., 299 F.2d 525 (5th Cir. 1962); Ging v. American Liberty Ins. Co., 423 F.2d 573 (5th Cir. 1970); Attleboro Mfg. Co. v. Frankfort Marina, Accident & Plate Glass Ins. Co., 240 F. 573 (1st Cir. 1917) (an insurer acts as agent of insured); Merrit v. Reserve Ins. Co., 34 Cal. App. 3d 858, 110 Cal. Rptr. 511 (1973).

Other potential conflicts include coverage for only a portion of the period of treatment involved in the allegations, or a situation in which the physician is provided with a free defense but not with indemnity for a judgment awarded by a jury.

There are also many situations in which a malpractice insurer voluntarily permits the physician to select her own counsel. If the doctor has been represented by a law firm in the past that is on the approved list of the carrier, the carrier will invariably accede to the physician's request. Even if the law firm is not known to the insurer, if it is reputable and experienced in malpractice, the insurer will often consent. Remember, insurers want to keep the good faith of their insureds. It is often in their best interest to consent to the insured's request, particularly if there may be litigation in the future over the manner in which the defense counsel defended the physician. In any potential conflict situation, the insurer is in a better position if the defense was conducted by counsel of the doctor's choosing so that there can never be any charges of collusion or impropriety between defense counsel and the company.

Another potential conflict that gives rise to the physician's right to choose her own counsel is when there are multiple codefendants insured by the same carrier. Because there may be cross-claims among the defendants, separate counsel should be appointed for each physician or hospital. Although this situation does not guarantee that the physician can select counsel, some carriers will voluntarily accede to the insured's request.

Finally, even in the absence of any conflict, the physician can always request counsel of her own choice. There is nothing to lose. In fact, even if the plastic surgeon has no particular firm in mind, she could at least interview several firms recommended by her malpractice counsel, in much the way a patient can choose from several potential therapists.

It should also be noted, however, that most insurance contracts reserve the right of the carrier to select counsel. Nevertheless, it may be in the insurer's best interest to negotiate or surrender the right. Remember that in all of the situations we have described, the insurer pays the reasonable fees charged by counsel selected by the doctor or chosen by the company itself.

Even in situations in which the physician is not entitled to free counsel of her own choosing, many physicians retain personal counsel at their own expense to monitor the case, make recommendations about strategy and investigations, and consider whether settlement should be consummated to save the insured from a verdict in excess of her policy limits. In any case with a potential for a large verdict or punitive damages, it is highly recommended that the plastic surgeon retain her own counsel.

What are the remedies of a physician who believes that the insurer or its selected counsel are guilty of negligence or bad faith? In 1987, an Oregon jury awarded $2.1 million plus attorney fees to a physician who sued his malpractice carrier for negligence in conducting his defense and for bad faith in not negotiating a settlement.[7] The jury in the underlying medical malpractice case had previously returned a verdict for $3 million, which was far in excess of his policy limits. The plaintiff's counsel had offered to settle the case for the policy limit. The insurer declined and never offered more than $150,000. In the subsequent action against the insurer, the jury awarded the doctor the $2 million excess he owed the patient plus additional money for lost income, lost business, and emotional damages. The jury found that the company failed to negotiate a settlement in good faith and was negligent in investigating and defending the case. One interesting issue that was raised during the trial was whether the plaintiff could discover the report of the peer review committee that evaluated the case for the insurer. The trial court held that it was privileged.

The doctrine of bad faith may even permit a plaintiff and an excess carrier to file an action against the insurer. The plaintiff could either be subrogated to the rights of the insured or could bring any action as a judgment creditor. With respect to the excess carrier, privity of contract gives viability to such a cause of action.[8]

Whether an insurance company acted in bad faith is a question for a jury, and the evidence is largely circumstantial. Refusal to tender the policy limit is not evidence of bad faith as a matter of law and depends on the overall circumstances at the time the demand was made, including the exposure to the insured and an evaluation of the liability prospects at that time. Interestingly, offering the policy limits in certain situations may not exculpate a carrier from a finding of bad faith if the offer is not timely.[9]

Expert testimony is admissible in a bad faith action, but such testimony is not a requirement to establish a prima facie case. Expert testimony is limited to industry standards regarding investigations and evaluation of a claim, as opposed to the expert giving his personal opinion as to whether there was bad faith in a specific case.[10]

The insurance company file can be subpoenaed on the ground that the file was prepared for the benefit of both the insurer and the insured. Additionally, the defense attorney can be called as a witness with respect to her discussions, recommendations, and work product.

Other factors that can be considered by a jury are how thoroughly the facts of the case were investigated, the failure to negotiate, the timing of the negotiation, whether the insured was informed of settlement possibilities, and whether the insured was advised of the realistic possibility of a judgment in excess of the policy limits and her right to obtain personal counsel.

---

[7] Stiff v. Continental Casualty Co., No. 840402347 (Or. 1987).

[8] Peter v. Travelers Ins. Co., 375 F. Supp. 1347 (C.D. Cal. 1974).

[9] Phelan v. State Farm Mutual, 114 Ill. App. 3d 96, 448 N.E.2d 579 (1983).

[10] Kulak v. Nationwide Mut. Ins. Co., 40 N.Y.2d 140, 351 N.E.2d 735, 386 N.Y.S.2d 87 (1976).

In one recent case, the doctor lost the underlying medical malpractice case and requested the insurer and defense counsel to file an appeal. While it was pending, the carrier settled within the policy limits. The doctor accused the carrier of bad faith and argued that he had a right to vindicate his reputation through the appeal. But the appellate court held that a physician had no cause of action against his insurer for settling a case on appeal without his permission and that he could not hold the insurer liable for any alleged negligence of the defense firm. The court held that there could be no bad faith when the insurance contract gave the insurer the right to settle. The insurer could not be liable for any negligence of defense counsel because the law firm was an independent contractor and not controlled by the carrier and enjoyed a competent reputation.[11]

In another case, an insurer was severely criticized for not splitting the defense until the eve of the trial after the malpractice panel had already exonerated one insured but not the other. The court held that this represented a potential conflict of the defense attorney in formulating strategy. The court even weighed imposing sanctions against the defense firm and declared a mistrial.[12]

Ironically, it also should be noted that an insurer can be liable for settling a case without the physician's permission, assuming that there is such a consent clause in the policy.

§ 5.3 Enlisting the Defendant's Cooperation

The surgeon must be made to understand the imperative need for cooperation with defense counsel chosen by the insurer. The defendant's input is absolutely necessary. There is no substitute for total commitment and cooperation between counsel and client. The defense will be no better than the doctor is willing to let it be. She is its fulcrum and persona.

A spirit of cooperation must be fostered from the initial meeting, which should take place as soon as possible after the lawsuit begins. This will help to establish the necessary rapport and make the case more than a mere pleading in counsel's mind. If there is a prayer for relief with a demand in excess of the policy limits, both the insurer and the insured or you as her personal counsel should be advised immediately. It is also essential that you and the client review strategy and plan prospective defenses immediately, not after the depositions. You should never merely rely on the

---

[11] Fe Liberty v. Damon, 129 A.D.2d 207, 517 N.Y.S.2d 632 (1987). *See also* Casualty Ins. v. Town & Country, 147 Ill. App. 3d 567, 498 N.E.2d 600 (1986); Marginian v. Allstate, 18 Ohio St. 3d 345, 481 N.E.2d 600 (1985).

[12] Hoolan v. New York Infirmary (N.Y. Sup. Ct. 1986), reported in Nat'l L.J., Oct. 28, 1986, at 1.

initial pleadings or summary reports from the insurer. A team spirit will invariably lead to better results, whether by settlement or verdict.

According to Dr. Richard Coburn, who is a plastic surgeon and a lawyer and has been a defendant in a malpractice case:

> [The physician] often behaves as though his head was in the proverbial sand, hoping the nightmare will go away if it cannot be seen or felt. If it is the doctor's first lawsuit, the lawyer may be quite surprised by the distress, hostility and fear. At least, be prepared to handle these emotions. The lawyer must remember that most physicians know little of pleadings and answers and will need a mini-course in the anatomy of a lawsuit. . . . The importance of this first exchange between the lawyer and doctor cannot be overemphasized. It will set the tone for the entire relationship, for while it is perfunctory business for the lawyer, it is traumatic for the doctor.[13]

Advise the doctor that you are in charge of the case and that there may be assistance from associates or paralegals. The physician must be disabused of the notion that she does not have to become involved because "it's the insurance company's problem." She must recognize that she is primarily responsible for her own defense and must assist in the plastic surgery aspects of the case. Ideally, she should be willing to provide names of pertinent medical books and assist in preparing a medical brief. Such involvement benefits the defense and prepares the doctor for subsequent deposition and the trial.

§ 5.4 Analyzing the Complaint

The defendant should review the causes of action pleaded in the complaint. Has a prima facie case been set forth? Are there causes of action for negligence only or are there other claims such as lack of informed consent or breach of warranty? Is the complaint properly pleaded or is it vague, ambiguous, or devoid of sufficient detail, perhaps being the proper subject of a motion to dismiss? See examples of complaints in **Appendixes A** through **F**.

§ 5.5 Checklist of Affirmative Defenses

The defense attorney's first attack on the plaintiff should occur with the answer. All relevant defenses should be considered in preparing the answer. Assert them if applicable, even if you are not sure that they have to

---

[13] R.J. Coburn, The Physician and the Malpractice Suit in Medical Malpractice Strategies and Practical Principles 44 (1986).

be specially pleaded as defenses. You don't want to risk being precluded at the time of trial. The following is a checklist of defenses that should be considered.

1. **Lack of personal jurisdiction.** This is the most critical defense to consider, because it is deemed waived in most jurisdictions if not pleaded. A motion to amend the answer later will be of no avail. Call the doctor and verify the method of service. Never rely on a note from the adjustor or the doctor that she was personally served. Only you can and should make that legal decision.

2. **Statutes of limitations.** Various statutes may apply for different causes of action. Check for expiration of statutes for wrongful death actions, which usually run only two years, as compared to the three-year negligence statutes. Remember that derivative actions for parents' loss of services and medical expenses may be barred even though an infant's action has been tolled.

3. **Workers' compensation.** Often the patient's injury may have arisen out of employment, or the defendant saw him in consultation for the employer as a coemployee and is entitled to this defense.

4. **Failure to state a cause of action.** Use this defense if the prima facie elements have not been pleaded or if there exists no such action at law (for example, emotional damages are not recoverable for relatives who only hear of the plaintiff's injury). A cause of action for malpractice might be improperly pleaded as one for breach of contract in order to take advantage of the longer statute of limitations.

5. **Therapeutic privilege.** This defense is available if, in the defendant's best judgment, informed consent was impossible to obtain, was unnecessary, or would have endangered the well-being of the patient. This may be codified by local statute or establish by common law. However, in today's society, which is especially concerned about patient rights, this is not a particularly viable defense.

6. **Contributory or comparative negligence of the patient.** The patient may have failed to follow advice regarding medication or treatment. In some jurisdictions, this defense is only a setoff or mitigation of damages. In others, it may act as a complete bar. In plastic surgery cases this is often manifested by the failure of the patient to undergo a corrective procedure.

7. **Assumption of risk.** An example is the patient's agreeing to undergo experimental laser therapy.

8. Failure to prove proximate cause. Even assuming that the plaintiff can prove a departure from the standard of care and damages, the case will be dismissed if the departure did not lead to or cause the alleged damage.

9. Best judgment of physician was exercised. This is a jury question that will exonerate the defendant from an error in judgment if she did a competent examination and considered all relevant factors and records.

10. A release signed by the patient. Such a release may exculpate the defendant. However, in most jurisdictions it is strictly construed against the defendant or held to violate public policy.

§ 5.6 Cross-Claims, Counterclaims, and Third-Party Complaints

While analyzing the complaint and preparing the answer, you as defense counsel must also consider cross-claims, counterclaims, and third-party actions. Although cross-claims may engender animosity early in the litigation and can be disastrous at trial, they must be considered to protect the defendant. They are particularly important if your client's insurance coverage is inadequate.

The defendant must decide whether it is appropriate to bring a cross-claim against codefendants. If it appears that the hospital committed negligence, the surgeon should plead a cross-claim. Often it is difficult to convince a surgeon that this is necessary and not a sign of disloyalty or anger.

If a patient refused to pay the doctor's bill, the doctor should counterclaim for services rendered. Do not hesitate to press this counterclaim. It is psychologically and legally consistent with your defense and will provide psychological solace to the defendant.

The defendant may also consider bringing a counterclaim against the plaintiff. In a plastic surgery case counterclaims that are frequently considered include those for fees outstanding. An action for defamation should also be considered if facts warrant it.

Consideration should be given to bringing in an appropriate third party. Third-party actions should be considered against such parties as equipment manufacturers, drug manufacturers, and another physicians or hospitals not named in the complaint. The plaintiff's counsel should first be encouraged to join them as direct defendants before the statute of limitations expires. Particular consideration must be given to manufacturers. For example, in a breast augmentation action the defendant may consider impleading the manufacturer of the implant when it failed to warn a physician that closed capsulotomies could cause damage to implants.

§ 5.7 Motion to Dismiss or for a More Definite Statement

When confronting the complaint, you must answer the allegations or oppose them with a motion to dismiss. If the pleading is too vague, then a motion to dismiss is the answer. Some plaintiffs' attorneys intentionally use short, concise, and intentionally barren and vague complaints. Others use prolix, rambling, and verbose pleadings. Many complaints name multiple defendants and are indistinguishable as to the allegations against them. Many fail even to specify the actual dates of malpractice.

Such boilerplate complaints, whether too fat or too lean, should be met promptly with a motion to dismiss as insufficient or for a more definite statement. If you have had success with such a motion in the past, attach the prior court decisions. They are very persuasive precedents, particularly if you catch the same firm repeatedly using the same condemned complaint.

Under Federal Rule of Civil Procedure 11, the federal courts impose severe sanctions for an attorney's failure to investigate the medical records before filing.[14] Federal Rule of Civil Procedure 12 permits a defendant to move for a more definite statement when the pleading is so vague or ambiguous that a party cannot reasonably be required to frame a responsive pleading. If the motion is granted and the order not obeyed within 10 days, the court may strike the pleading.

Courts have been vigilant in insisting that plaintiffs add some meat to bare bones complaints or face dismissal, although usually with leave to replead. A pleading must be sufficiently particular to give the court and parties notice of the transactions, occurrences, or series of occurrences intended to be proved and the material elements of each cause of action.[15] In a malpractice action, there must at least be reference to the times and types of treatment involved.[16]

The motion to dismiss or for a more definite statement has other advantages for the harried defense counsel. In most states, it provides an

---

[14] Albright v. Upjohn Co., 788 F.2d 1217 (6th Cir. 1986).

[15] Mo. Rev. Stat. § 509.310 (1986); Neb. Rev. Stat. §§ 25-803 to 833 (1943); N.Y. Civ. Prac. L. & R. 3013 (McKinney 1982); N.C. Gen. Stat. § 1A–d, Rules 8., 9., 12 (Michie 1986); Ohio Rev. Code Ann. § 3, R. Civ. Proc. 8 (Banks & Baldwin 1987); Wis. Stat. § 80206 (1985–86).

[16] *See, e.g.,* Fassnacht v. Hartman, 67 A.D.2d 676, 412 N.Y.S.2d 179 (1979).

automatic stay of the time to answer, thereby providing additional opportunity for investigation, research, and reflection.

§ 5.8 Defendant's Discovery

Plan your preliminary discovery now. This plan should be a blueprint for the building of a solid defense at trial. Prepare interrogatories and a demand for a bill of particulars, if appropriate. Serve a notice for depositions. These basic, standard demands must be served with dispatch, preferably with the answer.

§ 5.9 Postdeposition Discovery

Following your deposition of the plaintiff, you will uncover new information and need new discovery to prepare for trial. Serve notices to produce and move to compel if timely response is not received. Postdeposition discovery usually includes requests for the following items:

1. Subsequent treatment records of current and previously unidentified physicians
2. Other statements made by the plaintiff or witnesses or, applications for disability, Social Security benefits, or new employment
3. New depositions of potential witnesses including relatives or friends
4. Private records kept by some meticulous plaintiffs along with memoranda or diaries of their medical treatment are quite common, particularly if the plaintiff is paranoid. One woman kept a scrapbook about her psychiatric treatment and conversations with the doctor, which she did not even tell her attorney about. Do not miss the opportunity to inquire about such treasures and attempt to procure them. Move for all employment records, school records, and driver's license applications. The license application often asks about any mental condition that may affect the ability to drive a motor vehicle. A patient may have denied mental disability in order to keep a license.
5. Prescriptions. In any case involving chemotherapy or prolonged use of medications, it is essential to obtain authorizations for the prescriptions. Original prescriptions and pharmaceutical records are essential, particularly those involving side effects or adverse reactions. Patients often cannot recall if they got prescriptions or exactly when or where they were filled. Because many surgeons fail to keep careful prescription records, it is imperative to obtain the record of prescriptions from the pharmacist. Discovery from the pharmacy will

reveal whether the patient has even filled the prescription or if other doctors were prescribing similar or contraindicated drugs. Potential third-party defendants may be discovered among these physicians. At times the pharmacist himself will emerge as the culprit when he knew or should have known of overprescribing or contraindicated combinations prescribed for the patient.

§ 5.10 Selecting the Defense Expert

The most important time to select an expert is before discovery begins. However, this opportunity is often lost. Many insurers hesitate to incur the expense at this early juncture of litigation. However, it is preferable to enlist the aid of the expert as soon as possible to assist in planning the defense and evaluating the surgical aspects. The defendant can herself suggest experts. Medical schools and department chiefs at leading hospitals are excellent candidates. Resist the temptation to use a close friend of the defendant's or one who has previously testified for her; the impeachment and bias at trial would be insurmountable. It is similarly not wise to use an expert who is known as a professional defense witness or who advertises excessively in the legal trade papers.

Under the Federal Rules your expert and his report are discoverable.[17] A deposition can also be conducted by your adversary. Courts have ruled that the work product exception articulated in Federal Rule of Civil Procedure 26(b)(3) does not apply to experts who are expected to testify.[18] Your expert is protected, however, if he is employed as a consultant only. It is wise to have a consultant as well as a true expert because the consultant can be more objective and critical of your case. However, you cannot call him as a witness in a federal case if you have not disclosed his name and report to your adversary during discovery.

Also avoid the temptation of using the same expert over and over again. Some defense lawyers have adopted a habit of retaining current or prior clients as defense experts. But the danger is too great that an alert plaintiff's counsel will uncover the fact that your expert is or has been a defendant in a malpractice case and your firm represented him. Indeed, some jurors have told this author that they thought such an expert wants to "get even with plaintiffs" or "owed a debt of gratitude" to the firm and would testify regardless of the merits. A liberal court may then permit inquiry into the nature of the prior action or of your relationship with the

---

[17] Fed. R. Civ. P. 26(a). *See also* Fed. R. Civ. P. 26(b)(4).

[18] Quadrini v. S. Korsky, 425 F. Supp. 81 (D. Conn. 1977). However, *see* Beverage Mktg. Corp. v. Ogilvy & Mather Direct Concrete Pipe Mach., 98 F.R.D. 740 (E.D. Mo. 1983) (a nontestifying expert's report could be disclosed because a testifying expert had read it).

witness. In any event, it will cast doubt on the credentials and credibility of counsel and witness.

Consider retaining two experts: one to be a negative and critical consultant and the other to serve as your trial expert, assuming he has concluded there is no liability. It is best for you not to socialize with your experts and for them not to socialize with the defendant. Cross-examination might be brutal or embarrassing if you do. Examine the potential expert, particularly regarding his background, publications, and testifying history. Has he ever testified for your adversary? If so, opposing counsel may know of an Achilles heel to attack concerning the credibility of credentials of your witness. Has he testified for your partners or associates? Worse, has he treated you or them? If so, you may have your own Achilles heel.

§ 5.11 Expert Selection Checklist

The following list of dos and do nots should guide your selection of the defense expert:

Do not pick:

1. Friends (or your own doctor)
2. Clients
3. Repeaters
4. Ivory tower types
5. Professional witnesses

Do pick:

6. Doctors qualified in the specific specialty
7. Board-certified physicians
8. Teachers
9. Active practitioners
10. Strong and affable personalities
11. Experts who are reasonable and concede limits
12. Witnesses willing to meet with you.

CHAPTER 6

DEPOSITIONS

§ 6.1 Introduction

The deposition is perhaps the most useful discovery tool in an action based on negligence in the performance of plastic surgery. It allows the defense attorney to explore the vanity of the plaintiff and discover inconsistencies and collateral information about the basis of the plaintiff's claim. It provides the framework for cross-examination and impeachment at trial. For the plaintiff it is the best way of obtaining evidence of departures to submit to the expert and of evaluating the defendant's case and jury appeal.

§ 6.2 Purposes of Depositions

The plaintiff's deposition of the defendant can be used to:

1. Perpetuate the defendant's testimony
2. Authenticate the medical records and documents
3. Assess the credibility and jury appeal of the defendant
4. Ascertain the background, qualification, and credentials of the defendant
5. Ascertain the surgeon's or staff's undocumented conversations
6. Document the dates and course of the illness, the surgery employed, and the reasons for treatment and basis of any diagnosis. The details of surgical technique can be determined.
7. Establish, if possible, a prima facie case
8. Learn of consultations and conferences with other physicians who may be potential witnesses or even potential additional defendants
9. Probe the basis for the surgical treatment, diagnosis, or medication prescribed
10. Defuse potential defenses (for example, informed consent, comparative negligence, therapeutic privilege, best judgment, use of alternative therapy, or minority school of therapy).

The defendant's deposition of the plaintiff is more than a fact-finding mission. Its purposes are to:

1. Pin down the plaintiff's story
2. Gather information to impeach the plaintiff or witnesses at trial
3. Gather evidence to establish defenses
4. Discover and then obtain records concerning prior and subsequent treatment
5. Discover collateral source evidence that may lead to impeachable evidence (life insurance or other medical insurance applications, prior psychiatric problems, diaries, disability or workmen's compensation records, employment, physical or psychiatric examinations upon return to work)
6. Discover preexisting emotional disorder, trauma, or alternate etiology such as personality disorder

7. Assess the jury appeal, credibility, and disability of the plaintiff
8. Evaluate potential settlement value and potential jury verdict
9. Test the resolve and mettle of adverse counsel
10. Impress adverse counsel with your own resolve and the strength of the defense
11. Intimidate the plaintiff and/or plaintiff's counsel.

Of course, these partial lists of objectives are by no means exhaustive or complete. They are intended only as guidelines to be supplemented by counsel's own creativity, investigation, preparation, and the facts of each particular case.

§ 6.3 Psychology of Depositions

There is a definite psychology to taking or defending a deposition. Experts disagree on the appropriate approach, which varies from case to case, lawyer to lawyer, and witness to witness. However, in general, you want to extract as much evidence as possible from the witness or restrict as much as possible when defending.

Depending on your personality and the medical issues, consider one of the following approaches:

1. Intimidate the witness and your adversary (this may lead to early settlement or an overly defensive witness)
2. Cajole and humor the witness (this may result in a loquacious and cooperative witness)
3. Use a combination of both, but start with the second method.

With any technique, you must control the pace of the questions and extent of the answers. You must also be tenacious and resolve to get your answers. Establishing a good initial rapport with the witness is probably the best approach; otherwise he clams up, and no worthwhile admissions are obtained.

Establish and maintain good eye contact with the witness. Do not let it go. The eyes are the windows of the soul and the channels to the mind.

Ignore your adversary. Create an intense, almost therapeutic atmosphere between yourself and the witness. No one else in the room should matter or get in your way. The witness is yours; he owes you the answers. Help him, indeed encourage him, to respond. Most witnesses want to be truthful and cooperative and will be if the atmosphere does not become too custodial or adversarial.

§ 6.4 Preparation

There is no substitute for thorough and complete preparation before conducting or defending a deposition. The deposition should be scheduled only after you have received and reviewed all pertinent medical records and discovery documents. Do not wait until the surgeon's deposition to examine and analyze the medical records.

Plaintiff's Preparation

The plaintiff's counsel should exhaustively review the medical aspects of the case before the examination of the physician. Counsel should be familiar with the nature of the surgical technique employed and postsurgical care required. It is not necessary to disclose or boast of the extent of this knowledge because it may make the doctor too defensive. However, this review is a prerequisite to the orderly establishment of the prima facie case.

Answers to interrogatories should also be reviewed together with attendant documents. The responses and information form the basis for drafting incisive and penetrating questions. Under Federal Rule of Civil Procedure 30(b)(5) and (6), the plaintiff can designate documents that are to be produced at the deposition. However, production of these documents must take place before the deposition to avoid loss of time and opportunity for review.

In general, the following documents should be reviewed prior to the deposition:

1. The surgeon's office records
2. All hospital records including operative reports
3. Office telephone or log records
4. All billing records (they may contradict time and dates of treatment visits)
5. All medical insurance reports and billing (they may reveal discrepancies in billing, diagnosis, or purpose of request for reimbursements)
6. Any notes or correspondence written after treatment, subject to work product privilege
7. Any audio or video tapes of treatment sessions
8. Any peer review committee meeting memos, subject to claims of privilege recognized by many states
9. All hospital records, accident reports, nursing records, protocol records
10. Defendant's answers, admissions in pleadings, affirmations, or interrogatories

11. Any prior testimony of the defendant
12. Publications or tapes of the defendant
13. Relevant authoritative texts, journals
14. Consultations with your expert
15. Photographs (preop and postop)
16. Your own client's case, including allegation, pleading, and assessment of the therapist
17. Television or radio promotions by the defendant.

Defense Preparation

Defense counsel can be no less vigilant in procuring all necessary discovery in advance of the plaintiff's deposition. Answers to interrogatories, bills of particulars, medical reports and records, and a thorough investigation are necessary predicates for conducting a successful deposition. Conferences with your medical expert are also advised. Similarly, you should not permit your client to be deposed until all these documents are reviewed and the physician is thoroughly prepared.

Special Problems and Preparation for Both Sides

Overpreparation of the client is not a problem. Underpreparation is and must be avoided. The deposition is often a window to the trial. Sometimes it is the trial in miniature. Errors or misstatements may be impossible to correct. No defendant or plaintiff should undergo a searching examination without benefit of painstaking preparation, reviews, and rehearsal.

The doctor or patient should meet with counsel well in advance of the scheduled date and bring all pertinent records. A leisurely, informal, and nonconfrontational but informative conference should be held.

Special problems should be frankly and openly discussed, such as admission against interest, inculpating letters, and incomplete or incriminating records. No stone should be left unturned. The client should then be told to return in a week or two. At that time, solutions to these problems can be discussed and, with luck, the problems resolved. The last stage of preparation is a dress rehearsal in which you play the part of the examining attorney and an associate plays opposing counsel. At this point you should observe the witness's demeanor and critique his answers. One special problem that emerges for plastic surgeons is discrepancies in operative reports and insurance records. Some plastic surgeons will submit false insurance forms to help their patients obtain insurance coverage. A false diagnosis and operative description is given to give the impression that the surgery is medically necessary instead of an elective cosmetic procedure. Some surgeons do this out of altruistic motives. Others simply want to encourage business. But all such surgeons face embarrassment at trial and possibly even criminal prosecution for insurance fraud. This possibility must be fully discussed and dealt with at the predeposition meeting.

Another special problem for many surgeons is incomplete medical records. For a variety of reasons, a surgeon may fail to fully document the patient's records. Complaints, history, impressions, diagnosis, and medications are often left out or incompletely recorded. Occasionally, a doctor will ask if she should "correct" the record upon her justification that she had meant to put it all in but was too busy. Nothing could be worse! Besides violating the criminal law, such an alteration or addition will make a defensible case indefensible. The plaintiff's counsel may already have a photostated copy of the record. The altered record then becomes an indictment of the physician. Besides, alterations are easy to discover and discern. It is better to explain why something was not in the records than to try to explain an addition after the fact. The latter is an impossible task.

The tendency to alter the record is not exclusive to defendants. In one case, the plaintiff apparently altered her own insurance medical report after the doctor signed it. She checked the box for an ectropion (an eye that would not close) she alleged was caused by the defendant's malpractice during a blepharoplasty. The deception was discovered during cross-examination. A five-foot blowup of the document remained in the courtroom throughout the trial as a constant reminder of the perjury and fraud. The court impounded the evidence and invited the district attorney to monitor the trial. Both the plaintiff and her lawyer retained independent criminal counsel.

During the trial, the counsel for the defendant asked the plaintiff to retake the stand. She was asked point-blank who altered the record. Nervously looking at her attorney, she obediently and predictably took the Fifth Amendment. Each time a similar question was posed, she repeated that she "refused to answer on the grounds that I will incriminate myself." She would then look at her lawyer and ask, "Isn't that what I'm supposed to say?"

Needless to say, the jury returned a verdict in favor of the defendant doctor; the plaintiff and her attorney became defendants in a civil fraud suit filed by the doctor, and the matter was referred to the district attorney.

§ 6.5 Strategy

Taking the Plaintiff's Deposition. In a case involving a plastic surgery procedure it is generally preferable to permit the patient to talk uninterrupted. The patient is generally anxious to tell his story and will often volunteer information that will be useful in obtaining discovery or later at the time of trial. The deposition should cover all aspects of medical care rendered prior to and subsequent to the defendant's treatment, the exact conversation and treatment rendered by the defendant, and the complaints of the plaintiff. Detailed inquiry should be made into the witnesses present at the time of any conversations with the defendant and any individuals who referred the plaintiff to the defendant.

The Defendant's Deposition. The plaintiff's counsel should question the defendant on the technical aspects of the procedure performed. Often all of these are not contained in the operative note and it is important to discover if the surgeon will add anything to the procedure performed or if he will rely solely on the report. The defendant should also be examined as to his prior experience with the surgical procedure in question. Was it his first experience? Has he had special training in the procedure?

The names of standard medical texts should be asked for, which may prove useful at trial to contradict the doctor's statements. Specific details of the defendant's version of conversations and witnesses should be obtained. The plaintiff's attorney should also research the medical aspects of the case and ask detailed questions regarding the defendant's knowledge of this topic.

§ 6.6 Use of Deposition for Discovery: Films Expose Plaintiff's Lies

The deposition is the ideal time to discover facts that can lead to the impeachment of the witness. Interrogate the witness regarding all claims by asking for facts: dates, names, and places. If difficulty in working is claimed, demand the names of supervisors and job descriptions. If sexual problems are alleged, ask for the names of specific partners and details of the restrictions. Then follow up by investigation and/or deposition.

In one case in which a young woman alleged negligence in the performance of a rhinoplasty she complained that, not only did her nose look worse after surgery, but she couldn't breathe. She exaggerated the damage to the extent of claiming she couldn't even kiss as well. During questioning the plaintiff testified that a good friend had made some award-winning art films and suggested she have the plastic surgery in the first place. Seeing an opportunity to explore this, the defense attorney asked whether she appeared in these films. It turned out that the plaintiff had appeared in several films, some before and some after the surgery in question. A notice of discovery of the films was served because, not only did they show before and after evidence of her connected deviated septum, but the young lady had several torrid "love" scenes in them. The films were obtained and were far more valuable than still photographs. They not only depicted a good surgical result but also, when shown in slow motion, impeached the claims that she couldn't breathe normally or that her romantic skills were diminished (see §§ **6.8** through **6.24**).

§ 6.7 Use at Trial

The most important purpose of the deposition, often overlooked by both sides, is its use at trial. A deposition is not an end in and of itself. It is or should be a means to an end: victory at trial. It should guide preparation, questioning, and follow up. It becomes a potent weapon and can be used in all stages of the trial.

Jury Selection

Information gathered during depositions can be useful during jury selection, because you know what the adverse party has testified to and what types of jurors may be sympathetic or adverse. For example, if a party has been foolish enough to make disparaging remarks about a particular ethnic group, you can attempt to select a member of that group during voir dire.

In one plastic surgery case involving allegations of negligence in the performance of a blepharoplasty, the plaintiff indicated at her deposition that she did not undergo a second surgical procedure because she was afraid of looking Chinese. This statement later haunted her at the time of trial.

Opening

Admissions made during the deposition can be referred to in the opening with devastating effects. In one case, a plaintiff, in her deposition, testified as expected about her lack of informed consent and then added, as she looked at her counsel, "Isn't that what I'm supposed to say? I mean that's what you told me to say, right?" This was used during the opening and of course during cross-examination to impeach her credibility as well as that of opposing counsel.

Contradictions between statements made in the plaintiff's deposition and opening can also be exploited.

Cross-Examination

The deposition can also be used in cross-examination to impeach and discredit a witness with inconsistencies. For example:

Q: Do you recall testifying and being asked the following questions and giving the following answers?
Q: Weren't you sworn before God to tell the truth?
Q: Didn't you place your hand on the Bible?
Q: You never made any changes in your testimony?
Q: When you signed the transcript you swore before God again that what you said was true?

Prima Facie Case or Defense

The deposition can also be used to establish a prima facie case or a defense. In most jurisdictions, the plaintiff can read into the record portions of the psychiatrist's deposition and then have an expert testify as to the alleged malpractice. This is considered evidence in chief. Similarly, a defendant could read portions of the plaintiff's deposition testimony into evidence as admissions against interest to establish evidence of a defense. The court must charge that the jury consider the deposition not for impeachment purposes but for the truth of the statement in issue.

Thought should also be given to the method of presenting the dry transcript. Trials are dramas, and the courtroom is a stage. A monotonous reading can lose an already bored jury. If possible, have an associate take the stand while you read the questions and he reads the answers. For impeachment purposes, exploit the drama and immediacy of the moment by confronting the actual witnesses on the stand. Of course, during summation, relevant portions can be read as evidence to relive the best points of the case.

RHINOPLASTY CASE: DEPOSITIONS OF PLAINTIFF AND DEFENDANT

§ 6.8 Background

The plaintiff was a young South American woman who visited the doctor, clutching a picture of a model as an example of what she wanted to look like. In her deposition and bill of particulars she claimed that the operation was negligently performed and that her deviated septum was still deviated and she had trouble breathing. She even claimed that it interfered with her kissing. However, cross-examination revealed that she had acted in films after the operation in which she kissed and carried on other respiratory-related activities without any apparent difficulty. Close-ups in the movies also revealed dramatic before and after pictures showing an improvement in the deviation and appearance of her nose. The defense was based on her vanity, which blinded her to the improvement.

§ 6.9 Motivation

Q. When you saw the doctor, what did you tell him was the reason that you came?
A. I told him that I wanted to change my nose because it was too long, and that I wanted to correct the defect of the septum, my deviated septum.
Q. Did you tell him that you had any kind of a breathing problem?
A. Yes. I told him that I had difficulty breathing, that I had chronic bronchitis, frequent colds, and asthma.
Q. What did the doctor say to you on that day?
A. That he could perform the operation. Then, he introduced me to the nurse, and I saw the clinic; I was shown around the clinic.
Q. Did he examine you and your nose on that day?
A. He saw my nose, and he agreed that it was too long for the rest of me, and if I decided to have the operation, to come back.

Comment. This answer reveals the real reason for the operation: she believed her nose was too long.

§ 6.10 Friend Had Complications

Q. Did you tell him about your experience in observing your friend, who had a nose that still seemed crooked after the operation?
A. Yes.

Comment. It is important to establish proof of informed consent. Her prior knowledge of a friend's complications is a great advantage for the defense if the complications are similar.

Q. What, exactly, did you tell him about that?
A. That I think that I needed an operation of that type, but I had always been afraid because of the experience that my friend had suffered and undergone.
Q. Did he tell you sometimes after an operation that might be the result?
A. No. He gave me confidence and told me that would not happen with me.

Comment. This is a common response and may have jury appeal. But, psychologically, many vanity patients honestly have a selective memory.

§ 6.11 Possibility of a Corrective Procedure

Q. Did he tell you sometimes you might need a corrective procedure if there were any problems after the first operation?
A. Only on the first visit.
Q. On the first visit?
A. Yes.
Q. Did he ever tell you before the operation sometimes you may need a second procedure to correct or modify the way your nose looks?
A. He told me—no. He told me, no. He told me it would take about six months to know exactly how the nose would have resulted.
Q. Did he, also, tell you that any secondary, minor procedures for additional correction could not be done until, approximately, a year after the surgery?
A. No.
Q. Did he, some time after the first visit, tell you something like that?

Comment. In many cosmetic procedures, a second procedure may be necessary for additional corrections. The defense will claim that this is to be expected and is not evidence of malpractice.

A. Yes.
Q. When did he tell you that?
A. On the last visit that I went to see him, he told me I would definitely need a second operation.
Q. Did he tell you the possibility of a second operation before you had the surgery?

Comment. The plaintiff must prove that the second operation was not contemplated, but rather is evidence of a departure. The defense has claimed it was a normal complication that the patient was advised of before the first operation.

A. No.

§ 6.12 Witness Refreshes Recollection

Q. When you came in to the deposition this morning, did you look at anything to refresh your memory about the case, such as papers or photographs, or anything at all?
A. No.

Comment. Counsel should always inquire as to any documents used to refresh the recollection. They are usually not protected by the attorney-client or work product privilege because the cross-examiner is permitted to compose the document with the testimony given in court. Thus, counsel must be careful in preparing any witness and not use documents that may have to be turned over to the adversary.

§ 6.13 Language Barrier

The plaintiff asked for a Spanish interpreter for her deposition as a tactic to show that the defendant never explained the risks to her in Spanish, her native tongue. However, she spoke English fluently and was reading Marshall McLuhan's *Understanding Media,* a complex book, in English in the lawyers' reception room before the deposition.

Q. When you came this morning, and you began the testimony, were you carrying some type of paperback book with you?
A. Yes.
Q. What is the name of that book?
A. Marshall McLuhan, *Understanding Media.*
Q. The version in front of you, is that in English or in Spanish?
A. English.

§ 6.14 Risk Discussed

Q. Did [the doctor] give you anything to read about the surgery that you were going to have?
A. No.

Comment. Many surgeons provide printed literature on informed consent. Some even show professionally produced video tapes. The plaintiff's counsel should serve demand for these prior to the deposition of the doctor.

Q. At any time before your operation, did he give you something to read concerning the operation?
A. The instruction as to what I was to do two or three days before the operation, the medicine I was supposed to take.
Q. Did you read those instructions?
A. Yes.
Q. Where did you read them—at home, in his office?
A. I read them over several times; I read them in several places.
Q. Do you still have those instructions?
A. I don't think so. I don't know.
Q. Did you write any kind of diary or notations about the visits to [the doctor] at any time?
A. No.

§ 6.15 Her Friend's Experience

Q. What about a Mr. Romero?

Comment. This is the name of a friend who apparently referred her to the plastic surgeon. Counsel is trying to elicit that she already had prior knowledge of the risks and of the possibility of follow-up surgery based on conversations with her friend.

A. He is my friend who had the accident on the finger.
Q. Did your friend tell you anything about the risks of surgery or problems that he had after the surgery?
A. No.

§ 6.16 Plaintiff's Description of Problem

Q. What did you tell [the doctor] about what it is that bothered you about the way your nose looked?
A. That it was long and a little bit wide here.
Q. Why don't we have the witness point to it.
A. On the sides.
COUNSEL: She has pointed to the sides of her nose.

Comment. It is important to have the patient point to the problem in order to clarify whether it is in her mind or imagination. If it is deminimus the jury will discount both the injury and the liability.

Q. At the present time, is there anything that bothers you about the way your nose looks?
A. Yes.
Q. What is it that bothers you?
A. That the left side is shorter than the right side, and that the left side and the right side look different from each other.
Q. Do you still believe that your nose looks too thick on the left than the right side of your nose, as you just showed us a minute ago?
A. No. The left side is different; it is not that it is thicker, just that it is different.

Comment. This is a weak answer and suggests an emotional reason for the lawsuit. Her claim for damages was based on breathing difficulties but vanity obviously is the real motivation. Counsel could follow up on this by simply asking if vanity, not breathing, is the real reason for this suit.

Q. After the surgery, as of today, do you feel there has been no improvement as to the way your nose looks, of any kind?

A. No.
Q. Have you had anyone do another operation on your nose?
A. No.

§ 6.17 Mother, Brother, and Boyfriend Don't Like It

Comment. The following questions were asked to elicit whether peer or family pressure led to the operation or was the source of criticism that might have precipitated the suit. Her answer was very revealing: a boyfriend who acted with her in films didn't like it. Her answer opened up a Pandora's box that led to discovery of "before" and "after" movies in which she appeared in "love scenes" with him. The films impeached her image, credibility, and claim that the nose didn't look better and function well.

Q. Has anyone in your family told you anything about the way they think your nose looks since the operation?
A. Yes.
Q. What have they said to you?
A. They don't like it.
Q. Who in the family?
A. My mother, my brother, and my friend, who makes pictures—who makes movies and who says that he liked the way I looked better before, in the movies made before than now.

Comment. This could be the main theme of the defense—her boyfriend didn't like it. This emotional vanity defense makes sense.

§ 6.18 The Movies

Q. Have you been in a movie of some kind?
Q. A movie of any kind by your friend?
Q. When is the first time that [the boyfriend] took any movies of you?
A. 1978.
Q. What was the reason for him taking the movies?
A. He wanted to—he likes to make movies, and he wanted to participate in the film festival.
Q. How long was the movie he made in terms of minutes?
A. 17 or 18 minutes.
Q. Was it in black or white or color?
A. Color.
Q. Did you get a print, a copy of that movie?
A. I don't have it.

Q. Have you ever had it?
A. Yes. He has it; I don't.

Comment. We were trying to identify the movie for a subsequent motion to preview the film. Plaintiff opposed but the court granted the motion to produce both the before and after films, which demonstrated a corrected septum and apparently normal breathing in several love scenes. However, because some jurors might be offended by the explicit sexual nature of the films, stills and edited versions were used at the trial.

Q. In the first movie you did before the operation, was there any kissing involved?
A. Yes. There was one scene involving kissing. I was the main star in the picture.
Q. Who was your co-star?
A. There were several people.

Comment. Her movie star sexual image totally contradicted the demure, almost withdrawn, image she presented at the deposition and pleaded in her deposition claim of depression.

§ 6.19 Present Problems

Q. Do you presently have any type of cold or cold symptoms?
A. Apparently, no.
Q. Are you presently seeing a doctor because of any problem concerning breathing or your nose in any way?
A. No, not in connection with my nose.
Q. Do you have any plans to see any doctor for any problem with your nose that you claim as a result of this operation?
A. Intentions, yes, but no specific plans.

Comment. Her claim of serious respiratory distress evaporates as she admits that she is not being treated now and has no appointments in the future for medical assistance.

Q. What are your specific intentions?
A. Sometimes I think that I have to have a second operation.
Q. Did you ever talk to a doctor about having a second operation?
A. Yes.
Q. Who did you talk to?
A. Dr. [X].
Q. Anyone else?
A. Dr. [X].

Q. Any other doctor who told you that you might need a second operation?
A. Yes.

Comment. Defense counsel should demand on authorization to obtain records from the surgeons.

§ 6.20 Full Consent Given

Comment. The following questions document that an informed consent was properly obtained, particularly in view of [the patient's] claim that she needed an interpreter to get through this deposition.

Q. Were you asked to sign some type of consent form for the operation on that day?
A. Yes.
Q. Did you have any difficulty understanding anything that [the doctor] or his nurse had ever said to you up until this point?
A. No.
Q. Did you read the consent form that you signed?
A. Yes.
Q. Did you have any difficulty understanding it?
A. No.
Q. Did you have any difficulty understanding the materials [the doctor] gave you about the operation before?
A. No.
Q. Did he, also, give you an instruction sheet about the operation? How many pieces of paper did he give you about the operation?
A. The day before?
Q. At any time.
A. The day before he gave me, I think, one paper.
Q. Is this a copy of what he gave you the day before?
A. Yes.
Q. I show you a copy of a consent form, and ask you whether that is your signature at the bottom.

Comment. The doctor gave the patient an instruction sheet and a consent form. Further questioning revealed that a six-page information pamphlet was also given out. In the plastic surgery suit such actions are helpful in defending the doctor. The plaintiff's counsel must question her own client carefully about these sheets and booklets because they are easily forgotten in the heat of litigation. In fact, the plaintiff denied having ever seen the detailed pamphlet.

A. Yes.
Q. Do you recall reading that before the operation?

A. Yes.
Q. I now show you a six-page document concerning facts about nasal surgery, and I ask you to look at it, first.
A. Yes.
Q. I ask you, after you have had a chance to look at it, is that not one of the documents that [the doctor] gave you to read before your operation?
A. No, no.

§ 6.21 Breathing Problems Postop

Q. Did your ability to breathe become a little better since the operation?
A. No, no.
Q. Is it the same?
A. No.
Q. When did you feel for the first time that you still have difficulty breathing after your operation?
A. Two hours after they took out the plugs, my first visit after the operation.

Comment. Such difficulties may not be uncommon in the postop period. But if the complaint persists there may be cause for concern. Most surgeons advise their patients of the problems that are expected in the immediate postop period.

Q. How many days was that after the operation?
A. I think, three days.
Q. Hadn't [the doctor] told you that you may feel difficulty breathing for some period of time after the operation?
A. At that meeting, yes, he told me that.

§ 6.22 Postop Period

Comment. Very often, the defense will claim that complications are a result of the patient's failure to follow postop advice, thus constituting comparative negligence. In the following questions the defense attorney attempted to ascertain whether the patient massaged the nose as requested.

Q. What did he tell you to do for your nose?
A. Not to put my head down; not to lower my head at any moment, but to try to do everything with my head up, raised.
Q. Anything else that you can recall that he told you to do at home?
A. At which time, when he took the cast off? Yes.
Q. What else did he say?

A. That everything was well. The only special instructions were not to lower my head. I remember, now—don't take any sun; don't sit in the sun.
Q. Did he, also, tell you at some point in your treatment after the operation to massage the nose?
A. Yes.
Q. When did he tell you to massage it for the first time?
A. I think it was on the visit after the visit where he took the cast off, when I saw him, and I complained about the left side being higher than the right side.
Q. Did he tell you why the left side was higher than the right side?
A. Yes, he told me.
Q. What is it that he told you about the left side and the right side of your nose?
A. That it was—that the nose was scarring with keloid, healing with keloid.

Comment. It is essential to ask whether the plaintiff claims that the doctor made any admissions against interest. If this is alleged, then follow-up questions should be asked to determine whether there was an actual admission or misunderstanding, or whether the comment was taken out of context.

Q. Did he at any time tell you that he thought that he had done something wrong, medically?
A. Yes, on the last visit that I went.
Q. What did he say on the last visit?
A. That I needed a second operation.
Q. Did he ever say that the reason you needed a second operation is because he committed some kind of medical malpractice?
A. No.
Q. When he told you to massage your nose, did you follow his instructions?
A. Yes.
Q. Show me what it is that you did.
A. (Witness indicating.)

Comment. The doctor was present during this demonstration and would therefore be in a position to comment at the trial on whether she followed his instructions properly. Of course, for evidentiary reasons it would be better if this deposition were on video tape.

Q. Why did you stop doing it?
A. When I went to see the nose specialist at Mercy Hospital, and he told me that the operation was not right, so then, I stopped.

Comment. This answer may lead to the name of a potential expert witness (in venues where it is discoverable) and also may be evidence of comparative negligence or even grounds for a third-party suit.

Q. When was this?
A. The first week in May.
Q. What was the name of the doctor who told you this?
A. Dr. [X].

§ 6.23 Comparative Negligence or Mitigation of Damages

Q. Did he tell you that you could undergo a second procedure to correct any problems if you wanted to?
A. Yes.
Q. Did you tell him that you would undergo this second procedure?
A. Yes.
Q. Did you ask him to do a second procedure?
A. No.
Q. Why?

Comment. The plaintiff's unreasonable refusal to undergo a corrective procedure may constitute comparative negligence or proof of her failure to mitigate damages. In this case the plaintiff claimed that a subsequent treating doctor advised against the second procedure.

A. Because when I went to Dr. [X], and he told me that the surgery was not right, and not to have the second procedure done by the same doctor, he told me.
Q. This is what Dr. [X] told you?
A. Yes. So, I decided not to go back to the defendant.
Q. Did you tell [the defendant] you wouldn't be coming back for any more visits?
A. No, I didn't tell him.
Q. Did you have an appointment scheduled with [the defendant] that you never kept?

Comment. Defense counsel may now argue that she abruptly terminated treatment before the defendant had a full opportunity to treat her. The plaintiff, however, argued that she acted on sound medical advice and obtained a second opinion from the physician who advised her to stop.

A. I think so. I think there was supposed to be another visit that I didn't go to.
Q. Did [the defendant] tell you whether he would charge you for any second procedure?
A. No. He said that the second procedure I would not have to pay for.
Q. This Dr. [X] you mentioned, can you tell us if he is a plastic surgeon?
A. No.

Comment. The defense was trying to establish that only another plastic surgeon should give such advice. However, in many jurisdictions there may be an overlapping area of expertise between specialties. In fact, defense counsel later established that other plastic surgeons have agreed with the defendant in recommending a second procedure, thus enhancing the defense position and undermining the opinion of the rhinolaryngologist.

§ 6.24 Deposition of the Defendant: Doctor's Writings

Q. Doctor, in January of 1988, did you see a woman, a patient, by the name of [plaintiff]?
A. Yes.
Q. Was it the first time you saw her on the 10th of January of 1988?
Q. Do you want the records to try to refresh you?
A. Yes.
Q. Sure. (Handing.)
A. Yes, January 10th, 1988.
Q. By the way, doctor, to the present, have you authorized or written any texts or scholarly articles in your area of expertise, plastic and reconstructive surgery?
A. I edited and translated an encyclopedia and translated a work on abdominoplasty from French to English.

Comment. If the book contradicts anything in his deposition the doctor will be impeached at the time of trial. However, it is unlikely to be relevant because it is about abdominoplasty.

§ 6.25 Advice about Photographs

Q. I notice that on the back, stapled to the back of the patient information form marked Plaintiff's 1A for identification, is a clipping that appears to be from a magazine. Do you recall why that is there, what is the significance of it?
A. Yes.
Q. What is that?
A. She brought this clipping in showing a woman on either side of it from a magazine with a nose that she thought that she would like to have.
Q. Was that either or both or one of the women, to your memory?
A. Well, I pointed out that I didn't think the two were the same woman and the two noses were not the same, which led me into a discussion how nobody's nose should be for anybody else's face and every nose should be done individually to fit the face of the character of the patient.

Comment. This is a typical problem with plastic surgery patients who want to bring in photography. The patient must be cautioned that a photograph cannot be used as a sample.

FACIAL MUSCLE SLING CASE: DEPOSITIONS OF SURGEON AND PATIENT

§ 6.26 Background

In this case, the patient was a 39-year-old woman with facial paralysis. Her eye would not close properly and she couldn't smile. The defendant proposed a facial sling procedure after her psychiatrist suggested that plastic surgery might help her chronic depression.

§ 6.27 Diary Private

Q. When were you licensed to practice medicine in the State of New York, approximately?
A. '74, I think. No, I am sorry, '75.
Q. Doctor, you are referring to some piece of paper?
A. No, I got the date off of here, license number (indicating).
Q. Is this a diary of some type; may I see the diary, please?
DEFENDANT'S COUNSEL: No, you can't see the diary. Thank you.
PLAINTIFF'S COUNSEL: He just refreshed his recollection.
DEFENDANT'S COUNSEL: He referred to the date that you requested.
Q. Can I see the portion of the diary that you referred to, Doctor?
A. New York license April 4, 1975. New Jersey license date . . .
DEFENDANT'S COUNSEL: No, you can't see it. Do you want to make a motion to see it? It is a private diary. If you have any question that his license is somehow recollected by his memory of a book, you are entitled to check with New York State. This is not refreshing his recollection from some evidentiary matter. I am sure he did that so he can give you an accurate date as to when he received the license.
PLAINTIFF'S COUNSEL: I believe I am entitled to see any document that he is referring to, specifically, in connection with his testimony to refresh his recollection.
DEFENDANT'S COUNSEL: You asked if he could give you approximately. He gave you the best answer.
PLAINTIFF'S COUNSEL: He did look at a document.
DEFENDANT'S COUNSEL: I beg to differ with you.
PLAINTIFF'S COUNSEL: Mark that for a ruling.

Comment. If a witness uses anything, even a privileged document, to refresh his recollection, it must be surrendered. However, here the doctor merely opened his private diary to verify his date of licensing. The diary itself, other than that one entry, is still privileged.

§ 6.28 First Visit

Q. Doctor, when, for the first time, did you have occasion to see the patient for any reason?
A. The office records show August 5th, 1982.
Q. Where was it that you saw her?
A. The psychiatric ward at [ ] Hospital.
Q. Had you been requested by anyone to see the patient?
A. Yes.
Q. By whom?
A. By Dr. [H].
Q. Do you know what service Dr. [H] was with?
A. She was the chief resident in plastic surgery service.
Q. When you say she requested you see the patient, was that pursuant to a written request of some type?
A. No, it wasn't, it was an oral request.
Q. Approximately how much before August 5, 1982, was it that Dr. [H] asked you to see the patient?
A. Maybe a few days before, but I don't really remember.
Q. Well, Doctor, do you recall what Dr. [H] said to you in sum and substance in connection with your seeing the patient for the first time?
A. She told me that the patient was in the psychiatric ward with a facial weakness on the right side and she wanted me to see her.
Q. For what purpose?
A. If I could correct her problem of the facial weakness.
Q. Did she indicate whether the patient was a private patient?
A. I don't remember, but if Dr. [H] asked me, it usually is a service case.
Q. Did she indicate to you the reason why the patient was in the psychiatric ward?
A. Yes.
Q. What did she say in that regard?
A. Well, she was there for depression.
Q. Did she say anything else?
A. That I don't remember.
Q. Did she say anything about a suicide attempt?
A. I don't remember. She may have said it, but I don't remember.
Q. Before you saw the patient, did you view the patient's chart?
A. I think I did briefly.
Q. What do you mean when you say briefly?

A. Well, most of the information I got from Dr. [H] so I didn't have to go through in detail.
Q. Other than what you told us about Dr. [H], was there anything else that you remember as having been said by you or Dr. [H] in sum and substance, concerning the patient?
A. The only thing I remember, one of the reasons she had the problem in the psychiatric ward is that because of her facial deformity. She has had that a long time and maybe this deformity is causing her psychiatric problems.

Comment. This can be the best defense—the attempt to help her improve her emotional problems by plastic surgery. The defense argued that she had little to lose given her prior disfigurement and depression. Her present complaints, they argued, are part of her paranoid personality.

§ 6.29 Risk Discussed

Q. Did you indicate to [the patient] that there might be any difficulty in surgery considering how long the condition had existed?
A. I don't remember whether I said it at that time or not, but during the course of my seeing her, I am pretty sure I mentioned about because she had this condition for a long time, the spontaneous recovery is almost zero and if she wants correction, the surgery is treatment of choice.
PLAINTIFF'S COUNSEL: Move to strike the last portion as unresponsive.

Comment. Of course he does. This is the defense theme—she had nothing to lose. The doctor seems well prepared for this deposition.

§ 6.30 Psychiatric Problems

Q. Doctor, within the limits and parameters of your knowledge and training, were you able to form an opinion as to [the patient's] psychiatric condition when you saw her on August 5th?
A. She was getting treatment and I was under the impression she was under control.

Comment. The plaintiff is suggesting that the surgeon was negligent in not considering the patient's psychiatric problems. But the psychiatrist had recommended this surgery.

§ 6.31 Chief Resident to Do Surgery

Q. Was there any discussion or understanding with regard to who was to perform the actual procedure itself?

A. Yes.
Q. Could you relate to us what that discussion was?
A. I was the attending for the month of August, so I'm the attending for the case.
Q. You, yourself, would do the procedure?
A. No. I have to supervise Dr. [H] performing the surgery.
Q. How was it decided that Dr. [H] would do the surgery?
A. The chief resident.
Q. How was it decided that she would be doing the surgery?
A. The service cases, she has a choice to do surgery. If she doesn't want it, the junior resident would do the case.
Q. In other words, she opted to do the surgery, is that what you are saying?

Comment. Some jurors might be upset that a complicated procedure like this was being done by the resident. However, this is not unusual in a service patient case as opposed to a private patient.

§ 6.32 Plaintiff's Behavior

Q. Doctor, are you referring to a note of August 24th, 1982 in which she was described as exhibiting bizarre behaviorism?
A. Another note on August 23rd, patient became very agitated, hostile, and verbally abusive.
Q. Had you ever seen her exhibiting such behavior at any time you saw her until the time surgery was done?
A. No.
Q. Did you see her on August 24th, the day of the proposed surgery?
A. No.
Q. How did you come to learn that she had been mentally unstable once again?

Comment. Of course the inference is that she was not competent to consent to surgery in the future and not really a good candidate for this surgery at this time.

§ 6.33 Chief Resident Never Did Procedure Before

Q. Who was the operating surgeon?
A. The chief resident.
Q. Was she operating under your direction?
A. Yes.
Q. Do you know whether Dr. [H] had ever done such a procedure previously?
A. No.
Q. You don't know?

A. No, she has never done.
Q. Had you ever done such a procedure before?
A. Yes.
Q. Approximately how many times?
A. Three.
Q. All at [ ] Hospital?
A. No.
Q. How many from [ ] Hospital?
A. None of them.
Q. Was this as of September 17th, 1982, an unusual procedure?
A. No.
Q. A rarely performed procedure?
DEFENDANT'S COUNSEL: He answered no.

Comment. This has great jury appeal. Plaintiff can argue that neither the supervising surgeon nor his chief resident were really familiar with this procedure. However, this is a rare procedure for most surgeons.

Q. Was it a rarely performed procedure as of September, 1982?
A. It is relatively rare, because the facial paralysis is rare.

§ 6.34 Referred to Texts

Q. Doctor, before this operation was begun and this preparation for the operation, did you have occasion to refer to any medical texts or journals in preparation for this surgery?
HOSPITAL'S COUNSEL: I object.
A. I want—
DEFENDANT'S COUNSEL: This is when he was performing the operation?
PLAINTIFF'S COUNSEL: Prior to and in preparation for the surgery.
A. Yes.
Q. What texts or journals did you refer to?

Comment. This is a great question and probably catches the doctor off guard. He can be impeached later at trial with any book he recognizes as authoritative.

A. Well, I don't know exactly which one, but there is a journal of the plastic surgery and reconstructed surgery.

§ 6.35 Patient Presented to Board

Q. Doctor, discussing your note of [date] which indicates you made an appointment with her for a board presentation? How did you make an appointment—did you call her, did you send her a note, how did you make that appointment?

A. I think I called her.

Comment. It is not often that a doctor presents his patient to a board unless there are unusual complications or it is a rare case.

Q. What was this board presentation that you referred to?

A. The board is the American Plastic Surgery Board.

Q. What was the reason for the presentation of this particular patient to the American Plastic Surgery Board?

A. To take the boards you have to present eight cases. You have to correct the eight cases to present, so she was one of them.

Q. Was she ultimately one of the cases that was presented to the board?

A. No.

Q. What was the reason that she was not presented?

DEFENDANT'S COUNSEL: What difference does it make? You don't have to answer that. It has nothing to do with this.

Q. In connection with the presentation of this patient to the American Plastic Surgery Board, did you prepare any additional documentation in addition to what's here in the hospital chart?

A. No.

Q. Did you prepare any additional photographs?

Comment. The plaintiff's counsel is fishing to see if there are additional reports on this case given to the board.

A. No.

§ 6.36 Deposition of the Plaintiff

Comment. The plaintiff claimed that because of her prior psychiatric condition she was not a good candidate for this surgery. She was a fragile woman and the defendant's malpractice aggravated this preexisting condition. The defense counsel therefore delved into her past. But his intent was to establish that her present depression was a result of her prior condition only.

Q. Tell us, what were your problems that led to your attempted suicide and your admission to [ ] Hospital in July of 1982?

A. My father.

Q. Your father—

A. Every time he drank, he wanted to kill me.

Q. That's why you tried to commit suicide in July '82?

* * *

Q. Was this the only problem that resulted in your attempted suicide in July of 1982, or were there other problems that sort of added to the whole thing for you?

A. Well, I—that's the only problem, because I wanted to get out of there, and I wasn't working. I didn't have no money, so, you know, that's heavy on the head.

Q. Did you, prior to 1982, ever attempt to commit suicide because your father was chasing you or trying to kill you?

A. You mean before the surgery?

Q. Yes.

A. Yes.

Q. Do you recall in California that you attempted suicide also? I believe you did, didn't you?

A. Yes.

Q. Can you tell us what led you to attempt suicide in California?

A. My husband.

Q. Just problems with your husband?

A. Yes.

Q. Can you tell us what kind of problems? Was he also beating you?

A. Yes, he also beat me.

Q. What else drove you to this desperate act?

A. I caught him with another woman.

* * *

Q. Do you have any recollection of ever being confined at any hospital in Santo Domingo?

A. No, I don't remember.

Q. Do you recall receiving any kind of medical attention in Santo Domingo at any clinics or by any doctors?

A. I recall my mother giving me injections.

Q. Do you know what those injections were for?

A. She said it was for my paralysis.

Q. From as far back as you can remember, did you suffer from some form of paralysis?

A. When I was a little girl.

MAMMOPLASTY CASE: DEPOSITION OF DEFENDANT

§ 6.37 Hard Capsule Formation Complication

This case involved allegations that, as a result of an insertion of improper type and size of silicone breast implants, the patient was caused to develop a capsule or hardness within the breast caused by adhesions forming around the implant. She also claimed that she was never informed of this risk. The defense claimed that she had a tendency to develop scar tissue and she knew the risks from a prior procedure as well as a detailed discussion with the defendant.

Q. Did you give [the patient] any advice with regard to her subsequent course?
A. Well, I told her that sometimes the breasts become hard because of swelling but it also could be that she is forming further capsule around her breasts because she has had that experience before. I told her it's too soon to do anything about a closed capsulotomy that, that soon, from surgery, and we should wait at least another week.

Comment. The surgeon was asked to describe the procedure for breaking up the adhesion without further surgery. It should be noted that it is quite common for these adhesions to form even in the absence of any malpractice.

§ 6.38 Sedation Necessary

Comment. These procedures can be painful. This description of popping the breast has jury appeal for the plaintiff's side.

Q. What were your findings on that visit?
A. The breast continued to harden. We had arranged apparently that this capsulotomy then to be performed, would be done with some IV sedation. In other words, the patient was not looking forward to having the procedure done unless she was sedated, she wanted to be asleep. So we arranged for a nurse anesthetist from the hospital to come to the office and give her some sedation through an IV tubing in her arm.

* * *

Q. Could you tell us what procedures were performed on August 15, 1978?
A. Closed capsulotomy.
Q. Can you tell us the results of that procedure?
A. Well, according to the note, it seemed that I wanted to make provision for her to have it done again. So I think the problem was that it wasn't completely soft at that point.

* * *

Q. Did you perform any procedure on October 26?
A. I guess I tried to break the capsule on the left side.
Q. And could you tell us what the results were of that procedure?
A. I made a note that they were minimal, meaning a minimal improvement.
Q. Following October 26, when was [the patient's] next office visit?
A. December 30, 1978.

§ 6.39 Second Surgery Risk

Q. What were your findings on that visit?
A. Apparently the breasts were still hard. She had to—the breasts were still hard and I guess I tried to do a capsulotomy on the left side, where she had some excess drooping and the surgery was gone over with her, explained to her and she seemed to be looking forward to it.
Q. Can you tell us the sum and substance of your discussion with regard to the surgery?
A. Well, I told her that the capsule had continued to form, even though a smaller implant had been put in at the time of the original surgery. So I told her that obviously she was a scar tissue former, this she knew from the first time she had the operation, which is why she came to me in the first place, or in the second place, as it were. She told me she was willing to undergo more surgery because she wanted her breasts soft. And I told her that that couldn't be guaranteed because she continually forms a scar tissue.

Comment. Note how the defendant is alluding to the defense theme. This was the patient's second operation and she knew of this risk from the first one, which left her with scar tissue.

> Some people form it and some people don't. Here we had great evidence that she was one of the people who formed it; not once, but continually. Even though I was going to go in surgery and try to incise the capsule in one of her breasts, I couldn't guarantee that this scar formation wouldn't recur. In fact, I told her it probably would, based on the number of visits that we had already had together when it had. Nonetheless, I felt that going in surgery to repair the puckering would be necessary. And that is what we talked about.

BREAST AUGMENTATION CASE: DEPOSITIONS OF PLAINTIFF AND DEFENDANT

§ 6.40 Background

The plaintiff, Mrs. Margot, first consulted the defendant, Ralph Gibson, M.D., on October 9, 1988. Approximately four years before she had undergone a breast augmentation performed by her gynecologist, Dr. Bill Walsh.

Her complaints were that her breasts were too large and hard and that she lacked cleavage. She had surgery scheduled to be performed by Dr. George Byron at the time she saw the defendant. The defendant examined her and advised her that surgery could be performed to decrease the size of the breasts.

On October 13, 1988, the plaintiff advised the defendant that she decided to forego her previously scheduled surgery and to have the defendant perform the surgery instead.

Surgery was performed on October 27, 1988, at St. Mary's Hospital. Dr. Gibson removed the 225 cc Cronin implants from the previous surgery and replaced them with 200 cc Heyer Schulte gel implants. Mrs. Margot was discharged the following day. She returned to the defendant's office for follow-up care on October 30, 1988, and had no complaints.

On November 3, 1988, when the plaintiff returned to the defendant's office she noted that her breasts were hard. The defendant indicated that he would perform a capsulotomy of the breasts if this continued and also noted the excellent result obtained by the plaintiff. A capsulotomy is a routine procedure to be expected following this surgery as normal sequelae and not evidence of malpractice.

On November 17, 1988, the defendant performed a restrained closed capsulotomy by exerting pressure manually on the breasts, and thereafter noted that there was some improvement in the right breast but that the left breast still required additional therapy. He continued to perform closed capsulotomies on December 1, 15, and 29, 1988. Again some improvement was noted although recovery was not complete.

On January 26, 1988, the defendant abandoned an attempt at a closed capsulotomy when weakness was noted under the left nipple. He discussed the possibility of additional surgery with Mrs. Margot but recommended waiting an additional six months. On February 25, 1979, he made another attempt at a closed capsulotomy. However, he again noted that surgery was indicated. Mrs. Margot returned on April 30 and May 7, 1979, for the purpose of reexamination and planning for additional surgery.

Mrs. Margot was admitted on June 6, 1979, to St. Mary's Hospital for surgery. That day Gibson performed the surgical procedure, correcting the incision line on the right breast and removing the prosthesis, excising the capsule, and reinserting the implant on the left breast. Mrs. Margot was discharged with no complications noted.

On subsequent office visits on June 14, 21, and 28, 1979, hardness of the breasts was once again noted. Gibson refused to perform a capsulotomy on the breasts as it was too early. Mrs. Margot never returned to Gibson again although he did not discharge her from his care.

Mrs. Margot subsequently consulted Dr. J., who performed subsequent surgery on Mrs. Margot on several occasions.

§ 6.41 Claims

The plaintiff alleged that the defendant was negligent in failing to use reasonable skill and care in treatment, in failing to diagnose the plaintiff's condition, in failing to employ proper tests, in failing to administer proper medications, in failing to guard against complications, in allowing complications to progress, in failing to advise consultations with specialists, in failing to recognize the plaintiff was not a suitable candidate for surgery, in improperly excising the plaintiff, in neglecting to sterilize the plaintiff preoperatively, in operating where scar tissue was present, in using an improper implant size, in failing to use steroids, in failing to use a gel-type implant, in failing to properly dissect the pocket, and in failing to provide proper and adequate postoperative dressing. The plaintiff also alleged a lack of informed consent.

The damages the plaintiff alleged she sustained were a hard and distorted left breast, scarring, retraction and inversion of the nipple and adjoining depression which necessitated additional surgery, as well as emotional and psychological distress. The following testimony is taken from Mrs. Margot's deposition.

§ 6.42 Gynecologist Performed Breast Surgery

Q. Have you, prior to coming under defendant's care, ever had surgery of any kind?

A. Yes.

Q. Approximately how many as an adult, talking from the age of 16 or 17 on?

A. Before defendant I had the same type of surgery performed by a gynecologist, not a Dr. Walsh. . . .

Q. Did he care for you for any reason other than the breast surgery?

A. He was my gynecologist.

Q. When did you first come under his care?

A. I think—I was still married. May '71.

Q. When did he do the breast surgery?

A. '73.

Q. Where was that surgery performed?

A. I think it was Medical Arts, Medical Arts something Hospital in the 50s.

Q. Was there any particular reason why you discontinued your care by Dr. Walsh?

A. Yes. I realized immediately I was caught at a very vulnerable moment going through divorce. He had also proposed I have the same surgery when I was married, and you know, my exhusband said it is ridiculous or whatever, but you are vulnerable at that moment, but being very unhappy about the results, I lost trust in him. I didn't want to see him anymore.

Comment. Note the typical profile of the vulnerable vanity patient that emerges here. However, note how her gynecologist pushed her to let him do plastic surgery on her.

Q. When was breast augmentation surgery discussed either by you or by Dr. Walsh?

A. He brought it up as early as when I started seeing him—if it was '71, I think probably it was late '71, probably it was performed spring or summer of '73.

Q. What were the circumstances under which surgery was first raised as a topic of discussion?

A. He kept forms in his office, in his examining room and had just brought it up as a matter of discussion. "Have you ever considered breast augmentation," et cetera. I don't remember the exact dialogue now, but it was something to that nature.

Q. Were your breasts unequal in size before Dr. Walsh did surgery?

A. No. Just smallish.

Q. What were the reasons or arguments that Dr. Walsh raised in favor of the surgery to enlarge your breasts?

PLAINTIFF'S COUNSEL: I am going to object to the form, but I will allow you to answer.

A. He thought I would look better.

Q. On how many occasions before the surgery actually took place did you and he discuss the possibility of having this type of procedure?

A. I don't know. He was my gynecologist.

* * *

Q. What were the circumstances under which you ultimately agreed and arranged for breast augmentation surgery?

A. When I was separated from my husband at the time.

Q. That was the time. What were the circumstances?

A. I was going to him for regular visits. I think I probably felt extremely insecure. If a doctor had told me at that time, assuming I had a large nose, you need a nose job, I would have said, "Okay, probably I do."

Comment. This is a ludicrous answer. It's the sine qua non of the vanity patient and defense counsel should save it for opening.

* * *

Q. Did you and Dr. Walsh discuss before you agreed to have the surgery how much larger you wanted to have your breasts made or how much larger he planned to make them either in terms of bra size or any other measuring system?

A. Yes, he did. It stands out in my mind. He said about a bra size which would be medium, a B. Medium size.

Q. Did that represent an increase of one cup size or more than a cup size or what?

A. I guess—there are varying degrees even within bra sizes but I guess it would be one.

Q. Do you know what type of device Dr. Walsh intended to use to enlarge your breasts?

A. I think it was an implant with a silicone liquid or gel contained in the implant itself.

Q. Do you know or did you discuss with him the size of the implant itself?

A. He said it would be equivalent to a size B, which would be a medium.

§ 6.43 Surgery Not Satisfactory

Q. Was the result of that surgery satisfactory to you?
A. No.
Q. What was it about the results following surgery that were unsatisfactory to you?
A. Basically the hardness of the implants themselves, and the size, I felt it was a little large for me. Basically the largest complaint was it felt unnatural and hard.
Q. When after the surgery that Dr. Walsh performed did you notice a sense of hardness?
A. Probably within a week, 10 days.
Q. Was this in both breasts or only one?
A. Both.

Comment. This is the same condition she suffered from after the defendant's surgery, thus impeaching her lack of informed consent case.

Q. Did you feel pressure when you did not touch it or only if you touched the breast or when pressure was applied to it?
A. Yes. It would be very uncomfortable to lie on my stomach, for example. I can feel the hardness of the implants. It would be an uncomfortable position.
Q. Did you feel hardness throughout your breasts or only in certain areas of each breast?
A. Throughout.

* * *

Q. Did you bring this to Dr. Walsh's attention?
A. Sure.
Q. What was his response?
A. He dismissed it. He said, "Oh, that is nothing. It will improve with time." In effect, it got worse, not better.
Q. How long did you remain under Dr. Walsh's care following the surgery itself?
A. I don't know. Maybe several months waiting to see what this improvement would be and then realizing there was no improvement, naturally I lost trust in him. I left. I left his care.

§ 6.44 Friend Recommended a New Doctor

Q. Did there come a time after you left Dr. Walsh's care that you sought out another physician with respect to surgery or treatment for your breasts?
A. Yes. Quite a bit later. I think at the time I felt this was what I am stuck with—
Q. Who was it you went to next?

A. A friend of mine who was a surgeon had recommended that I see Dr. Byron who he knew very well, and said that, you know, "I think maybe there is something that can be done for you. There are improved methods today. He supposedly was quite good in this area, see him." I did.
Q. Did you at one point make arrangements with Dr. Byron to have surgery?
A. Yes.
Q. What was Dr. Byron's first name?
A. I think Jerry.
Q. Where was his office located?
A. Great Neck.
Q. Do you know what type of physician he was or what his specialty was?
A. Plastic surgeon.

* * *

Q. How many visits did you make to Dr. Byron's office before ultimately deciding to go forward with the surgery?
A. I think I was there two or three times.
Q. On the first visit to Dr. Byron, what complaints do you recall making to him?
A. I really didn't have to say. Examining me he saw exactly what my complaint was.
Q. Did you make any verbal complaints?
A. I said, "I feel that my breasts are very unnatural and hard, and I am unhappy. Can anything be done?"

* * *

Q. Did Dr. Byron—
A. He was angry that a gynecologist should be performing this surgery.

* * *

Q. Did he discuss in any fashion his intention to use a smaller implant?
A. Yes. It was also my request and he agreed with me.
Q. Did he discuss the type of implant he planned to use?
A. I believe it was a silicone gel or saline solution. I don't know. I am confused. It would have been one or the other.
Q. Were you aware before you went to see—
A. I think it was saline.

* * *

Q. Had you done any reading on the subject of breast implant surgery between the time you were under the care of Dr. Walsh and when you went to see Dr. Byron?
A. Consumer information, naturally. I had read articles and seen photographs of successful operations, ones that weren't successful, whatever. But of course they were designed for the layman. I had never seen a medical journal on what was available.

Comment. A good question to elicit her sophistication about common risks.

Q. As a result of your consumer publication reading, what did you understand about this type of surgery, what it could do or what problems might be associated with it?
A. A number of things could go wrong naturally.
Q. Such as?
A. I don't know. Some cases I think came out unequal sizes, or had some altered spacing between breasts, some were lumpy, I guess, or had hardened.

* * *

Q. Had you learned of capsule formation from consumer reading or some other source?
A. In a vague way I think from magazines, whatever. They don't go into any great depth. It is okay, you know this type of surgery can be successful. On the other hand you know, there are things that can go wrong.

Sometimes it is not successful, which I wish I had seen then before I ever went through it.

§ 6.45 Plaintiff Consulted Defendant

Q. How did you come to contact defendant?
A. A friend of mine.

* * *

Q. What made you decide to ask defendant on that first visit if he would do the surgery?
A. Because I had been nervous. It is unfortunate, I think, for Dr. Byron that he has a couple of people working in his office that would scream with that Long Island accent being very rude and impersonal and that unnerved me, plus thinking what if anything was wrong. I don't have a car in the city and I am going to have to try to get back and forth to Great Neck on the train.

* * *

Q. What was it that you were seeking from defendant on your first visit?
A. His opinion.
Q. As to what?
A. As to could I be helped, that Dr. Byron had said that it should be a fairly easy matter to help my condition.

* * *

Q. . . . Did you know him to be a very reputable doctor?
A. That I had had glowing reports of defendant from my friend, and another friend of hers that had also been to him, and could he perform the same type of surgery?

What hospital did he work out of? I would have felt comfortable knowing there was a doctor I could see close by to me.

Q. Did you go to the defendant with the thought of asking defendant to do the surgery?
A. Yes.
Q. Do you know where the incision was that Dr. Walsh used to place the implant?
A. Quite evident, under the breast.
Q. At the lower fold of the breast or some place else, the crease between your chest wall and your breast or at some other location?
A. Under the breast.
Q. Right in that crease.
Q. Did Dr. Byron discuss with you that he proposed to use the same incision or did he intend to use a different spot?
A. He would use an incision in the same area, of course.

* * *

Q. What was defendant's comment or response to you at that first visit after he examined you and explained to him what you have described?
A. His response?
Q. Yes.
A. I was upset at the time and I am sure was very nervous. I had this date set for surgery and I didn't know what to do. I was nervous.

He said, you know, calm down. Things don't have to be rushed. Think about whatever this is, and yes, a successful result can be obtained, and there are improved implants, on and on.

* * *

Q. Did you ask defendant on that first visit if he would perform the surgery himself?
A. Yes.

* * *

A. I asked him at that time, I felt like I had learned a lot in my conversations with Dr. Byron, and his concern about the implant not being positioned deep enough, and as I can imagine there was professional pride there and my comment about what another doctor's viewpoint was. You know, "I know what to do"—that type of thing.

§ 6.46 Doctor Described Surgery

Q. What did defendant tell you about the surgery he intended to do?
A. Remove the other implant and use a newer implant, silicone gel which he felt was improved over the old kind.
Q. Did you ask defendant if he had opinion as to what had caused the hardness following Dr. Walsh's surgery?
A. I don't remember who said what, but I am sure most every doctor would agree that it had encapsulated.

§ 6.47 Patient Sought Another Doctor

Q. Did Dr. J. indicate to you, ever, that the placement of the implants by defendant was in any way responsible for the capsule formation?
A. No.

Comment. It's always a good idea for the defense to ask if one's subsequent treating doctor has expressed an opinion about malpractice.

* * *

Q. When for the first time did Dr. J. advise you that you were ready physically to have further surgery and have the implants replaced?
A. Between November and March 24th, I called him naturally being anxious to be in a normal appearance again, and I thought things seemed to be healing so far as I could see and that, you know, many months had gone by since he initially removed them. Could he examine me and see if he thought that I was ready?
Q. Did he examine you?
A. Yes.
Q. Did he tell you you were ready?
A. He said he would have been happy if from day one I could have lived through everything and just waited like a year. But of course, I think he understood from a patient's standpoint it is difficult being you have to live in that body.

* * *

§ 6.48 The 1988 Surgery

Mrs. Margot's initial complaints to Gibson were that her breasts were too hard and too large. The hardness of the breasts which Mrs. Margot complained of is quite common following breast augmentation. Such firmness is usually the result of a contraction of the fibrous capsule. The contraction generally occurs as a physiologic response to foreign bodies in which tissue forms fibrous bands. It is reported to occur in between 25 to 45 percent of patients. Such firmness can occur bilaterally or unilaterally and can occur even years after surgery. The exact cause of capsular contracture has not been determined although it appears that scar formation may be a contributory factor. Other factors that have been implicated in capsular contracture are hematoma, seroma, and chemical impurities.[1]

---

[1] *See* J. Baker, *Augmentation Mammoplasty,* in Plastic Surgery (Brown & Co. 1979); Baker & Bartolz, *Closed Compression Technique for Rupturing a Contracted Capsule Around a Breast Implant,* 58 Plastic & Reconstructive Surgery 137 (Aug. 1976).

It has also been found that the incidence of capsular contracture is more prevalent in patients who underwent breast augmentation using implants attached with Dacron or Teflon patches. A study conducted by Williams documented firmness in 65 percent of a series of patients augmented with Cronin implants with Dacron patches.[2]

Although the defendant considered the possibility of performing a closed capsulotomy, also known as "popping" or "squeezing" of the breasts, the fact that Mrs. Margot also wanted a smaller breast size led the defendant to recommend an open capsulotomy with replacement of the implants. In fact when given the options available—that is, a closed capsulotomy or an open capsulotomy—Mrs. Margot chose the surgical procedure specifically because she now wanted her breasts to be smaller. Previously, she wanted larger breasts when she had surgery with Dr. Walsh. Open capsulotomy is an acceptable procedure for treatment of breast firmness.[3]

The defendant also discussed with Mrs. Margot that there might be continued hardness. This he based upon the fact that a patient who already has experienced scar contraction is more likely to have the problem recur. From her readings and her discussions with the defendant and with Dr. Walsh and Dr. Byron, the plaintiff was fully aware that the surgery would not necessarily decrease the hardness in her breasts.

The defendant chose to use 200 cc Heyer Schulte gel implants. This size provided for the decrease in breast size desired by the patient. By using a small implant there was also a possibility that the small degree of increased space would provide additional give and decrease pressure. Interestingly, the plaintiff alleged that the defendant was negligent in failing to use a gel implant. However, defendant did actually use a gel implant.

The use of a gel implant was appropriate because the patient had prior capsule formation, which put her more at risk for another occurrence of capsular contracture. If such occurred, a closed capsulotomy may have been necessary, and there is a risk of the capsule rupturing with the inflatable implant during a capsulotomy.

Experimental studies have shown that there is no significant functional difference between a gel-filled, inflatable, or double lumen prosthesis.[4] Moreover, there have been no demonstrable differences in the formation of capsules based upon the type of implant used, and thus implant choice is generally one of personal preference.

The plaintiff's counsel neglected to even question the defendant about whether he used a gel or inflatable implant. He had also advised us it was

---

[2] S. Aston & T. Rees, Mammary Augmentation, *Correction of Asymmetry and Gynecomastia,* in Aesthetic Plastic Surgery (W.B. Sanders 1980).

[3] W. Grabb & J. Smith, Plastic Surgery (Brown & Co. 1979).

[4] *See* T. Rees, Aesthetic Plastic Surgery (W.B. Sanders 1980).

a gel and the plaintiff admitted this in her deposition, yet the bill of particulars claims negligence in not using a gel implant.

The defendant, in performing the surgery, used an inframammary incision. Again this is an acceptable procedure. Although there are alternative approaches for an incision, an inframammary incision is one of the most common incisions and provides easy access and excellent exposure. Many authorities consider this the method of choice.[5] The other available approaches, the peri areolar and transaxillary, have certain disadvantages. Specifically, the peri areolar approach has been implicated in greater loss of nipple sensation and the transaxillary approach may cause problems if there is capsular formation because the prosthesis may be pulled up and out. The inframammary approach also allows simpler reentry if the need for drainage or surgical capsulotomy is necessary. Because the plaintiff had already undergone surgery using an inframammary incision line, it was also clinically indicated to use the same incision line.

Postop care was also within the standards of medical care. The defendant issued a postop brassiere and directed the plaintiff to return in a few days. There was certainly nothing that suggests a failure to properly follow-up postop. Indeed, the defendant couldn't complete his care because the plaintiff abandoned him.

§ 6.49 The Closed Capsulotomies

After several postop visits Mrs. Margot once again complained of hardness of the breasts. As discussed in **§ 6.48** this is the most common complication. Closed compression capsulotomy is the primary treatment for fibrous capsules. The advantages of the closed capsulotomy are the simplicity of the technique and the noninvasive nature. The procedure can be repeated as necessary so long as effective.

In the instant case the defendant noted hardness occurring approximately one week after the surgery. He additionally noted that the shape was good and the result excellent. He waited two weeks and performed the closed capsulotomy noting some improvement. This was an appropriate period of time to wait to perform closed capsulotomy because development of tensile strength and collaginous maturity does not occur until the third week.[6] Because it was only three weeks postop the defendant limited his capsulotomy to a restrained version. Despite the capsulotomy, the plaintiff again developed hardness of the breasts. Multiple closed capsulotomies are often required to maintain softness of the

---

[5] W. Grabb & J. Smith, Plastic Surgery (Brown & Co. 1979).

[6] Terino, *Essential Concepts in Prosthetic Breast Surgery,* 6 Aesthetic Plastic Surgery 25.32 (1982).

breasts and again the defendant's actions were consistent with standards of medical care.

Generally the procedure used in a closed capsulotomy is to exert force circumferentially and horizontally to the breasts. Thus, the defendant's description of his technique of exerting slight pressure on the breast between the fingers on the palm of the hand is the standard employed.

During the performance of the closed capsulotomies the defendant noted that some of the capsule broke superiorly but not inferiorly and that therefore the breast prosthesis had migrated to the superior pole. The defendant generally felt that the problems stemmed from the proclivity of the patient towards scar formation as was evidenced by her postop recovery from her initial breast augmentation performed by Dr. Walsh. This was exactly what the defendant had felt could occur, which the plaintiff was fully aware of.

§ 6.50 The 1989 Surgery

After performing multiple closed capsulotomies it became apparent to the defendant that an open capsulotomy would be necessary. His decision to operate again was clearly warranted because it was his judgment that further closed capsulotomies would not be effective. The defendant fully informed the plaintiff as to the possible need for surgery on January 26, 1989. Again the defendant indicated to Mrs. Margot that he could not guarantee that her breasts would be softened by additional surgery because of her tendency toward scar formation.

This second surgery was also within the prescribed technique for an open capsulotomy. The superior capsule was removed from the left breast to allow more room and the implant was temporarily removed and reinserted. The defendant sutured the right breast capsule. Such procedures are clearly acceptable and were indicated in this patient.

Postop Mrs. Margot again developed firmness. She discontinued treatment before any additional treatment could be provided by Dr. Gibson. The defense's argument, through their expert, was that:

> The pre- and postoperation case rendered by defendant as can be ascertained from the hospital and office records appears quite in keeping with acceptable plastic surgical procedures. Capsule formation following the silicone implantation is certainly the most frequent problem associated with this surgery and although not a complication it certainly occurs in 35 to 40 percent of the patients that have this type of implant. Capsulotomies as described by defendant are the method of choice for the initial treatment and open capsulotomy is certainly a well-established and accepted procedure. The choice of implant by defendant, in that he chose a smaller

implant than the original one, was well thought out. In summary in my opinion defendant's pre- and postoperation case was in keeping with high plastic surgical principles and that there is nothing from the medical respect that suggested malpractice is an issue in this case.

In the following section, we have extracted the most pertinent sections of the defendant's deposition.

§ 6.51 The Defendant's Deposition

A. Well, it was a continuation of the original complaint voiced four days prior to that second meeting.
Q. And at that time, did she request that you render any treatment?
A. According to the notes, she stated that she decided not to have surgery with the other doctor. But that she came back to me because she wanted me to do the surgery on her.
Q. Did you indicate to her that you could and would perform that surgery?
A. I did.
Q. Did you discuss with her the proposed surgery at that time?
A. Yes.
Q. Can you tell us the sum and substance of what you discussed?
A. I discussed the possibility of doing a closed capsulotomy with her or an open capsulotomy, which is in fact surgery. And I told her if her breasts were too large for her, smaller implants could be put in for her and, by definition, that would make her breasts smaller.
Q. Did Mrs. Margot indicate to you a desire to have performed either of the procedures that you just mentioned to me?
A. Yes, she did.
Q. What did she say?
A. She said she wanted to have surgery. She wanted the breasts made smaller.
Q. Did you indicate to her that you could and would perform that surgery?
A. Yes.
Q. At that time, did you discuss with Mrs. Margot the risks and complications of the proposed surgery?
A. Yes.
Q. What did you tell her about the risks and complications?
A. I told her that she could die from the anesthesia, I told her she could be allergic to any of the medications used. I told her that she could have continued hardness, because it seemed that her body formed scar capsule. I told her it was easier to be aware of that in her case, because she had already had an augmentation mammoplasty, which is the formal name for this operation. I told her that, if a woman comes in for this operation the first time, there is no good way we have of knowing what degree of scar tissue the body will form. We could only guess. But if somebody comes in with a problem of this dimension, we have a good indication that this problem may recur.

And doing an operation to make the breasts smaller would make them smaller but I couldn't guarantee that they would make them softer. However, there was a possibility that with a smaller implant, smaller than the implant that was already in there, the capsule formation might be less, because it had already been done once and it might be softer. But the preponderance of the chance or whatever you want to call it, is that it might be the same as it was before.

Q. When you met with Mrs. Margot, saw her in your office on October 13, 1988, did you have a discussion with her concerning photographs, concerning preoperative photographs?

A. I am sure I did. I don't operate on patients without photographs.

Q. Would these photographs be contained in your office records?

DEFENDANT'S COUNSEL: You have to ask your client that.

PLAINTIFF'S COUNSEL: I would like to know what the doctor's understanding was, as to why Mrs. Margot was seeing him.

DEFENDANT'S COUNSEL: Again, I think what you are asking is whether she had a particular complaint.

Q. Did she have a complaint?

A. She had a complaint.

Q. What was that complaint?

A. She had a problem with her breasts.

Q. What was the nature of that problem?

A. Well, according to her, she claimed that her breasts had been augmented by a gynecologist in 1973. She complained that they were hard at the time that I saw her, and they didn't move when she lied down. Or is it lay down?

Q. Doctor, did you examine Mrs. Margot on that date?

A. Yes.

Q. What were your findings?

A. I found that she had breast implants.

Q. Right breast?

A. No.

Q. Did you have any opinion at that time, Doctor, as to the cause of the problems which manifested themselves on January 26?

A. Well, apparently this woman had the proclivity to get scar tissue which resulted in a capsule around these implants. This was apparently the same tendency which she had demonstrated after her first augmentation mammoplasty was done in 1973.

Q. Is it your opinion that a new capsule formed between January 11 and January 26, or is this the old capsule that was causing the problem?

A. You see, when the capsule is broken during these closed capsulotomies, it allows the implant more room in which to move. What happens in women of this sort is often a new capsule will form to pull the two open ends of the previously opened capsule together. So new capsule formation is occurring at a constant rate.

Q. Did you discuss any further potential treatment with Mrs. Margot on January 26?

A. Yes, I did.
Q. Could you tell us the sum and substance of your conversation?
A. Well, I told her that we had tried to break the capsule and apparently the reformation of scar tissue was becoming obvious; even though closed capsulotomy was being done. I suggested that perhaps what we would have to do is an open capsulotomy to break or to incise the scar tissue surgically.
Q. Did you discuss with Mrs. Margot when that procedure could or should be performed?
A. Well, my feeling is that no surgery should be done for at least a six-month period from the other surgery, so that would put it past May of 1979.
Q. Do you recall what if anything Mrs. Margot said to you during this conversation?
A. No, I don't.
Q. When did you next see Mrs. Margot?
A. I next saw her on Monday, February 26, 1979.
Q. What were your findings on examination at that time?
A. Hardness of the left breast, puckering of the right breast in the lower lateral area.
Q. Was that puckering the rent which we discussed before?
A. Yes.
Q. Did you have a discussion with Mrs. Margot at that time as to what further treatment was necessary?
A. Yes.
Q. Could you tell us the sum and substance of that conversation?
A. That she probably need surgical intervention. That she would probably have to have this puckering in the right side stitched surgically and reinforced surgically. That is on the right breast, and on the left breast the capsule would have to be incised.
Q. Did you perform any procedure on February 26?
A. I guess I tried to break the capsule on the left side.
Q. And could you tell us what the results were of that procedure?
A. I made a note that they were minimal, meaning a minimal improvement.
Q. Following February 26, when was Mrs. Margot's next office visit?
A. April 30, 1979.
Q. What were your findings on that visit?
A. Apparently the breasts were still hard. She had to—the breasts were still hard and I guess I tried to do a capsulotomy on the left side, where she had some excess drooping and the surgery was gone over with her, explained to her and she seemed to be looking forward to it.
Q. Can you tell us the sum and substance of your discussion with regard to the surgery?
A. Well, I told her that the capsule had continued to form, even though a smaller implant had been put in at the time of the original surgery. So I told her that obviously she was a scar tissue former, this she knew from the first time she had the operation, which is why she came to me in the first place, or in the second place, as it were. She told me she was willing

to undergo more surgery because she wanted her breasts soft. And I told her that that couldn't be guaranteed because she continually forms a scar tissue.

Some people form it and some people don't. Here we had great evidence that she was one of the people who formed it; not once, but continually. Even though I was going to go in surgery and try to incise the capsule in one of the breasts, I couldn't guarantee that this scar formation wouldn't recur. In fact, I told her it probably would, based on the number of visits that we had already had together when it had. Nonetheless, I felt that going in surgery to repair the puckering would be necessary. And that is what we talked about.

Q. Following the visit on April 30, when did you next see Mrs. Margot?

A. May 7.

Q. What were your findings at that time?

A. The right breast needed to be tucked underneath because of the small opening, although the breast seemed soft that day. The left breast was hard. I kept trying to soften it up for her. I kept trying to hope that the closed capsulotomy would obviate surgery; but it didn't.

Q. Again the small opening that you just referred to and that is mentioned in your notes, is that the rent which we have discussed previously?

A. Yes.

Q. Doctor, in your office record which we have marked as Plaintiff's Exhibit 1, there is a document from Lenox Hill Hospital, captioned: "Physician admission justification," and I'm wondering if you could tell us just what that form is and what its significance is?

A. The significance of that form is to allow the admitting office to know what the diagnosis is, what the justification is to allow, for instance, third-party payment. To allow them to know what the proposed surgery would be, the extent of the hospital stay and any type of post-hospital home or office care that we intend to give to the patient.

CHAPTER 7

TRIAL TECHNIQUES

OVERVIEW

§ 7.1 Introduction

Successful trial techniques are universally applicable to any type of litigation, but the plastic surgery case merits some special consideration. This chapter discusses the best juror profile for your case and analyzes actual trial transcripts of the plaintiff and physician witness in blepharoplasty and mammoplasty cases.

§ 7.2 Preparing Juror Profile

After discovery is over counsel should begin to formulate an ideal juror profile. Indeed, you might be thinking of this from the first day you get the case. Consider education, race, religion, economic class, prior experience, sibling and peer pressure, age, neighborhood, employment, and a host of other factors. Then draw a profile, and select jurors who come as close as possible to that profile.

The plastic surgery case involves some unique considerations. Some jurors dislike patients who undergo elective surgical procedures such as face-lifts and breast augmentation. They may feel the plaintiff is simply vain and thus they may react unfavorably. Other jurors look upon plastic surgeons as specialists who benefit monetarily because of the vanity of patients. These considerations must be evaluated.

§ 7.3 Plaintiff's Best Jurors

Select jurors who can identify with the reasons your client sought surgery in the first place. Don't be afraid of nurses or those who have related medical experience. They are privy to medical errors and do not defy doctors or hospitals.

Look for educated people who will understand the technical aspects of the surgery and who believe in the value of plastic surgery. There is no magic formula, however. Jury selection is at best an imperfect science. You must rely upon the skills and experiences you have developed. Professional upscale people who have considered the merits of plastic surgery will identify with your client. Sometimes even older women or men, in the midst of their own midlife crisis, will relate well to the desires of the vanity patient.

§ 7.4 Defendant's Best Jurors

Generally, the lower economic classes and working class people will not identify with a plaintiff who undergoes plastic surgery. Defense counsel must be wary of jurors, particularly male jurors, who will be sympathetic towards a beautiful female. Counsel might also choose professionals who will identify with the doctor's status and responsibility. They are generally more amenable to defense arguments such as error in judgment, bad result not necessarily being malpractice, and alternative treatment.

§ 7.5 Avoiding Prejudice

No list or profile can be complete or accurate in every case. However, if you thoroughly question the jurors on their attitude towards plastic surgery in the voir dire you will eliminate any undue prejudice or at least minimize it.

§ 7.6 Model Jury Questionnaire

The following model jury questionnaire is intended as a guide for use in the average plastic surgery malpractice case. The comments are generalities and must be adapted to the facts of a particular case.

Personal Background

1. Name
2. Address
3. Occupation
4. Marital Status
5. Spouse's occupation
6. Children's occupations (if relevant)
7. Parents' occupations (if relevant)
8. Own or rent property? (This reveals the prospective juror's stake in the community and may bear upon knowledge of rising insurance rates.)

Prior Litigation Experience

1. Any prior litigation of any kind?
2. As plaintiff or defendant?
3. As auto driver or passenger?
4. Medical cases?
5. Witness for relative, friend, employer or other?
6. Legal professional in family?

Prior Juror Experience

1. Civil
2. Criminal (if so, juror may hold plaintiff to the higher "criminal" burden of proof).

Expectations from TV Experience

1. Do you watch Perry Mason, L.A. Law, or Judge Wapner and the People's Court?
2. Are these shows realistic?

General Medical History

1. Family physician (if long and trusted relationship, this juror may lean to defendant)
2. Specialist (equate referral to plastic surgeon to referral to any other specialist)
3. Hospitalization (family or close friends)
4. Serious illness
5. Disputes with doctors
6. Medical personnel in family
7. Knowledge of medications taken
8. Attitude about plastic surgery.

Major Themes

1. Defense
   a. Just because the plaintiff sues, does that mean we have to be at fault or that he must get a huge verdict?
   b. Mirror, mirror on the wall vanity concept? Can the plaintiff be at fault?
   c. Is beauty in the eye of the beholder? (psychological inability to express satisfaction or recognize natural aging process).
2. Plaintiff
   a. Can someone be sick or ill in the mind?
   b. Does the plastic surgery patient deserve the same compassion and help as any other kind of patient?
   c. Do you feel that an emotionally ill person can be like a child depending on the doctor for help?
   d. Do you think that the patient may have impaired judgment and may not be responsible for her own conduct?

Probing Issues

1. (Defense) Will you or can you be swayed by sympathy? (Or can you be tough enough?) We all feel sorry but must leave emotion outside jury and courtroom doors. Only facts should count.
2. (Defense) Manipulation: Can you be easily manipulated or persuaded?
3. (Defense) Meritless complaint: Should you pay a bill that is not your responsibility?
   a. Should we (defendant) pay for a bill (claim or complaint) that is not our responsibility or fault?

b. Should the plaintiff pay if she is partially or fully responsible (comparative negligence)?

c. Should we reject or give bill (complaint) back to the plaintiff's attorney and fight for justice before "you people"?

4. Mirror, mirror on the wall

a. (For men or women) Do you use cosmetic creams, cologne, hair coloring, makeup?

b. Do you diet regularly, exercise, belong to health clubs, enjoy jogging? Would you have cosmetic surgery? Is beauty in the eye of the beholder?

5. (Defense) Jury role: In this country anyone can bring a lawsuit against anyone else. Thank God, that is one of our basic rights. But if it is a groundless claim, then our system looks to you, the jury, as the remedy—to vindicate us. That too is one of our most basic and cherished rights.

6. (Both sides) Identification: Do you identify with plaintiffs? With patients? With doctors?

7. (Both sides) Law: Can you agree with the law the court gives you?

8. (Defense) We all make judgments without benefit of hindsight. If things go wrong, does that mean you were negligent?

9. (Defense) Burden of proof: The burden of proof is the plaintiff's responsibility to you. That is why the plaintiff opens first and sums up last; that is why the defense does not have to present any evidence.

10. (Both sides) Objections: Will you understand my obligation to object and not hold it against my client?

11. (Both sides) Cross-examination: Will you understand my obligation to cross-examine sympathetic witnesses?

12. (Defense) Sympathy: Plaintiff will not attempt to sway you with sympathy, I am sure. But if they do, will you let emotions blind you to your duty to be impartial?

13. (Both sides) Damages: Can you evaluate damages as you would everyday purchases and values (food, clothing, furniture)? If not warranted, can you return a small verdict or a large one based on evidence?

14. (Both sides) Motives: Are some stories exaggerated? Do witnesses have motives to lie?

15. (Both sides) Jury function: You are the judge of the facts. Can you still call them the way you see them, like an umpire, fair and square?

16. (Both sides) Personal: Personalize the defendant (age, family, practice; explore any problems) or plaintiff (a patient with family, friends, and fears, hopes, and dreams like you).

17. (Both sides) Skepticism: We will explore and investigate this claim together just like a good detective.
18. (Defense) Comparative negligence: Do patients (plaintiffs) have responsibility to follow orders, take medication, give complete history, and be honest about their part and their complaints? If they do, can you find them at fault? Can they not be responsible for their condition?
19. (Defense) Burden of proof: What if the defense presents no case? We have no burden. (This is generally a poor strategy because the defense should accept that they really do have a burden of proof.)
20. (Defense) Codefendants: Our independence from codefendants: we are not responsible for them.
21. (Both sides) Lawyers and witnesses: Personality of lawyers or parties not to be a factor.
22. (Defense) Complications and cures: Do you understand that, despite the best of care, patients do not always recover or escape from complications? There are no guarantees. Result of treatment depends on many variables including condition of patient and complications—problems resulting need not be result of any malpractice.
23. (Defense) First and last impressions: Are first impressions lasting impressions? The defendant is last, but not, I hope, least in your mind. (Can a first impression of the plaintiff be misleading?) Keep your mind open.
24. (Both sides) Knowledge of witnesses: Any knowledge of any parties or witnesses to be called?
25. (Both sides) Special problems: Drinking, intoxication, handicaps, drug history, sexual problems, no witnesses, no defendant in court, no plaintiff in court, changes in deposition testimony.
26. (Plaintiff) Do you deify doctors?
27. (Plaintiff) Are you affected by publicity of recent malpractice cases? Can you judge this case on its own merits?
28. (Both sides) Thank the jury for their time, patience, and cooperation now and during the remainder of the trial.

§ 7.7 Opening Strategies

The psychological importance of your opening cannot be overstated. It is the jury's first real impression of your case. The jurors' interest is at a peak. Many studies report that the opportunity to persuade is greatest at this time and that more than 80 percent of jurors actually make up their minds during the opening.

Both plaintiff and defendant should avail themselves of the opportunity to put their best foot forward. Tell the story in sufficient detail, with the most compelling facts. As Federal Judge Herbert Stern is fond of saying in his trial seminars, "Be the firstest with the mostest." However, do not overstate the case and do not exaggerate. You should not promise evidence that you cannot deliver. Do not ask the jury to wait and keep an open mind. Tell them the reasons why your client should prevail. Both sides should reveal and defuse the weaknesses in their case at this time. Liability and damages should be thoroughly addressed.

The plaintiff's counsel must convince the jury of the righteousness of her cause and the carelessness of the defendant's. She must persuade the jury to identify with her client while being suspect of the defendant. Sufficient facts should be revealed to convince the jurors that they are part of a crusade to determine the truth and help right a wrong.

Defense attorneys, on the other hand, generally seek to infuse doubt, cynicism, and skepticism in their openings. They are the great counterpunchers. They should reveal everything favorable to the defense and everything that the plaintiff has failed, forgotten, or intentionally neglected to tell the jury. However, the best defense is a good offense, as demonstrated by the captivating testimony of Lieutenant Oliver North at the Iran-Contra Congressional hearings in 1987. Even though he was later convicted, his strong persona helped to win acquittal on 10 of 13 charges.

This is not the time to keep the defense a deep dark secret. This is not the time to ask the jury to wait. Give the jurors your reasons for a defendant's verdict now. You need not be overly argumentative. In fact, you must not argue obviously. Simply tell them what the evidence will show. Be assertive, confident, perhaps even righteously indignant, if appropriate to the case. Tell them you will prove it. This will preclude any attempt by your adversary to object that you are too argumentative.

§ 7.8 Direct Examination

Plaintiff's Strategy

Counsel should generally begin with the defendant surgeon and cross-examine him as an adverse witness. This technique is quite effective because the jury views the defendant in a negative posture, restricted basically to yes and no responses.

The strategy is to establish the lack of good care and departure from accepted practice. Later, the plaintiff's expert will comment on the testimony and establish the departure from accepted practice.

Any strange behavior of the plaintiff can then be explained well before he testifies. Of course, by that time the jury will sympathize with him and have already begun thinking about the malpractice of the surgeon.

The plaintiff's testimony, when it is proffered, should not be too long or exaggerated. He is the victim. The defendant's conduct should be the issue for the jury, not the plaintiff's. The plaintiff should be kept in the background as the sympathy and suspense build to a climax.

Defense Options

Defense counsel usually will counterpunch and look for openings and inconsistencies in the plaintiff's case. If the plaintiff calls the doctor to the stand, one must decide whether to rehabilitate him then or reserve his direct testimony for the defendant's case. I favor immediate rehabilitation. Personalize the doctor defendant now. Psychologically the jury must relate and warm up to him now. Of course, if your witness has been good and told his story on the plaintiff's direct it may not be necessary to question him or recall the witness later. This may only give your adversary a second chance to make his case or correct any of his oversights.

The defendant's direct case should be professional and straightforward. A prominent expert in defendant's specialty should testify in his behalf. But other experts in other specialties should be considered to compliment the plastic surgeon's treatment and confirm that it conforms to good practice.

It is also a great advantage to have a subsequent treating doctor of the plaintiff testify for the defendant as to limited damages and liability, if possible.

Defense Counterattacks

The defense should be aggressive if it has developed evidence of exaggeration, similar prior hidden claims, or inconsistent statements. The days of the laid-back option are gone.

Of course, if the plaintiff has not presented a prima facie case, then you must move for dismissal and insist on a decision before putting on your witnesses.

Any contradictory evidence that the plaintiff has malingered or withheld evidence should be pursued. Jurors want to see the plaintiff pressed hard. They were weaned on Perry Mason and will not hold it against defense counsel if he defends vigorously. Simply use good taste and be consistent with your own style and personality.

§ 7.9 Cross-Examination

No concise treatment here of this classic and revered subject could possibly do justice to the great books already devoted to it. However, in brief, one should observe the following guiding principles:

1. What Are the Goals?
   - **a.** To prevent adverse testimony before it is offered (objections on direct and voir dire)
   - **b.** To discredit and impeach the witness
   - **c.** To bolster and support your case
2. When Does Cross-Examination Begin?
   - **a.** In Preparation—EBTs, Investigation, Medical Information, Pre-cross Notes
   - **b.** When Witness Enters the Courtroom
     - **i.** Intimidation
     - **ii.** Body Language
     - **iii.** Conferences—Actions with Adversary
   - **c.** When Witness Testifies
     - **i.** Notes on contradictions and exaggerations
     - **ii.** Body Language and Lies
     - **iii.** Refresh Recollection and Documents
   - **d.** Objections during Direct
   - **e.** Voir Dire of Qualifications—
     - **i.** Challenge
     - **ii.** Move to Strike
     - **iii.** Overnight recess
3. When Should It End?
   - **a.** When you make your point
   - **b.** End on high note
4. Methods of Cross-Examination
   - **a.** Don't if not necessary
   - **b.** Limit and plan attack
   - **c.** Elicit favorable testimony
   - **d.** Impeach credibility (bias and prejudice)
     - **i.** Financial interest
     - **ii.** Relationship between parties
     - **iii.** Prior litigation experience
     - **iv.** Prior testimony

e. Never ask why—best "yes" or "no" questions
f. Attack merits and basis of opinion
   i. Preparation
   ii. Review of materials
   iii. Errors or fact
   iv. Visit situs (opportunity to observe and test)
   v. Substance of opinion
g. Demeanor
   i. Polite but firm
   ii. Your personality controls.

Cross-Examination of the Expert

In a plastic surgery case an expert can be attacked on several grounds. These include the following:

1. Unfamiliarity with plastic surgery procedures. This is particularly useful when plaintiffs place an expert on the stand who has a background in dermatology, otolaryngology, and/or dermatology
2. Inexperience with the procedures
3. Testimony based upon one limited examination
4. Expert unaware of all pertinent facts.

§ 7.10 Summation

Plaintiff's Approach

The summation should be the highlight of your case but the days of mandatory great oratory are past. The idea that a great and stirring summation will win the case is a terribly naive misconception. You should have already convinced the jury. Everything that has gone before is part and parcel of the closing. Like a squirrel preparing for winter, you should have been "squirreling away trial testimony acorns" for your summation.

Appeal to the injustice done to your client and the jury's opportunity to help and send an important message to the medical establishment. Invest them with a sense of purpose and mission and the verdict will be substantial. Devote the bulk of your summation to the strongest portions of your case. Don't try to rebut every point raised by the defendant. Be sincere, be honest, and thank the jury for its consideration and acceptance of responsibility for the great burden "you have been carrying" for the plaintiff.

Defendant's Strategy

Defense counsel is the "spoiler." Inveigh against the inconsistencies, the exaggeration, the broken promises of the plaintiff.

Read the plaintiff's opening back to the jury if it has been grossly exaggerated and impeached by the testimony. Return the plaintiff's theme with sarcasm, but now add a touch of righteous indignation, even outrage that "the defendant and this jury have been misled, used and abused." (Only in the appropriate case.)

The rest of this Chapter discusses representative trial transcripts showing direct and cross-examination techniques in plastic surgery cases on both liability and damage issues.

ILLUSTRATIVE CASE: BLEPHAROPLASTY

§ 7.11 Background

Comment. In this cosmetic case, the plaintiff was a 77-year-old woman who underwent her third blepharoplasty. She was a plastic surgery addict. She claimed that too much tissue was removed from her lower eyelids and that the procedure was negligently performed resulting in a drooping or permanent ectropion of the lower lids and permanent infection. The defense claimed that the ectropion was only temporary and that her conjuctivitis was a result of her soaking her contacts in Perrier water with lime. The expert witness was an ophthalmologist, not a plastic surgeon. He examined her only once and testified as to damages only. During the trial, the defense called her treating ophthalmologist who testified that she did not have the ectropion. He was confronted by an alleged copy of his report which indicated that she did in fact suffer from an ectropion. However, subsequent evidence proved that the record had been altered. When the defense called the plaintiff to the stand to confront her with the fraud, she took the Fifth Amendment. The judge referred the case to the district attorney who had an assistant district attorney sit in the courtroom every day and took possession of the evidence.

§ 7.12 Qualifications of Plaintiff's Expert

The plaintiff called an examining ophthalmologist to testify to the existence of an ectropion. However, his close relationship to the plaintiff's counsel and his 11th-hour introduction into the case severely impeached his credibility.

Q. Dr. [ ], are you a physician duly licensed to practice medicine in the State of New York?
A. Yes.
Q. And, Doctor, have you concerned yourself with a particular field of medicine?
A. Yes.
Q. And what field is that?
A. Ophthalmology.
Q. Now, Doctor, did you examine Mrs. Davis at my request?
A. Yes.
Q. And when did you examine her?
A. July 27, 1981.
Q. And did you obtain a history with reference to her eye condition?
A. Yes.
Q. And what was the history given to you?
A. She reported that in December 1974 there had been a blepharoplasty.
Q. And what is a blepharoplasty?
A. It's a repair of the condition of the lid.
Q. Is that surgery to the upper as well as the lower lids?
A. It can be either. There was a blepharoplasty of all four lids.
Q. That's the upper and lower?
A. Both sides.
Q. Does a blepharoplasty concern itself with the removal of excess of skin for cosmetic purposes from the eyelid?
A. That's briefly where a blepharoplasty is done.
Q. Is that the understanding, that the nature of the operation that she had performed?
A. Yes.

* * *

A. She reported that in December of 1974 there had been a blepharoplasty of all four lids which represented a repetition of a similar operation within the previous year.

She stated that she "felt something" in the left lower lid and the latest surgeon had advised a revision of all four lids because the fissures were not equal.

Comment. The plaintiff claimed that she never knew that the defendant was going to do all four lids. Yet she apparently admitted that she did know to this doctor. Defense counsel interrupted to highlight this admission and express his surprise. The answer gets repeated four times.

DEFENSE COUNSEL: Sorry?
THE WITNESS: Had advised revision of all four lids because the fissures were not equal.

DEFENSE COUNSEL: Sorry. Did you say, doctor, that he advised a revision of all four lids in—

PLAINTIFF'S COUNSEL: Judge, what is this?

THE COURT: He asked for a repetition of the last answer and I said there could be a repetition of it at the time he cautioned the doctor to read more slowly. So if you would please repeat the last answer?

THE WITNESS: The latest surgeon had advised a revision of all four lids because the fissures were not equal.

Q. Thank you. Doctor, what is meant by "the fissures were not equal"?

A. The space between the lids.

Q. Now please continue with the history that you obtained.

§ 7.13 Voir Dire on Doctor's Qualifications

Comment. A failure to call the treating doctor should be highlighted because that physician should be the best judge of the patient's condition.

DEFENSE COUNSEL: May I make an objection? I don't mean to interrupt, but I think, based upon what has been testified—well, to this extent, I don't believe that this doctor is a treating doctor. I think that's been stipulated or mentioned before by plaintiff's counsel. If he is not a treating doctor and gives the report after the case is on the calendar, I would like a voir dire because I think it's improper for him to testify to any complaints or any permanency.

PLAINTIFF'S COUNSEL: Judge, I never heard of this kind of stuff.

THE COURT: As to voir dire on what?

DEFENSE COUNSEL: As to the qualification to testify as a treating doctor. If he is not [the] treating doctor, then he shouldn't be testifying as to her condition of permanency. May I add that this doctor's name was never given to us when this case was placed on the trial calendar.

Comment. The best cross is to prevent the direct in the first place. If one can show through a voir dire of the expert's qualifications that he is not qualified to testify there will be no adverse testimony. Psychologically it always helps to cast doubt on the testimony before it is given.

THE COURT: I will permit the history but I will not permit the complaints. I will permit the witness to testify.

Q. Doctor, when you examined Mrs. Davis, please tell us what your objective findings were and I recall your examination about her eyes—withdrawn. Please tell us the nature of your examination of her eyes and what your findings were.

A. There was an examination of her eyes, including the lids and their function. The findings at that time showed that the revision of the right eye could be corrected with glasses 20-20, and the left to 20-25ths. I'll quote from my records. There is a substantial ectropion—

Q. And what is an ectropion?

A. Ectropion is the position of the lid in which the lid border changed outward from the eye.

Q. Is that in reference to the lower lids?

A. Yes.

Q. And what effect does that have on the closure of the eye?

A. It makes it difficult and sometimes impossible for the lids to come together.

Q. And what effect does that have on the function of the eye?

A. Tearing—

DEFENSE COUNSEL: Objection, unless it's related specifically to Mrs. Davis and not some theoretical pertinent with other problems or conditions.

Q. Is it related to the condition that you found?

A. Yes.

Q. Please continue, what effect does the ectropion lower lid have on her function?

A. The first thing that it does is to change the appearance of the lids from what it would be if the ectropion were not present.

Q. In what way?

A. The lid hangs outward, exposing the inner lining of the lid; hence, there is an area which normally would not be seen and a lake of tears collected between the globe and the lower lid occasionally spills over.

Q. What does that mean in lay terms?

A. Because the lid was turned outward, tears collect in that area. There are scars seen in all four lids.

Q. What were these scars from, in your opinion, with a reasonable degree of medical certainty?

A. They appear to have been related to the previous operations and there was a millimeter of lag of thalmus, which is to say that the lids could not be proximated or brought together.

Q. What distance is a millimeter in inches?

A. A millimeter lag of thalmus on a forced closing is in the order of a 25th of an inch, but on relaxation this increases to 3 millimeters, the order of an eighth of an inch.

Q. Now, Doctor, what effect would that space have when a person goes to sleep?

A. It exposes the cornea to the air.

Q. What is the cornea?

A. The cornea is the round front part of the eye.

Q. And what effect does that have on the function of the cornea when it's exposed to the air?

A. The cornea is normally kept moist by tears. When the lids do not close, the cornea is exposed to the air and it dries out.

Q. And what effect does that have on the first one, such as who has this condition?

A. Gives rise to discomfort, irritation, sensitivity to light.
Q. Do you have an opinion with a reasonable degree of medical certainty as to what treatment or what procedure a person of this type should use to minimize the effects of the drying?
A. An ointment is placed in the eye each night and the lids are brought together with adhesive tape.
Q. Now, Doctor, after examining Mrs. Davis, did you arrive at an opinion, with a reasonable degree of medical certainty, as to what was the cause of this ectropion?
DEFENSE COUNSEL: Objection. I would like a voir dire in order to determine this witness' qualifications concerning this case, in terms of evidence and background to answer this question.
THE COURT: All right, you may do that. Bear in mind it is voir dire for that purpose, not a cross-examination.
DEFENSE COUNSEL: Of course.

§ 7.14 Second Voir Dire

Q. Dr. [ ], is it true that you only saw this patient on only one occasion?
PLAINTIFF'S COUNSEL: I object to that. That's cross-examination, not going into the doctor's qualifications as to whether or not he is qualified to give an answer with regard to this type of procedure.
THE COURT: The witness' testimony has been that he saw her.
Q. Doctor, what records, if any, have you reviewed as to the past medical history of this patient, before you saw her?
PLAINTIFF'S COUNSEL: Judge, objection. He objected to the use of the history—or he allowed the history to go in.
THE COURT: Yes, objection overruled. You may answer.
Q. Of course. Doctor, what records, if any, did you review before writing this report?
A. I saw no other records before writing the report.
Q. Do you know how many plastic surgery procedures this patient had had prior to 1974?

* * *

A. I was aware or had been informed of—I believe I stated earlier that she had had operations of all four lids.
Q. Well, I think, sir, you said reading from something that she was advised that she was going to have an operation for all four lids, is that what you told us?
A. If I may quote from what I said earlier?
Q. Please do.
A. She reported that in December of 1974 there had been a blepharoplasty of all four lids which represented a repetition of a similar operation done within the previous year.
Q. Go on.

A. So, in answer to your question there was a similar operation done in the previous year.

* * *

Q. Did you look at any other records relating to the prior surgery?

A. No.

Q. Do you know if she had any surgery since 1974, the surgery on all four lids that she told you that she was advised of since that time up until this time that you examined her this past year?

THE COURT: Once again, limited to the surgery which would have effected the findings; not other surgery.

Q. Since the surgery, do you know of any other plastic surgery that she has undergone?

A. Dr. [ ] is the doctor who did this?

Q. He is the doctor this lady sued.

A. I didn't know his name.

Q. You mean when you were questioning this—

THE COURT: We are dealing now with the voir dire and not with the cross-examination.

DEFENSE COUNSEL: Respectfully, your Honor, if he was never advised of the name of the doctor, it goes to his ability to testify in the case, not in terms of his expertise in general, but on his background in this case, what records he has seen, what he even knows about the procedure before he testifies to anything.

THE COURT: And the question is—

Q. Do you know if she had undergone any plastic surgery procedures since the 1974 surgery on all four lids that she told you her surgeon had advised her to have?

A. I am not aware of any other operations.

Comment. Again, the strategy here is to show he is unprepared. He doesn't know the patient's past medical history or even the name of the defendant. Where did they get him from? The answer is surprising (see § 7.23).

* * *

Q. Would it be important to know before giving your educated opinion to this jury whether or not she had undergone plastic surgery procedures concerning the area of the eyes, both before the operation by the defendant and after the operation, up until the time that you saw her this past summer?

* * *

THE COURT: Bearing in mind, counsel, we are dealing with a voir dire and not a cross-examination.

DEFENSE COUNSEL: But if it's determined that he doesn't know the proper records or background, I would respectfully submit that the opinion cannot be given to this jury, and that's why I am asking.

PLAINTIFF'S COUNSEL: Well, Judge, I think he is going far beyond the purpose of a voir dire. He is going into cross-examination which he will have his chance to if he lets me finish with my direct.

THE COURT: Go to your next question on voir dire.

Q. Do you know if this patient had worn contact lenses since the operation in 1964? This could be subject to connection.

A. Yes.

Q. Do you know whether or not the contact lenses were the cause of the irritation to her in the years before you saw her on that one occasion on July 27th, 1981?

Comment. This is the defense claim—that her contacts washed in Perrier caused her conjunctivitis.

PLAINTIFF'S COUNSEL: Judge, I'll object to this.

THE COURT: Sustained.

* * *

THE COURT: Counsel, you are getting into cross-examination and I limited it to a voir dire on what I previously said.

* * *

Q. Did you know that this patient had testified that [she] was seen by Dr. Steven Bloomfield, an ophthalmologist, after this surgery?

PLAINTIFF'S COUNSEL: Objection.

THE COURT: Sustained.

PLAINTIFF'S COUNSEL: Judge, I think he is finished with his voir dire. I think I should be permitted to go on with my case.

THE COURT: Yes, the witness has testified.

DEFENSE COUNSEL: I submit that the witness has no knowledge of a list of doctors that I would like to read now of their treatments or records, his opinion based on one visit would be incompetent in terms of his knowledge of the case and the history of the patient, with all due respect to the doctor, and that's why I would like to ask which doctors, if any, that she has seen. Inasmuch as there was no pretrial discovery, I have not had a chance to question her because I have taken this witness out of turn and consented to it, and I have a right and the jury knows it, I have a right to know whether he has knowledge of this treatment, these doctors and their treatment, before he could make a record on the ultimate issue.

THE COURT: Overruled at this time on the voir dire.

PLAINTIFF'S COUNSEL: May I continue?

DEFENSE COUNSEL: May I make a motion that this witness should not be permitted to testify on permanency, based on his lack of knowledge and background in the specific case, with all due respect to the doctor?

THE COURT: That motion is denied.

DEFENSE COUNSEL: Respectfully accept.

Comment. Even though the Court denied the motion, the defense had actually cross-examined before the plaintiff even had his direct. The seeds of doubt had been sowed.

§ 7.15 Treatment of Problem: Mitigation of Damages

Comment. Ironically, this testimony is also evidence for the defense of mitigation of damages. In fact, the plaintiff had testified in her deposition that she would rather suffer than undergo this correction because in her mind she might turn out looking "Chinese." This ridiculous answer was used on her cross-examination to attack her vanity, sanity, and credibility. It was also not lost on defense counsel during jury selection—the last juror the defense chose was of Chinese ancestry.

Q. Doctor, I think you were telling us about what steps a person with a condition that you found Mrs. Davis in should take in order to alleviate the impact of that condition. Would you continue on with what you feel should be done by such a person?

A. I have already mentioned that lubricating ointments are used at night and lubricating drops are now mentioned during the day, and the lids are brought together with adhesive at night.

Q. Now, Doctor, is there some sort of treatment which could have been adopted by Mrs. Davis which would change this condition such as a surgical—some sort of surgery which might correct this failure of the eyes to close?

A. Yes.

Q. What type of procedure would that be?

A. It would have been possible to do a skin graft for the shortened lower lids.

Q. Now, where would you take the skin from in order to apply it to the lower lids?

A. In the normal circumstance, it could be taken from the upper lid, but she has already been operated [on] twice, so that would not be suitable. From behind the ear or supraclavicular area.

Q. Meaning the shoulder?

A. Yes.

Q. Would the color of the skin that would be grafted to the eyes be different from the natural skin surrounding the eyelids?

A. Yes, possibly would.

Q. Would such a surgical operation leave her with pronounced scars on both eyes?

DEFENSE COUNSEL: Objection, the doctor has already said, "probably would." There is no definite opinion that there would be any scars whatsoever.

THE COURT: Sustained.

Q. With a reasonable medical certainty, do you have a medical opinion as to what would be the effect of such an operation on the cosmetic appearance of the person submitting to such an operation?

A. Yes.

§ 7.16 Risk of Future Treatment

Q. Please tell us.

A. The skin taken from elsewhere than the lids would be different from the skin of the lids, probably in color, and probably inconsistent in the wrinkles and so on would be different.

Q. Would it be noticeably different?

DEFENSE COUNSEL: He is leading the witness. He never said, "noticeably."

THE COURT: Sustained.

Q. Please continue.

A. It would be apparent that the skin graft would be apparent.

§ 7.17 Permanency

Comment. Although the doctor testified as to permanency, the truth is that the condition can be corrected. However, the plaintiff refused because she irrationally believed she could end up looking "Chinese." Defense objections were to remind the jury that she had permanency only because she wanted it.

Q. Incidentally, this condition that you found on Mrs. Davis, do you have an opinion with a reasonable degree of medical certainty as to whether or not it was a permanent condition?

A. Yes.

Q. And what is that opinion?

A. I believe that it's permanent, in the absence of treatment.

DEFENSE COUNSEL: In the absence of treatment, Doctor?

THE WITNESS: Yes. This is what we are discussing now.

Q. Would you say that ectropion that you have in the lower lid was a permanent condition with reasonable medical certainty?

A. Yes.

DEFENSE COUNSEL: Objection. The doctor just testified in absence of treatment. I move to strike the answer.

THE COURT: The prior answer may stand.

Q. Assuming with reasonable medical certainty that such a corrective operation was performed, do you have an opinion as to what period of time would have to elapse between the operation, the blepharoplasty, and the corrective surgery?

DEFENSE COUNSEL: Objection. Before the doctor answers, we are now asking questions about plastic surgery. I have not heard one qualifying question as to this witness' background, experience, knowledge, and expertise in plastic surgery. This is totally a different area that he is attempting to draw from him as an expert.

PLAINTIFF'S COUNSEL: I will withdraw the question.

§ 7.18 Witness Qualified in Plastic Surgery of the Eyes

Comment. A key to the prior voir dire on qualifications was that this doctor was not an expert in plastic surgery. The witness attempted to prove he was but this made him very vulnerable on cross.

Q. Doctor, have you had any experience with plastic surgery around the eyes?

A. Yes.

Q. Please tell us what type of experience you have had with this type of procedure.

A. All ophthalmologists do surgery around the eye, including plastic surgery around the lids.

Q. Have you observed such operations during the course of your professional life?

A. Yes.

Q. Have you been assisting in this type of operation?

A. Yes.

Q. Doctor, based on your experience, with a reasonable degree of medical certainty, what period of time, if any, would be required to pass between the blepharoplasty which led to the ectropion—withdrawn.

DEFENSE COUNSEL: I was going to object, but was waiting for you to finish.

THE COURT: Yes, he has withdrawn it.

PLAINTIFF'S COUNSEL: I withdraw the question.

DEFENSE COUNSEL: Please may I finish? I will submit that the qualifications procedures have not been completed yet. If he is going to ask another question and opinion, I ask that the doctor be qualified on plastic surgery or he may not. I haven't heard anything yet of a concrete, specific nature, and that's why I want to object, and perhaps that would save time. Do you have more questions as to the background of this doctor, or is that it?

PLAINTIFF'S COUNSEL: That's it.

DEFENSE COUNSEL: Then I move that he is unqualified to testify as to plastic surgery, based on what has been elicited so far.

THE COURT: You may testify.

DEFENSE COUNSEL: May I have a voir dire on that qualification?

THE COURT: On that qualification and only that qualification.
DEFENSE COUNSEL: Yes, absolutely.
THE COURT: Yes, sir.

§ 7.19 Voir Dire Examination by Defense Counsel

Comment. Here we go again—a second precross voir dire. This time defense tried to weaken the foundation of any opinion the expert might proffer on damages of liability with respect to plastic surgery.

Q. Doctor, how many blepharoplasty procedures have you, yourself, conducted on your patients in your career?
A. Oh, 75.
Q. And how long have you been in practice in medicine?
A. 30 years.
Q. And when was the last time that you performed such a procedure?
A. Six months.
Q. Was this in the function of an assistant or surgeon in charge?
A. No, I was the surgeon.
Q. In your practice at the hospitals, which you have privileges, do you have an application on file asking for the privilege to perform plastic surgery procedures?
A. Those applications have been approved at all these hospitals.
Q. And do they include blepharoplasty specifically?
A. They specifically include blepharoplasty.
Q. Have you taken any specific residency in the area of blepharoplasty or plastic surgery?
A. Our training includes training in blepharoplasty.
Q. Have you taken a specific residency in blepharoplasty?
A. In ophthalmology it specifically includes work done on blepharoplasties.
Q. Have you done any teaching in the area of blepharoplasty?
A. Yes, sir.
Q. Where?
A. At Columbia.
Q. Have you written any articles in blepharoplasty?
A. No.
Q. Have you a degree or title or entitled as a diplomate in the area of plastic surgery?
A. Plastic surgery around the eyes is included in our diplomate of the American Board of Ophthalmology.
Q. That's not what I asked you.
A. Examinations include plastic surgery.
Q. Are you board-certified in plastic surgery? I heard that you give plastic surgery. I don't recall hearing if you are board-certified in plastic surgery.
A. No.

Comment. Counsel must not let a witness, especially a medical witness, equivocate. Pin him down. Keep asking the question until the witness answers it.

Q. Do you hold yourself out in the credentials that you gave for the medical directories as a specialist physician, specializing in plastic surgery?
A. Plastic surgery around the eyes is done by an ophthalmologist.
Q. With all due respect, there is a book called Medical Directory of New York?
A. Yes.
Q. Are you listed in that book as a specialist in plastic surgery?
A. No.
Q. Is there also a book known as the Directory of Medical Specialists which lists doctors across the entire country as well as the New York area in their respective specialties?
A. Yes.
Q. And do you hold yourself out in that book under the area of a specialty in blepharoplasty?
A. All ophthalmologists do blepharoplasty and plastic surgery.
Q. And is there an area in this book, in the book known as the Directory of Medical Specialists divided up into areas, into specialties such as ophthalmologists and plastic surgeons, is that not correct?
A. Yes.
Q. You are listed in the area of ophthalmology?
A. Yes.
Q. And you are not listed in the area of plastic surgery are you, sir?
A. That is correct.
DEFENSE COUNSEL: You are not. Thank you. I would move that this witness, although certainly qualified as a physician and an ophthalmologist, is not qualified in the area to give opinions in plastic surgery.
THE COURT: He may testify as to plastic surgery insofar as discussing blepharoplasty.
DEFENSE COUNSEL: Respectfully accept.

Comment. Although the court overruled the objection, the jury should have already been suspect of the witness' credentials in the plastic area.

§ 7.20 Discrediting Opinion

Comment. One of the plaintiff's claims was that she had *exposure keratitis*—that is, an inflammation of the cornea—because she could not keep her lids together.

Q. Thank you. I have no further questions. One other thought: does exposure keratitis have anything to do with the condition that you found on Mrs. Davis?

A. Yes.
Q. What is exposure keratitis?
A. Exposure keratitis is a condition in which the cornea shows changes because the lids cannot be brought together, the cornea is exposed.
Q. And did you find any such indication in Mrs. Davis' eyes?
A. Yes.
Q. Do you have an opinion with a reasonable medical certainty as to whether or not his surgery, this blepharoplasty, was the cause of this condition?
DEFENSE COUNSEL: Objection. This doctor doesn't know the medical history of this patient. Admitted, he didn't read the medical records or other hospitalizations. How could he give an opinion with any kind of certainty as to the conditions that he thinks he sees was competently produced by a procedure years before? There is no foundation from this man.
THE COURT: Overruled.
THE WITNESS: Yes, I do.
Q. And what is that opinion?
A. I believe that the operations on the lids resulted in shortening of the lids to the extent that the lids could not close, and this resulted in exposure keratitis.
PLAINTIFF'S COUNSEL: Thank you. I have no further questions.

§ 7.21 Cross-Examination by Defense

Comment. Of course this man's testimony had to be discredited or at least minimized. Defense attempted to do this by showing a prior relationship between him and the plaintiff or her counsel.

Q. Doctor, you have certain materials before you that you referred to?
A. Yes.
Q. And do they include a report that you rendered to this attorney?
A. Yes.
Q. May I see it, sir?

(Handing document.)

DEFENSE COUNSEL: (Examining document.) I would like the doctor's letter to plaintiff's counsel on September 21st, 1981, to be marked at this time for identification.
THE COURT: Mark it.

(Document marked Defendant's Exhibit C for identification.)

Q. Doctor, on the one occasion that you saw Mrs. Davis on July 27, 1981, was she alone or was she accompanied by someone?
A. She was not alone. She was accompanied by someone.
Q. Who was she with?
A. Plaintiff's counsel.
Q. And did plaintiff's counsel talk to you about the case at that time?

A. Yes.
Q. And at that time you took the history from Mrs. Davis?
A. Yes.

§ 7.22 Highlighting the Plaintiff's Admission

Comment. Defense counsel had the doctor impeach the plaintiff's claim that she never knew all four lids would be revised.

Q. You've told us before in reading from that record that she told you, "She stated that she felt something in the lower left lid, and the latest surgeon had advised a revision of all four lids because the fissures were not equal." Sir, is it correct that that's taken from your report of September 21st, 1981, which is Defendant's Exhibit C, right now, for identification?
A. Yes.
Q. When Mrs. Davis told you that she was advised—withdrawn. When Mrs. Davis told you that the latest surgeon had advised an operation, you knew that to be the surgeon who was being sued in this case, did you not?
A. I think so, yes.
Q. But did you know his name was Dr. [ ] at that time?
A. No.
Q. When she told you that the surgeon who she is suing, "The latest surgeon had advised a revision of all four lids," was plaintiff's counsel present at that time or were you alone?
A. He was present.
Q. Did you know that her claim in this case before this jury is that the doctor never told her there would be a revision to all four lids, but only the upper lids?
PLAINTIFF'S COUNSEL: Objection.
THE COURT: Overruled.
Q. Did you know that her claim to this jury today is that she was never told that there would be an operation on her lower lids?
A. No.

§ 7.23 Expert's Relationship with Counsel

Comment. It is always good to discover that the expert has a professional relationship with counsel. But it is even better to learn that he is his own doctor. Credibility flies out the window for both doctor and lawyer.

Q. Do you know Mrs. Davis from some social acquaintance or a friend before Mr. [ ] brought her to your offices on July 27th of this past year?
A. No.

Q. Had you ever met her before at some type of capacity, medical or otherwise?
A. No.
Q. Had you ever known plaintiff's counsel or his law firm before the visit that she made this past summer?
A. Yes.
Q. Will you kindly tell me what your prior relationship or association with plaintiff's counsel was?
A. He had been a patient in my office on a number of occasions.

Comment. This is a terrible admission to have to make. The plaintiff's counsel must have been desperate or very sloppy to have had to resort to his own doctor.

Q. I will not ask you what the conditions were, sir.
PLAINTIFF'S COUNSEL: You can ask.
Q. Was it for an eye condition, I would assume?
A. Correct, for an eye examination.
Q. I don't mean to pry into plaintiff's counsel's personal affairs, but for how long had plaintiff's counsel been a patient of yours?
A. I cannot recall, I don't have the record here. A number of years.
Q. Does it go back as much as five or 10 years or longer perhaps?
A. Probably not longer, between five and 10 years would be my recollection.
Q. As many as 10?
A. Five and 10.
Q. And have you treated other members of his family as well, sir?
A. I think I have seen other members of his family.
Q. He has two sons, does he?
A. I don't recall.

Comment. Even his children? Plaintiff's counsel should never have called this witness.

Q. Which members of his family did you—
PLAINTIFF'S COUNSEL: I personally don't see the relevance of my family in this lawsuit, and I'll object to anything further as irrelevant.
DEFENSE COUNSEL: Your Honor, I will stipulate that the members of his family and the conditions are irrelevant, but the relationship of the witness and plaintiff's counsel who called him in a case of malpractice, or any case, is certainly proper as to bias or background or any number of influences that may be operating.
THE COURT: I'll permit it.
DEFENSE COUNSEL: Thank you.
THE WITNESS: I have no recollection of seeing other members of his family.

Q. Sorry, I thought you told us a moment ago that you treated other members. And I asked if it was two sons?

Comment. The doctor is retreating out of embarrassment but now he looks untrustworthy.

A. I don't recall whether I had seen his wife or not.
Q. Do you know his wife?
A. I cannot say that I know his wife. I don't mean to offend him. I don't remember seeing any other members of his family.
Q. Have you ever had any other type of social circumstance with plaintiff's counsel or any member of his family, any other dinner or drink or show or something of that nature?
A. No.
Q. Have you seen plaintiff's counsel in your offices at 165th Street?
A. I think I saw him in the White Plains office.
Q. When you were sworn in, the court clerk asked you to give your office address, I believe. You gave 165th—
A. 635.
Q. Yes, what was the address?
A. Yes, sir, 165th Street.
Q. That's the address here in Manhattan?

§ 7.24 Attack on Credentials

A. Yes.
Q. But, sir, isn't it a fact that you are listed in the Medical Directory of New York and in the American Medical Directory of Medical Specialists with an address on Maple Street, I think it is, in White Plains?
A. Yes, that is correct.
Q. Did plaintiff's counsel ever ask you to help him out on a case before this one?
A. I have not been asked to help him out on any case.
Q. Well, I'll rephrase it, sir. Has he ever asked you to give testimony in cases in which he was a lawyer before this Davis case?
A. No.

§ 7.25 Expert's Prior Testimony

Q. Have you ever given testimony in a court of law before involving a malpractice action?
A. Yes.
Q. On how many different occasions, sir?

A. Some number, smaller than five.
Q. Was it five or more than five?
A. Smaller than five.
Q. Which courts?
A. To my recollection, it's very vague, but I know that I testified in the Westchester Supreme Court.
Q. In front of what judge was that?
A. Oh, I can't remember, it's years.
Q. How long ago was that, what year was it?
A. I've been in the practice 35 years. If I testified three times, I don't remember what the problems were.
Q. No, sir, perhaps you didn't hear me. What year did you testify in the Supreme Court?
A. I don't remember.
Q. What about the other occasions, what courts were those actions pending in?
A. I've only testified in Westchester and in this court is my recollection. So it's one or the other on one or more occasions.
Q. When was the last time that you were in New York?
A. I don't even know that was a malpractice case, I don't remember. I don't do this very often.
Q. In those other cases, were you testifying on behalf of a patient?
A. I don't have that information or even the recollection.
Q. Well, were you testifying against the patient and for a doctor? Don't you recall even that for or against?
A. I really don't.
Q. Is there some place that I can get a transcript of this testimony that you gave that you can't seem to recollect? Can you tell me the name of the case, the lawyer, the court, so I can go and try to find the transcript of it? Could you help me out with that?
A. I'm not withholding anything, I don't remember.
Q. What [are] the name[s] of the other lawyers that you testified for, surely you remember their names?
PLAINTIFF'S COUNSEL: I object to the form of the question, "Surely you remember," your Honor.
THE COURT: Sustained.
Q. Please tell me the names of the lawyers for whom you testified?
A. I don't know if I ever testified in a malpractice case, I don't remember.
Q. Sir, I asked you the names of the lawyers. I didn't ask you whether it was a malpractice or not. I understand you are no longer sure about that one. Are you sure [about] the names of the attorneys who asked you to testify?
A. I remember one case in which I testified in which Mr. Dempsey was representing the plaintiff and Mr. Rendy (phonetic) of the office in White Plains was representing the defense.
Q. Do you remember any other attorneys?
A. (No answer).
Q. If not, if you have no recollection, I won't burden you any longer.

A. I do not.
Q. Do you know or did you ever in your professional capacity know either one of plaintiff's counsel's sons?
A. No.
Q. Do you know if they are doctors or physicians?
A. I do not.
Q. When did plaintiff's counsel first approach you and ask you to come to court to testify against the defendant?

§ 7.26 Why Are You Testifying?

A. Prior to my examining the patient, he indicated there may be a suit and I might be asked to testify.
Q. Did you tell him at that time, "But I never treated this woman, why are you asking me to go to court"?
PLAINTIFF'S COUNSEL: I object to that.
THE COURT: Sustained.
Q. Did you ask him why, if you were not the treating doctor, he was going to ask you to testify as to her condition?
PLAINTIFF'S COUNSEL: Objection.
DEFENSE COUNSEL: It goes to his background.
THE COURT: Sustained.
Q. When was this that he came to you?
A. I don't recall. Prior to the patient's visit.
Q. When was the patient's visit, your patient, what day was it?
A. I don't remember. It's in the record which you have in front of you.
Q. What month was it?
A. It's in that record. I don't recall. Was it in July of last year?
Q. Who else was present besides plaintiff's counsel and Mrs. Davis?
A. Myself.
Q. Was there a nurse present?
A. No.

* * *

Comment. Incredibly, this witness admitted that he agreed to testify without ever seeing the patient. Obviously his close friendship with counsel was a factor.

Q. When did you agree to testify in this case?
A. I don't recall. I suppose it was shortly before I first saw the patient.
Q. So, you agreed to testify before you even saw the patient, Doctor?
A. Absolutely.
Q. Without knowing what the patient looked like, without examining her and without seeing any medical records relative to her medical history, you agreed to testify?

A. Yes.
Q. Was it some time that you agreed to testify, when you agreed on the amount of money?
A. I never agreed to the amount of money. I had agreed to testify. I didn't say that. I said I agreed to examine her.
Q. When you wrote your report on September 21st, 1981, that it was based on a visit back in July, didn't you think it was necessary to have seen not only the operative report but the whole hospital admission that's involved in this case since 1974?
A. No.
Q. You agreed to come and testify before this court and this jury without thinking it was necessary to see the hospital record?
A. Yes, after seeing the record, the medical record, it concerns my—
Q. Have you ever seen the entire record?
A. I saw substantially a record that could have been the complete hospital record, the ones that I saw.
Q. Wouldn't it be important for you to know before testifying exactly what was everything that was in that hospital record?
A. No.

§ 7.27 The Cursory Examination

Comment. As further proof of the shallowness of this testimony, defense counsel established that this doctor's examination was done earlier the same day in the vestibule of the courtroom instead of in his office.

Q. How long did the entire examination take?
A. An hour and a half, an hour and a quarter.
Q. I didn't hear you testify as to the use of any equipment. Did you use a slit lamp?
A. A slit lamp is so ordinary to our work that we don't mention it.
Q. Please, could you answer yes or no?
A. Yes.
Q. So, you did use it?
A. Yes.
Q. Did you perform a Schirmer's test?
A. Not on that day.
Q. But you told us that you had only seen her on that day.
A. I performed a Schirmer's test today.
Q. Today on whom?
A. Mrs. Davis.
Q. Today you took the examination of her?
A. Today.
Q. Did you feel it was important that you take that particular kind of test?

A. Well, it could be helpful.
Q. Would you please tell the court and jury why that test is important?
A. That test is a measure of tear formation.
Q. Doctor, this important test which is a measure of tear formation was one you did not bother to take when you did your examination in July and then wrote a report to plaintiff's counsel, isn't that correct?
A. No.
Q. So you based your opinion then, knowing it would be the same opinion given to this court and jury without taking this very important test, is that not correct?
A. That's correct.
Q. Are there other important tests that you did not take back in July of 1981 when you had this one opportunity to examine this individual so that you could come before this jury and give them the benefit of your expertise and knowledge and opinion in a malpractice action against the defendant?
A. No.

§ 7.28 Paid for His Testimony

Q. I assume you are being paid something for your time here today?
A. That's correct.
Q. Would you please tell the court and jury how much you are being paid for your testimony?
A. I'm not being paid for my testimony, your Honor.
Q. Aren't you giving testimony today?
A. I'm being paid for the time and preparation.
Q. Of course, I'm sorry. That's what I meant.
A. Yes.
Q. What are you charging?
A. In order to make this day available, the fee was $2,000.

Comment. This was a considerable sum for a half day's pay in 1980.

Q. Now, you also gave us a report of July 27th. What was the fee that you charged to write this report to Mrs. Davis?
A. I do not recall.
Q. How about the fee that you charged to do the examination before you can write the report?
A. I don't recall.
Q. Well, we have three separate fees. We have the court testimony, the report, and the examination. Can you give us your best estimate of what the fee for the examination and the report was?
A. There are only two fees.
Q. What was the other fee?
A. The one fee for examination and report, and today's fee.

Q. Today's fee is the $2,000 that you are getting to testify against the defendant?
A. Yes, sir.
Q. What was the fee for the report and examination?
A. I don't recall. Ask plaintiff's counsel or Mrs. Davis.
Q. Didn't he give you a check for it?
A. Pardon?
Q. Did he give you a check for this work?
A. For that report?
Q. Yes, that goes back to July.
A. I don't know who paid for it. I don't know, I don't remember.
Q. I'm suggesting, perhaps, you have a check or record that would tell us?
A. I don't have it here.
Q. In your office?
A. Oh, the office has a record of payment.
Q. Did he pay you or did Mrs. Davis pay you?
A. I do not recall that.

§ 7.29 Curriculum Vitae Limitations

Comment. Here defense counsel had a chance to renew an attack on the witness' lack of substantial experience in blepharoplasty.

Q. In looking at your curriculum vitae, is that up to date, which was marked as an exhibit?
A. To the best of my knowledge, unless I omitted something.
Q. Sorry, I didn't hear.
A. To the best of my recollection, it's up to date, it's accurate, unless I omitted something.
Q. Well, you correct me if I'm wrong. I'm looking at it for the first time now. It talks about teaching courses and being members of academies in ophthalmology and being certified in ophthalmology and about being a fellow in ophthalmology and having training in ophthalmology. Would you tell me, sir, where on your own curriculum vitae, which you prepared, and would you please point out where it says that you have specific training, experience, residency, fellowship, or publications in plastic surgery?
A. Every time the word "ophthalmology" appears, there is implied confidence—
Q. Sir—
PLAINTIFF'S COUNSEL: Let the doctor answer.
THE COURT: The witness may answer.
Q. Please answer the question.
A. It is commonly understood that where the word "ophthalmology" appears it includes surgery to the lids with plasty experience with all due respect.

Q. Would you please answer my question? Where does it say that you have any qualifications or training?
A. Ophthalmology in there includes any particular grounds or expertise in plastic surgery.
PLAINTIFF'S COUNSEL: Judge, that was already answered. The doctor said blepharoplasty.
DEFENSE COUNSEL: I object to speeches to the jury.
THE COURT: Both objections are sustained.
Q. Doctor, does it say plastic surgery?
A. Would you repeat the question?
DEFENSE COUNSEL: I would like to have this marked in evidence. I would like to offer it in evidence.
PLAINTIFF'S COUNSEL: I have no objection.
THE COURT: Received.

(Received the doctor's curriculum vitae as Defendant's Exhibit D in evidence.)

Q. Dr. [ ], one more question on ophthalmology and plastic surgery. Aren't there some ophthalmologists who take special training, residencies, and programs in the area of plastic surgery?
A. Yes.

§ 7.30 No Special Training

Q. You have not taken any special training?
A. No.
Q. Other than what you have learned and what you learned in medical school and your initial internship and residenceship in the 1940s?
A. You don't intend to minimize that?
Q. Not at all, sir. Just since that time, since medical school and your internship?
A. I have taken further training.
Q. When was the last time that you took training?
A. November of '81.
Q. And what was that?
A. American Academy of Ophthalmology.
Q. How long did that training last?
A. Hours.
Q. Years?
A. Hours.
Q. Well, that's not equivalent to a residency in a particular subject or attending day in and day out of a particular hospital, for months to a year. This is more in the nature of what, a little speech or seminar?
A. No, it's called continuing medical education.
Q. It's a one-time course?
A. No, several.
Q. A couple of hours?
A. Several hours, not a couple. A couple is two.

§ 7.31 Available Remedy

Comment. Defense counsel used the witness in a friendly manner to establish the defense of mitigation of damages. He eventually had to admit that she could easily have a revision.

Q. In either event, in the type of [revision] it's a relatively simple procedure that could be performed?
A. No.
Q. Could the operation have been performed back in 1975?
A. Yes.
Q. So that as we sit here in 1982, she has gone some seven years with this condition that she complains is so troublesome to her eye without undergoing this corrective procedure that she could have undergone the same year with the surgeon?
A. I don't understand the question.
Q. I will rephrase it. Sorry. Sir, isn't it likely that this procedure, whatever, no matter who it's done by, might very well leave no strips, no scars whatsoever, and nothing perceptible?
A. It's unlikely.
Q. It's possible?
A. Possible.
Q. Do you know whether in the past seven years that she has had an opportunity to undergo this corrective procedure, if she ever made an appointment with a plastic surgeon or an ophthalmologist to have this corrective procedure done, so she could eliminate all her problems?
PLAINTIFF'S COUNSEL: Objection.
THE COURT: Come up, counselor.

Comment. The point proves that she could have mitigated her damages for all of these years. She, of course, claims that she might wind up looking "Chinese" if she has the correction.

Q. Doctor, we are going to take a break in a minute and I believe one last question. Did Mrs. Davis ever tell you that she had agreed in the past seven years to go ahead and have this corrective procedure which would have ended all her problems?
A. She told me that she had consulted a doctor who advised her against it.

Comment. Of course, no such doctor was ever called to the stand.

Q. Did she tell you whether she had ever made plans to have such a procedure?
A. No.

§ 7.32 Attack on Preparation

Q. For example, suppose this patient had had a prior history of plastic surgery involving the eyelids before the defendant—I'll stop there. Would it have been relevant to you to know whether or not she had had a prior blepharoplasty?
A. I did know that.
Q. Did you know it at the time?
A. It's in the record.
Q. Wouldn't it have been important for you to see what that procedure was like before commenting and making your report?
A. There's only one way to do the operation.
Q. Sir, did you see the prior hospitalization?
A. No.
Q. Sir, do you know if she had any complications from the prior surgery—that's in 1971—to the lids that resulted in the exposure keratitis and the ectropion that you testified that she has today—

* * *

THE WITNESS: Sorry?
THE COURT: You may answer.
THE WITNESS: The operation that was performed could not have been performed if she had already had this problem.
Q. Do you know whether she did or not?
A. I had evidence that she didn't.
Q. Have you ever seen any records or asked to see any records in evidence or asked whether she had any problems before?
A. The patient knew that she had a problem before.
Q. The patient has testified that she did not, that she had no problems before this.
A. Then I accept that.
Q. Would it be important to know if she did have this problem, in fact, a year before?
A. The patient's history is very important in evaluating the total situation.
Q. Thank you. Now, with respect to that history, did you know that she had a blepharoplasty in 1968?
A. I didn't know the exact date, but I knew it was prior to her recent operation, more recent operation.
Q. Since the history is important, as you say, could you please tell the court and the jury what history you know of this woman, prior to the defendant procedure in 1974?
A. Can I have my records, please?
Q. Sure, Doctor, do you have any independent recollection before ever looking at that sheet?
A. No. My records indicate that she had an operation a year earlier than the operation in question, that would be in 1973.

Q. Do you know the doctor who performed that operation earlier?
A. No.

Comment. The following line of inquiry demonstrated that this witness never bothered to review the patient's prior plastic surgery history. He therefore appeared to be more interested in helping his friend—plaintiff's counsel—than in being fair to the defendant. There was also another, more subtle, strategy at work here. Defense counsel wanted to portray the patient as a frivolous, vain woman—a plastic junkie who was never satisfied with the results.

Q. Would the name of Dr. Hogan ring a bell or refresh your recollection?
A. I said I do not know his name.
Q. Did she ever tell you his name?
A. If she told me, I would know, but I do not know.
Q. You didn't see those records, did you sir?
A. No.
Q. Did she tell you the procedure was before Dr. Hogan's involving plastic surgery?
A. Of her lids?
Q. Of her lids.
A. No, she did not.
Q. Did she tell you of any other plastic surgery?
A. There were other operations on her, other operations on her face and scalp.
Q. Do you know whether or not she had a breast operation?
A. No.
Q. That is, she didn't or you don't know?
A. I don't know whether she had it or not.
Q. Did you know whether or not she had any type of chemical peel procedures done to her face?
A. I didn't know it at the time that I wrote this, no.
Q. Do you know it now, sir?
A. Yes.
Q. When did you first learn of this, that she had chemical peel procedures?
A. Today.
Q. How did you learn that information?
A. By communication.
Q. With?
A. Plaintiff's counsel.
Q. With plaintiff's counsel? Were you speaking with him after you left the stand the past few minutes?
A. We had a great discussion on skiing, skiing at Stowe.
Q. Did it include this case at all?

A. This case wasn't at Stowe. It was purely on skiing at Stowe.
Q. When did you get this information about chemical peel?
A. Prior to my entering the court today.
Q. Who gave you that information?
A. Plaintiff's counsel, I just said so.
Q. Do you know if she had plastic surgery done in Beverly Hills by Dr. F.?
A. No.
Q. Now, keeping in tone with this history which you say is important, do you know the names of any doctors who she saw for treatment after she left the defendant about a week or so after the operation?
A. I don't know when she saw him, but I know the names of two doctors that she had seen.
Q. She saw you in 1981?
A. Correct.
Q. Did she ever tell you the name of the two doctors that she saw?
A. That's how I know there were two. She gave me their names.
Q. Do you recall?
A. Yes.
Q. They are?
A. One was Dr. S., and the other one was Dr. Byron S.
Q. Do you know either one of these gentlemen?
A. What?
Q. Do you know these gentlemen, either one of these gentlemen?
A. Yes, I know them both.
Q. Dr. Bloomfield is an ophthalmologist also?
A. Yes, sir.
Q. And Dr. Smith is what?
A. An ophthalmologist, a plastic surgeon or an ophthalmologist. I think he may have both interests.
Q. He specializes in both areas doesn't he? Is he one of the physicians who has taken advanced, specialized training in plastic surgery as well as ophthalmology?

Comment. Defense counsel had a chance to get in a dig about his lack of qualifications or boards in plastic surgery.

A. I don't know what his training is. I know that he has a special interest, yes.
Q. Do you know how many times she has seen Dr. Bloomfield?
A. I know that he was treating her.
Q. She has told the court and the jury that she has seen him something like 75 times, according to my notes. Do you know if it was over a period of many years?
A. Yes.
Q. Did you look at his records?
A. No.

Q. Did you request his records from plaintiff's counsel?
A. No.
Q. Did you ever speak to—
PLAINTIFF'S COUNSEL: Now, there is an assumption that I have his records. I object.
DEFENSE COUNSEL: Were there records served from your office to me with Dr. Bloomfield's name on it?
Q. Sir, I would like to show you the records of Dr. Bloomfield that I have been supplied by plaintiff's counsel.
A. Yes.
Q. These records, incidentally, are about one month postoperatively, January '78—
PLAINTIFF'S COUNSEL: Judge, I don't think that he should supply him the records.
DEFENSE COUNSEL: I asked him whether there was anything in Dr. Bloomfield's records that show any ectropion of the eyelids whatsoever.

Comment. We later called this doctor to prove that she never had the ectropion. He was the doctor who was confronted with an altered version of his records that indicated ectropion. However, it was not listed in the diagnoses and was checked off in an irregular manner, rather than as if she was being treated for it. The only diagnosis was conjunctivitis. Ectropion is more serious and would have been written out if diagnosed. We later blew up the original report and the altered one to five-foot cardboard models. Obviously, the jury found for the defense.

* * *

Q. Doctor, would looking at this record be helpful to you in rendering an opinion, since it is based on a treating physician right after the incident itself?
A. No.

Comment. This answer was incredible and destroyed any impartial objective image he may have still had with the jury.

Q. Did you know whether or not Mrs. Davis has undergone any treatment at Duke University Medical Center?
A. No.
A. Could I say that everything I know is in this report and I don't have to sit through this and that. I know it's all in here.
Q. Doctor, I don't mean to harass you. Don't take offense.
A. I know. But everything I know is in this record.
Q. Exactly doctor—and that doesn't even begin to tell you the whole story, does it?
PLAINTIFF'S COUNSEL: Objection.
Q. Withdrawn—never mind.

§ 7.33 Suggesting Alternative Causation

Comment. This witness claimed that her keratitis resulted from the operation. We suggested that it could also come from problems with her contact lenses. Her treating doctor would testify later that it was a result of soaking the lenses in Perrier and lime.

Q. Keratitis is a word meaning an irritation of the cornea, is that correct?
A. That's correct.
Q. Couldn't such an irritation that you say you found come from an irritation agent such as overuse of contact lenses in the eye?
A. Not if the lens is properly fitted.
Q. Doctor, isn't one of the causes of keratitis found to be the use of contact lenses?
A. Not lasting seven or eight years.
Q. Now, Doctor, we don't know—please confine yourself to what you know. You only saw her once in 1981—
PLAINTIFF'S COUNSEL: I object to the admonition made by counsel.
THE COURT: Please listen to the question, Doctor, and answer only that which is asked. Don't volunteer.
THE WITNESS: All right.
Q. Would you agree, Doctor, that the contact lens use could be an irritant causing keratitis?
A. Yes.
Q. Doctor, I'm going to rephrase the question and make it subject to connection. Hypothetically, if there was evidence that she had a preexisting keratitis and an ectropion before surgery, could that have been a competent producing cause of what you find today in 1981?
A. Yes. (End of testimony).

§ 7.34 Altered Medical Record

Comment. At the end of the trial defense counsel called the plaintiff to the stand. In the following dramatic testimony, she was forced to take the stand and answer questions over objection about the altered record. She took the Fifth Amendment. Obviously, this is devastating to her case before the jury.

DEFENSE COUNSEL: For the convenience of the jury, your Honor, I have made photostats of the exhibits so that they could follow along.
THE COURT: We will use only the exhibits, not copies of the exhibits.
Q. Mrs. Davis, this is a document your attorney offered in evidence as a form filled out and signed by Dr. Bloomfield on September 15, 1981, this

form before you has Box No. 40 ectropion of lower lid checked off and underlined, do you see that before you, Ma'am?

A. I refuse to answer on the grounds it will incriminate me.

Comment. Counsel didn't even ask the question yet. Notice how defensive the plaintiff was already. Her answer was even worse than it constitutionally had to be.

PLAINTIFF'S COUNSEL: "It may" incriminate you.
DEFENSE COUNSEL: Objection to his speech.
THE COURT: Counsel, please.
THE WITNESS: That it may incriminate me.
Q. Mrs. Davis, will you be so kind as to tell the court and jury where that photostated copy of this report came from?
A. I refuse to answer on the grounds that it may incriminate me.
Q. Can you tell me, have you prepared that photostated copy?
A. I refuse to answer on the grounds that it may incriminate me.
THE COURT: Mrs. Davis, if Mr. Robertson were to ask you other questions concerning this document, would your answer be the same as it has been up until now?
THE WITNESS: Yes.
DEFENSE COUNSEL: Your Honor, I believe I have a right to inquire a little further.
PLAINTIFF'S COUNSEL: Now, Judge, we have gone through this before. He knows that is the procedure and this is unfair advantage being taken. That was the agreed upon procedure.
THE COURT: If this is something which has escaped me?
DEFENSE COUNSEL: May I approach the bench, your Honor?
THE COURT: Yes.

(Discussion off the record.)

THE COURT: I will permit one further question.
PLAINTIFF'S COUNSEL: And that will be it, Judge, right?
THE COURT: Based upon the witness' assertion that her answer would be the same, yes.
PLAINTIFF'S COUNSEL: I have advised her.
DEFENSE COUNSEL: I object to speeches before the jury.
THE COURT: It is what the witness does, not your advice which is material.
Q. Mrs. Davis, please direct your attention to Box 40 on Dr. Steven Bloomfield's photostated record which says "Ectropion of upper lid/lower lid." There is a check mark in Box 40, and apparently someone has underlined the words "lower lids."
Now, did you place your check mark in your own hand in Box 40 and underline the words, "lower lids," yes or no?
A. I refuse to answer on the grounds that it may incriminate me.
DEFENSE COUNSEL: No further questions in that event, your Honor.

Comment. This is devastating testimony and totally destroys the plaintiff's credibility. In fact, by this point in the trial the court had a marshal take possession of the evidence, the district attorney was sitting in court monitoring the trial, and the news media were watching with bated breath. The jury returned a verdict for the defendant. However, they wanted to look at the before and after photographs from the surgery. Even though there was no evidence that the photos proved anything, the jurors wanted to see if Mrs. Davis had enough skin or fat to justify her eyelid lift.

ILLUSTRATIVE CASE: BREAST REDUCTION

§ 7.35 Qualifications of Expert

It is essential to establish the credentials of your expert to impress the jury because malpractice cases often come down to the battle of the experts.

The plaintiff was a 17-year-old girl admitted for a bilateral reduction mammoplasty. After surgery she discovered that her right nipple was 1 ½ inches higher than the left and not in the proper anatomical position near the center of her breast. The plaintiff claimed, among other things, that the defendant did not properly mark the breasts prior to surgery.

The plaintiff's lawyer called his expert to the stand to testify to the departures. The expert testified that the presurgical markings should have been done with the patient in a sitting or standing position instead of when she was lying down. Note the authoritative way counsel established the credentials of the expert. He elicited his academic background in addition to his practical, hands-on experience in performing this surgery. The expert then carefully explained the departures from accepted practice and the bases for his opinions, at one point even exclaiming that he had never heard of the method of measurement utilized by the defendant.

Q. Good morning, Doctor. Sir, are you a physician and surgeon duly licensed to practice medicine and surgery in the State of New York?

A. I am.

Q. And do you limit your practice to any particular speciality?

A. Yes, I limit it to plastic surgery.

Q. Tell us, Doctor, please, tell his Honor and the jury a bit about your educational background, where you went to medical school and where you received your training thereafter.

A. I went to medical school at Penn State University at Hershey Medical Center from 1973 to 1977. After completing my medical school, I did a residency in general surgery at Montefiore Hospital and Medical Center from 1977 until 1982. At that time I completed a chief residency in general surgery and was certified by the American Board of General Surgeons and did a residency in plastic and reconstructive surgery at Montefiore Hospital and Medical Center in 1982 and 1984. Since 1983 I have served as chief resident in general surgery at the Medical Center in the College of Medicine.

Q. Doctor, have you ever been awarded any faculty appointments?

A. Currently I am on the faculty of the College of Medicine and have a teaching appointment to that institution.

Q. And what are your duties consistent with that teaching position?

Comment. The image of the expert as a teacher is a strong psychological analogy to his role as advisor to the jury.

A. I am involved in the teaching of residents in plastic surgery and general surgery, the procedures that we do in plastic and reconstructive surgery, and lecturing to medical students.

Q. Doctor, prior to coming to court today, were you provided with certain materials by my office pertaining to this case?

A. Yes, I was.

Q. And did they include the hospital record and the doctor's office records and some photographs?

A. They included photographs of present and postoperative photographs, the pretrial examination of the defendant, the office records and hospital records of the patient, and letters from Dr. Bromberg and Dr. Roth, including the examination of the patient.

Q. Doctor, based upon your experience and training, have you become experienced with the performance of breast reduction surgery?

A. Yes, I have.

Q. And approximately how many of these procedures have you performed in your career, Doctor?

Comment. Jurors are impressed by experts who have had a lot of hands-on experience with the particular procedure at issue.

A. Somewhere in the neighborhood of 50 to 75.

Q. And have you ever taught plastic surgeons or people?

A. Yes.

§ 7.36 Critique of Hospital Record

The expert was asked to review the record as a foundation for testimony about specific departures from good practice.

Q. Doctor, does that anesthesic record indicate that anesthesia was commenced at eight o'clock in the morning?

A. Well, that is what it seems to indicate: at the top of the graphic chart there is a notation "8:00 A.M.," and in the middle of the bottom section there is—it says "Operation 8:00 A.M. to 3:10 P.M."

Q. Doctor, based upon that, are you able to state an opinion based upon a reasonable degree of certainty as to how long the surgery in this particular case actually took?

A. Well, that time period is seven hours and 10 minutes.

Q. And can you tell us how long of that seven hours and 10 minutes was actually involved with the performance of the cutting and the suturing and all the various steps in the surgery performed by the defendant?

A. This is a little blurry. I am trying to sort it out. It appears that it started after the first hour or the first—wait a second—35 minutes; the first 35 minutes were preparation period. Then it seems that the surgery started.

Q. So how long did it actually take, Doctor, for the defendant to do the surgery?

DEFENSE COUNSEL: Objection. No foundation for that question. All we know it is 35 minutes past 8:00 A.M.

THE COURT: I think it is sufficient foundation assuming, of course, that the doctor can answer the question from the anesthesia record. Overruled.

A. Seven hours and ten minutes minus 35 minutes.

Q. Six and a half hours?

A. Correct.

Q. For an operation that customarily takes three-and-a-half to four hours, Doctor?

§ 7.37 The Hypothetical Question

Q. Doctor, I want to assume that on February 20, 1980, Marcy James, a 17-year-old, was admitted to the Brunswick Hospital in Amityville for performance of bilateral reduction mammoplasty or surgery to reduce the size of both of her breasts. Please further assume that that evening, the evening of the 20th, the defendant came to the patient's room, used certain instruments and marking pencils and made certain measurements and made certain markings on the patient's breasts. Assume that the following morning the patient was taken to the operating room and, before she was put to sleep, before she was anesthetized, the defendant had her sit up in the upright position on the operating table and he again checked some of the markings and either reinforced them or changed them. Assume further, Doctor, that the defendant thereafter performed the surgery which is described in the official operative report contained in the hospital record. Please further consider, Doctor, in forming your opinion that, after the surgery was performed, the patient was bandaged with heavy support bandages which were removed and replaced over the next couple of weeks and that approximately two weeks after surgery on

March 5th the bandages were removed and the doctor testified that he removed all the sutures. Assume further, Doctor, that prior to that time the patient had not been able to see her breasts but on the date that the bandages and sutures were removed, she examined herself in the mirror and noticed that the position of the nipples was the same as the position shown in this photograph, Doctor, which you have testified you have seen before, I believe, and in this photograph. Assume further, Doctor, that since that time the position of the nipples has never changed. Please further consider that in September of 1981 Dr. Bromberg examined the patient, measured the patient and found that the right nipple was one-and-a-half inches higher than the left nipple and that it was more towards the sternum or midline, as the patient had testified, than the other one. Assume that throughout the postoperative period the patient had no infections or sicknesses that could interfere with healing and, as testified by Dr. Bromberg, the patient had no anatomical conditions before surgery which predisposed her to asymmetrical placement or asymmetrical scarring. Please further consider, Doctor, that throughout the postoperative period, as noted in the doctor's own office records, the patient healed well and entirely satisfactory.

Assuming those facts to be correct, Doctor, are you able to state an opinion, based upon a reasonable degree of medical certainty, as to whether or not the defendant departed from accepted standards of good medical practice in performing the surgery on February 21st, specifically with regard to the nipple graft?

Comment. The use of the hypothetical question is traditional in malpractice cases. It has the advantage of providing a minisummation but runs the risk of boring the jury if too long.

§ 7.38 Departure No. 1: Misplacement of Nipples

Q. Please, Doctor, explain the basis for your opinion that there was a departure from proper care in performing the surgery.

A. The operative markings that are done with the patient in the upright position either the day of the surgery or prior to surgery should accurately depict where the nipples need to be placed on the breast. This should be done symmetrically and if the nipples were placed asymmetrically, that is a departure.

Q. Doctor, how could such misplacement occur?

A. The measurements that one makes in performing a reduction mammoplasty either were made inaccurately or, if they were made accurately, the lines that were drawn were not followed during the execution of the procedure.

Q. Doctor, if the lines were not measured and marked accurately, would that be a departure from proper practice as it existed at this time?

A. Yes, it would.

Q. And, Doctor, if the lines were marked accurately but were not followed carefully and properly during surgery, would that be a departure from proper practice as it existed at the time this surgery was performed?

A. Yes, it would.

Q. Doctor, are you able to state an opinion as to whether the departures you have just described were a competent producing cause of the position and placement of the nipples on the patient's breasts as noted by Dr. Bromberg on the patient and as you observed in those photographs?

A. Yes, I am. The nipples are asymmetric and they are asymmetric because they were placed asymmetrically.

Comment. Of course, a departure that does not lead to specific damages is not legal malpractice. The proximate cause must be established or the case will be dismissed.

§ 7.39 Departure No. 2: Method of Determining Breast Size

Q. Doctor, I want you to further assume that, during the course of the operation, in order to determine the amount of tissue to remove from each breast, the defendant had a brassiere sterilized which was then brought into the operating room which during the course of surgery he placed over the patient's breast in order to judge the size of the achieved breast. Assume that this was done while the patient was in the supine position, flat on her back. Assuming that to be correct, Doctor, are you able to state an opinion based upon reasonable medical certainty as to whether or not such a method of determining—excuse me—able to form an opinion, Doctor, as to whether such a method of determining the size of the achieved breast was a departure from proper practice as it existed at that time?

A. Yes, I am.

Q. What is your opinion, sir?

A. The use of a—

Q. Is it a departure or is it not?

A. Yes, in my opinion it is a departure.

Q. Please explain the basis for your opinion.

A. Well, first of all, a bra or brassiere is made of elastic material for the most part which allows a certain degree of stretchiness. Number two, a breast, especially a large breast, in a patient or a person lying flat on her back, can assume almost any position that one wants to make it assume. It can be moved from the armpit to above the shoulder. There is a lot of flexibility as to where the breast can be placed and, in addition, typically speaking, markings and judgments done in breast reduction are done with the patient either sitting or standing because of these inherent inaccuracies when the patient is lying flat.

Q. Is that method which I have just described a reliable method of making such a determination?

A. I am not familiar with it. It seems inherently unreliable.

* * *

A. This was a departure, if—I must clarify though the fact that, if the only thing that the doctor relied upon was the brassiere size, the residual hypertrophy appears to be related to the use of this method.

Comment. The expert was trying to qualify his answer and the defense counsel jumped to his feet to try to keep him from giving an explanation and stop the plaintiff's counsel from helping him.

Q. Well, Doctor, if it wasn't the only method, but he relied at least in part on that determination, by using the brassiere, would that be a departure?

DEFENSE COUNSEL: Objection, your Honor. Counsel has asked the question. He's gotten his answer. I think he is stuck with it.

PLAINTIFF'S COUNSEL: Judge, first of all, to make that sort of comment, I have no objection to the answer—

THE COURT: Mr. Lewis, let's not have such comments.

DEFENSE COUNSEL: I am objecting to the form of the question. It's leading.

THE COURT: Read the question back.

(The question was read by the court reporter.)

THE COURT: It is leading to some extent.

Q. Doctor, I want to assume that the defendant has testified that he didn't rely solely upon the brassiere but used it as a check. Assume that to be correct. Would that be a departure from proper practice?

A. Yes, it would, because the brassiere can be misleading and in itself is inherently inaccurate in measuring breast size.

Comment. The plaintiff learns he got the departure by persevering and being alert to the witness' answers.

§ 7.40 Departure No. 3: The Unnecessary Scar

Q. Doctor, I want you to assume that the position, shape, and size of that scar as noted in that picture was the same as it was when the patient first saw it postoperatively approximately two weeks postoperatively, but further assume that since two weeks postoperatively, the position, shape, location, and angle of that scar have remained the same. Are you able to state an opinion, sir, what caused that scar and its position and location?

A. Yes, I am.
Q. And what is your opinion, sir?
A. The scar is there. That is where the surgeon made the incision during the course of his surgery.
Q. Is that something the surgeon would control, where he puts the incision?
A. Yes, the scar, the incision is dictated by the preoperative markings.
Q. Doctor, are you able to state an opinion based upon a reasonable degree of medical certainty as to whether or not it was a departure from proper practice for defendant to make an incision on the right breast in that location and at that angle?
A. Yes.
Q. And what is that opinion?
A. That it was a departure. There does not seem to be any reason during the—either from the patient's preoperative photographs or his records that would indicate why it would be necessary to make the scars asymmetric.

§ 7.41 Departure No. 4: No Informed Consent

Q. Doctor, are there any risks associated with this procedure?
A. Yes, there are risks.
Q. I want you to assume for the purpose of my question, Doctor, that neither the patient nor her parents were ever advised of any risks of untoward procedures or untoward results associated with this operation. Assuming that to be correct, would that be a departure from proper practice as it existed at the time the surgery was performed.
A. Yes, it would be.

§ 7.42 Doctor Paid for His Time

Q. Doctor, you just indicated you and I met prior to today to discuss the case. Are you being paid for the time that you spent in reviewing the records and discussing the case with me?
A. Yes, I am being reimbursed for the time we have met.
Q. Have you taken time off from your practice today and your duties at the university to come to court today?
A. Yes, I am.
Q. Are you going to be paid for the time that you are spending in court today?
A. Yes, I am.

Comment. It is customary to let the jury know that the expert is being paid for his time, not his testimony. If the plaintiff doesn't reveal it, the defense will on cross-examination in a pejorative way.

§ 7.43 Cross-Examination by Defense Counsel: Witness Never Examined Plaintiff

The defense attorney's strategy was to attack the expert both collaterally (he never examined the patient) and later by insisting that the patient's weight gain affected the size and ultimate symmetry of her breasts and that they were asymmetrical even before surgery. He also tried to have the expert concede that the defendant used his best judgment—thus even an error would not subject him to liability.

Q. Doctor, you have indicated that you have used certain written material to make an evaluation in this case. I think you mentioned the hospital record, the preoperative photos of Marcy James, the pretrial deposition of the defendant, his hospital or the hospital record, and his office records and letters of Dr. B. and Dr. R.?
A. Correct.
Q. Have you seen or have you examined the plaintiff herself before you came to testify today?
A. No, I have not seen the patient.
Q. So that, as far as what the scars on this young girl's breast and under the breasts look like today, you don't know, do you?
A. Just what I have seen in the pictures.
Q. And, Doctor, is it fair to say that, as time goes on, the appearance of scars changes?
A. Absolutely.

Comment. This was a good tactic. It suggested that the doctor didn't do a complete job and that his opinion concerning the scars may no longer have been accurate. Of course, her condition must have improved or defense counsel wouldn't raise this point.

§ 7.44 Increase in Weight Affects Breast Size

Q. Doctor, does an increase of weight in a female, can that have an effect on her breast size?
A. It can.
Q. And can you tell us what a female breast is composed of?
A. Female breast is composed of adipose tissue, which is fat. It is composed of glandular tissue. It is composed of ducts and it is composed of skin and subcutaneous tissue. The nipple is a different type of tissue that is related to the ducts and the glandular tissue.
Q. When a woman gains weight and the size of her breasts increases, what type of tissue in her breast is it that causes the increase in size? Is it the increase in the adipose or fat tissue or the glandular tissue or other tissue?
A. It is usually an increase in the adipose tissue, fat tissue.

Q. So that if a woman were, the converse of that, to lose weight, conversely the size of her breasts should also decrease?
A. They may.

§ 7.45 Judgment Proper in Measuring Breast

Q. Doctor, when a surgeon performs this type of surgery, a bilateral mammoplasty, how does the surgeon determine the size of the breast? Let me put it to you this way, how did the surgeon do it back in 1980?
A. Most of the time the surgeon does it by measuring positions of nipple height in relationship to certain landmarks on the patient's body, to give the breast symmetry and then by more of a judgmental type of analysis from experience, to get the proper shape and size of the breast.
Q. And, Doctor, you mentioned the term "judgmental type of analysis"—how is that judgmental analysis made? Are there any instruments that the physician uses for that?
A. No—for determining size?
Q. Size, that's right.
A. There are methods of determining size which are also inherently inaccurate. People have tried to used things like volume displacement to measure breast size. That is known to be a very inaccurate measure of breast size. What one usually relies on and what I rely on is my experience from prior surgery and from surgery during my training and from the experience of people who have done the surgery before me.
Q. Doctor, you look at the breast, you eyeball it and you try to determine whether or not the size is the desired size, is that fair enough?
A. Correct.

§ 7.46 Expert Only a Resident at That Time

Q. Doctor, at the time in 1980, what were you doing as a physician?
A. I was a resident in general surgery at Montefiore Hospital, the Albert Einstein College of Medicine.
Q. While you were a resident, were you performing this type of operation?
A. Occasionally as a resident.
Q. Occasionally. When you say "occasionally," how occasionally were you doing this?

Comment. This is a very effective tactic. The expert was still learning as a resident and inexperienced at the time the defendant was performing this procedure.

A. Probably during that particular year, I couldn't give you an exact number but certainly no more than five times.

Q. And whenever you did engage in this type of an operation, is it fair to say that you were supervised when you did it?
A. Correct.
Q. And as far as plastic surgery is concerned, as I understand it, you did not begin your residency in plastic surgery until 1982?
A. Correct.
Q. And you continued your training from 1982 to about a year ago, 1984?
A. Correct.

§ 7.47 Breasts Asymmetric Preop

Q. If you looked at the preoperative photographs that the defendant took, there is no doubt in your mind that this young lady had quite enlarged breasts?
A. Correct.
Q. And, as a matter of fact, the right breast was quite a bit larger than the left one?
A. Correct.
Q. Doctor, is it fair to say that in the preoperative photographs that were taken of Marcy James, the nipples are grossly stretched?
A. They are asymmetric preoperatively.
Q. Asymmetric preoperatively.
A. Yes.
Q. When you say they are asymmetric preoperatively, tell us why you say that; what is it that you see in that photograph that leads you to state that they are asymmetric?
A. The right one is larger than the left breast preoperatively and the nipple height or the location of the nipple is lower on the right side than on the left side preoperatively.
Q. The nipple is lower on the left than on the right?
PLAINTIFF'S COUNSEL: Lower on the right.
Q. It's lower on the right than on the left?
A. Yes.
Q. And of course the right breast in those photographs is the breast that is quite a bit larger?

§ 7.48 Good Results Not Always Possible

Q. Doctor, in the field of plastic surgery, is it possible for a physician, even if he follows good and accepted medical practice, to obtain a good result during each and every operation that he performs?
PLAINTIFF'S COUNSEL: Objection.
THE COURT: Sustained.
Q. Doctor, in the field of plastic surgery, is it not a fact that revision surgery, meaning a second surgery after an initial surgery, is many times warranted

in a procedure such as we have in this case even though good and accepted medical practice was followed during the course of the original procedure?

PLAINTIFF'S COUNSEL: Objection.

THE COURT: What is the objection?

PLAINTIFF'S COUNSEL: Form, your Honor.

THE COURT: Sustained.

Q. Doctor, have you read any studies concerning the percentage of revision surgery that occurs or that is necessary as a result of a bilateral operation such as was done in this case?

PLAINTIFF'S COUNSEL: Objection as to form and also calls for hearsay.

THE COURT: Overruled. He asked him whether he read any studies. Calls for a yes or no answer.

A. I honestly don't recall.

Q. Doctor, do you know from any information you may have whether or not there is an accepted percentage in cases reported where revision surgery is warranted and necessary?

A. I am not aware of a certain percentage.

Q. Let's get away from the percentages then. Are there times when revision surgery is necessary even though good and accepted medical practice has been utilized during the course of the initial surgery?

A. Yes.

§ 7.49 Plastic Surgery Is Art and Science

Q. Doctor, is it fair to say that medicine in and of itself is at best an inexact science, if we can even call it a science at all?

A. All medicine?

Q. Plastic surgery, let's say.

A. Many of these things that we do have a certain amount of inaccuracies associated with them so there is a certain amount of inaccuracies in the results.

Q. And would you say that plastic surgery is more of an art than a science?

A. Certain procedures that we do are very artistic. Other ones are very straightforward.

Q. What about the bilateral mammoplasty, what would you say about that?

A. It has—it probably stems from both the art and the science.

Q. Plastic surgery is a form of medicine practiced by inexact people on inexact people, is it not?

PART II

COSMETIC SURGERY

CHAPTER 8

ABDOMINOPLASTY

§ 8.1 Introduction

Although abdominal surgery has been done for hundreds of years, cosmetic abdominoplasty is a relatively new procedure. It has gained popularity recently because it alleviates certain conditions in the abdominal area that cannot be cured by dieting or exercise.

An *abdominoplasty*—the cosmetic or aesthetic repair of the anterior abdominal wall—is sought by patients who wish to improve the appearance of their skin, remove adipose tissue, or tighten the muscles to better hold the abdominal contents in place.

The abdomen which this operation seeks to correct takes on many shapes: it may be a little too fat, or be extremely obese, with a hanging abdominal *panniculus,* or apron; it may be an abdomen rife with stretch marks or the *striae* of pregnancy; it may have little fat, but sagging wrinkled skin. This surgery attempts to correct an abdomen swollen in girth due to weakness of the *rectus abdominis* or strap muscles of the abdomen. When these muscles stretch out, the abdominal contents tend to pour into the submuscular layer, causing the abdomen to be large and paunchy. An abdominoplasty can also correct scars from previous surgeries and can repair a ventral or umbilical hernia, as well as strengthen the loose tissues around the strap muscles.

§ 8.2 Consultation

Before coming to the plastic surgeon, patients often hear tales from well-meaning friends, relatives, and old wives regarding abdominoplasty. These days, many people regard themselves as experts on surgery as well as many other topics because of television talk shows and advertising.

Many plastic surgeons and attorneys have taken it upon themselves to publicize their wares to a very disheartening degree in newspapers and on television. Newspaper advertisements for face-lifts and cosmetic surgery are often sandwiched in between nylon sales and hemorrhoidal creams. Television tells people exactly how they should think, whom they should consult, and how they can have a consultation for no fee at all (which is often all that consultation is worth). These advertisers do harm to the unsophisticated and uninformed public by making them think that the operation is simpler than it actually is. Even the term "tummy tuck" suggests with some degree of levity that a small tuck or a pleat is taken in the abdomen similar to the way a seamstress might take a pleat in a skirt. This is far from accurate and is very misleading.

A consultation for an abdominoplasty should cover the indications for the surgery, the type of patient who would benefit from it, what the surgery itself is like, and what type of anesthetic will be used. The patient should be instructed regarding postoperative care, degree of pain, and the restriction of activities. Furthermore, it should be made clear that certain inconveniences will occur for the first few days, such as intravenous feedings and a tube inserted through the nose into the stomach to relieve tension on the bowel.

The discussion of the incision in an abdominal operation is very important because frequently a patient does not think that there will be a scar if a plastic surgeon operates. A scar is the result of the healing of any traumatic or surgical intervention to the skin. The patient must understand thoroughly that a scar is inevitable but that a plastic surgeon will attempt to get the best scar possible.

Limiting postoperative movement is very important for abdominoplasty patients. They must be told that they cannot get up the day after surgery and walk. They must keep their knees flexed and the head of the bed in an upright position to relieve the tension from tight abdominal flap. They can sit in a chair but should not stand up perfectly straight. They can certainly take care of themselves with relative ease, but there will be discomfort if not occasional pain for several weeks after the surgery. They usually feel almost normal after the third postoperative week.

During the consultation, it is necessary to take a careful medical history so the surgeon is aware of any systemic diseases which would preclude elective surgery. For example, any bleeding problem or easy or prolonged bruising following a relatively minor injury should be investigated before surgery is undertaken.

During the consultation, the incisions, which can be made in several ways (see **§ 8.10**), should be drawn on the patient with a felt-tip pen to indicate the length of the scar. The type of scarring should be explained very carefully, from the possibility of a fine line scar to the possibility of a wide, red scar. Unsightly scarring is often a common cause for a lawsuit, when the patient claims that the doctor did not discuss it thoroughly enough.

§ 8.3 Clinical Indications for the Surgery

The indications for an abdominoplasty are:

1. Abdominal panniculus or apron caused by weight gain or loss
2. Diastasis recti (weakening of the abdominal muscles), often associated with either childbirth or relaxation of the muscles due to aging
3. Excess abdominal skin, often seen after pregnancy when there is no fat to remove
4. Scars from previous surgeries, which are removed with the abdominal reconstruction
5. Ventral or umbilical hernias, which can be repaired during the abdominoplasty.

Patients with these conditions would benefit from an abdominoplasty. The vast majority of patients seeking or requiring abdominoplasties are females, although some males are candidates for the surgical procedure.

§ 8.4 —Obese Abdomen

The most common reason for having an abdominoplasty or abdominal lipectomy is obesity. But before any surgery is contemplated, the causes for the obesity must be considered. Generally speaking, an abdominoplasty is not indicated in a patient who has gained weight and refuses to lose it. Before a patient with an obese abdomen who is trying to lose weight is taken to surgery, an internist should be consulted. Does the patient have a metabolic disorder which makes weight loss impossible? If the patient is losing weight and still has a large abdominal panniculus or hanging apron of skin and fat from obesity, an abdominal lipectomy may be the procedure of choice. This is different from an abdominoplasty because it is a direct excision of the roll of fat and skin usually below the umbilicus. The skin edges are sutured directly to each other and no attention is given to the rest of the abdomen. The rationale for doing an abdominal lipectomy before a patient has succeeded in losing all his excess weight is to alleviate the burden of excess abdominal skin and fat, at the same time encouraging him with his new body image to continue on his diet, and to lose and keep the weight off.

Once the desired amount of weight has been lost and the desired weight maintained for six months to one year, the patient is a candidate for an abdominoplasty. His abdomen has been obese and, because of the usual relaxation of the rectus muscles, the patient is unable to assume a proper posture. It is during this operation that the rectus abdominis muscles are sewn together and thereby strengthened, allowing the abdominal contents to be held in a smaller, more compact space.

Formerly obese patients who have attained or nearly attained their desired weight constitute the majority of patients seeking lipectomy and abdominoplasty.

§ 8.5 —Abdomen with Surgical or Traumatic Scars

Patients with scarred abdomens are good candidates for abdominoplasty. Their traumatic or surgical scars with their underlying adhesions often cause functional as well as cosmetic problems. Such scars are common after appendectomies, exploratory laparotomies, cesarean sections, or cholecystectomies and can cause the patients abdominal pain as well as an unsightly appearance. These scars can often be removed entirely or in part during an abdominoplasty.

§ 8.6 —Abdomen Distended from Pregnancy

Many young women who are small and relatively slender who have had multiple or large pregnancies find their abdomens are greatly distended and flaccid. The skin is wrinkled and creased and there are stretch marks or striae present on these abdomens, which have lost their tone. The rectus abdominis muscles have been pushed apart and the abdominal contents pour into these spaces between them. This is called a *diastasis recti.* These women may not show obese abdomens but may be victims merely of flaccid skin and decreased muscle tone. They can benefit a great deal from an abdominoplasty, which often restores their bodies to a prepregnancy state. These women should seek an abdominoplasty only if they do not plan another pregnancy because the end result of an abdominoplasty could be ruined by subsequent childbearing.

§ 8.7 —Herniated or Weakened Abdomen

The fourth group of abdominoplasty patients are those who have a diastasis recti with a ventral or an umbilical hernia. If a diastasis recti accompanies these hernias, it can be repaired by approximating the medial edges of the two muscles while a formal hernia repair of the umbilicus and/or the ventral hernia is done at the same time.

The abdominoplasty is contraindicated when:

1. The patient plans to become pregnant
2. The patient is emotionally or psychologically unstable
3. The patient's expectations regarding scars and postoperative results are unrealistic or
4. The previous abdominal incisions are so large or badly placed that they would jeopardize the blood supply to the abdominal wall flap.

§ 8.8 Informed Consent

An informed consent for an abdominoplasty should include the indications for the surgery, the surgical procedure itself, the incisions, the risks, the complications, and the limitation of activities relative to the abdomen. These should be explained to the patient in clear lay terms and should be understood as completely as possible in order to allow her to make up her mind intelligently based on the facts given. If there is a language problem, or if English is not the patient's first language, an interpreter should be present. The complications of abdominoplasty appear in **§ 8.12**.

Some attorneys feel that a written informed consent is undesirable because, if an unusual or unexpected complication occurs which was not listed in the informed consent, the patient can claim that this was not discussed by the doctor, thereby constituting a lack of informed consent on that issue.

Most authorities feel that all the normal, possible complications of both the abdominoplasty itself and those secondary to general anesthesia should be discussed with the patient and even written down, so that there is some evidence that the patient has heard the complications.[1] This written list of complications should be signed by the patient as proof that it has been read and hopefully understood, then entered as part of the chart. Many surgeons draw the abdominal scars on the patient's body with a marking pencil and photograph it, including this as part of the chart to provide proof that scarring, a major cause of litigation, was discussed with the patient. The patient must be made to understand that the quality of the scar is not necessarily proportionate to the skills of the surgeon but that some of it has to do with the ability of her own body to heal.

The surgeon should discuss the position and character of the umbilicus with the patient because this is a visible landmark on the patient's abdomen. Although most people never notice an umbilicus or a belly button if it is normal, it becomes the object of great concern in a patient who has a distortion in this area.

Photographs of abdominoplasties can be shown to new patients, although a release should be obtained from the patients whose photographs are used.

The complications of general anesthesia should be discussed with the patient as well as the specific complications of abdominoplasty (see **§ 8.12**).

The most significant element of the informed consent is a clear understanding on the part of the patient, as well as careful notation in the doctor's records of this discussion.

§ 8.9 Anatomy of the Abdomen

For the attorney to clearly understand what could go wrong in an abdominoplasty, it is essential to know something about the anatomy of the area.

The bony landmarks of the abdomen are the lumbar and sacral spines which are posterior to the abdomen and give the patient posture. Superiorly, the rib cage and the diaphragm separate the chest from the abdomen. The bases of the abdomen are the pelvic bones, the pubic bone, and the iliac bones.

The muscles involved in abdominoplasties are the rectus abdominis muscles, the transverse abdominal muscles, and the external and oblique muscles, which all help form the muscular abdominal wall. When

[1] *See, e.g.,* T. Rees, Aesthetic Plastic Surgery (1980) and R. Goldwyn, Unfavorable Results in Plastic Surgery (1981).

these muscles, particularly the rectus abdominis muscles, have been weakened, they constitute a diastasis, or a spreading apart, and they should be strengthened by suturing them together.

The abdominal skin, measuring approximately 2 to 4 mm, is quite thick compared to the skin of other parts of the body. Its rich blood supply allows it to stretch easily in obese patients and during pregnancy. Its elasticity is limited, however, and it may not regain its original shape after the cause of distention has been removed.

Distribution of adipose or fat tissue is one of the major distinctions between the male and the female abdomen. *Adipose tissue* is a connective tissue composed of round fat cells whose diameters vary between 50 and 150 mcg, each containing a large fat globule. This tissue is abundant in the abdominal wall and the accumulation of it is one of the well-known reasons for doing a panniculectomy or an abdominoplasty.

The abdominal wall, like the abdominal skin, is rich in arterial blood supply. Many perforating arteries pass through the muscular and fascial sheaths. Clamping or coagulating these vessels during the procedure is necessary.

The abdominal veins and lymphatic vessels are significant in the study of the abdomen because venous return is essential to decreasing the edema of an abdominal flap.

There are many superficial sensory nerves to the skin of the abdomen and, because of this nerve supply, all abdominoplasties with the exception of the vertical ones will cause a paresthesia of the lower portion of the flap for at least 6 to 12 months and perhaps longer. It is for this reason that the patient complains of numbness of the area around the incision, particularly in the lower portion of the abdominal flap.

An attorney should make a more detailed study relevant to the abdominal anatomy in each specific case in order to examine and cross-examine even the expert witnesses more impressively. Although most surgeons have a good working knowledge of the areas on which they operate, detailed study, including names of vessels and nerves, is sometimes clouded after years of practice. This doesn't mean that they are not familiar with the anatomy, it simply means that they may be hazy in the recounting of it. It is for this reason that an attorney who makes a recent study of the anatomy of the area can discredit the testimony of an expert witness on the stand and embarrass her in front of the jury.

§ 8.10 Surgical Techniques

A low, transverse abdominal incision from one anterior iliac spine to the other across the supra pubic area is usually considered the standard incision for an abdominoplasty. See **Figure 8–1**.

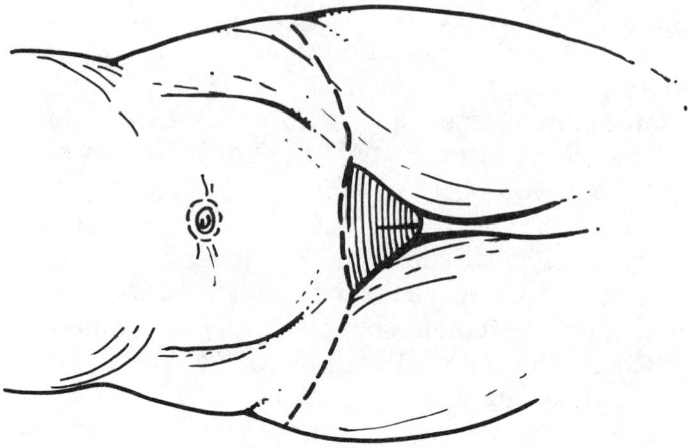

Figure 8–1. Standard suprapubic transverse abdominoplasty incision.

There is a fairly wide variation in techniques and incisions. None of these popularly used techniques will alone correct every type of lesion in every patient. Therefore the problem must be evaluated and the technique to be used must address the particular deformity.

The three most common types of incisions for abdominoplasty are:

1. Transverse incisions
2. Vertical incisions
3. Combined procedures.

The transverse incision is the most popular one and has been used by many plastic surgeons. One technique utilizes a low horizontal incision from one iliac bone above the pubic hair across to the other iliac bone. Another technique modifies the first incision by bringing its lateral extension upward and straight across the abdomen rather than dipping down into the groin (see **Figure 8–2**). A very popular technique is called the *W incision of Regnault* in which the lateral limbs of the incision dip into the inguinal area while the medial portion of the "W" comes over the pubic hair (see **Figure 8–3**). This reduces some of the strain on the transverse abdominal flap and allows the final scar to be more pleasing anatomically.

The vertical incisions are used when there is an exceptionally large amount of abdominal skin and muscular laxity. Certain abdomens require a vertical incision to reduce their tremendously stretched, striated skin. When this incision is used, it is crucial to inform the patient that a vertical scar will remain after the surgery, extending upward from the pubis, around the umbilicus, and sometimes into the upper abdomen.

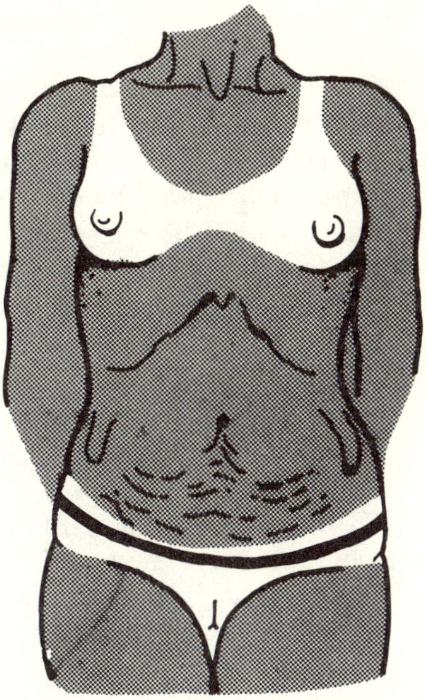

Figure 8–2. Lower abdominal suprapubic incision with the lateral extension directed upward.

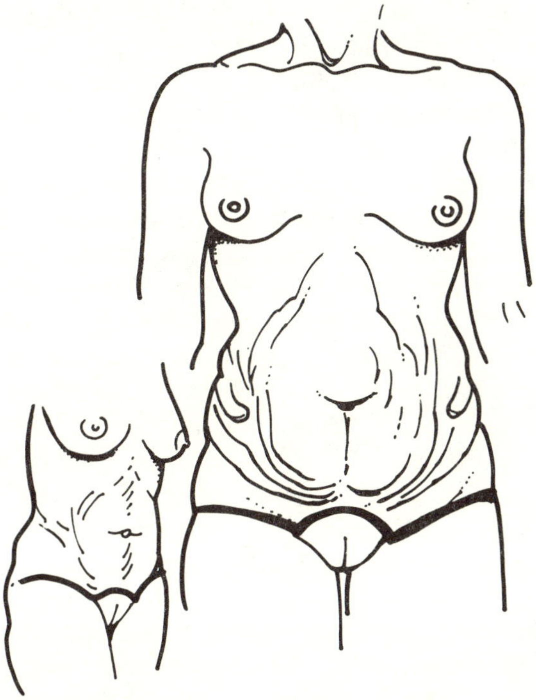

Figure 8–3. The "W" incision.

A combined procedure uses several combined incisions, allowing a resection and even a reduction on both the horizontal and the vertical planes. The disadvantage of this is the multiplicity of unattractive scars, often giving rise to infection or superficial necrosis at their junction.

A belt lipectomy or circular lipectomy involves the excision of the entire circumference of the abdomen from back to front. This was designed to improved the entire midsection of the body during the same procedure but is not commonly done these days. This technique is limited to special problem cases in which large abdominal, gluteal, and dorsal fatty deposits present.

§ 8.11 Description of a Standard Operation

An abdominoplasty is performed under general anesthesia so that the anesthesiologist can achieve total muscle relaxation and complete control of the patient. The patient is placed in a supine position with the knees and head slightly flexed to reduce tension in the abdominal area. See **Figure 8–4**. Preoperatively, a high colonic enema is given to the patient to decompress the bowels and to remove as much of the intestinal contents as possible. A needle is introduced into a vein in the arm for the administration of fluids and medication. A nasogastric tube is passed through the nose into the stomach to relieve it of its gastric juices while the patient is asleep. This tube is left in place for two days after the surgery until the bowel sounds have returned, indicating normal peristalsis.

Prior to surgery and in an upright position, a marking is made on the patient from one iliac bone to the other through the midline and above the pubic hair. When the patient is asleep and has been prepared and draped in the usual manner, incision is made on this marking with a scalpel or an electric cautery to control the bleeding. The incision continues through

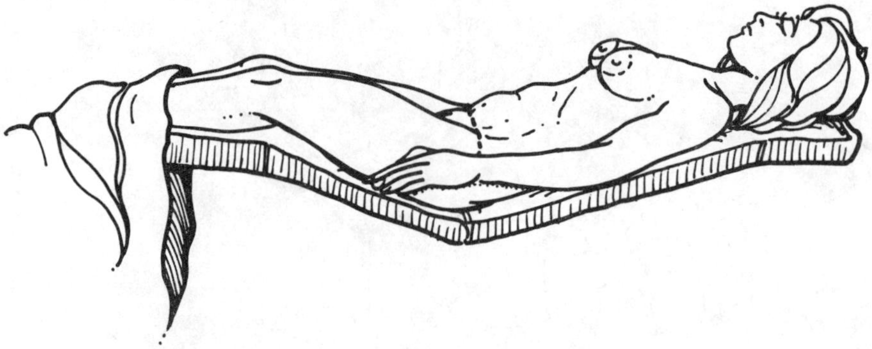

Figure 8–4. Patient's position on operating table.

the skin to the fascial layer. The flap, consisting of skin, subcutaneous tissue, and fat, is developed from the incision upward to the umbilicus (see **Figure 8–5**). The perforating arteries should be clamped or coagulated to reduce the blood loss as the operation progresses. The flap is undermined; that is, the skin, subcutaneous tissue, and fat are loosened up from the underlying musculofascial compartment to the area of the umbilicus. Then the scalpel is used to circumscribe the skin of the umbilicus (see **Figure 8–6**), leaving it on its stalk so that it can be reinserted when the abdomen is reconstructed (see **Figure 8–7**). The flap proceeds upward toward the costophrenic angle or lower border of the rib cage. The perforating arteries are clamped and coagulated and the flap is elevated to expose the muscles and fascia.

The abdomen is usually wide and somewhat bloated at this point and the rectus abdominis muscles, which have been separated because of pressure from within, are now reconstructed (see **Figure 8–8**). They are approximated with heavy dissolvable sutures of dexon or vicryl. The sutures are placed in one muscle sheath and then across the gap into the other muscle. They extend the whole length of the rectus abdominis muscle, originating below the rib cage around the umbilicus and on to the

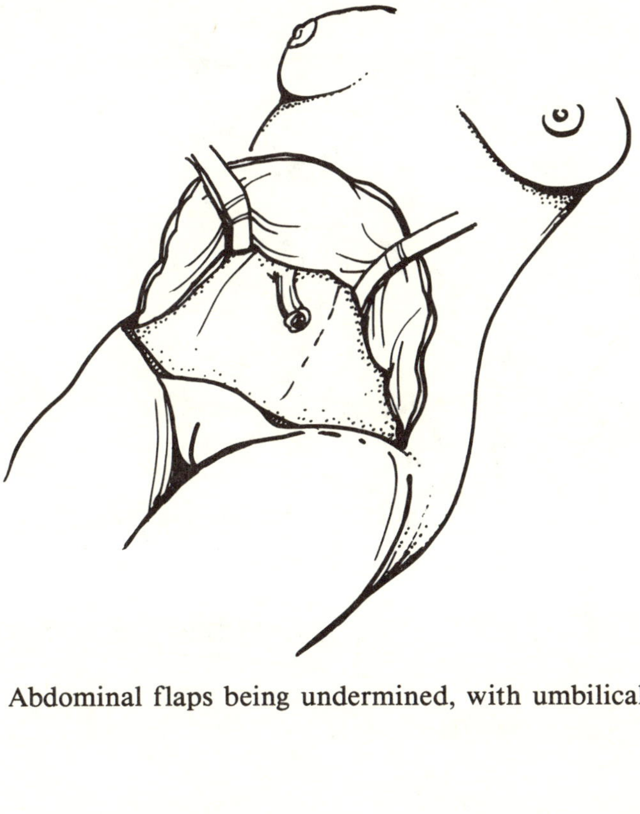

Figure 8–5. Abdominal flaps being undermined, with umbilical stalk still in place.

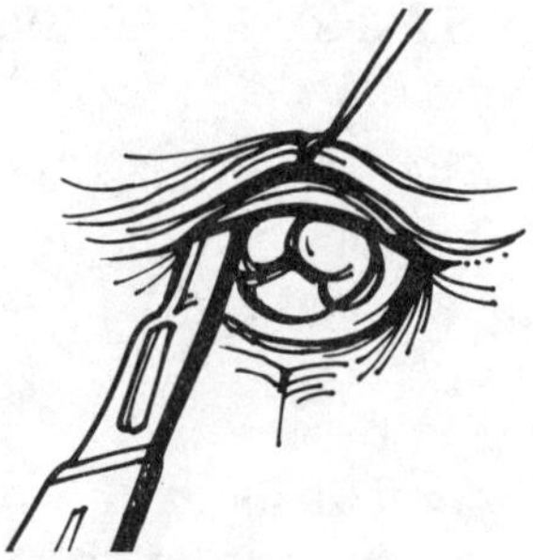

Figure 8–6. Umbilicus being buttonholed and cut away from abdominal flap.

Figure 8–7. Umbilicus is pulled through the sheet between the two rectus muscles on its stalk.

Figure 8–8. Repairing the diastasis recti.

suprapubic area. All these sutures are then tied, so that one rectus muscle is brought toward the other to form once again a strong, straight abdominal wall to hold the abdominal contents in place (see **Figure 8–9**). When the muscles are brought together, the girth of the abdomen is decreased.

The intestines slowly reestablish their normal peristaltic movements. The nasogastric tube is left in place for a day or two to put the intestines at rest until the bowel tones return. It is only then that we know the intestines are once again functioning normally to accommodate food for digestion. If this does not occur, then a complication called *ileus,* or atonic bowel, is encountered, giving rise to tremendous problems. This will be discussed more thoroughly in **§ 8.12**.

With the new decreased girth of the abdomen, the abdominal flap is then pulled down and the excess skin, fat, and subcutaneous tissue is removed at the suprapubic incision (see **Figure 8–10**). Sometimes the hole in the abdominal flap where the umbilicus was originally located can be pulled down to the incision and excised entirely. If it cannot, then as much as is excised, but a small vertical scar remains in the suprapubic midline from the previous hole in the umbilicus. The flap is sutured into place with a three-layer closure.

The umbilicus, which remains on its stalk inside the flap, has a metal button attached to it so it can be easily identified and delivered to its new central position in the abdominal wall (see **Figure 8–11**). An incision is made with the scalpel over this button and the umbilicus is presented through the flap and sutured in place. It is important to place the umbilicus properly as malpositioning is a major complication, not functionally but because it gives asymmetry where symmetry had previously existed. Once the umbilicus is delivered, the flap is sutured in place from the lateral portion of the wall to reduce the chances of hematoma and seroma.

Figure 8–9. The rectus muscles strengthened into their normal position and the umbilical stalk ready to be placed into the abdominal skin flap.

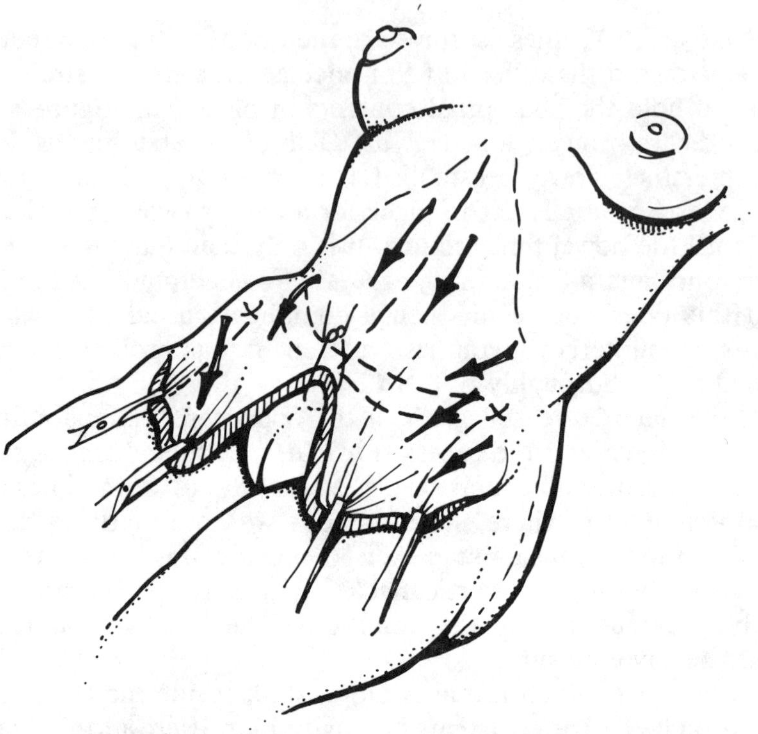

Figure 8–10. The abdominal skin flap is pulled down over the lower incision in preparation for excising the excess tissue and sewing it into place.

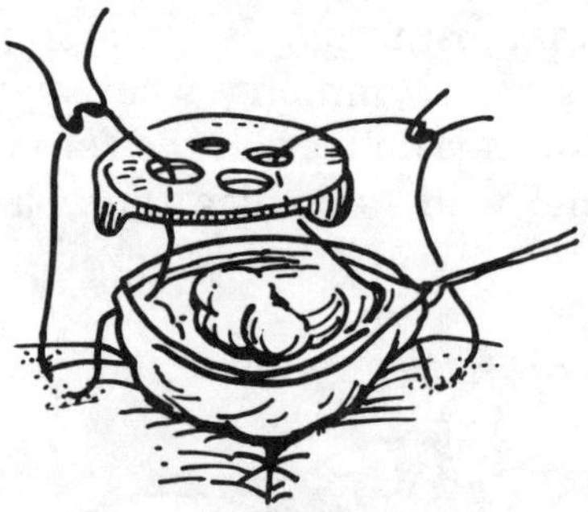

Figure 8–11. A plastic or metal button is attached to the umbilicus so that it can be felt underneath the abdominal flap, thereby avoiding malpositioning of the umbilicus in the flap.

The operation is now complete and the dressings are applied. The patient is moved onto a stretcher and then into bed in the jackknife position, with the knees flexed and the back and the head up. This decreases the tension on the abdominal flap, to avoid sloughing in the midline portion of the flap, its weakest area.

The patient is maintained with intravenous feedings and antibiotics and the nasogastric tube is attached to low suction. The patient can get out of the bed the following day and can walk with assistance. She can sit in a chair or lie on her back. She should not lie on her abdomen or on either side for several days.

There is usually some discomfort but not severe pain. Ordinarily the drains are removed 48 hours after surgery, the nasogastric tube is removed when the bowel sounds reappear, and the patient can start taking full liquids before progressing to a regular diet. The usual hospital stay for an abdominoplasty is two to three days.

§ 8.12 Complications and Unfavorable Results

Unfavorable results can occur in all fields of surgery, and particularly in the area of cosmetic surgery because some patients have unrealistic expectations. They want to trade what they perceive as unattractive features for a Madison Avenue model's body, frequently refusing to allow for the limitations which their anatomy imposes. Many patients want surgery for all the wrong reasons, such as to get a spouse or become a model, or to solve problems that have nothing to do with the part of the body they would like to change. It is incumbent upon the plastic surgeon to recognize these patients who are emotionally unprepared for surgery before the operation takes place. An unhappy patient can be a great disappointment and frustration for the surgeon for many months or years, even long after the abdomen has healed.

§ 8.13 —Psychological Complications

Obviously, it is impossible to predict with certainty the result of the surgery or the patient's acceptance of it. It is not reasonable to assume that the surgeon can predict patients' psychological states when they first see themselves after surgery. The result is always different from the expectation because the reality overshadows the patient's further hope of perfection.

In the preoperative period, surgeons must be mindful of the messages the patient is sending to them and, despite their enthusiasm to do another operation, they must try to determine whether this patient would be a stable subject and a good risk.

It is often said that the surgeon is in charge until the surgery is performed, and after that it is the patient who is in charge. This means that the patient has legal recourse after the surgery if something has gone awry. Most patients come to the plastic surgeon wanting to have the operation performed and so they will be pleasant, conciliatory, and even seductive until the surgeon consents to do the operation. Many patients change their mood entirely once the enthusiasm and the excitement of the promised youthful or flattering result has passed into the stage of postoperative distortion caused by edema and discoloration.

If the surgeon feels that the patient is in any way unstable emotionally, the advice of a psychologist or a psychiatrist should be sought prior to surgery. A consultation and an evaluation should be done, and the surgeon should follow this recommendation.

§ 8.14 —Complications of General Anesthesia

Often, complications are not due to the surgery itself but to the effects of general anesthesia on the body. It is important for the surgeon to discuss these possible complications with the patient, although they should also be discussed by the anesthesiologist on his visit to the patient prior to surgery.

Several things can happen to the system during surgery, none of which has to do specifically with the cosmetic procedure being performed.

A pulmonary embolism or a blood clot breaking off from the vein traveling to the lungs could lead to death. A pulmonary embolism can be nonfatal, however, and if treated with anticoagulants such as heparin or Coumadin after it is diagnosed, the patient can withstand the insult to the system. However, the diagnosis itself of a pulmonary embolism is crucial. The doctor must make sure that the patient is not taking birth control pills or other medications such as vitamin K which cause blood clotting. Care should be taken that the patient wear constrictive stockings during surgery because the immobilized limb can give a rise to pulmonary embolism especially in older patients. In addition, other pulmonary complications such as *atelectasis* (collapse of a lung) or postoperative pneumonia are not uncommon after general anesthesia. A fat embolism sometimes occurs during an abdominoplasty. This is a piece of fat breaking off and getting into a major blood vessel and traveling to the lungs, heart, or brain, causing obvious deleterious effects.

Cardiac complications such as arrhythmia, ventricular fibrillation, and myocardial infarction can occur as a result of general anesthesia or coincidental to the surgery and the patient should be aware of the possibilities.

§ 8.15 —Ileus

Ileus is a medical term for paralyzed bowel, which sometimes follows general anesthesia. After an abdominoplasty and the plication of the rectus muscles, the intestines are contained in a smaller space. This means that they may lose their normal intrinsic movement.

An ileus can occur when a nasogastric tube is not used. The nasogastric tube tends to decrease the incidence of paralyzed bowel because it decompresses the bowel and removes the air and intestinal contents from it, allowing it to accommodate more easily to a smaller space. An ileus can lead to the more serious complication of bowel obstruction, which may require surgery. One very effective method of preventing postoperative ileus is to use a nasogastric or rectal tube.

§ 8.16 —Infection

Infection can be caused by a number of factors including nonsterile intraoperative technique or bad postoperative care. An infection is a very common surgical complication and should be mentioned in every informed consent. The prophylactic use of antibiotics reduces the incidence of infection in cosmetic surgery. Although many surgeons feel that prophylactic use of antibiotics is overdone, it seems warranted in most cases to avoid the aesthetically disastrous results an infection can give.

§ 8.17 —Hematoma and Seroma

A *hematoma* is a collection of blood underneath the abdominal flap. This is an easy complication to diagnose as it usually causes a large area of swelling that is tender, warm, and red. The incidence of hematoma in abdominoplasty is small because most of the bleeding can be visualized, clamped, and coagulated before the flap is closed. The bleeding usually comes from the large perforating vessels rather than the small oozing ones. However, if the patient is taking aspirin or any other antiplatelet medication with aspirinlike activity, an oozing can occur in the operative site. Hematoma can also occur when the patient is extubated after anesthesia because of coughing, vomiting, or wretching.

The treatment for hematoma is to remove the stitches and evacuate the blood clot as soon as possible.

A *seroma* is a collection of serous or proteinlike fluid which weeps from the wound, especially in a large operative area. It can cause swelling, discomfort, and pain, as well as discoloration of the flap. Usually a seroma can be aspirated with relative ease if it hasn't escaped through the Penrose drain sites—sites where opened-hole rubber tubings were placed underneath the abdominal flap during suturing of the abdominal flap to allow a point of exit for any bleeding or serous fluid.

§ 8.18 —Fat Necrosis, Dehiscense, and Skin Loss

In areas where large amounts of fat are removed and some fat remains, there can be necrosis of the fat due to compromised blood supply to the area. The same is true with wound dehiscense or loss of skin. This usually occurs because there is too much tension on the area. It can also be caused by inadequate blood supply to the flap or by a flap being developed too superficially. Part of the blood supply to the skin comes from the subdermal plexus. A combination of thin skin and tension on the flap plus any edema or bleeding from within can cause a skin slough. This usually appears within 12 to 36 hours after surgery and presents with a dusky, purplish color signaling ecchymosis. When the skin slough appears, an immediate possible solution is to loosen the stitches in the area, thereby relieving the tension on the blood vessels. When this is done, the slough should be treated conservatively with soaks and antibiotics. The skin will reepithelialize within some weeks and if necessary a split-thickness skin graft can be applied in the area.

The patient's own postoperative care can contribute to sloughing of skin. If a patient goes home and does any number of things that could cause tension or weight on her body, such as exercise, stretching, carrying children, lifting heavy things, or engaging in sexual activities involving the abdomen, a normally healing abdominal flap can become ischemic, losing its blood supply because of the patient's lack of caution.

Consider the case of a 35-year-old woman who was the manager of a tennis shop at a country club. She did not have a large amount of fat in her abdomen but she had sagging, stretched skin after several pregnancies and she wanted it tightened. The abdominoplasty was performed and she went home two days after surgery. She was young and healthy; the operation had been properly done and she felt good. Instead of taking care of herself conservatively, she went to work early and before two weeks were over, she even played tennis. When she developed a skin slough in the middle of the abdominal flap, at the area of the greatest tension, she blamed the plastic surgeon for the complication, although when the patient was discharged from the hospital there was no sign of infection nor of skin loss. She instituted a suit against the plastic surgeon for negligent surgery and, after the case had been settled for a fairly large amount, she admitted that she not only had played tennis but had had sexual relations within the two-week postoperative period.

§ 8.19 —Scars, Umbilical Scarring, and Necrosis

Scarring is the natural result of healing. Although some patients think that plastic surgeons can perform an operation without the present of a scar, this is a myth. *Scarring* is the term used to indicate the growth of fibroblasts from one side of an open incision to the other, thereby gluing it together.

Good scarring is largely a function of good skin chemistry. Patients are told that the scarring can be affected by three things:

1. The surgeon's skill at closing the wound properly
2. The patient's postoperative care of herself
3. The patient's skin chemistry and its capability of forming a good scar.

Many patients complain about scar contraction around the umbilicus. This is often due to the tension put on the umbilicus and can be corrected by leaving a larger area of skin around the umbilical incision at the time of surgery. Mattress stitches can be applied subcutaneously to keep the umbilicus well positioned. The location of the scar is important. Again, it should be explained to the patient before surgery and be drawn on the patient's abdomen with a pen or marker. A photograph should be taken and included in the chart so that the patient can see that she was told a scar would be present.

§ 8.20 —Umbilical Malpositioning

Umbilical malpositioning or displacement of the belly button has gained importance recently because of a case brought against a plastic surgeon by a woman who claimed that her belly button was one centimeter off center and that this caused her tremendous psychological upheaval. She sued the surgeon and the jury awarded her $850,000. On appeal, the amount was reduced to $250,000.

The plaintiff was not a belly dancer nor did she use her belly button for business purposes, but apparently she was offended aesthetically by the asymmetry visited on her abdomen. She felt that financial compensation might lessen her embarrassment. Prior to that lawsuit, not many people were concerned about the exact location of their belly buttons.

The belly button, by the way, is a remnant of the umbilical cord in utero. It has become an important aesthetic concern. Actually an abdomen without a belly button would be abnormal and displeasing to the eye. Except for the usual jokes about belly button use, there is no real function of this vestigial apparatus in adult life. However, it is important to replace it symmetrically if, in fact, it was centered in the first place. (Preoperative photographs can settle this point.) Before the surgery is concluded, the umbilicus should be aligned with the xiphoid process of the sternum superiorily and symphysis pubis inferiorily. An efficient way to find the belly button is to suture a metal marker to the umbilicus for its easy detection through the abdominal flap.

§ 8.21 —Sensory Changes

After surgery there is usually a numbness surrounding the incision at the lower part of the abdomen. This is due in part to the cutting of the sensory nerves to that area of skin and partly because of edema descending to the point of the abdomen. Patients have complained about insensitivity in this area for up to two years after surgery. The patient should be alerted to this possibility prior to the surgery during the informed consent, as it is a common postoperative complaint.

Sometimes, while the sensory nerves are healing, the patient may experience unpleasant sensations in the lower abdomen when a garment touches her skin; this is *hypersensitivity.* A hardness also develops around the lower abdominal incision due to the edema and the normal scarring of body healing. There is nothing extraordinary about this, and the doctor should assure the patient that this will go away within six months to a year.

§ 8.22 —Peritoneal Perforation and Peritonitis

It should be mentioned that, during reconstruction of the abdomen, the surgeon may encounter scars and adhesions from previous surgeries such as a hysterectomy or an appendectomy. Care must be taken to avoid making a pinhole incision in the peritoneum, the covering of the abdominal cavity. This can be easily done due to scars and adhesions. If even a pinhole incision is made in the peritoneum, an abdominal fistula can occur. This is a serious complication because fecal contents can escape the periotneum cavity, causing severe infection under the flap and demanding further surgery to correct it.

Although the abdominoplasty is not a technically difficult operation to perform, great care must be taken to avoid these pitfalls of surgery.

§ 8.23 Bibliography

J.M. Converse, Reconstructive Surgery Plastic (W.B. Saunders, 1977).

J.S. Elbaz & G. Flageul, Plastic Surgery of the Abdomen (Translated by W.T. Keavy, M.D. Masson Publishing, 1979).

R.M. Goldwyn, The Patient and the Plastic Surgeon (Little, Brown & Co., 1981).

W.C. Grabb & J.W. Smith, Plastic Surgery (Little, Brown & Co., 1984).

S.H. Miller, Yearbook of Plastic and Reconstructive Surgery (Year Book Medical Publishers, Inc., 1989).

T.D. Rees, Aesthetic Plastic Surgery. Vol. II. (W.B. Saunders, 1980).

CHAPTER 9

COSMETIC EYELID SURGERY

§ 9.1 Introduction

Our eyes have looked at so many things; they have seen so much in our lifetimes. The eyelids get very tired with all this looking because they blink open and shut every eight to 12 seconds while we are awake, whether we want them to or not. It is an involuntary movement.

The eyelid skin is the body's thinnest and most delicate skin. With all this movement, it is not surprising that these areas, which receive so much wear and tear, are the ones that wrinkle first and most easily.

§ 9.2 The Consultation

When people who are interested in their appearance and want to stave off the effects of facial aging as much as possible look into the mirror, they notice the first evidence of skin degeneration in the eyelids. Women in their late thirties find that it is difficult to apply eye shadow to their upper lids because of the "shelves" of skin that have gathered there. Men in their forties are suddenly aware that there is puffiness and swelling under their eyelids that does not go away with a good night's sleep. Some people complain that they look like they have a "hangover" that won't go away. Their friends tell them that they always look tired, that they need a good rest or a vacation. It is then that they will seek a consultation with a plastic surgeon.

The consultation is a very important part of the plastic surgical experience, because it is during that first meeting that the initial impressions are formed of the patient by the surgeon and vice versa. After the initial consultation the surgeon must determine if the person would be a good candidate for eyelid surgery. A surgeon, in making such a determination, may consider, inter alia, (1) whether the patient's expectations are unrealistic, (2) whether the patient is psychologically suited for the surgery at that time or at any future time, and (3) whether there is sufficient indication physically to justify a surgical procedure.

During the initial consultation the patient should also evaluate the surgeon's manner, and be aware of developing confidence or a lack thereof in her and a sense of rapport between them. These are all crucial elements to be considered by a patient when selecting a surgeon to perform an elective, cosmetic operation.

Once favorable initial impressions are formed, and the patient has decided to undergo the surgery, the preoperative preparations and the postoperative care must be carefully explained to the patient. The surgeon must detail thoroughly the possible complications that might occur (see **§ 9.8**). Eyelid surgery is quite common today and many patients with friends or relatives who have had the surgery become self-proclaimed experts about the surgery, the postoperative care, and the results. However, without regard to the extent of the patient's asserted knowledge of the procedure, the surgeon must explain completely all aspects of the procedure, and this should be carefully documented in the surgeon's office notes immediately following the consultation. This will provide the necessary documentation to defend against any future claim based on lack of informed consent. Nothing is too commonplace or well-known to the patient to allow the physician to exclude it in the preoperative consultation.

During the initial consultation the surgeon should obtain a careful medical history from the patient. Although the diagnosis of the need for cosmetic eyelid surgery is not difficult to make, there may be serious underlying causes for the condition. In addition to aging and a general laxity of the eyelid skin, the edema or swelling under the lids may come from a number of different systemic causes. The surgeon should carefully examine all patients to determine whether they are suffering from any one of them. Some of the more common causes of periorbital edema are:

1. Cardiac
2. Renal
3. Hepatic
4. Pulmonary
5. Hormonal (thyroid, and so on)
6. Allergic
7. Menstrual
8. Excessive alcohol intake.

The plastic surgeon who is a clever diagnostician and is careful in analyzing the reasons for the cosmetic procedure can often spot an underlying condition in the patient which may postpone the immediate eyelid procedure in deference to treating the systemic illness.

Once it is determined that the patient desiring to have an eyelid operation is in satisfactory physical condition, and is psychologically sound, the surgeon's next step is a thorough examination of the eyes themselves. Although the surgeon may perform a funduscopic examination and ask the patient to read an eye chart, it is probably more beneficial from a medical point of view and more prudent from a medical-legal point of view to have the patient examined by an ophthalmologist or an optometrist. (Of course, these reports should be included in the patient's chart.) Hopefully, this will clarify a situation in which a patient complains postoperatively of difficulty with vision or something else relative to the eye/eyelid apparatus, when the preoperative documentation reveals that the condition predated the surgery. One can easily see the importance of the preoperative examination in such an instance.

It is good practice for the surgeon to see the patient once again after the initial consultation and before the surgery is performed. This will provide the patient with an opportunity to ask any last minute questions that need to be answered, or to articulate fears that need to be allayed.

The last essential element of a consultation is the preoperative photography. This is absolutely crucial. No surgeon should perform a blepharoplasty without photos. Two essential purposes are served. First, the surgeon uses the photos during the operation to see how the patient's eyelids looked while standing in an upright position and without the additional swelling of local anesthesia. Second, in the postoperative healing period, patients forget how their eyelids really looked in the preoperative state. If there are any questions about the results, the surgeon can refer to the photos, thereby clarifying any misconceptions the patient may have, as patients often see themselves in an unrealistic fashion. Although patients may wish to argue with the surgeon and disagree with her opinion, one must concur with the old adage that a picture is worth a thousand words!

Ideally, photographs should be taken professionally by a photographer who specializes in medical work, who has a precision camera and lens, and who can provide the exact lighting to get the necessary detail in the photograph. Some surgeons have employees in their offices who are clever at taking photos, and occasionally the surgeon with the hobby of taking pictures will want to do so herself in an attempt to save the patient inconvenience and money. However, preoperative photos must be precise; therefore, if in-house photography produces poor quality photos, a professional should be used. Preoperative photos are an essential part of the patient's chart, and often are an essential piece of evidence in litigation.

§ 9.3 Clinical Indications for the Surgery

When a patient consults a plastic surgeon for an eyelid operation, it is usually for one of two reasons: (1) sagging or drooping of the upper eyelids (*ptosis*) or excess upper eyelid skin (*blepharochalasia* or *dermatochalasia*) with wrinkling, or (2) fat pouches, bags, or swelling under the lower lids and sometimes in the upper lids (*herniated periorbital fat*).

The diagnosis of eyelid deformity is made by a precise identification of the anatomical components that can reasonably be corrected by the various surgical procedures which are available. Castanares[1] made the following classification of the more common eyelid deformities:

---

[1] S. Castanares, Classification of Baggy Eyelid Deformity Plastic Reconstructive Surgery 215 (1971).

1. Skin deformities
   a. Blepharochalasia—generally a young patient subject to recurrent attacks of edema, with thin, atrophic skin; generally accompanied by some degree of
   b. Dermatochalasia—loose, hypertrophic skin brow ptosis
2. Protrusion of orbital fat
3. Orbicularis hypertrophy
4. Ptosis (hooding) of eyebrows

The type of surgery performed should be based on the particular anatomical element that is affected—that is, the skin, muscle, fat, lacrimal gland, eyebrow, or bone.

§ 9.4 Informed Consent

It is important to instruct the patient carefully on all aspects of the procedure, preoperative and postoperative. A surgeon should take extra caution here because patients are generally extremely nervous about their eyelids. Indeed, the shape of the eyelids changes the entire expression of the eyes and of the face. Although everyone wants to have more attractive-looking eyelids, not many patients want to have their expressions changed. At any rate, the patient should be told that his expression will not change as a result of the surgery, unless this is a result that is specifically desired, and when it is the surgeon should suspect the psychological status of the patient. Included in the surgeon's instructions to the patient should be some variation of the following: (1) not to eat or drink anything after midnight on the eve of surgery, (2) not to wear makeup to the operating room, (3) postoperative instructions for rest and application of iced saline soaks to the eyelids for a certain period of time, (4) limitation of postoperative activities, including athletics, exercise, and sexual activities, and (5) the manner for washing the skin of the face and eyelids and washing the hair.

During the consultation some patients ask to see pictures of former patients who have had similar eyelid operations. A good method to circumvent the patient/doctor confidentiality is:

1. Show patients photos from a printed text where the eyelid operation is explained
2. Get releases from certain patients who will show their photos
3. Or actually bring a patient in who has had the operation done and show the operative photographs and the postoperative status. This is the best method because then you are assured that the patient knows

that the photographs are being shown and that he is being shown. Secondly, the patient can talk to the perspective patient and discuss any points of the perspective patient's interest in the operation.

Perhaps the most important aspect of informed consent is to explain in detail to the patient the possible complications that can result from the eyelid operation. It is only then that a reasonable person can make an intelligent decision whether to have the surgery performed. Informed consent is the consent for the surgeon to operate on the patient after he has been informed of all the risks. Of course the risks of general anesthesia or local anesthesia exist in the eyelid operation, as in all other operations, and must be explained and stressed. The risks involved in eyelid surgery are discussed in some detail in §§ **9.8** through **9.21**.

§ 9.5 Anatomy of the Eyelids

The eyelids (*palpebrae*) are two thin, moveable folds of skin located in front of the eyeball primarily for protection. The upper lid is larger than the lower, and is the one that moves and blinks constantly and involuntarily every eight to 12 seconds. It can move voluntarily as well. The basic structure of the upper and lower eyelids is similar, except for the *levator palpebrae superioris muscle,* which assists in the movement of the upper lid.

The *palpebral fissure* is the space between the lids. The corners of the palpebral fissure are known as the (medial and lateral) *canthi,* and are quite different from one another. They are important because patients often want them altered in order to change the shape of their eyes. Patients frequently ask to have their eyes made "almond-shaped," which implies widening the lateral canthus, which rests directly on the globe, or eyeball, at the acute angle of the lids at the side of the eye. The medial canthus is separated from the globe by the small, irregular reddish mound of mucosa called the *lacrimal caruncle,* which empties into the lacrimal lake, or tear pool. The importance of the tear apparatus is examined later in this section.

The eyelashes are attached to the free edges of the eyelids. They are short thick hairs arranged in a double or triple row, and are thicker on the upper lid than on the lower.

According to *Gray's Anatomy,* the eyelids are composed of the following structures, taken from without inward: integument, areolar tissue, fibers of the orbicularis oculi muscle, tarsus, orbital septum, tarsal glands, and conjunctiva. The upper eyelid has, in addition, the aponeurosis of the levator palpebrae muscle. The integument, or skin, is extremely delicate, and continuous at the margins with the conjunctiva. The subcutaneous areolar tissue is very lax and delicate, and seldom contains any fat. The palpebral fissures of the orbicularis oculi are thin, pale in color, and possess both an involuntary and a voluntary action.

The *tarsal plates* are two thin, elongated plates of dense connective tissue about 2.5 cm in length. There is one in each eyelid, contributing to its form and support.

The *orbital septum* is a membranous sheet attached to the edge of the orbit. In the upper eyelid it blends with the levator muscle and the superior tarsus, and in the lower eyelid it connects with the inferior tarsus. The septum is perforated by the vessels and nerves which pass from the orbital cavity to the face and scalp.

The *tarsal glands* are located on the inner surfaces of the eyelids between the tarsi and the conjunctiva. They are modified sebaceous glands.

The *conjunctiva* is the mucous membrane of the eye. It lines the inner surfaces of the eyelids, and is reflected over the sclera and cornea.

The *lacrimal apparatus* consists of (1) the lacrimal gland, which secretes tears, and its excretory ducts, which carry the fluid to the surface of the eye, and (2) the lacrimal ducts, the lacrimal sac, and the nasolacrimal duct, by which the fluid is conveyed into the cavity of the nose.

It is only proper to assume that a surgeon operating on the eyelids and the surrounding areas would have a good knowledge of the anatomy of the region. Although some of the finer points of the anatomy which are not used everyday may be forgotten once a routine for surgery has been established, it would be well for the surgeon to review the particulars of the eyelid anatomy periodically.

The attorney trying a case should have a rather thorough awareness of the general anatomy outlined above, and even the ability to delve into the finer points of anatomy as an aid to discredit an expert witness.

§ 9.6 Description of a Standard Blepharoplasty

A standard blepharoplasty is usually divided into two separate procedures: one to correct an upper lid deformity and the other to improve a lower lid problem. The two procedures can be done separately or during the same operation.

Upper lid blepharoplasty in the Caucasian lid is a relatively simple operative procedure, especially in the hands of an experienced surgeon. Black skin tends to scar differently than Caucasian skin because of excess melamine in the skin. Black eyelids present other difficulties as far as configuration but many blacks can have a successful eyelid operation except for the potential of scarring. Oriental eyelids present problems because of the difficulties in eradicating the Mongolian fold characteristic in the upper eyelids.

Attention should be given to the three important components for correction of the upper lids: (1) the redundant skin, (2) the orbicularis oculi muscle, and (3) the herniated periorbital fat.

Prior to surgery, the patient is medicated with a mild sedative or tranquilizer such as Valium. Many surgeons do this procedure with premedication and a local anesthetic agent alone, such as Xylocaine (lidocaine) with epinephrine. Other more cautious surgeons seek the aid of an anesthetist who gives the patient supplemental anesthesia as the operation is about to begin. Although their patients do not undergo intubation and general anesthesia, they are given some short-acting agent, such as Pentothal, and Versed, a relatively new drug which induces amnesia for the duration of the surgery. These drugs are administered through intravenous tubing in the arm, and the patient can be well-maintained throughout the procedure, feeling and remembering little if anything about the surgery. Often a certain amount of pain can be felt when the local anesthesia is injected directly into the eyelids, and more discomfort is felt when the deep fat pads are pulled during their removal. A further argument for the presence of the anesthetist in the operating room is to monitor the patient's blood pressure, pulse, and electrocardiogram during surgery. Certainly the surgeon cannot do this while operating, and although some operating room nurses are competent to perform these duties it is advisable to use an anesthetist.

The local anesthesia is injected into the eyelids whether an anesthetist is present or not. The upper eyelid is marked with a felt-tip pen to include the excess, ptotic skin to be removed (see **Figures 9–1** and **9–2**). Both upper eyelids are marked at the same time to achieve symmetry. The incision is placed from 7 to 10 mm above the lid margin, and the skin is removed by sharp dissection with a scalpel (see **Figures 9–3** through **9–5**). The bleeding is meticulously coagulated with an electrocautery, and then the two fat pads of the upper lid are identified. Pressure is gently exerted on

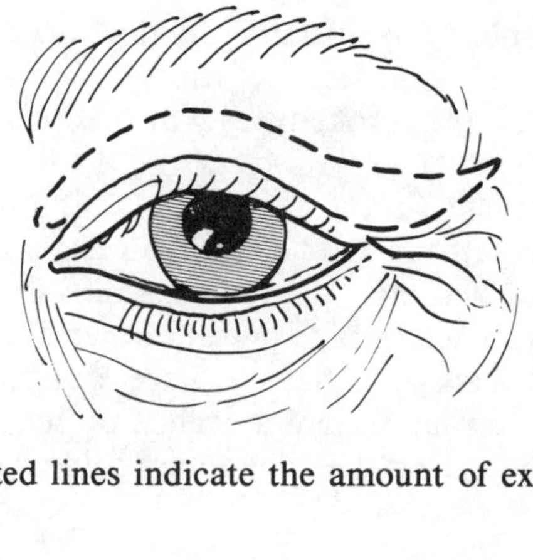

Figure 9–1. The dotted lines indicate the amount of excess ptotic skin to be removed.

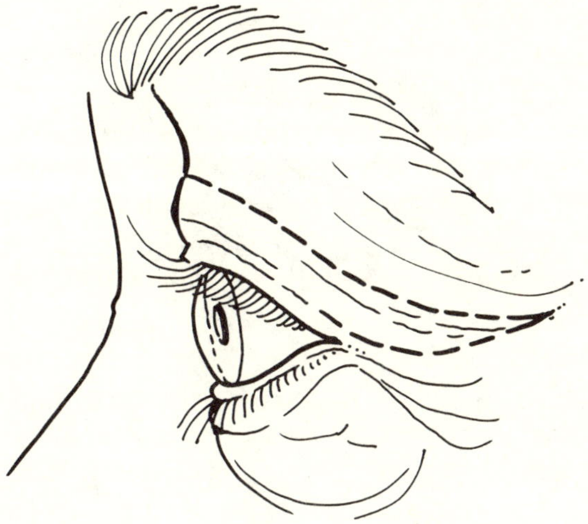

Figure 9–2. The dotted line outlines the excess ptotic skin to be removed.

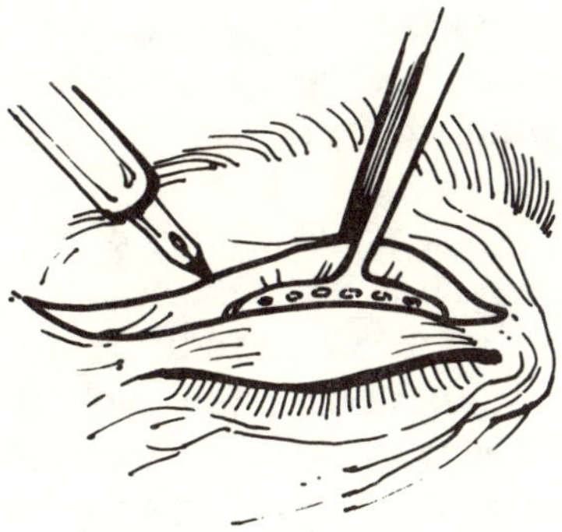

Figure 9–3. A Green forceps grasps the excess ptotic skin in a preincision test to make sure that the eye will still be able to close after the excess is removed.

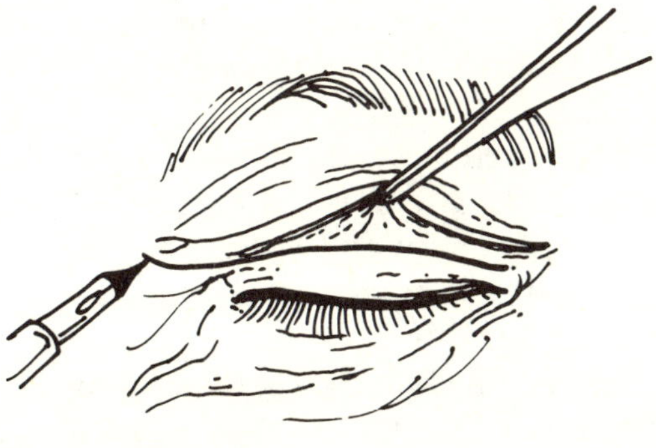

Figure 9–4. The excess ptotic skin in the forceps is raised so that the lateral extension of the line can be drawn.

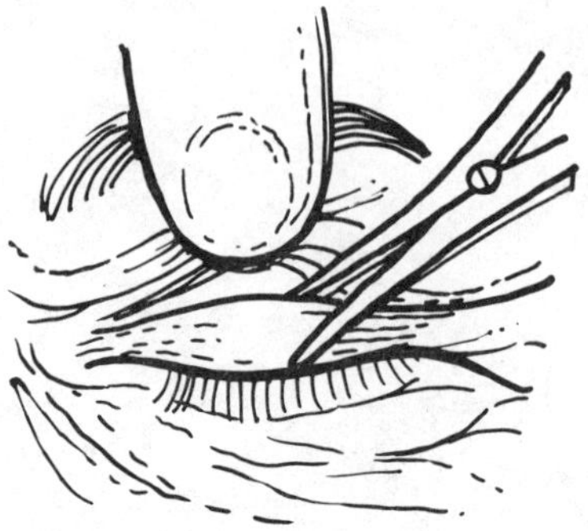

Figure 9–5. A calliper measures the distance from the upper lash to the inferior upper lid incision.

the eyeball, causing the herniated fat to protrude. The two fat pads—one which lies toward the medial portion of the eyelid, and the middle one, which is more laterally located—are then coagulated. This is important because there are blood vessels within the fat that must be coagulated. If they are not they will bleed when the fat retracts into the periorbital area, causing a hematoma around the optic nerve. This will be discussed more thoroughly in **§ 9.9**.

At this point many surgeons excise a strip of the orbicularis oculis muscle, which surrounds the eyelid. This excision seems to enhance the appearance of the upper lid and allows it to drape more attractively over the globe. It does not impair function of the eyelid in any way. The suture material used for these operations differs from surgeon to surgeon. It is common to use a 5-0 nylon suture in the layers below the skin in a back and forth fashion. This suture can be pulled out at the end of several days. The 6-0 silk is a smaller suture made of different material with less tensile strength but can be used for the through-and-through stitches on the skin, and should be removed in 2 to 3 days.

If the wrong size or type of suture is used, it does not necessarily mean malpractice. However, if a surgeon used a very large suture on the eyelid like 2-0 suture, it would seem to be contrary to the standard of care in the plastic surgical community.

The skin of the upper eyelid can be sutured in several different ways. Some surgeons use an *intracuticular suture,* one which goes in and out between the upper and lower skin edges, approximating them (see **Figure 9–6**). This is usually a 5-0 nylon suture. If the surgeon decides to use a stitch specifically for the skin, it is usually of 6-0 silk, and can be either interrupted or continuous. These suturing techniques depend on the individual physician's routine, and usually vary from one surgeon to another.

The eyelids are not routinely bandaged with any sort of constrictive dressing, although occasionally a surgeon will put a firm dressing around

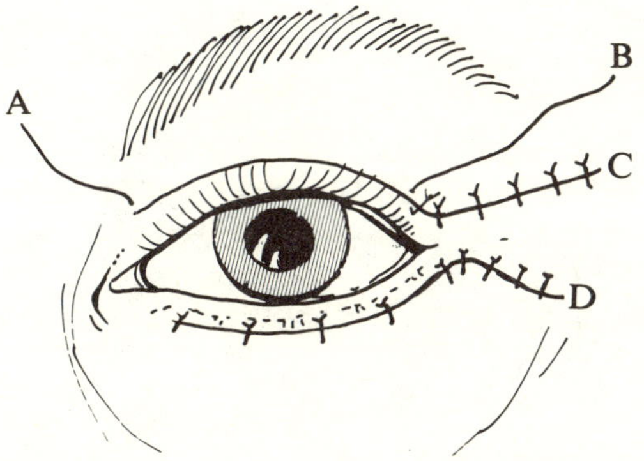

Figure 9–6. "A" shows the intracuticular suture starting at the inner canthal area near the nose, going underneath the skin, and exiting at the outer canthal layer, "B." "C" shows the interrupted sutures of the lateral canthal incision and "D" shows the lower lid incision sutures.

the eyelids for 12 to 24 hours in an attempt to decrease swelling postoperatively. Most physicians use iced saline soaks applied almost constantly to the eyelids for the first 24 hours and thereafter for the next several days, and then for a short time each morning and evening, until all the swelling is gone. The cold saline makes the eyelids feel good, as well as having an important effect on the reduction of edema.

The standard technique for lower lid blepharoplasty includes incision, development of a skin-muscle (or just a skin) flap, excision of herniated periorbital fat, possible removal of a small amount of muscle, conservative excision of skin, and closure. It is crucial to remember that the lower lid skin is very delicate and, although it is often tempting to remove all the bags or all the wrinkles, the results will be terrifying if too much skin is removed, causing a starry-eyed look.

The incision is outlined with a marking pen approximately 1 to 2 mm from the inferior ciliary margin. It begins at the medial canthal area, and proceeds laterally to the lateral canthus, and usually turns obliquely downward for about 1 cm (see **Figure 9–7**). A number 15 blade is used to make this incision, which penetrates the skin and orbicularis muscle into the subcutaneous area. Then the dissection is continued with a small pointed scissors, and the skin-muscle flap is undermined (loosened from its underattachments) with these same scissors. (The technique of developing a flap at this point varies from surgeon to surgeon. There are physicians who feel it is better to undermine only the skin, leaving the muscle intact, while others feel that the development of a skin-muscle flap gives a better shape to the lower lid, and allows less chance of eversion and even ectropion in the early postoperative period.)

The undermining is facilitated by placing countertraction on the skin of the cheek opposite the exact site of dissection. The degree of undermining

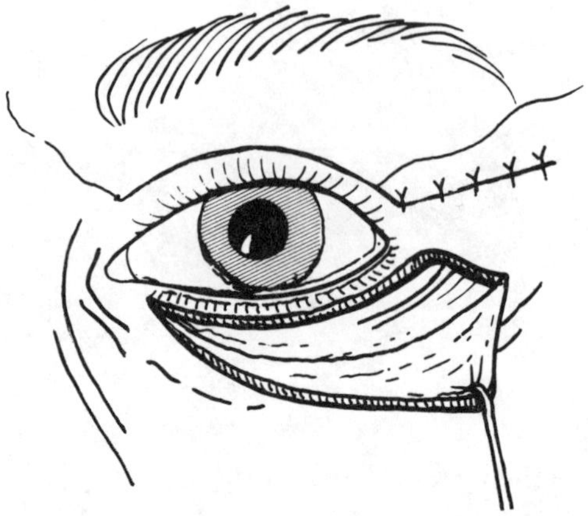

Figure 9–7. The lower lid skin flap is pulled down to expose the areas for removal of the fat pads.

varies, but is usually limited by the inferior orbital rim or upper limits of the cheekbone. It is at this point that hemostasis must be meticulously achieved—that is, every small, bleeding vessel must be coagulated with the electric needle (see **Figure 9–8**). If this is not done, the possibility of hematoma postoperatively is markedly increased.

The next step in the lower lid blepharoplasty is locating the fat pockets to be reduced (see **Figure 9–9**). They are identified by exerting mild pressure on the globe, and watching them bulge through the orbicularis muscle. There are three fat pockets in the lower lid, and they are thought to be separate entities. A sharp scissors is introduced through the septum in the

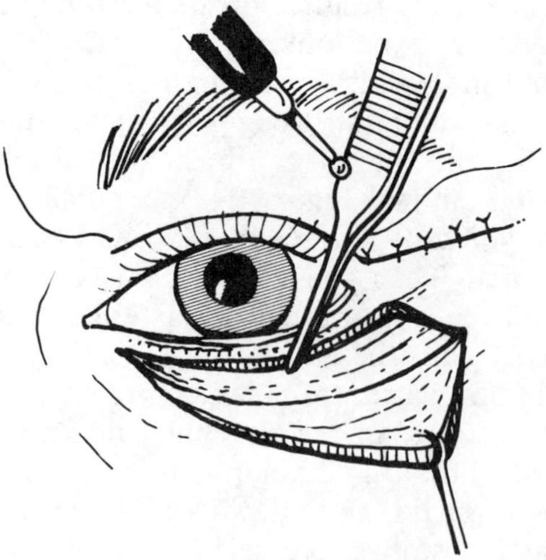

Figure 9–8. An electric cautery machine is touched to a small forceps to coagulate the small blood vessels.

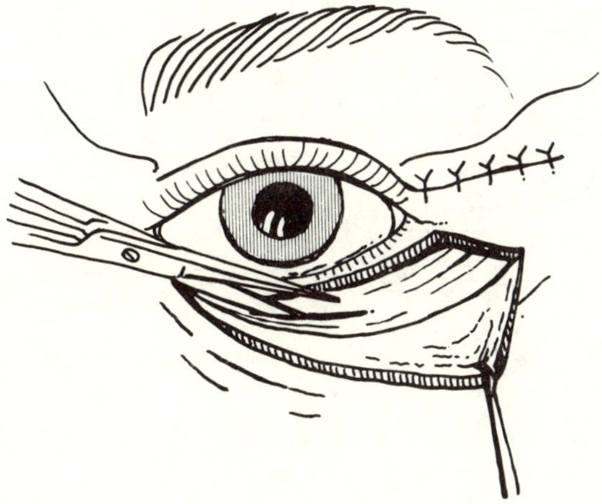

Figure 9–9. A scissors is used to incise the orbicularis oculis muscle to find the fat pads in the lower lids.

medial, middle, and lateral areas to expose these fat pads. They are then identified, and a small clamp is placed at the base of each one separately (see **Figure 9–10**). A number 15 blade or a scissors is used to excise the section of the fat pad on the upper surface of the clamp. Then the fat is coagulated, to avoid any bleeding in this rather vascular fat pad once it has slipped back into the orbit and behind the eyeball. (*Retrobulbar hematoma* is the bleeding caused by not coagulating the fat pad before it slips back into its place. The buildup of blood in the space surrounding

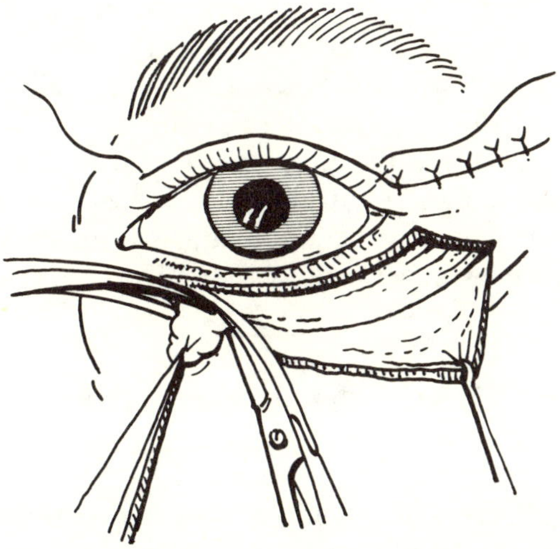

Figure 9–10. A small fat pad is pulled forward with a forceps, clamped on the right side, and cut with a scissors from the left side.

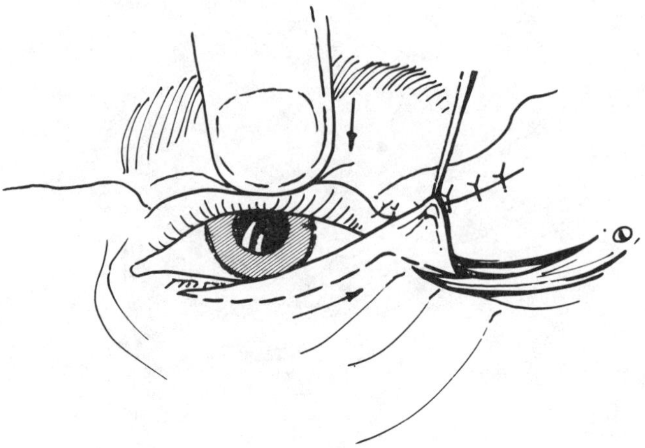

Figure 9–11. The excess skin of the lower lid is pulled up into the lateral canthal area and excised.

the all-important optic nerve will exert pressure on the nerve, and could ultimately cause blindness, if this complication is not discovered in time.)

Once all three fat pads are identified, reduced, and coagulated, and the entire eyelid field is dry, the surgeon is ready for the removal of excess skin. The skin should be advanced over the lower lid, and lie there without tension before any marking to remove it is made. Some surgeons like to ask patients operated on under local anesthesia to open their eyes wide and look toward the ceiling, while at the same time opening their mouth. This demonstrates all the possible pull to the lower lid under normal conditions. The skin is then marked and cut with a knife or scissors (see **Figure 9–11**), and the small blood vessels in the skin are again coagulated. When the skin is laid into place comfortably, and not under tension, the edges are approximated, usually with a 6-0 interrupted silk or nylon suture. Many surgeons use iced saline soaks on the eyelid once it has been completed and while they are operating on the other lids. Although some surgeons bandage the eyelids for 24 hours after the surgery, most do not, but are content to place cold saline soaks on them for the first 24 hours, and even several days thereafter.

§ 9.7 Postoperative Care

The postoperative period after blepharoplasty is extremely important for the patient and surgeon alike, and careful instructions with definite restrictions must be given both before and after the surgery. While the eyelids are being operated on for a cosmetic improvement the eyes themselves could be in jeopardy, and visual impairment or loss could occur as a result.

Rest and conservative care in the immediate postoperative period are essential. The surgeon must tell the patient to lie still for the first 12 to 24 hours after the operation, so no unnecessary bleeding will occur. Too much movement could cause a retrobulbar hematoma, which could impair the patient's vision.

From a medical-legal point of view, this period is absolutely crucial, because the desired result of the cosmetic procedure can be impaired or compromised. An operation can be performed in a technically perfect manner; the results after the surgery, however, cannot be guaranteed. Patients can leave the hospital or surgical unit and go home and ruin the results of their operation by their own negligence, excessive activity, or failure to heed instructions.

Accordingly, the pertinent legal question is: How can we determine whether a bad result (which is not in and of itself malpractice) was the direct effect of the surgical procedure, or was in fact brought about by the patient's ignorance about instructions or his failure to heed them?

There is a long list of things that patients can do to themselves to cause harm inadvertently after surgery. Patients have been known to apply the wrong medication or ointment to their incisions. Often, in an attempt to be overzealous, a patient will apply Vaseline, olive oil, mineral oil, or cod-liver oil to the incisions, either before or after the sutures have been removed, perhaps because a friend, a grandmother, or even an article in the newspaper or on television has suggested that this would bring about more rapid healing. Some patients apply vitamin E to the incisions the day of surgery, before they have healed sufficiently. Some patients think that if a little is good, more is better, so if told to soak the eyelids for a certain amount of time, they will soak five times longer. If they are told to massage a certain area of the eyelids after surgery, and to do it gently, they will massage the entire area, and will do it with too much force.

Reading or watching television after eyelid surgery is not advisable. Putting too much strain on the eyes immediately after surgery can cause fatigue, and create edema and discoloration that will take much longer to subside than it would otherwise. Certainly washing the eyelids, which includes taking a shower, can restrict good healing. It can cause maceration to the suture lines, and sometimes even infection or inflammation, if soap is introduced into the area at too early a stage.

Again, one aspect of informed consent covered instruction regarding the type of activity that is allowed postoperatively. This includes every day activity, athletics and exercise, and sexual activity. Most every day activity is allowed a day or so after surgery, but the surgeon must know from the consultation what exactly the patient considers to be "normal." The patient may be a stevedore or a trapeze artist, and consider that particular activity normal; therefore, defining "normal activity" is important. Many patients who care enough about their appearance to have a cosmetic surgical procedure done typically also want to keep trim, and will be anxious to get back to their fitness program. This could be a problem, because not only can the increase in vital signs potentially cause bleeding, but the perspiration can carry contaminants to the incisions. The same is true of early sexual activity. It is important for the physician to mention the restriction on sexual activity, and to chart that it has been discussed.

The primary reason for being so explicit with postoperative instructions is so that the patient will know how he can best care for himself to enjoy a good healing period and achieve an excellent result. Another important reason for giving and carefully charting these instructions should be obvious by this time. It is the only defense a surgeon has against a case gone awry after the surgery is over, when the patient is out of the care of the physician or nurse. It cannot be overemphasized: negligence is a two-way street. If there is an undesirable result, it may be the result of the surgeon's negligence. It may also be the result of the patient's faulty postoperative care. It is imperative for surgeons to chart the restrictions as best they can, because an attorney will cross-examine the patient on his postoperative activity, and find out exactly what was done to contribute to the problem.

Often women will apply eye shadow and liner and mascara to the operative site earlier than it is thought to be beneficial because of the pressures of business, or just because of vanity. Sometimes they will not even remember when they applied it, just as patients may honestly have difficulty remembering when they resumed exercise or sexual activity. Sometimes they will remember, and try to conceal the facts, because they know that what they did was not advised. These experiences make it necessary for surgeons to chart their instructions carefully. If at all possible, they should give printed instructions to the patients to take home and read preoperatively so there will be no surprises, and so they will have enough time to prepare themselves for their postoperative courses. Suffice it to say that the postoperative instructions and adherence to those instructions are extremely important to the ultimate surgical result.

§ 9.8 Possible Complications and Unfavorable Results

Because we look so frequently into each other's eyes, any aberration or abnormality of the eyes or their surrounding tissues is of the utmost concern to the patient, and is immediately noticed by others. Perhaps a minor complication to an operation on a part of the body which is covered by clothing would not be so distressing to many patients but, because the eyes are such a mirror of our feelings and emotions, and because they are such an essential part of our facial expressions, it is crucial that any surgery done to improve or beautify them be done extremely well.

Complications from eyelid surgery can be either serious and permanent, or minor and temporary. A minor complication or *sequela* (a natural, usually temporary condition which is expected after the surgery, and lasts for a relatively short period of time—for example, swelling, or discoloration—and is not truly a complication) will disappear with time or with a minor adjustment. A good example of this is the appearance of a small hematoma, which demonstrates as a swollen, discolored area and can disappear quicker if the patient applies saline soaks or even massages the area gently. Before the surgery is done, the surgeon should prepare the patients for any minor occurrence that can be expected or anticipated, so that if and when it does happen, they do not become alarmed or frightened. Most patients are reasonable, and will be guided by their surgeon's experience in a given matter. Patients who have given their informed consent should understand the difference between something that will happen as a natural consequence of the surgery and will disappear, and something that is considered a serious and undesired complication. They should of course be warned about both types of complications, and should learn to distinguish between the two.

A serious complication may require a minor surgical procedure to correct it, and patients should understand the possibility of this happening before they consent to the surgery. It is for these reasons that the informed consent is of such importance. If the patient understands this, the concepts of complication (usually not malpractice) and negligence (malpractice) will be much better understood by both patient and attorney.

Short of death, the most serious of all complications is blindness, and this is irreversible. This complication, above all others, should be discussed by the surgeon, so that the patient consents to the operation with the full knowledge that, although this seldom happens, it can, on rare occasion, occur.

§ 9.9 —Blindness (Retrobulbar Hematoma)

Retrobulbar hematoma is a clot of blood that forms behind the eyeball. This complication is usually seen in the lower eyelids, although it can occur in the uppers as well. It is most often caused by a small (and obviously unnoticed) bleeding vessel in the periorbital fat. In order to visualize these fat pads, pressure is gently exerted on the globe, causing this fat to protrude through the muscle before it is excised. After the fat pads are reduced, the surgeon must carefully coagulate the end of the fat, which then retracts into the retrobulbar, or intraorbital, space. If a small vessel is hidden in this fat, and accidentally starts bleeding after the fat has retracted, it is impossible to see. As it bleeds, a collection of blood builds up in an area behind the eyeball and adjacent to the optic nerve. The pressure that this blood exerts on the optic nerve could cause damage to it because of the lack of blood to the nerve itself during this period. If this is allowed to occur for any significant period of time, the resultant retrobulbar hematoma will lead to blindness.

The possibility of this complication should be uppermost in the surgeon's mind during every blepharoplasty, and until the danger period passes, which is usually between six and 12 hours. The primary symptom heralding this complication is severe pain in the involved eye, and it is usually unilateral. Direct vision of the globe is essential. It takes on a characteristically wooden appearance. This is probably an excellent reason not to bandage the patient's eyelids after surgery. If a hematoma should occur, it is preferable that the patient be in a hospital environment or an outpatient surgical facility. Good and quick nursing care is very important at this time, because the tragedy can be averted if the diagnosis is made, the surgeon is notified at once, and the sutures are removed in the affected eyelid.

Once the sutures are removed, and the blood is allowed to escape the area around the optic nerve, the blood supply to the nerve will be reinstated, and the danger will have passed. Then the fat pads must be carefully re-examined, and the incriminated blood vessel coagulated.

There is a classic case of an ex-soldier who, during his early fifties, and some years after he had been discharged from the military, decided to have a blepharoplasty. The doctor failed to have a visual examination done prior to surgery but the operation was performed well. After the surgery, the patient reported blindness in one eye, and instituted an action against the surgeon. It was a very clever and thorough attorney who thought to check back into an old military medical record, only to find that the patient had had faulty vision in the involved eye at that time, with the prognosis of partial or complete blindness in a matter of years.

§ 9.10 —Hematoma

A hematoma under the skin is a much less serious complication; however, it can cause some problems later on if not treated properly. The cause of hematoma is bleeding and often, if the doctor is not meticulous in obtaining hemostasis in the eyelid area, a small vessel will bleed and cause a swelling under the delicate eyelid skin. Iced saline soaks usually prevent postoperative bleeding of this nature, and can often arrest a small amount of bleeding that has started.

If a small, or spot, hematoma is noticed postoperatively, it should be watched for seven to 10 days. Blood usually liquifies at this time, and can often be aspirated with a needle, or expressed through a tiny incision in the adjacent skin.

If a blepharoplasty is done under general anesthesia, as it was years ago, or even today if the blepharoplasty is done in conjunction with a face-lift and is done under general anesthesia, a potential problem arises. Although the surgeon has achieved complete hemostasis, and there is a perfectly dry field when the eyelid skin is sutured, a coughing spell or vomiting could ensue when the patient is being extubated. This will inevitably raise the blood pressure and could cause one of the small, coagulated plugs at the end of the vessel to break forth and cause this bleeding under the skin.

Of course, it would seem better to perform such surgery under local anesthesia with standby, thus averting most problems due to a postoperative rise in blood pressure. (A standby anesthetist or anesthesiologist monitors the patient's vital signs, starts the IV, and gives tranquilizing or anesthetizing drugs. While under general anesthesia, the patient is not intubated. This type of anesthesia is much safer and reasonable for this type of surgery.) It is for this reason that conservative postoperative care is so important. Many patients experience similar hypertensive episodes on their way home from an ambulatory surgical unit if their taxi or auto jostles them, or throws them unexpectedly forward against the dashboard.

A recent case involves an action taken by a 45-year-old woman against her plastic surgeon after a blepharoplasty. The patient presented with heavy upper eyelids and large amounts of periorbital fat underneath both eyes. The operation apparently was explained to her and was performed in an acceptable manner by the surgeon. After a coughing spell, a hematoma developed under the skin of the right lower eyelid. The surgeon tried to evacuate the hematoma at the proper time. He asked the patient to use cold soaks on the eyelids, which she did. After the hematoma had been mostly absorbed by the body (as it will be after several weeks to months), a hardness remained underneath the delicate eyelid skin, which was caused by the fibrin clot giving rise to scar tissue underneath. At the patient's behest because she was unhappy with this hardness and refused to wait any longer, the surgeon injected the lower lid with small amounts of Kenalog, a steroid medication used to help dissolve soft tissue and particularly scar tissue. The patient seemed to have a favorable result from this injection and after a relatively short period of time the swelling went away. All that was left under the lower lid was a slight pinkish discoloration caused by a change in the vasculature because of the hematoma and the injections. The woman had an excellent result from her eyelid operation and her appearance was remarkedly changed. However, she sued the plastic surgeon for the minimal amount of discoloration under the right lower lid. In this situation, the patient was aware that this could happen, having been given the proper informed consent, which however she denied hearing. The case did not go to trial; after the depositions were taken and the defendant's expert could ascribe no negligence to the surgeon, the case was closed.

§ 9.11 —Scleral Hematoma

This occurs when a small blood vessel in the sclera breaks and causes a bright red color to appear in the white part of the eye. It often occurs in the white portion of the eye lateral to the pupil and it is frightening and alarming to the patient. It is neither dangerous nor painful and will always go away. A satisfying treatment for this is the application of cold soaks to the eyelids. This allows the edema and discoloration to recede at a quicker rate. The ecchymosis is gone at the end of one week to 10 days; the edema usually takes three weeks to disappear.

§ 9.12 —Infection

Because the blood supply to the skin of the eyelids is so rich, there is not a great incidence of infection in the area. There are usually no contaminants, such as the hair in a face-lift operation, to infect the area. However, an infection does occur from time to time. The most frequent cause of this infection is interference from the patient, either by touching or rubbing the eyelids, or by application of some foreign substance, such as an oil or a cosmetic, before it is safe.

Of course a break in the sterile technique on the part of the surgeon or one of the staff can cause an infection, as can multiple surgeries performed during the same operation. There is a much greater incidence of infection when the eyelids are done at the same time as a rhinoplasty, for example. When the fractures of the nasal bones are done, there is a distinct possibility of contamination from nasal bacteria.

Any eyelid infection should be treated with antibiotics and warm soaks. A culture of the drainage should be taken, so the bacteria can be identified and the proper antibiotic prescribed.

§ 9.13 —Ectropion

Many patients who have some sagging in the cheek area request that it be alleviated by excising skin from the lower eyelids. Of course this is not possible, because the skin of the cheek is heavier. Rather than the desired result of lifting up the cheek skin, the opposite will occur, and the lower lids would be pulled down, causing perhaps the most common complication of lower lid surgery: ectropion.

The word itself is derived from two Greek words, *ek,* meaning "out of," and *tropos,* meaning "place." So an ectropion is the skin of the lower lid being out of (its) place. It gives a starry, wide-eyed look, like a bloodhound, very unnatural and undesired.

Two categories of ectropia are seen, one temporary and the other permanent. The first ectropion is caused by swelling and scar tissue that has not gone back to its normal status in the eyelid, and is often seen from two days to six weeks after surgery. This condition is known as cicatricial ectropion. It causes great unhappiness to most patients, because they look unnatural during this period and are often either ridiculed or pitied by their friends.

If not too much skin has been removed at the time of surgery, the lid will return to its normal position in a relatively short period of time. Massaging the lid helps, and sometimes warm soaks help, but the best treatment for this is patience and time. It is during this time that the lid can be everted, or turned out, showing the pink part of the inside of the lid, known as the conjunctiva. This is always very alarming to patients, but constant assurance on the part of the physician will usually help the patient through this emotionally difficult period.

The real problem ectropion is the one which, without further surgical intervention, is permanent. It is caused by the removal of too much skin at the time of the operation. It is usually the fault of an inexperienced surgeon, who is trying quite hard to make a perfect lower lid, leaving no wrinkling or lines. This is a pitfall to be avoided. The lower lids should be operated on very conservatively, and usually not more than 2 to 4 mm of skin should be removed. If the ectropion is a result of excess excision of skin, the treatment for it is skin grafting to fill in the deficit, thereby restoring the lower lid to normalcy. If the surgeon knows that too much skin has been removed, he should do the skin graft relatively soon, to alleviate the patient's anxiety and avoid the possibility of further or permanent damage to the cornea caused by exposure and lack of lubrication. If, however, the etiology of the ectropion is in doubt—that is, if it may be cicatricial—then it would be advisable to encourage the patient to wait for several months to see if the lid will return to its normal position spontaneously.

It will sometimes be difficult to convince patients to wait for any time to elapse, because this is such a difficult condition for them to bear. They are confined to dark glasses, and usually refuse to go to any social events and sometimes even to the office to work. Because indeed the purpose of the surgery was to improve the looks of the eyelids, no one wants to look into the mirror and see this worsening of their looks.

§ 9.14 —Scleral Show

The sclera is the white part of the globe, and when a little too much skin has been removed, or in the early stages a bit too much swelling or scar tissue persists, the resultant wide-eyed look is known as *scleral show.* It is really a mild ectropion, it is unattractive, and will usually disappear in time if too much skin has not been removed. This condition is more commonly seen in patients whose lower eyelids have been operated for the second or third time.

In one case a woman in her middle sixties went to a doctor for an eyelidplasty. Although there were wrinkles in the periorbital area, the doctor did not want to operate on this patient because he felt she was not psychologically a good candidate for the operation. However, the doctor was young, somewhat inexperienced, and slightly intimidated; the patient was older and quite wise in the ways of the world, and inveigled the surgeon to operate on her. She did not give her complete history, however, and lied about the number of times she had had plastic surgery, fearing that the truth might discourage the surgeon.

The operation was performed on her eyelids, and postoperatively she developed cicatricial ectropia, with a resulting *keratitis,* or infection of the keratin layer of the eyeball. This manifested itself by pain (which is often quite severe) in the eyeball itself, excess tearing, and generalized discomfort. The doctor was upset when the plaintiff attorney approached him asking for a settlement and telling the surgeon that it might be inconvenient for him to give time from his practice to go to court, it might be embarrassing, and so on. The surgeon agreed that all these things would be true but, nonetheless, he felt it would be better to bring the case to trial, because he felt that no malpractice had been committed. The doctor had been attentive to his patient, and had performed the operation well, with the limited knowledge of medical history.

The case went to trial, and the woman was exposed as a "plastic surgery junkie" who would go to any lengths to have an operation, even to the point of concealing her true medical history. In addition, the lawyer brought enlargements of the patient's medicare statements from her ophthalmologist, who had made the diagnosis of chronic keratitis long before the plastic surgical operation had taken place. The jury returned a verdict in favor of the defendant doctor. Incidentally, by the time the case came to trial, the lower lids had returned to their normal position without further surgical intervention. Defense attorneys should beware of the plastic surgery junkie.

§ 9.15 —Dry Eye

Lagophthalmos is the inability to close the eye when too much skin has been removed. The exposure of the eye without the protection of the lid can cause a dry eye, which can lead to keratitis or other infection of the conjunctiva and sclera. This condition can be temporary or permanent. If it is temporary, it is the result of swelling and scar tissue preventing the lids from closing. If it is permanent, it is the result of excessive skin excisions, and a skin graft will have to be done to alleviate the symptoms. When the eyelids do not close, the reason is usually that too much skin has been removed from the upper lid, making it unable to close. This can result in other complications such as *desiccation* (drying of the globe), *exposure keratitis* (infection of the keratin layer), and ulceration of the anterior chamber or cornea. Taping the eyelids shut at night, and lubricating them with false tears, is the immediate treatment for this problem.

§ 9.16 —Epiphora or Excess Tearing

Epiphora is produced by excess secretion of tears and can be the result of mild trauma to the lacrimal gland, lacrimal sac, or tear ducts during surgery. This can be caused by the injection of local anesthesia in the obicularis muscle, exposure because of a lack of skin of the lower lid (ectropion), or exposure because of a lack of skin of the upper lids (lagophthalmos). Epiphora is usually temporary and is resolved within several days to several weeks unless some anatomic abnormality is present.

§ 9.17 —Loss of Lashes

Occasionally, when the lower lid incision is made in the skin adjacent to the lower lash line, some of these lashes will be sacrificed. Furthermore, the upper lid lashes will occasionally drop out because of the vascular changes of the eyelids after surgery. In both situations the lashes will return spontaneously unless there is some extenuating metabolic reason. However, it may take several months for the eyelashes to grow back. A loss of eyelashes is usually produced by direct damage to the hair follicles from desiccation or cauterization or incision placed too close to the lid margin.

§ 9.18 —Excess Scarring

Although the eyelid skin is the thinnest skin in the body and has the potential to give the best scars, occasionally there are heavier reddened scars in this area. Conservative treatment is usually best, using vitamin E or steroid cream on the scars. The scar beneath the lower lashes is the first to disappear and is usually imperceptible within one week. The upper lid scars take longer because of the constant movement of the eyelids, and the lateral scars take longest to heal.

Often patients have an allergy to some creams such as vitamin E. Recently a patient reported to her surgeon that her scars were red and inflamed for several months. It was not until a careful history of her postoperative period was taken that it was learned that she used mineral oil on the scars in an attempt to soften them. This was not done with the instructions of her physician.

§ 9.19 —Sunken Eyelids

The surgeon's goal is to take out fat to relieve the patient of a baggy appearance. Sunken eyelids are caused by removing too much fat from the lower lids, giving them the appearance of having caved in. If this occurs, nothing should be done for at least one year. During this time the condition can alleviate itself by the appearance of more fat through the muscle. If, however, the eyelids remain sunken, occasionally a small fat graft will have to be placed in the eyelids.

§ 9.20 —Milia or Inclusion Cysts

One of the sequelae of a blepharoplasty is *milia,* the small sebaceous cysts on the suture line. These small white nodules usually disappear spontaneously but, if they persist, they may be incised and their contents expressed. They are normal sequelae of eyelid surgery, but they may be disturbing if the patient has not been warned prior to surgery of their possible postoperative occurrence.

§ 9.21 —Skin Wrinkling

Often after a blepharoplasty a patient sees that the eyelids, especially the lower lids, have more wrinkling than they did prior to surgery. This is a result of the relaxation of the skin after the tension placed on it by the fat has been removed. This is particularly true if the surgeon was conservative in the excision of lower lid skin. The patient should be warned prior to the surgery that there will be wrinkling in the lower and lateral portions of the eyelids, especially during laughing and certain expressions.

§ 9.22 Patient Dissatisfaction

The successful plastic surgeon must be acutely aware of the unrealistic expectations of some cosmetic surgery patients. Some patients have selective hearing, which allows them to screen out all the important caveats regarding their surgery, leaving them contemplating only the idyllic ends to their venture. Many patients' expectations exceed that which can realistically be done, even by a competent and experienced surgeon. Despite having been told what to expect from a surgery, some patients are disappointed that more was not achieved. This is why a plastic surgeon must be acutely aware of the importance of the informed consent and make sure that the patient understands clearly all of the complications that could happen at any time. Although most patients can accept a result that may not reach their level of expectation, those who are unhappy may become increasingly difficult to manage, becoming hostile and angry with their surgeon. Anger is one of the most common motivational forces for litigation.

§ 9.23 Illustrative Cases

In blepharoplasty cases the issues generally revolve around patients who claim such complications as ptosis or ectropion.

In order for a plaintiff to succeed in proving a case, the emphasis is often on the informed consent cause of action.

Moser v. Stallings & Plastic Surgery Institute[2]

The plaintiff was 52 years old at the time she sought treatment from the defendant in July, 1979. Prior to that time Mrs. Moser had undergone five surgeries on her nose but was not satisfied. She became aware of the defendant through a national television show.

The defendant examined the plaintiff but recommended that instead of merely having surgery on her nose the plaintiff should have a facial and eyelid plasty, forehead plasty, chin implant, and dermabrasion of the upper lip. The defendant performed surgery on August 2, 1979 encompassing all of the procedures mentioned except for the chin implant.

The plaintiff alleged that as a result of the surgery she suffered a displaced hairline and a rearrangement of the face, scalp, and neck area. She sued on grounds of battery and lack of informed consent. The court stated that

> A medical battery claim is appropriate in circumstances when a doctor performs an operation to which the patient has not consented. . . . A battery occurs when the patient consents to one type of treatment and the doctor intentionally deviates from the consent and performs a substantially different treatment.[3]

---

[2] 387 N.W.2d 599 (Iowa 1986).

[3] *Id.* at 600.

The plaintiff alleged that Dr. Stallings' failure to perform the implant and his performance of a rearrangement of the chin muscles instead constituted a battery. The court found that there was no deviation from consent. The consent form authorized "the defendant to perform such surgical procedures as Dr. Stallings deemed necessary for the purpose of attempting to improve appearance with respect to the following conditions. Facial and chin deformity." The battery cause of action was dismissed.

The jury found against the plaintiff on the informed consent issue.

Burton v. Youngblood[4]

On November 17, 1978, the defendant Youngblood, a board-certified plastic surgeon, performed an upper eyelid blepharoplasty. Excessive bleeding occurred and Youngblood cauterized the bleeding areas.

Subsequent to surgery the plaintiff developed ptosis of the eyelid and was unable to close her left eye when she blinked. Her eye became unusually dry, resulting in an infection. Youngblood drained the infected area and told the plaintiff to use hot packs. After being treated by Youngblood for an additional year postoperatively without relief Mrs. Burton consulted an ophthalmologist who performed two surgical procedures to correct the ptosis, without complete success.

At trial Burton relied upon her own testimony, the testimony of Youngblood, and that of the ophthalmologist. The court excluded the testimony of the ophthalmologist when the plaintiff's counsel failed to lay an adequate foundation to show that the ophthalmologist could testify as to the procedures which a plastic surgeon should have followed.

In examining the plaintiff's claim of lack of informed consent the court found that, while proving that ptosis was a substantial risk of eyelid surgery, she failed to meet the requirements of the Utah informed consent statute which reads as follows:

> For a patient to recover damages from a health care provider in an action based upon the provider's failure to obtain informed consent, the patient must prove the following:
>
> (a) That a provider-patient relationship existed between the patient and health care provider; and
>
> (b) The health care provider rendered health care to patient; and
>
> (c) The patient suffered personal injuries arising out of the health care rendered; and
>
> (d) The health care rendered carried with it a substantial and significant risk; and

[4] 711 P.2d 245 (Utah 1985).

(e) The patient was not informed of the substantial and significant risk; and

(f) A reasonable, prudent person in the patient's position would not have consented to the health care rendered after having been fully informed as to all facts relevant to the decision to give consent. In determining what a reasonable, prudent person in the patient's position would do under the circumstances, the finder of fact shall use the viewpoint of the patient before health care was provided and before the occurrence of any personal injuries alleged to have arisen from said health care; and

(g) The unauthorized part of the health care rendered was the proximate cause of personal injuries suffered by the patient.[5]

Thus the court found that the action must be dismissed.

§ 9.24 Bibliography

J.M. Converse, Plastic Reconstructive Surgery. (W.B. Saunders Co., 1977).

R.M. Goldwyn, The Patient and the Plastic Surgeon. (Little, Brown & Co., 1981).

R.M. Goldwyn, The Unfavorable Result in Plastic Surgery 456–516. (Little, Brown & Co., 1984).

W.C. Grabb, & J.W. Smith, Plastic Surgery. (Little, Brown & Co., 1984).

H. Gray, Anatomy of the Human Body. (Lea & Febiger, 30th ed. 1985).

Habal, Morain, Lewin, Parsons, & Woods, 5 Advances in Plastic and Reconstructive Surgery. (Year Book Medical Publishers, Inc., 1989).

S.H. Miller, Year Book of Plastic and Reconstructive Surgery. (Year Book Medical Publishers, Inc., 1989).

T.D. Rees, II Aesthetic Plastic Surgery. (W.B. Saunders Co., 1980).

R.B. Stark, Plastic Surgery of the Head and Neck. (Churchill Livingstone, 1987).

---

[5] *Id.* at 249 Utah Code Ann. § 78-14-1 (1977).

CHAPTER 10

FACE-LIFTS

§ 10.1 Introduction

Face-lifts have become increasingly more popular as life in the eighties changes. Partly because science is developing treatments to keep people living longer, people have become increasingly more aware of their health. Fitness programs and gymnasiums are flourishing. People smoke less, drink less alcohol, eat better, and live longer. Competition in the work place is keener, and retirement ages are being extended. Many people feel they have to look better to keep up with these changes.

The first surgical attempts at improving the appearance of facial skin occurred in Europe around the turn of the century. By 1920 a famous French surgeon, Madame Noel, was doing face-lifts in Paris secretly because the public's disapproval of vanity augmented its disdain for facial surgery at that time. Many people considered plastic surgery trivial, unnecessarily risky, and contrary to the laws of nature; growing old gracefully was their hue and cry.

The American Board of Plastic and Reconstructive Surgery was established in 1936, and from that time on cosmetic facial surgery became not only more accepted, but widely done. The Second World War was a major factor in increasing the acceptance of cosmetic and reconstructive surgery. In Sussex, England, a large hospital was organized to take care of the facial injuries of the American and Canadian flyers who were burned in the war. This unit is still in existence today and enjoying great acclaim. Reconstructive plastic surgery is done there now, and a renowned burn unit is attached to it.

When face-lifts were discussed in the United States in the 1930s and the 1940s, most people visualized vain, wealthy women and movie stars secluded in a clinic somewhere in the Hollywood hills. They would enter under the shade of night and emerge several weeks later looking rejuvenated and radiant, hoping that the public would not know whether the change was from makeup, lighting, or plastic surgery. Now cosmetic surgery is available to the population at large—to secretaries, clerical workers, and other people of moderate means.

The cost of plastic surgery has decreased in some areas because of advertising and the desire on the part of some surgeons to accommodate the masses it attracts. Some other plastic surgeons in practice for a longer time seem to limit their practice by keeping their fees high. These surgeons do no public advertising, relying instead on their patients' favorable results to publicize their reputations.

Today it is estimated that 20 percent of all face-lift patients are males. This can probably be attributed in part to the fact that older men must now compete for jobs and promotion not only with younger men but with women, who have in recent years entered the work place in large numbers. These men realize that appearance is a crucial factor in job success.

Because so many people want cosmetic facial surgery today, physicians must understand which patients are good operative risks. The surgeon must explain to the patients how he prepares them for surgery, what the operation and the postoperative care entails, and what the patients' realistic expectations should be.

§ 10.2 The Consultation

Which patients should a competent plastic surgeon select for face-lift surgery? The consultation gives the doctor and the patient an opportunity to interview each other. The surgeon must decide whether the patient is in fact a good candidate emotionally as well as physically for this highly elective procedure, while at the same time the patient can form an opinion of the surgeon.

The ideal patient for a face-lift is a person who is psychologically stable, in very good health, a nonsmoker, and someone whose facial skin will be greatly improved by the operation. The majority of these patients are between their early forties and their middle sixties, but age is not an important factor.

The patient should have good facial bone structure, should not be overweight, and have no fat beneath the chin or in the neck. Skin texture is important. Optimally it should be neither too dry nor too oily, free of acne scars, and without those small, fine wrinkles so difficult to remove.

The patient should be a stable individual, with proper motivation for having the operation—namely, to look better and to feel better about herself. Most importantly, the patient should have realistic expectations about the operation.

That describes the ideal patient. Many of the people who actually come in for plastic surgery are few or none of those things. The surgeon must use his experience in weeding out those who would not get a good result or who would become hostile and litigious after the surgery, especially if there are complications.

Patients must also use their experience and knowledge in selecting the proper surgeon. How does one choose the surgeon to do this delicate and highly specialized surgery? Perhaps the best ways are to ask one's own family doctor for a recommendation, to call the medical society or the local hospital to find out whom they would recommend, or to consult with the surgeon who has given a good result to a friend. The consultation is a time when patients should learn whether they are a good risk for surgery. Is a patient ever too old? Probably not, as long as their health is good. A 40-year-old smoker with diabetes and heart disease is certainly a much less attractive candidate for surgery than a 70-year-old nonsmoker in good health.

Smoking should be discussed during the consultation, because it is a very definite contraindication to facial surgery. The skin of the face is rich in blood supply, and because nicotine seriously affects the blood vessels of the facial skin causing them to bleed much more, a smoker would have a much greater risk of bleeding, both during and after a face-lift. An attorney examining a patient who has suffered a hematoma after a face-lift should question her smoking history and ascertain whether the surgeon insisted she stop smoking prior to surgery.

Is there an ideal age to have a face-lift? The ideal age is the age when one feels she needs it. Everybody ages differently because of certain factors in their lives. People of Mediterranean ancestry such as Italians, Greeks, Spaniards, and blacks have more melanin in their skin than people from northern Europe. Melanin is that substance in the skin that protects it against the sun's harmful rays and also gives it its color. People of Irish, English, and Scandinavian backgrounds, on the other hand, have been exposed to difficult weather, winds, and cold for centuries, and this is etched on their faces. Their skin tends to be lighter and more delicate, with less melanin but more vascularity, and therefore more wrinkling.

Hormonal problems contribute to the condition of one's facial skin. After a hysterectomy, women often notice that their facial skin wrinkles and sags much more easily due to a lack of estrogen.

Certainly the amount of sun that one gets over the years is a factor in the deterioration of facial skin. In addition, heavy sun exposure causes a greater incidence of basal cell carcinoma (a common, slow-growing skin cancer) as well as other spots, marks, and lesions.

Last, but certainly not least, stress plays a large part in the aging of the skin. One who has had a difficult life, has had any sort of tragedy—for example, has sustained the loss of a mate or a child, has had a severe reversal in her business, or has gone through a divorce—can show the effects of this loss on her face and in the texture of her skin.

Therefore, the best time for anyone to have a face-lift should be when she needs it, and that time will be different for each of us.

§ 10.3 Informed Consent

Patients contemplating a face-lift often neither hear nor concentrate on the negative aspects of the operation. They are exhilarated at the prospect of having the surgery, because at that point in their lives the effects of aging show on their faces, and they are very anxious to look more youthful. In addition, many patients are no longer terribly frightened by facial surgery because of advertising, the patient's willingness to discuss the surgery, and the state of the art itself. It is because of the patient's exuberance that a second consultation is necessary.

During the first consultation, certain questions were asked and topics discussed. After the patients have had time to contemplate both the surgery and the initial discussion, the surgeon should see them a second time to review their photographs with them and answer any further questions. Then the all-important informed consent information should be given.

The informed consent information for a face-lift consists largely in preparing patients for the emotional trauma of seeing themselves swollen and discolored after the surgery. Patients have facial surgery to improve their appearance. They may go in the operation wrinkled or with sagging skin but they are shocked when they see themselves coming out in various degrees of edema and ecchymoses. Each patient is unique and, because of the physical and emotional factors already discussed, each postoperative period is different.

It is during the consultation that the patient learns of the swelling and discoloration, and that the face may look somewhat distorted for the first few weeks. Some surgeons feel that, in addition to discussing the complications of the surgery with the patient during this informed consent consultation, it is wise to mention that many patients go into a postoperative depression after facial surgery. The reason for this is obvious: they come in for improvement and when the bandages come off, the swelling, discoloration, and distortion of their faces look worse to them than their wrinkles did before. Some patients find it difficult to endure a period of relative unattractiveness when they may be confined to their homes, segregated from society. They should be told of this before the surgery and prepare to develop some activities that they can perform by themselves. They should be relaxed about taking a certain amount of time away from their work.

It is during this informed consent consultation that the surgeon goes over the location of the incisions on the face with the patient and tells them of possible complications that could occur.

An older patient who has a face-lift looks good for the first six months to one year until the swelling is totally gone, and then there is a certain relaxation of the skin of the face and neck. Many surgeons feel that some patients will have to undergo a secondary procedure a year or so after the operation to tighten up the slack that has occurred due a lack of elasticity in older skin. Therefore the patient should be aware that a secondary procedure, although not inevitable, may be necessary and the surgeon will advise her of it if and when the time comes. It is during the second consultation also that the medical history and physical examination should be carefully reviewed. The laboratory work should be done, any bleeding problem should be addressed prior to surgery, and any allergies to anesthetics or medication should be discovered. If there are any cardiac problems, such as mitral valve stenosis or arrhythmias, an internist and/or cardiologist should be consulted. A medical clearance for surgery must be obtained in writing from this specialist.

Many malpractice suits are brought because of a systemic medical problem that was not thoroughly investigated by the plastic surgeon. One case involved a woman who was diabetic and had arterial disease of the leg for which she was medicated with an anticoagulant. Her local internist stopped the patient's Coumadin 10 days before the surgery, which she had discussed with him. After surgery the patient did well as far as the cosmetic improvement went, but formed a blood clot in her leg because of her immobility during the general anesthesia. She then developed a pulmonary embolism. When the case came to trial, the family doctor denied knowing about the operation, much less giving his consent. The defense attorney questioned the internist and found that he had stopped the Coumadin in preparation for surgery. When asked why he stopped the anticoagulant, he said that the patient requested it. His testimony was discredited and a settlement was made in favor of the defendant based on the defense's ability to discredit the internist. However, it would have been better for the plastic surgeon had this internist given a written consent and clearance for the surgery.

If there is a medical problem, many specialists will be hesitant to give the patient medical clearance for surgery, because they will have to share some of the liability if anything should happen during the surgery. Nonetheless, it is essential for the plastic surgeon to obtain medical clearance for any elective procedure if there is any questionable medical history.

A similar consultation should be obtained from a psychologist or a psychiatrist if the plastic surgeon suspects any emotional or psychiatric problem on the part of the patient. If these are present, and if the patient is on any medication or has any history of psychiatric illness, it might be better to postpone the surgery until a definite psychiatric clearance is obtained.

§ 10.4 Clinical Indications for Surgery

Many plastic surgeons divide the face conceptually into three thirds. The upper third includes the forehead and eyelids, the middle third is comprised of the cheeks and mouth, and the lower third takes in the jaws, jowls, chin, and neck. The skin of the eyelids, of course, is usually the first place where degeneration is seen (see **Chapter 9**). Most patients see degeneration in the nasolabial area and the jowls and neck next. These are the areas that gravity attacks first, pulling the skin downward because of a lack of elasticity. Many patients who come for a face-lift do not have wrinkles as such, but have sagging in these areas, especially those patients who tend to be slightly overweight.

These *nasolabial lines* are furrows that go from the corners of the nose to the sides of the lips. They are the natural boundaries of the cheek muscles. These furrows have on one side tight skin above the lip with no subcutaneous fat beneath it and, on the other side, the loose, sagging skin of the cheek with more generous areas of fat and subcutaneous tissue within, causing them to sag lateral to the nasolabial lines.

Patients should be told that, although the nasolabial lines can be softened, they can never be taken away totally. Patients who feel that this operation will cure that problem are ill-advised by their surgeons or have unrealistic expectations themselves.

The jowls and jawline are areas that patients like to have corrected because they show clearly the signs of aging. Patients without wrinkles may have sagging of the skin in this area, or may have fat jowls. If this is just a skin problem, a face-lift can correct this. If there is fat present, some liposuction may be necessary.

The wattle under the chin and the columns of skin seen in the neck can cause problems. Patients with disturbances in this area have either a problem with excess skin or a laxity of the platysma muscle. The platysma muscle has recently achieved popularity in the area of facial surgery. Ligation of the platysma muscle may enhance the look of the neck and chin and lessen the "turkey gobbler" deformity. A suctioning or a direct excision of fat in the submental area often enhances the result.

Patients with small wrinkles and senile changes of the skin of the neck because of atrophy from constant exposure to the sun over the years sometimes expect a total rejuvenation, but this is seldom the case. The areas of small wrinkles on the skin of older patients are usually not corrected completely with a face-lift but are only improved for a period of time because of the loss of elasticity in this type of skin.

Some deep lines or furrows of the face in the glabellar area (the area between the eyebrows) cause patients considerable difficulty. It is often difficult to treat these areas. Various cosmetic procedures have been tried over the years, including excision of the deep furrows between the brows, filling them with collagen or silicone, and obliterating the muscle underneath to stop the continuous force on this area. Nothing is very successful. The newest procedure of injecting the patient's own fat into these lines seems as successful as anything else, but the patient should always be advised that, if the lines are due to frowning, a permanent line is etched in the face and, even though the skin around it can be pulled, evidence of a furrow will remain.

Adjunctive procedures to improve the looks of the face are:

1. Forehead or frontal lift for patients with deep wrinkles or furrows in the forehead

2. Malar implants to augment the cheek bones
3. Liposuction of the face to give a more shallow appearance to certain areas in the cheeks, the neck, and submental area
4. Augmentation of the chin with an implant.

These will all help improve the appearance of the face if the indications are present.

§ 10.5 Anatomy of the Face

The skin of the face usually ages more quickly than the skin of the rest of the body. The rate of aging depends on so many factors that it is difficult to standardize them. Certainly exposure to the elements as well as heredity, chemical composition of the skin, the degree of elasticity, life-style, and other factors account for one individual's face aging more than another's. Skin folds and wrinkles develop in several different places and are the result of a combination of gravitational, dynamic, and orthostatic forces. The muscles used in facial expressions are intimately involved with the inner portion of the skin. The overlying skin develops wrinkles and lines because of the constant and continuous movement of these facial muscles.

The lines around the eyelids develop first because of the constant smiling, laughing, and blinking of one's eyes. This, coupled with the fact that eyelid skin is the thinnest skin in the body, accounts for the fact that many people need an eyelid operation before they need a face-lift. Gravity deepens the nasolabial folds and brings the skin of the cheeks down to the relaxed condition of the jowls. Glabellar frown lines develop at variable ages depending on individuals' expression patterns. These lines are caused by the action of the *corrugater supercilii muscles,* or the muscles that wrinkles the eyebrows. The forehead shows frown lines because of expression. Some people's foreheads wrinkle very early in their lives. The gravitational lines develop usually around the age of 40 in the area of the orbit, the zygoma, and the mandible.

In addition to constant use and movement of the facial muscles, there is an atrophy of subcutaneous tissue in many areas of the face as one ages. This, coupled with a lack of elasticity and continued constant movement, causes wrinkles, furls, and lines as well as a doughy quality to the skin. The force of gravity on the skin of the neck over the medial portion of the platysma muscles can form two long, vertical folds, often called "turkey gobbler neck." The intervening submental fat pad can increase, forming a noticeable wattle beneath the chin.

When considering doing a face-lift, the surgeon must be aware of the crucial structures to be encountered in the dissection, particularly the five branches of the facial nerve. The facial nerve is the seventh cranial nerve and it gives motor function (movement) to the muscles of facial expressions. It is usually protected from the subcutaneous tissues especially over the temporal, cheek, cervical, and rectoauricular areas (see **Figure 10–1**).

The cheek consists of two distinct compartments, the preauricular and the parotid/masseteric areas. These are covered by deep fascia with the superficial temporal vessels, the parotid gland, and the facial nerve beneath. The skin is closely connected to the fascia in these areas. There is a fat pad anterior to the masseter muscle that is referred to as the *buccal fat pad* and it has a posterior extension between the masseter and the buccinator muscles. The duct of the parotid gland is seen in the area of the buccinator muscle. The parotid gland travels along the lateral surface of the buccinator muscle and empties into the mouth through the duct in the oral mucosa. The skin in the area over the buccal fat pad can be raised by careful blunt dissection as far as the nasolabial folds. The buccal branches of the facial nerve lie at a deeper level than the subcutaneous tissue and can be avoided unless the muscle itself is entered. The buccal fat pads help to protect the parotid duct.

In the temporal area, the scalp is intimately involved with the deep fascia. Dissection of scalp tissue should be performed below the level of this aponeurotic layer to prevent destruction of the hair follicles. If large spots

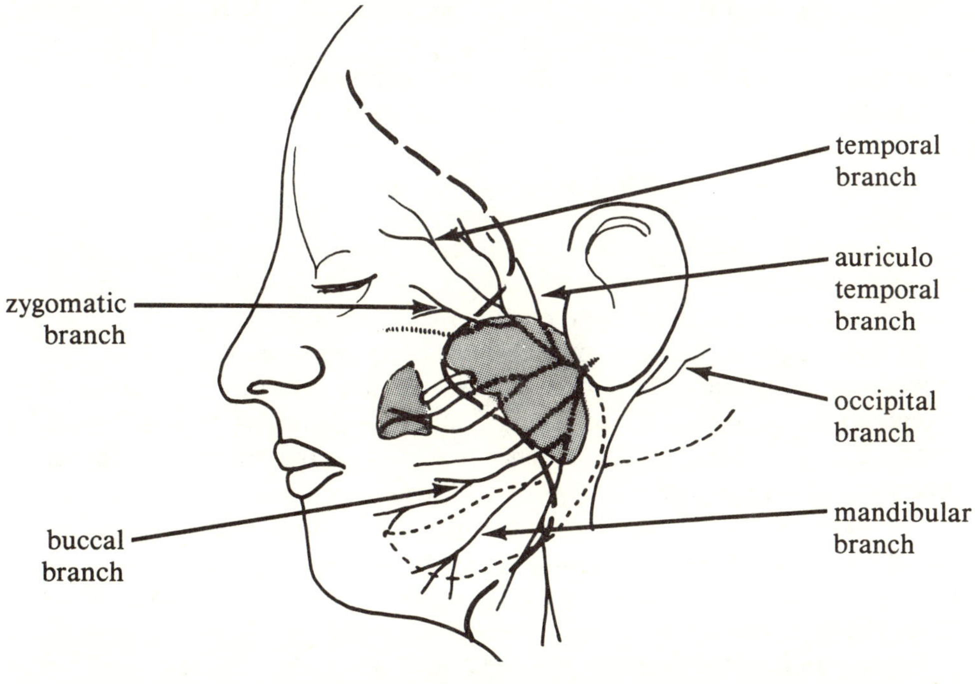

Figure 10–1. The facial nerve exits through the sternomastomastoid foramen near the ear and breaks into its five branches.

of alopecia or baldness are seen in the temporal area, it may be because the hair follicles have been interfered with and the dissection was carried out on too superficial a plane. As the dissection goes toward the lateral portion of the eye, it should become very superficial right underneath the skin to avoid the frontal branch of the facial nerve. Although on many anatomical specimens and drawings the course of the branches of the facial nerve can be followed, there are individual differences, and many times an aberrant branch can cause difficulty by not being where it is anticipated.

The superficial temporal artery is a branch of the external carotid artery and is found in the area of the parotid gland. It divides into two smaller branches, which are found beneath the superficial layer of the temporal fascia. These are important to know because excessive bleeding will result if these vessels are cut. Other arteries of the face—such as branches of the transverse facial artery, a branch to the superficial temporal artery, or the middle temporal artery arising above the zygomatic arch and perforating the temporal fascia—are often cut and coagulated.

One of the most frequently injured structures in the course of a face-lift operation is the greater auricular nerve. This is the largest of the nerve branches from the cervical plexis. The nerve goes upon the sternomastoid muscle beneath the platysma into the parotid gland and provides sensory intervention to the mastoid process, the back of the auricle, and the earlobe. Cutting of this nerve results in anesthesia in the areas mentioned. Sectioning of other nerves in this area such as the lesser occipital nerve, the greater auricular nerve, and the posterior auricular branch of the facial nerve often results in permanent loss of sensation in the innervated areas.

Platysma muscles extending over the lower part of the mandible are delineated by a line extending from the tragus of the ear to the edge of the mouth. Beneath the platysma are the branches of the facial nerves. The marginal mandibular branch lies under the platysma muscle at varying levels and can become involved when a *SMAS* (Superficial, musculoaponeurotic system) procedure or cutting of the platysma muscle is done.

With the new techniques in face-lifting, the platysma muscle becomes even more significant than it had been. It is a broad, thin muscle connected by the superficial fascia which is divided into superficial and deep layers. The platysma muscle extends upward to the tragus of the ear. It goes toward the medial portion of the neck and reaches the superhyoid region where it sends fibers to the mental or chin bones (see **Figure 10–2**). A section of this platysma muscle in the submandibular area can produce a weakness that may simulate injury to the marginal mandibular branch of the facial nerve.

The platysma muscle joins the platysma from the opposite side below the chin, leaving a triangular area devoid of either muscle. This forms the border of the submental triangle where the submental fat is frequently seen and often excised during a surgical procedure.

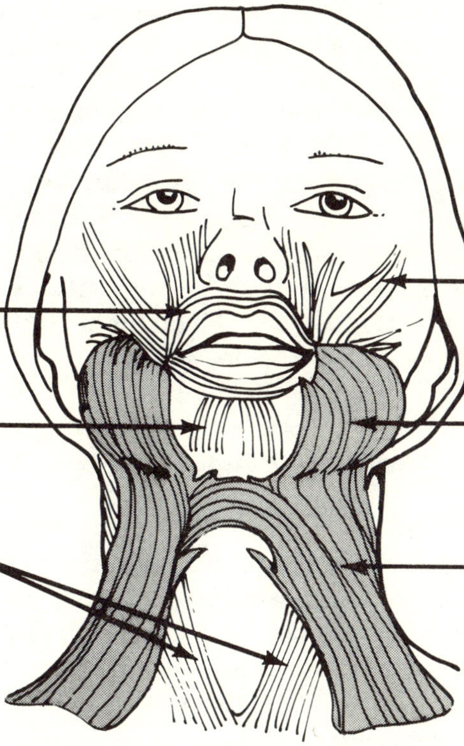

Figure 10–2. Anterior view of some of the muscles of facial expression.

The two techniques presently used for face-lift surgery are:

1. The superficial or subcutaneous dissection, which is the classical method of skin lift operations. This operation is performed by separating the platysma muscle from the overlying skin, leaving all muscles in place.
2. The second and more modern technique is based on the superficial musculo-aponeurotic system described by Skoog in 1974[1] and is now known as the SMAS technique.

§ 10.6 Anesthesia

The type of anesthesia used must be carefully discussed with the patient prior to surgery. Anesthesia is usually one of the patient's greatest fears. The type of anesthesia used for many face-lifts in this country today is a combination of local anesthesia with a "standby" anesthesia. The local medication is Xylocaine (lidocaine) for the anesthetic effect, in combination with a small amount of Adrenaline (epinephrine) for vasoconstriction.

---

[1] Skoog, T., Plastic Surgery—New Methods and Refinements (1974).

A standby anesthesia calls for an anesthesiologist or nurse anesthetist to administer preoperative medication and keep an intravenous line open during the surgery. At the same time they inject Pentothal or Valium, and Versed, which gives amnesia during the time of surgery. The anesthetist will maintain the patient's airway, make sure that the blood oxygen saturation level is adequate throughout the procedure, and monitor vital signs (blood pressure, respiration, pulse, and heart beat) for the duration of the surgery. This makes the operation safer for the patient and easier for the surgeon, who does not have time to concentrate on these vital things while she is performing the surgery. The patient is assured of a safer and more peaceful journey through the operation.

§ 10.7 Description of a Standard Operation

Prior to surgery the patient is taken to the operating room and the face and hair are washed with a cleansing solution. The hair is combed and separated in the temporal and postauricular areas where the incisions will be made. The patient lies supine with the head turned toward the left, leaving the right side ready for surgery. The facial skin is marked with a felt tip pen in the area of the incisions and out to the limits of the undermining. Local anesthesia is then injected. Pentothal has already been given, so the patient does not feel discomfort from the injection of local anesthesia. The Pentothal lasts for several minutes, at which time the patient returns to a greater state of consciousness and the operation begins.

The incision is made in the appropriate area of the temple, in front of the ears, under the lobe, onto the back of the ear and into the hair-bearing postauricular skin (see **Figure 10–3**). The skin is then undermined (separated from its underlying attachments), approximately from 3 inches on the front of the face to between 4 and 5 inches on the jaw and neck, leaving it free and flexible and able to be moved and repositioned.

Hemostasis, the coagulation of the blood vessels, is obtained now with great care. If even a small vessel bleeds postoperatively, a hematoma could develop, threatening the ultimate good result of a face-lift.

The facial skin is pulled upward and backward behind the ear, carefully redraping it over the face in a smoother, tighter fashion (see **Figure 10–4**). The excess, lax skin is measured, so the same amount is removed from each side, and excised in preparation for reapproximation of the edges. Stitches are placed above and beyond the ear under tension, to hold the skin firmly in its new position. The excess skin is now marked and excised and the remaining skin is sutured to the scalp and the areas around the ear with different types of sutures, depending on the thickness of the skin in that area (see **Figure 10–5**). A similar procedure is then carried out on the other side of the face.

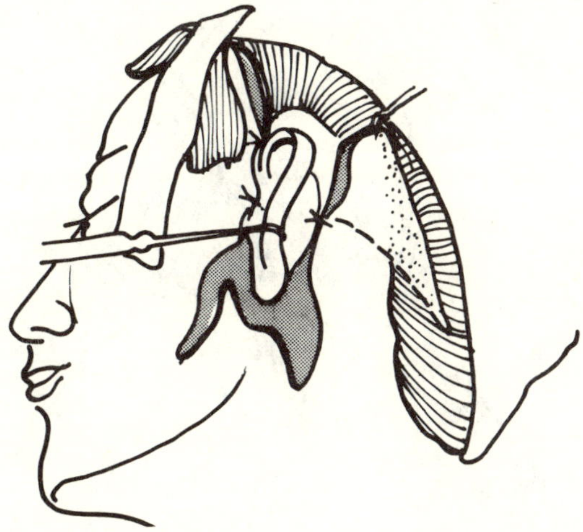

Figure 10–3. The standard face-lift incisions start in the temporal area and extend in front of the ear, behind the tragus, under the lobe, behind the concha, and backward into the hair-bearing postauricular skin. The darkened area represents the skin to be excised. The two tension stitches above and beyond the ear provide the greatest point of fixation for the facial skin.

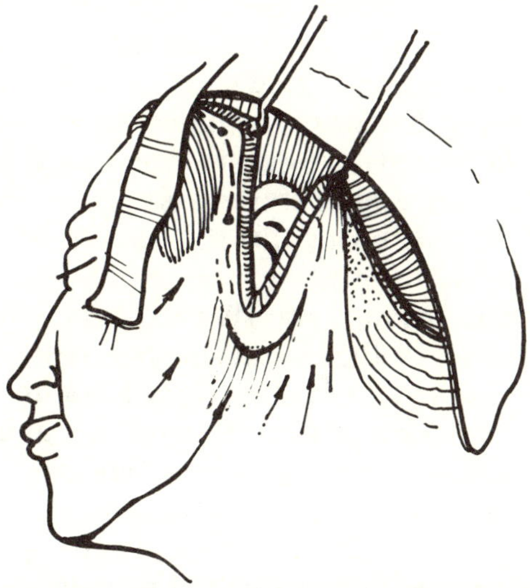

Figure 10–4. The skin is undermined with a standard face-lift incision and is pulled upward and backward, draping it over the ear from which it will eventually be excised.

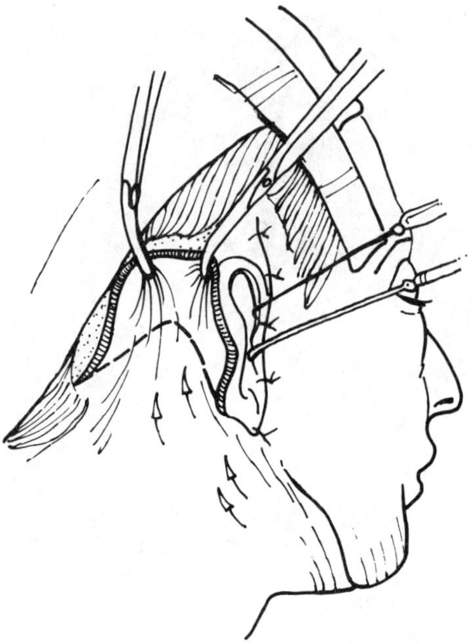

Figure 10–5. The preauricular and temporal portions of the face-lift incisions are sutured in place in front of the ear and the posterior portion of the face and neck are pulled upward and backward. The dotted line shows where the excess skin will be excised.

§ 10.8 Postoperative Care

The postoperative period is of great importance for good healing. The patient should remain quiet, lying supine with the head slightly elevated. For the most part visiting with friends is discouraged. One family member might remain with the patient for a short time, but should not encourage talking. Telephone conversations are not allowed. Good monitoring by the staff is essential, as it is during this period that hematomas arise, and must be detected immediately.

The patient has a firm pressure dressing around the head and neck after the operation, but enough of the cheeks are exposed to detect an expanding hematoma. The intravenous feeding should continue until the patient is fully reactive. Oral intake is limited to ice chips and clear liquids with some soft food on the day of surgery. A soft diet may be resumed the following day and care should be taken not to chew meats and other substances that would require too much activity in the cheek area.

There is minimal pain with this operation, therefore a mild analgesic should be enough to make the patient comfortable. She may feel some pulling and tightness in the neck area due to the edema; this will begin to recede a few days after the surgery. On the day following the surgery, the patient can be out of bed and go home to continue resting postoperatively in a familiar setting. Activities should be strictly limited. The patient returns to the surgeon's office after six to seven days for removal of the sutures in front of the ears. It is at this time that the patient may take a shower, but care should be used not to disturb the areas of incision, as the stitches are still in place and healing has not been completed. The remainder of the stitches are removed 12 to 14 days postoperatively. Working and other normal activities should not be resumed for approximately two weeks and any exercise or athletic activity should be limited until one month has passed.

During this two-week period the normal postoperative sequelae will be: discoloration of the skin of the face and abnormal swelling that may distort the patient's look and cause alarm. These are not complications; they are simply the results of a normal surgery and normal healing. There may be stiffness in the neck; the head should not be turned very much for the first few days because of the tension placed on the neck. The degree of discomfort is a good limiting factor for activity.

Smoking should be prohibited at least 10 days prior to surgery and definitely during the postoperative healing period. Sexual activity should be avoided as well as anything else that could cause a rise in blood pressure and vital signs.

An example of bad postoperative care can be seen in the case of a registered nurse, age 48, who had a face-lift. The operation was uneventful, and the results before the dressing was applied were good. The patient was an overly energetic woman who wanted to prove to herself and others that even surgery could not keep her down. Although she was carefully warned by the surgeon about smoking, the nurses on the ward reported that the night of surgery, she smoked several cigarettes, and was sitting up in her bed moving around as if to prove she did not have to take the normal care that most people do because she was stronger. The following day she was on the telephone constantly with friends and family and when visited by the surgeon she was quick to douse a cigarette in an ashtray that she concealed in the night table drawer. She was warned about her overactivity and was sent home with the usual caveats.

The patient confided to one of the nurses that when she went home she had to drive her neighbors back and forth to various places. She felt it necessary to mow the lawn three days after surgery. When she came to visit the surgeon, she was constantly chided about this type of activity and warned that this could lead to serious and permanent bad results. She retained a pleasant affect, bright and cheery, assuring the surgeon that she would be able to get through this: after all, she was a nurse and she knew her own body better than anyone else did.

The patient developed a superficial epidermolysis on the right side of the neck: the skin flap on the right side of the neck shed its epidermal layer because of her overactivity and smoking. In continuing to turn her head to the side where the telephone was located during the day after the surgery, she exerted too much pressure on the skin and caused blood vessels in that area to die. She was treated for the infection with antibiotics and soaks and the area had "granulated in," eventually healing with a predictable discoloration to the skin. When she realized several months later that the result of her behavior was an unsightly scar going down the right side of her neck, she instituted a malpractice action against the surgeon.

It is easy to see that malpractice in this case was committed by the patient and not the surgeon. Good documentation of nurses' notes, confidence given to the nurses by the patient, caveats, and the careful informed consent consultation by the surgeon were crucial in this case to avoid liability and culpability.

Although the operation and the skills of the surgeon of course are of utmost importance, the necessity for the patient's smooth postoperative period is of equal importance and can be determinative of the result.

§ 10.9 Complications and Undesirable Results

Complications of facial surgery fall into two categories: objective or physical, and subjective or psychological. The subjective complications of a face-lift arise from patients expecting to acquire a beauty or a look previously unknown to them or expecting to look substantially younger than before. These patients are disappointed with any surgical result no matter how good it is, and they become hostile and angry with the surgeon because the dream that was sought was not realized. These are the patients who will cause more disruption in the doctor/patient relationship than any other kind. They are upset and angry. They possibly have some mild to severe emotional disturbance and should not have been chosen as candidates for the surgery in the first place. If the surgeon could detect these traits in a patient before surgery is undertaken, there would be far fewer problems for all concerned.

Even the experienced surgeon, however, may find it difficult to decide which patients will have an inordinate number of subjective complaints after the surgery. The patient reacts completely differently before surgery than after. Before surgery, patients are excited, anticipatory, and eager to have the surgery, if somewhat anxious about the discomfort and the outcome. Once surgery has been performed and reality sets in, patients become more vulnerable. They become impatient with waiting for a good result, they are unhappy when they look in the mirror and see their faces distorted with swelling and discoloration. They do not want to wait for their eventual good result but often wish they could go back to their preoperative state, because many times they look worse during the healing period than they did before the surgery.

It is during this period that a certain amount of complaining and questioning takes place on the part of the patient. Patients are often anxious and scared when they see the distortion in their faces, and must look to the surgeon for guidance about the outcome, which is based on experience and expertise. Surgeons, on the other hand, should not become too defensive about queries and complaints during this period, for it is often frightening for patients to see themselves distorted, even though a clear and fair warning has been given prior to their surgery. Reading about swelling and discoloration is certainly a different experience for the patient than looking into a mirror to see the face to which she has been accustomed looking totally different. An identity crisis may take place, and patients with any emotional disturbances at this point will have a more difficult time coping with this temporary condition than others do.

The surgeon and staff must be supportive of the patient at this time and yet must remain firm, not subjugating their authority to the whims and aggression of the patients.

The objective or physical complications following surgery are certainly more real, and any or some of them may occur with any given patient. The importance of the informed consent now becomes obvious. A patient who is not trained in facial surgery nor experienced in the viewing of postoperative swelling and discoloration will not be able to make the proper decision about having surgery unless informed of all the potential complications. Many things can happen to a patient postoperatively. The common complications are:

1. Hematoma
2. Infection
3. Skin slough
4. Pigment changes
5. Excessive scarring
6. Alopecia
7. Nerve injury
8. Numbness, sensitivity, and hypersensitivity
9. Pain
10. Need for secondary surgery.

§ 10.10 —Hematoma

A large or expanding hematoma is a serious problem if it is not immediately detected. The intrusion of large amounts of coagulated or clotted blood can cause tension on the skin, causing it to slough or die. The immediate treatment for this type of hematoma is to remove the stitches in the area and evacuate the hematoma—that is, clear away the clotted blood, and find and coagulate the incriminating blood vessel or vessels—and allow the skin to go back to its new attachments.

Expanding hematomas are usually unilateral, although they can be seen on both sides. When a hematoma occurs on one side, the difference in the two sides of the patient's face is remarkable. The usual place for the expansion of a hematoma is in front of the ear, although it can occur in the neck or behind the ear at the same time or separately. Most hematomas occur within the first 12 hours after surgery. This is caused by a rise in blood pressure due to any number of factors. Blood pressure can rise while the patient is being moved from the stretcher to the bed, coughing and vomiting would certainly stimulate bleeding, and extubation of a laryngotrachial tube after general anesthesia disturbs a patient's blood pressure. A small plug can be loosened from the end of a coagulated vessel at this time and trickle blood into the subcutaneous area.

In one case, an older female patient who was hypertensive but was being controlled by medication during the surgery had an uneventful operation. An inexperienced nurse anesthetist came into the room as the surgery was being finished because the anesthesiologist was called to another room. Not realizing the difficulty of extubation with this patient, the anesthetist administered a drug called Narcan, which reversed the effects of the sedatives and caused the patient to become awake and agitated before the dressings were applied. Bilateral hematomas were immediately seen and had to be evacuated. In this case the anesthetist was negligent, and responsible for causing the hematomas because of the lack of a quiet transition from anesthesia to consciousness.

Small hematomas or spot hematomas can occur any time after the operation for the first 24 hours to the first several days. These are less problematic but should be aspirated or expressed as soon as detected. A failure to evacuate these small hematomas could result in organization of the clot. The result of this could be a discoloration of the overlying skin, and it may take several months before the skin regains its normal appearance and texture. This change in pigmentation may even be permanent, and has been the basis for many lawsuits. Small areas of bleeding under the skin will be detected as the generalized edema recedes, usually in the first week to 10 days after surgery. It is often at this time that a liquifying blood clot can be aspirated with a 20 gauge needle.

A blood study should be done prior to surgery to rule out any serious blood disorders and, if they are present, the face-lift should either not be done or a hematologist should be consulted.

§ 10.11 —Infection

Because of the rich blood supply to the skin of the face, infection is rare in face-lift patients. The most common sight for infection is behind the ears because of the proximity of the hair. The greatest amount of pressure and tension is exerted on this area, and it is also the area where the skin flap is the thinnest. The hair, no matter how well washed or cleansed, is never completely free of bacteria. It is advisable to have the patient wash her hair with a cleansing preparation the night before surgery, and then to wash again in the operating room with a Betadine-type preparation.

It is often advisable to start the patient on antibiotics a day or two before surgery or at the time of surgery to prevent this type of infection. Although antibiotics are often thought to be too readily prescribed for common colds and other minor infections, it seems that prevention of an infection in an important operation like a face-lift, thereby preventing possible permanent damage and irreversible scarring to the skin, would justify the use of any antibiotic therapy prior to and after the surgery. The use of a broad spectrum antibiotic is recommended, particularly Erythromycin, Ampicillin or Keflex. It may be used for a period of five to seven days until the patient gets past the initial healing period, during which time most infections occur.

One patient, who had an uneventful face-lift, had a certain amount of swelling in the postauricular areas. In addition, she had long stringy hair that she did not seem to keep away from the area. She developed an infection in the left postauricular area because the hair was near the wound, the flap was thin, and she had a moderate amount of edema. When given an antibiotic, the patient failed to fill the prescription, but instead brushed her hair to keep it out of the area. She returned to her home state before the stitches could be removed. When she developed an infection in this left postauricular area and the skin sloughed due to infection, it granulated in in a discolored fashion. She then started a suit against the surgeon, although she had received all the appropriate instruction and warnings. The suit was eventually thrown out in a pretrial hearing because there was no liability on the part of the surgeon.

§ 10.12 —Skin Slough

Skin slough is a disaster to a face-lift. It is a result of compromised marginal circulation in the skin flaps, and is frequently caused by a hematoma, but can be caused by edema, or external pressure on the skin. Furthermore, when the skin is dissected and the flap is developed there should be a small area of subcutaneous fat on the flap to make sure that the subdermal blood supply is intact. Development of too thin a flap can cause skin slough, especially in the areas of greatest pressure, behind the ears. The postauricular area is the most common place for this to happen, because that part of the flap is farthest from its base where blood supply originates. Occasionally skin can slough in front of the ear because of either too tightly or too thinly developed flaps, hematomas, edema, or external pressure. Too tight a dressing can cause unwanted pressure. When this happens in front of the ear, it is even more disastrous because it is more visible. The postauricular skin slough, however, is behind the ears and not apparent to most onlookers. The result of a skin slough is the formation of an eschar or scab behind the ear. This should be gently debrided from time to time to allow the skin to reepithelialize.

The usual result, six months after the operation, is not as bad as it looks at the beginning, but it does have a discoloration, a redness, and a different texture of tissue. The possibility of skin slough must be carefully discussed with the patient before surgery.

§ 10.13 —Pigment Changes

Occasionally a pigment change is seen in the skin of the face and around the neck, particularly in the area of the greatest tension. Two types of pigment changes are noted. The first is a whitish scar that can occur with an infection (**§ 10.11**) or skin slough (**§ 10.12**). This white scar tissue heals over in the areas when a partial or a full thickness of skin has been lost due to tension, infection, or pressure on the delicate skin flap.

The second type of pigment change is seen when a pinkish hue appears on the skin. This results from a recanalization of the blood vessels, again caused by even normal amounts of tension upon the skin flaps after the operation is done. This is not abnormal in some subjects and should be mentioned in the informed consent before the surgery. It often appears as a slightly reddened or subtle inflammation in the neck area and, although it will decrease, it may not disappear entirely and may be a permanent change. It should be treated with vitamin E and/or steroid cream. It is a minor complication but one that seems to annoy some patients.

§ 10.14 —Scarring

It must be made clear to the patient prior to the surgery that any time a surgical incision is made on any part of the body the resulting healing is called a scar. What is important is how the scar will heal. This has been discussed previously in these chapters and of course it is difficult to predict prior to the fact. Scarring in the normal incision areas can be reddened and thick, depending on the patient's ethnic or racial background as well as the degree of tension placed on that part of the wound. Incisions in front of the ears should have no tension placed on them so that the skin will have the best opportunity of healing without an unattractive scar.

The scars in the back of the ears and into the hairline have been described in **§§ 10.11** through **10.13**. Scars can be reddened and thicker, however, without an infection or a skin slough. The stitches should be removed in front of the ears approximately six to seven days after the surgery to relieve the tension, thereby allowing that all-important visible preauricular scar to heal well. The stitches behind the ears should stay in for somewhat longer, perhaps 10 to 14 days in all, depending on the patient's healing, to make sure that there is no separation in this area. These are usually thicker stitches (3-0 nylon) than the stitches in front of the ears (6-0 silk). The reason for this is the degree of pull and tension that is transferred to the areas above and behind the ear and not where the scar can be seen.

§ 10.15 —Hair Loss

A certain amount of hair loss occurs after a face-lift. Some surgeons shave the areas in which the incisions will be made; others do not, but instead part the hair and make the incisions by removing a certain portion of hair. As the facial skin is advanced upward and backward, the excess is removed. When the skin edges are approximated, a scar will be formed and no hair can grow on this (hopefully thin) scar. However, if there is too much tension put on the area and the skin flap in the temporal area is too thin, thereby interfering with the hair follicles, a certain loss of hair will be demonstrated in these areas. Although it may spontaneously regrow, some subjects show permanent damage to the hair follicles with resulting baldness in these areas called *alopecia,* which is considered a complication of this procedure.

Often when a surgeon is performing a face-lift on a female patient, he should question her as to the way she likes to wear her hair. It cannot always be guaranteed that the hair will be able to be worn pulled back, because sometimes the scarring behind the ears will show. It is important for the surgeon to indicate to the patient where exactly these scars will be, and if that interferes with her wearing her hair in certain styles she may want either to reconsider having the operation or to discuss a modification of the surgery with the surgeon.

Another problem exists as far as the hair distribution in males. Certain men who are bald cannot tolerate a face-lift because the scarring, especially in the temporal area, will be visible on the naked scalp, and this would be undesirable. A surgeon should not operate on a totally bald man, in whose case the incisions cannot be concealed, because even though the patient may initially think that he wants it, more likely than not, after the surgery has been performed and the excitement of a younger-looking face has been experienced, there will be recriminations about the appearance of scars on a bald head and the patient will be unhappy.

Similarly, in the male patient the preauricular incision comes down adjacent to the sideburns, and the sideburns are usually advanced somewhat closer to the front of the ear. This is not usually a problem but it should be explained to men preoperatively so they will know that the sideburns may be narrower, or the hairless space between the ear and the lateral edge of the sideburns may be decreased. In addition, the male patient should be forewarned that in the advancement of the large neck and facial skin flaps, the skin bearing the beard will be advanced behind the ears, and it will be necessary for him to shave an inch or two farther back into his neck and scalp. Most men do not mind this, but they must be informed about it before the surgery is performed.

§ 10.16 —Nerve Injury

The facial nerve (the seventh cranial nerve) innervates the muscles of facial expression. It comes out of a foramen in the bone in front of the ear and forms five secondary branches that move the muscles of the forehead, eyelid area, cheek, mouth, and jaw. The branches most often incriminated in facial nerve palsy as a result of face-lifting are the frontal branch, the temporal branch, and the buccal branch of the facial nerve. These branches become superficial at certain points in the face and are intimately involved with facial muscle movement.

A small branch of this facial nerve could be inadvertently cut during surgery if the surgeon goes into the muscular planes or if there is an aberrant branch in the normal plane of dissection. If the buccal branch of the facial branch is cut, there will be drooping at the side of the mouth. If the frontal of the facial nerve is cut, there will be an inability to frown or flex the forehead. This can be the result of trauma caused by electrocautery while the blood vessels are being coagulated, or can be caused by edema of the surrounding tissues. In secondary face-lifts, the amount of scar tissue can sometimes obliterate the endings of the facial nerve. In the instances of edema or coagulation of the nerve, paralysis will improve as the swelling recedes or the function of the nerve returns. This usually takes about six months and the patient should be warned that most paralyses are temporary. If the nerve is cut, however, the paralysis is permanent, and grafting must be done at an early date, the sooner the better. This procedure of nerve grafting has somewhat limited results.

As important as the preoperative evaluation of a patient for facial surgery is the evaluation of the facial nerve. Often a patient has a weakened or decreased function of a branch of the facial nerve prior to surgery. The unwitting surgeon will operate on this patient and notice the slow muscle function postoperatively, attributing it to the surgery, when in fact it was there all the time. A helpful way of finding out a weakness in the facial nerve branch is through the preoperative photographs. The photographer should encourage the patient to smile, wrinkle the forehead, and make other facial grimaces to discover any such preoperative weakness. This is certainly one reason why preoperative photographs are essential.

§ 10.17 —Numbness and Hypersensitivity

An insensitivity or numbness in the face is caused by the cutting of the small sensory (not motor) nerves to the skin of the face. This is a normal sequela of all facial surgery, because the facial skin must be undermined and separated from the underlying tissues. These nerves usually regenerate two to four months after surgery but the face will be numb during this period. It can take longer for feeling to return and occasionally, although infrequently, the insensitivity is permanent. This must be explained to the patient prior to surgery. One very important reason for explaining the postoperative numbness to a patient is that otherwise it will be thought to be a complication and not a normal occurrence after surgery. Secondly, the male who must shave and cannot feel his face as he could before can inadvertently cut his face if he is not aware that it is numb.

Occasionally, the face becomes hypersensitive because of a change in the nerve pattern to the skin. This hypersensitivity usually goes away but it is a rare condition in patients and is not normal after surgery.

§ 10.18 —Pain

The patient may have pain from the surgery but it is usually just discomfort. Pain comes when a nerve has been cut or damaged in some way and a neuroma, which is the scar tissue surrounding a nerve, forms. Usually this does not happen with face-lifts and the patient is pain-free. If there is pain however, analgesics, warm soaks, and massage can be effective measures of relief. Usually after several months the scar tissue decreases in the area around the nerve and the pain or discomfort diminishes.

An unstable patient might blame a surgeon for pain that is unrelated to the surgery. In one case, a 72-year-old female had undergone her second face-lift with the same surgeon. The operation went well, the results were objectively excellent, but what the surgeon didn't know was that, in the seven years between the face-lifts, the woman's mental status had deteriorated and she had become an unreliable reporter of circumstances. She complained of pain in the top of her head, and described it as a "toothache." She became so obsessed with the alleged pain in the top of her head that she went to a neurologist who facetiously told her that sometimes a cut nerve could cause this type of pain after a face-lift.

In fact, no nerve in the operative site of a face-lift could cause the kind of pain that she described, especially the occipital nerve, which was suggested. The patient sued the surgeon, using the words of the neurologist as her proof of negligence. The neurologist tried to deny his statement. The patient's personality continued to deteriorate, and she exhibited unusual slovenliness in dress, abusive talk to her staff and associates, and garbled and incoherent talk. None of these psychological factors were caused by the face-lift. A psychiatric consultation done on this patient prior to the second surgery might have persuaded the physician not to operate.

§ 10.19 Adjunctive Procedures

Many other new advancements have been made in facial contouring in addition to the classical face-lift operation. These new and additional techniques provide other modalities by which the surgeon can improve and change the shape and dimensions of the patient's face. Some of these procedures are:

1. Frontal or forehead lifts
2. Submental lipectomy
3. Liposuction of the cheeks and neck
4. The SMAS procedure
5. Fat transplant in the nasolabial and glabellar lines
6. Chemical peel
7. Dermabrasion
8. Injections of silicone or collagen.

Some of these procedures are discussed in other chapters, and some of them are discussed in the following sections.

§ 10.20 —Frontal or Forehead Lifts

A frontal or forehead lift is not a new concept in face-lift surgery. It was described as early as 1910 but has become popular since the early 1970s when patients realized that an ordinary skin face-lift would not correct deep forehead wrinkles.

In a patient with overactive frontalis muscles, deep furrows form in the skin of the forehead and, as the muscles contract, the furrows become deeper. Many methods to obliterate deep forehead furrows have been tried, including the injection of liquid silicone, injection of collagen, and even bilateral section of the frontalis branch of the facial nerve. This is not a good solution to the problem; because the frontalis muscle elevates the eyebrows, a progressive downward look appears in this area.

However, a more successful surgical approach to smoothing out forehead wrinkles is found in the procedure called the *forehead lift.* The superior extension of the normal face-lift incisions ending in the temporal area are extended over the forehead and 4 to 5 cm behind the anterior hairline. The dissection is taken down to the aponeurotic layer above and the frontalis muscle below and a scalp flap is raised and developed from this incision in the hairline down to a point above the eyebrows (see **Figure 10–6**). Therefore, the sensory innervation of the frontal flap is preserved. At this time the scalp flap is pulled backward tightly and, while some hair-bearing skin is excised approximately 2 to 3 cm of it, the two areas of hair-bearing scalp are approximated and the forehead seems much less wrinkled (see **Figure 10–7**).

The patient must be warned that frequent complications in these areas are paresthesia and lack of sensation in the area of the incision, and even down farther into the flap.

If the sensory nerves are severed or a neuroma occurs, there can be intractable pain in this area, and this has been experienced by more than a

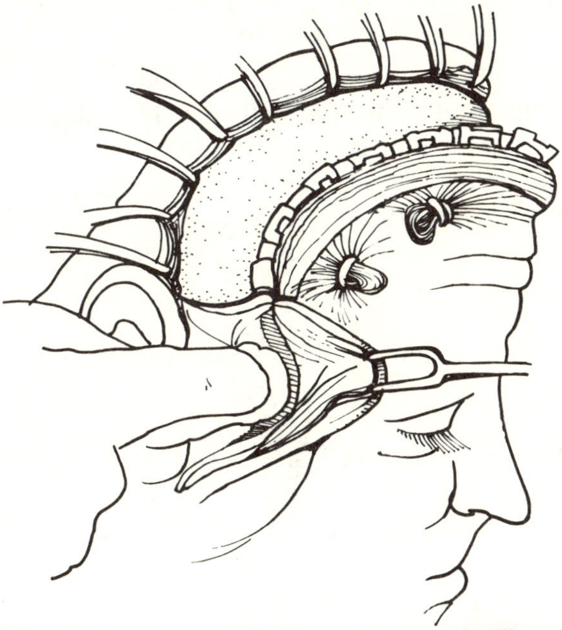

Figure 10–6. The frontal lift. The posterior-frontal scalp is pulled backward with clamps. The frontal skin is pulled forward and undermined down to the forehead, then pulled backward.

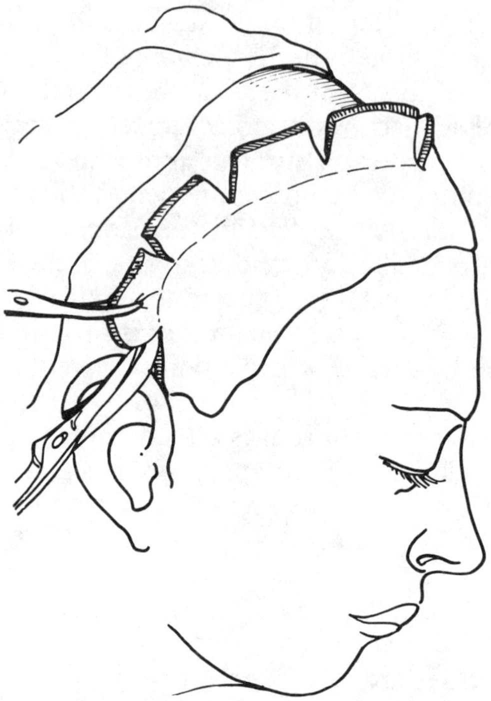

Figure 10–7. The excess frontalis or scalp skin is excised at the dotted line, pulled backward, and approximated to the posterior frontal scalp skin.

few patients who have had this procedure. Furthermore, baldness is a definite complication of this incision, as the hair follicles may be damaged in the pull or in the incision itself.

The forehead lift is not commonly done with the face-lift, but there are certain surgeons who think that this is an excellent procedure.

§ 10.21 —Superficial Musculo-Aponeurotic System (SMAS)

SMAS, which has received a fair amount of press in the last five years, stands for the superficial musculo-aponeurotic system. It refers to the area below the skin which is made up of aponeurosis or fibrous tissue, and muscle and subcutaneous tissue. This involves the platysma muscle which can be resected to change the shape of the neck (see **Figure 10–8**). In patients with long columns of skin and muscle in their neck, the platysma muscle is sectioned below the jaw and contours given to the neck. In addition, the subcutaneous tissue and aponeurosis is brought up underneath the skin and attached to the preauricular fascia (see **Figure 10–9**).

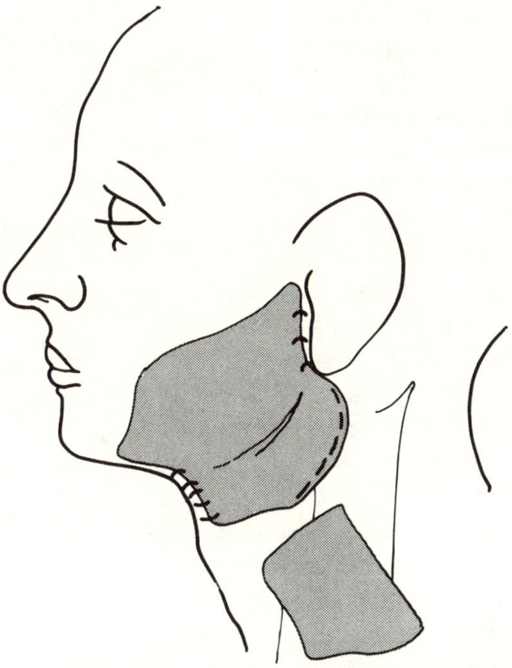

Figure 10–8. The platysma muscle is dissected and sutured to form a more desirable neckline.

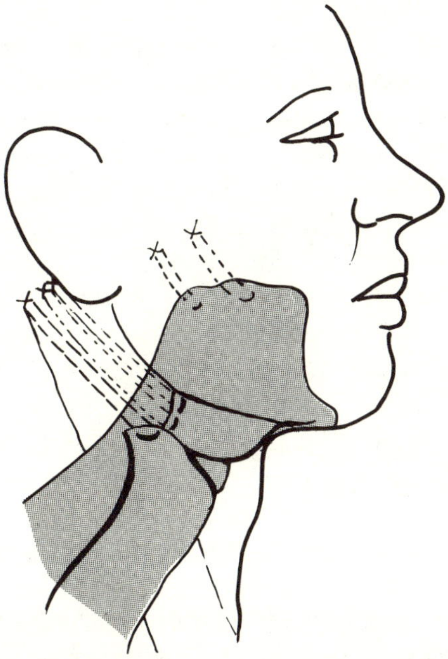

Figure 10–9. In the SMAS procedure the pre- and postauricular fascia is brought up in front and behind the ear to ligate it, giving the neck and jaw a cleaner line.

The SMAS divides the subcutaneous fat into two layers: a superficial layer and a deep layer. A thorough understanding of the SMAS and the related anatomy is crucial to the surgeon undertaking this relatively new face-lifting procedure. It is essential to understand that this fibrous tissue makes the facial muscle tense from the frontalis down to the platysma muscle, and anteriorly to the obicularis oculi muscle. Inferiorly, its tension is preserved by the platysma and it attaches posteriorly to the fascia of the tragus and the mastoid area. It is for this reason that adding a SMAS procedure to a classical face-lift on some patients becomes important. However, because of the increased dissection in this area, the risks are far greater than those of the classical skin undermining.

A thorough discussion of the SMAS and platysma portion of the operation can be found in the reference reading, **§ 10.27**. This procedure should not be done on every patient, and patient selection for this procedure is of upmost importance.

The most frequent sequelae of surgery of the SMAS are the irregularities and the ridges in the neck surfaces along the route of the transected borders of the platysma muscle. When the muscle is tensed postoperatively, the irregularities are more exaggerated. Sometimes minor deformities improve with time but often they are permanent. Failure to excise certain superficial fat can result in bulges along the course of the transected muscle. The thickness of the patient's neck as well as the thickness of the muscle, the age of the patient, and the type of skin should all be noted before the procedure is undertaken. Older female patients with delicate thin skin through which these irregularities may show more easily should not be candidates for this procedure. Younger patients with thicker skin can withstand the potential irregularities better. Obviously, nerve damage is more common in this procedure because often the branches of the facial nerve reside within these facial muscles.

Injury to the ramus mandibularus is not uncommon and, although permanent loss of function is rare, it can happen, and the patient should be informed of this before the procedure is undertaken. As in the classical facial skin operation, nerve damage here can be caused by trauma of the electrocautery or to excess edema or scar tissue from previous surgery. These paralyses will recede in time (anywhere up to two years), but the risk of cutting the nerve in this procedure is definitely greater.

§ 10.22 —Submental Lipectomy

When there is a heavy neck, a small incision measuring approximately 2 cm is made in the submental crease below the chin. The skin is transected and the submental fat pad is excised under direct vision and the bleeding is carefully coagulated. It is at this point that the digastric muscles under the neck are plicated. An elliptical portion of skin is removed from the lower portion incision and the incision is sutured with interrupted sutures to finesse the larger lower portion of skin edge to the smaller upper portion. Submental lipectomies have been replaced at the present time largely with liposuction of the chin.

§ 10.23 —Liposuction and Facial Contouring

During a face-lift, be it traditional or with the SMAS, a certain amount of submental fat can be suctioned through a small stab wound in the submental area or through both sides of the face-lift incision. Fat suctioning is done in the area of the cheek and underneath the malar bone where large buccal fat pads may be present. Great care must be exercised during this procedure as bleeding may be magnified or a small portion of nerve may be traumatized during the suctioning causing paralysis, which may again be permanent. Liposuction is discussed further in **Chapter 13**.

§ 10.24 —Excision of Glabellar and Nasolabial Lines

Glabellar and nasolabial lines are difficult to treat. The glabellar lines pose more of a problem than do the nasolabial lines, because the former are actually lines etched in the skin from constant use of the corrugator muscles. Filling them with silicone has been a temporary solution, as has been filling them with collagen. In more recent years some surgeons have sectioned the corrugator muscles, and other surgeons have excised the lines and sutured them, believing that a well-sutured fine-line scar in this area would be preferable to a deep furrow in the skin. Additionally, the frontal lift can improve the glabellar lines. However, there is no totally satisfactory answer to this vexing problem, and the complications for each of these procedures are sometimes worse than the problems themselves.

Nasolabial lines often present are a problem because patients seldom understand that these will not be totally eradicated with a face-lift. It is important that the surgeon discuss the diminution of the nasolabial lines with the patient but to be sure that it is not promised that these lines will completely disappear with a face-lift. When the nasolabial lines remain after a face-lift, patients often say that the reason they came for a face-lift was to get rid of these lines. They should have understood before the surgery had taken place that these lines would be diminished only and not be completely eradicated.

Correction of these lines includes silicone, which is not recommended, or collagen, which disappears in a short period of time. Perhaps the best-known method for improving and decreasing the lines at this point is to inject the patient's own fat into them. This is a fairly simple procedure done under local anesthesia in the office. It occurs by taking 10 cc of fat from the thigh, washing it, and injecting it through a large gauge needle into the nasolabial lines. This procedure may have to be done two or three times, because a certain percentage of fat resorption will occur, but this is now considered a good solution for this difficult problem.

§ 10.25 When Should a Face-Lift Be Done?

Patients commonly ask when a face-lift should be done. Should it be done before it is really necessary? Is it better to do at an older age or a younger age? If it is done once, must it be done again, and if it is done, how long will it last? It is difficult to give an honest answer to these questions because it differs from patient to patient. Perhaps the best answer is that a face-lift should be done when the patient looks older than he feels, or feels younger than he looks. As was discussed in § **10.2**, everybody's skin ages differently and the factors that influence the aging of one's skin are many. A consultation with a reliable plastic surgeon who is honest and forthright about the need for the patient to do this elective procedure, and the results that can be achieved, is the only guideline that can be given to patients who are contemplating this surgery.

§ 10.26 Illustrative Cases

Malpractice cases involving face-lifts generally fall within several areas. The first area involves allegations of damage to the nerves. For a plaintiff, this is an easier case to prove because it relies upon objective findings—something a jury can more easily identify with.

In other areas of face-lift litigation the plaintiff claims a bad result has occurred: the jowls continue to be pronounced or his facial expression has changed. Unless dramatic photographic evidence is present, the plaintiffs have a great deal of difficulty in proving these cases. Jury selection becomes even more important in these situations.

Campesano v. Claiburn[2]

The plaintiff brought an action against the defendant surgeon alleging that the defendant assured her she would only have hairline scars following a face-lift. The plaintiff suffered major scars.

---

[2] 196 A.2d 129 (Conn. 1963).

At the time the action was brought a cause of action for negligence would have been barred by the applicable statute of limitations.

The court found, however, that this was a contract action based upon the failure to perform an agreement and therefore the longer contract statute of limitations would apply permitting the action to continue.

Bush v. St. Paul Fire & Marine, Inc.[3]

The plaintiff underwent a rhytidectomy (face-lift) performed by the defendant surgeon. Postoperatively Mrs. Bush developed an area of necrosis of the face, a scar on her cheek, and pleated skin on the neck.

The defendant testified that the necrosis was not an expected result and proposed several theories for its occurrence. She also testified in detail as to the procedures she performed. Expert medical testimony supported the defendant's position that there was no deviation from accepted medical practice in the performance of the surgery.

The court dismissed the action against the surgeon citing the failure of the plaintiff to present expert evidence and stating that the occurrence of a poor result does not shift the burden of proof to the defendant.

The court also rejected the informed consent argument, pointing out that the plaintiff signed a special consent that detailed certain risks and further that there was evidence the plaintiff thought the surgery out in detail.

Burns v. Bell[4]

In 1968 June Burns consulted Dr. Bell for a face-lift, and surgery was performed in August of that year. Mrs. Burns suffered what she categorized as gross scars. Dr. Bell assured her they would shrink in time. Mrs. Burns also experienced wrinkling and pain. The pain became worse and Mrs. Burns took analgesics for the next nine years.

In 1970 Dr. Bell performed a second procedure to correct the previous scarring and new wrinkling. However, the scars were still noticeable. Dr. Bell continued to assure Mrs. Burns that she would improve. Mrs. Burns' last visit to Dr. Bell was in 1970.

In 1974 Mrs. Burns referred a friend to Dr. Bell for a face-lift. After her friend had a better result Mrs. Burns filed an action for medical malpractice.

The defendant moved to dismiss the action on the basis of the expiration of the statute of limitations.

---

[3] 264 So. 2d 717 (La. Ct. App. 1972).

[4] 409 A.2d 614 (D.C. 1970).

The court refused to grant summary judgment, finding that there was an issue of fact as to when the negligence was discovered.

§ 10.27 Bibliography

J.M. Converse, Plastic Reconstructive Surgery. (W.B. Saunders, 1977).

R.M. Goldwyn, The Patient and the Plastic Surgeon. (Little, Brown & Co., 1981).

R.M. Goldwyn, The Unfavorable Result in Plastic Surgery. (Little, Brown & Co., 2d ed. 1984).

W.C. Grabb, & J.W. Smith, Plastic Surgery. (Little, Brown & Co., 1984).

H. Gray, Anatomy of the Human Body. (Lea & Febiger, 30th ed., 1985).

S.H. Miller, Year Book of Plastic and Reconstructive Surgery. (Year Book Medical Publishers, 1989).

T.D. Rees, II Aesthetic Plastic Surgery. (W.B. Saunders, 1980).

R.B. Stark, Plastic Surgery of the Head and Neck. (Churchill Livingstone, 1987).

CHAPTER 11

RHINOPLASTY

§ 11.1 Introduction

Galen is generally considered to be the first scientist to perceive the key functions of the nose and actually describe its anatomy, some 2,000 years ago. However, it is only since the early 1930s that surgeons have made large strides toward refining both functional and cosmetic nasal surgery.

§ 11.2 Functions of the Nose

The nose is a very complex organ with many functions, but breathing is its primary duty. During respiration, air is brought into the lungs through the nose by means of two openings separated by a partition, the *nasal septum.* The air is taken into the nasopharynx through the trachea, and into the major bronchi, infiltrating the lungs with oxygenated air. On its way in, several things happen. The small hairs or *vibrissae* in the anterior portion of the nose filter and clean the inhaled air by removing soot and other foreign materials from it. Smaller particles such as dust, pollens, and bacteria reach the mucosal covering of the nose, where they are caught and retained, to be disposed of by the pharynx through swallowing. The incoming air is moistened as it passes over the *turbinates,* a portion of the internal structure of the nose; 90 percent of it is humidified before reaching the lungs, meaning that approximately 1 liter of water is admitted by the nose every 24 hours. In addition, the turbinates heat air as it enters the nose. Because turbinate bones house a dense arrangement of blood vessels that permit rapid accommodation of a large blood volume, they circulate and radiate heat.

The nose cleanses itself by producing mucus from the cilia and the mucus glands. Approximately 1 liter of mucus is produced every 24 hours by these glands. Mucus contains antibodies that are active against viruses and bacteria.

In addition to its function during respiration, the nose is also used to smell. This special sense is not as well developed in man as it is in lower forms of animal life. The olfactory apparatus, including the olfactory or the first cranial nerve, is located above the nose. It is important to know that the olfactory apparatus can be damaged during a rhinoplasty.

The nasal cavities also serve as a resonating chamber for certain sounds. In addition, they can improve one's singing capabilities and therefore it is important to consider this function when nasal surgery is performed on people who earn their living by singing.

§ 11.3 Nose Anatomy

The nose is a multistructured organ in the center of the face and is made up of several quite different components. The outside is covered by skin. There are two passageways through which air is inhaled and exhaled. These passages are lined on the inside by the nasal mucosa, a tissue different from skin, and made of secreting glands with many different functions. The mucosa and the skin are the inner and outer coverings of the structures which form the architecture of the nose, namely the bones and the cartilages.

The two nostrils are separated centrally by the nasal septum, which, if deviated or uneven, forces the air to enter unequally and may cause an obstruction on one side. This may result in many pathological conditions caused by the sedimentation of bacteria, soot, and other contaminants from the outside air en route to the lungs.

The nose is also made up of muscles, blood vessels, nerves, and lymphatics that must be considered when one is contemplating a nasal surgical procedure. Some of the important components of the nasal anatomy are considered in §§ **11.4** through **11.7**.

§ 11.4 —Muscles

The muscles of the nose are all part of the muscles of facial expression and are therefore innervated by the facial or seventh cranial nerve.

The *procerus muscle* starts at the forehead and goes down to the top of the nose. The other important nasal muscles are the nasalis muscle, attaching from the nose to the top of the gums, and the *levator* and *depressor muscles* which move the tip of the nose up and down when the nose is crinkled.

The nose is innervated by the nasal branch of the supraorbital nerve and branches of the infraorbital and anterior ethmoidal nerves. The olfactory nerve comes out of the *sphenopalatine ganglion,* which supplies sensory innervation from the maxillary division of the fifth cranial or trigeminal nerve.

The blood supply to the nose is primarily through the external *carotid artery,* via the external and internal maxillary arteries, and the *ophthalmic artery,* which is a branch of the internal carotid artery. The facial or external maxillary artery provides major blood supply through several of its branches. The internal maxillary artery, or the infraorbital artery, contributes some branches to the nose as does a small branch of the ophthalmic artery.

§ 11.5 —Soft Tissue

The skin plays an important part in the appearance of the nose. Its type and texture can alter the result of a rhinoplasty and the experienced surgeon can often anticipate those changes, based on the thickness and oiliness of the preoperated skin. A plastic surgeon must be able to recognize certain skin types and ethnic background plays a part in this determination. Individuals of Mediterranean background, who have increased amounts of pigment and sebaceous glands in their skin, have thicker and oilier skin. Thinner, finer, drier-skinned individuals enjoy the advantages of having their skin redrape itself more evenly and more easily over the renovated architecture of the bones and cartilage after surgery, usually allowing them a finer, more defined rhinoplasty.

The nasal tip contains more sebaceous glands than other parts of the nose. It is for this reason that the tip stays swollen longer and will take longer to reform itself after surgery.

It is imperative to warn the patient with thick, oily skin that plastic surgery will improve the nose but will never give them a thin, refined nose. Often patients see pictures of actors or models who have a nose that they long to have. Their expectations are unrealistic, however, because they do not take into consideration the skin type and thickness when selecting this nose. If a patient brings a photograph to the plastic surgeon and asks for that type of nose, the surgeon must be able to immediately tell the patient whether it is possible for them to have that type of nose or whether their particular skin type prohibits their desired result. Most litigation from nasal surgery turns on the result of the skin type and the discrepancy between what the patient sees in her mind's eye and what the surgeon can actually produce.

§ 11.6 —Bones

The framework of the nose is made up of bone approximately two-fifths of the way down the nose and cartilaginous septum from there to the tip. The nasal septum is made of firm cartilage from the central hanging portion of the nose, or *columella,* up to the medial nasal bone, or quadriform plate. The nasal bones are projections from the nasal processes of the maxilla on each side and from the frontal bone above. The upward limit of the nose is the nasofrontal suture line. The lateral boundaries are the areas where the nasal bones come off the maxilla. The nasal bones are quadrangular and thicker above than below. Nasal bones are seldom equal and are often not evenly placed in the midline of the face. The lower portions of the nose, where the columella reaches the upper lip, surround the vomer bone, which is contiguous with the maxilla and the palatine bone posteriorly. When the anterior portion of the septum has to be moved, the anterior nasal spine is fractured from the vomer bone.

During the rhinoplasty operation, a chisel or saw is used to remove the hooded covering of the nasal bones that form a hump on the nose. When this is done, the nose takes on a flat appearance. In order to make it a pyramid again, the lateral portion of the nasal bones must be cut with a saw or chisel and moved inward several millimeters to give the nose its normal appearance. One of the problems of nasal surgery is the possible collapse or malposition of one of these bones. This is frequently the result of bleeding in the channel where the bones have been fractured or from undue pressure from inside or outside the nasal dressing. It will take approximately six weeks for these nasal bones to mend themselves after a rhinoplasty is done. Therefore, it is incumbent on the patient to be sure that during the postoperative course she is careful not to hit, touch, or allow another to interfere in any way with her nose.

One month after her rhinoplasty, one patient, who had seemed pleased with the results immediately after surgery, complained that the left nasal bone was pushed in and had fallen in of its own accord, that she had not touched it. Litigation was started. It was not until careful examination by a meticulous attorney that it was discerned, during the deposition, that the patient's baby, while playing with her mother's face, had inadvertently hit the nose with its fist. The mother, not wanting to recall the episode, had convinced herself that it had happened spontaneously. This is an example of why an attorney, during deposition, has to elicit a careful chronological history of the events postoperatively, asking all sorts of questions pertinent to any events that could have changed the condition of the nose in its fragile new state.

§ 11.7 —Cartilage

Cartilage of the nose is the firm tissue in the nose formed from chondroblasts. It is a whitish tissue which is flexible but firm. It is not hard like bone nor is it soft like skin. It is a median tissue that gives support to certain structures in the body, particularly the nose.

The septal cartilage is the firmest cartilage in the nose and forms the main partition between the two nostrils. The quadrangular cartilage borders superiorly and posteriorly on the perpendicular plate of the ethmoid bone, and inferiorly and posteriorly on the vomer bone.

Contrary to popular opinion, a dorsal nasal hump is not made entirely of bone. Part of it is nasal cartilage and the hump is seen where the cartilage and bone join. The dorsum of the nose is also comprised of a portion of the upper lateral cartilage; therefore, when the nasal bones and the septal cartilage are removed during a rhinoplasty, a small portion of the upper lateral cartilage must be removed to decrease the height of the nose. Except for the septal cartilage, the other cartilages that form the nose are the right and left upper and lower lateral cartilages.

The *lower lateral cartilages* above the nostrils are those structures that give shape to the lower portion of the nose and must be altered to shorten the nose. The *columella* is the extension of the septum, and is the column between the nostrils at the base of the nose. It is composed of skin on the outside, cartilage in the middle, and mucosa on the inside. When this columella hangs too low and must be reduced, it is not skin that is excised but mucosa and cartilage.

The *alae* of the nose are the winged extensions of skin and mucosa at the lateral portion of the nostrils. When the nose is too wide, it is the alae that must be reduced. This should be the only surgery that leaves an external scar on the nose because a wedge of nostril skin must be excised and sutured to reduce the width of the nostrils.

§ 11.8 Consultation and Informed Consent

Of all the operations a plastic surgeon is called on to perform, perhaps the most difficult aesthetically is the rhinoplasty. Good judgment is required in performing rhinoplasty and, even then, the results are not assured because postoperative healing varies so much from one patient to another. Selection of patients for rhinoplasty is an extremely important consideration for the surgeon. Emotional factors are very important as are the patient's expectations.

Many patients who seek a rhinoplasty are in their mid to late teens. The nose begins to grow after the age of 12 or 13 and is complete by age 16. Often a young person with a relatively normal-looking nose develops the characteristic features of a dorsal hump and wide nasal bones between the ages of 13 and 16. It is at this time that it becomes evident to them or their parents that a nasal correction might be considered. It is often interesting to see parents with large noses swell with pride at the fact that their 10- or 11-year-old child has a nice, average-looking nose, only to learn several years later that their own hereditary traits are soon to be visited on the noses of their children.

The optimal age to do nasal surgery is at 16 years of age. Some children mature sooner and perhaps 15 to 15 ½ would be the early stopping point. Recently articles have been written about starting rhinoplasties at the age of 13 but in the opinion of most operating surgeons this is too early.

Teenagers seek rhinoplasty with the idea of reducing criticism and ridicule by their peers, and they also think that changing their nose will change their lives. This is also true of people in older age groups who want to have a "perfect nose." Patients seek rhinoplasty well into their later years.

Certain patients have good reasons to wait until later in life to have their noses changed. One woman at the age of 70 decided that, when she wanted to have a face-lift, she wanted to have her nose changed at the same time. When questioned why she waited until that age in life to do her nose, she explained that when she was 20 she wanted the operation but her father forbade it, when she was 40 she again wanted to do it but her husband forbade it, and when she was 60 she still wanted her nose changed but her children did not want her to. Now that they were all either dead or living far away, she decided to have the operation that she had been wanting for 50 years. This patient not only had an excellent result from her face-lift, but her nose changed the appearance of her face into what she had envisioned for herself for all those many years, and she was able to go into old age as a happy and infinitely more attractive person, both physically and emotionally.

It is often the parents who want the operation for their sons or daughters. This surgery must be looked at carefully and the physician should speak confidentially with the patient alone at some point. If the patient wants the operation for himself, then it is fair to continue the discussion with the parents present.

In discussing a rhinoplasty with a patient, be he older or younger, it is very important to include all the possible things that can happen in the postoperative period. A rhinoplasty well done at the time of surgery can change entirely as the healing takes place, as swelling recedes and the scar tissue accrues. Rhinoplasty patients, because they are usually in younger age groups, become anxious and excited about the result. They must be advised that when the splint is removed after seven days, the nose will not look as good as it will look several weeks later; the swelling and the discoloration will still be there. Patience is the greatest virtue for the postoperative rhinoplasty patient. It is difficult for patients to look at themselves after a rhinoplasty and have to wait for one year before the final result of the work is achieved. A nose with a good structure one week after surgery will change completely and hopefully for the best during the ensuing year. The patient should be warned that, although two to three weeks after surgery they will look usually very well, the nose will continue to change and the swelling will continue to recede for 12 to 18 months. Patients who expect an early perfect result are the ones who will be most dissatisfied when they see the swelling, and will be moved by impatience and even hostility toward the surgeon to be legally dissatisfied with their noses.

A case in point is a 35-year-old woman who came to a plastic surgeon for a rhinoplasty. Although she was adequately warned about the length of time it takes for the swelling to recede, five weeks after the operation was done, because one side was more swollen than the other, the patient enlisted an attorney to start suit against the plastic surgeon because the nose was uneven. It was difficult if not impossible to convince her that the five-week period was nowhere near the time it would take to see the final result of her nose. She was told this in the informed consent and this was written into her chart, so at deposition it was revealed that the suit was not timely because she admitted she knew of the one-year waiting period.

Most patients, especially younger patients, are very excited about the prospect of having a rhinoplasty so they can have the nose they have always wanted. They engage in what is often called selective hearing. Although most plastic surgeons discuss frankly and openly with the patient the pros and cons of plastic surgery, and discuss in detail the complications and the limitations of the surgery, patients often do not hear all this. They focus on the beautiful result they expect, and they do not hear the caveats of waiting for the final healing to take place.

Therefore, postoperatively, when the swelling and discoloration and other sequelae do occur as they often do, the patient may not be prepared for these predicted eventualities. Experience demands that patients must see something in writing about the nose operation in the form of a pamphlet or a written instruction booklet. They must know what to be prepared for after the operation and what the operation itself consists of. This booklet should inform them about the anesthesia, the type of scarring, how long they should stay in the hospital or clinic, how long the bandages, packing, and splint will remain, and when the sutures will be removed. They should also know when they can return to work, exercise, wash their hair, shower, and engage in sexual activities again.

It is sometimes difficult for the plastic surgeon to get a full appreciation of the patient on the first consultation. It is reasonable therefore to have the patient discuss the nose during this first consultation, send him to an outside photographer for photographs, and schedule a second appointment for discussion of these photographs. Practically speaking, this is another opportunity for the surgeon and patient to meet again and further formulate their opinions of one another.

Although nasal surgery is done very often on young people whose careers and ways of life have not been settled, the surgeon must be particularly careful when an older patient seeks a rhinoplasty. When a patient around the age of 30 consults a plastic surgeon for a rhinoplasty, he must be carefully evaluated. His education is usually finished at this point; his career and lifestyle have already been formed. He must be carefully examined from a psychological point of view, which might reveal a basic dissatisfaction within himself that he thinks will be altered by a new nose. This would make him a less desirable candidate for surgery on an emotional basis.

A detailed medical history should be taken on the patient, especially regarding bleeding disorders, blood dyscrasias, and smoking habits. If the patient smokes, it is fair to consider not doing the nasal operation until there has been a cessation of smoking for at least two weeks prior to surgery. The nose has such a rich blood supply that, under normal conditions, a large amount of bleeding can take place. In smokers the bleeding can be increased. Similarly, if the patient is on any drug like aspirin, which can decrease the platelets and cause more bleeding, the medication should be stopped before any surgery is considered.

A careful history should be taken regarding old traumas to the nose, fractures, difficulties in breathing, excessive sinusitis, or an allergic condition of the nose. The septum should be carefully examined to see whether there is even a minimal deviation that might cause difficulty in breathing. Often the patient with a markedly deviated septum is promised complete relief in breathing, but the septum will be corrected and the breathing problem will still exist. Therefore the breathing problem should be further investigated, perhaps with the help of an ear, nose, and throat surgeon. The breathing problem may be caused by an impairment of the sinuses or other allergic conditions. A thorough physical examination as well as a full examination of the patient's blood studies are essential prior to any surgical procedure.

It is very important that the surgeon understand precisely the type of nose the patient wants to achieve. After the photographs are taken, a profile view should be presented to the patient with an uncorrected and a corrected photograph which has been sketched on by the surgeon. This will give the patient an approximation of the new profile. It is at this time that a patient should try to communicate with the surgeon, to discuss whether too much or too little has been taken off in their opinion, and whether the projected profile is satisfactory. The patient's concept of a good nose might be completely different from that of the surgeon, and there must be a meeting of the minds before any surgery occurs. One's concept of beauty is a very subjective thing, and it is influenced greatly by one's past experience and ethnic background as well as the size, shape, and features of the face. A surgeon of one ethnic origin may find that her choice of a good nose reflects her background, while the patient of another origin seeking surgery might have a totally different idea of what constitutes beauty.

Some patients present photographs of a currently popular movie actress and expect that nose to be put on their face. They do not take into consideration that the other features are completely dissimilar to theirs. Also they may not consider the difference in skin types. These patients must be treated very carefully because it will often be difficult to fulfill their expectations. When they register dissatisfaction postoperatively and are impatient to wait for whatever good result can be achieved, even after too short a time, they will go to a lawyer for their subsequent postoperative visit rather than relying on their plastic surgeon.

Another important part of the preoperative consultation is the discussion of a secondary minor procedure. When a nose operation is done, an increase in the amount of scar tissue, movement of cartilage, or difficulty in reduction of edema may occur. Sometimes the cartilage will heal in an unusual or uneven way, so that a secondary procedure may have to be done to rectify it. This is not unusual, and the patient should be made aware of this possibility prior to the surgery. Often a patient will seize upon the opportunity of a misplaced cartilage or a small amount of edema to start litigation when the situation could have been alleviated with a minor correction done under local anesthesia in approximately 10 minutes. Although no surgeon likes to admit that a less than excellent result might occur, there is always the possibility that this can happen, and can be easily corrected.

The nose, with its diverse tissue types—namely skin, cartilage, bone, and mucosa—heals in a unique way. As the healing occurs, it may be slightly irregular for a period of time, and eventually may need minor correction.

§ 11.9 Location of Surgery

Plastic surgery is being done more frequently than ever before. More rhinoplasties and submucous resections are being done as office procedures so hospital beds are not tied up for these relatively harmless procedures and so the patient does not incur excessive hospital bills. Many surgeons in larger metropolitan areas have office/operating facilities where rhinoplasties are done and the patient is sent home shortly thereafter. It is usually good practice for the patient to remain in the operating suite anywhere from 12 to 24 hours following surgery. If he leaves a tranquil atmosphere to take a taxi or an automobile home, many things can happen to the blood pressure, causing bleeding and clotting to form in the nose and affecting the final result. A little prudence in the immediate postoperative period could prevent many difficulties from occurring later on that harm the result of the surgery.

§ 11.10 Anesthesia

Nasal surgery is best done under local anesthesia. Xylocaine or lidocaine, usually 1 percent with 1:100,000 epinephrine for control of the bleeding, is frequently used. Often this procedure is done in conjunction with an anesthetist (nurse) or an anesthesiologist (doctor), who gives Pentothal or other tranquilizing drugs to keep the patient in a subdued state, particularly during the somewhat painful injection period. Most surgeons prefer not to do this operation under general anesthesia because they feel that there is an increase in bleeding because of some of the anesthetic agents used.

§ 11.11 Standard Rhinoplasty Procedure

The usual time required to perform a rhinoplasty with a submucous resection is approximately 45 minutes to an hour and a half, depending on the speed of the surgeon and the ease of the operation.

The operation is usually started after the standby anesthesia is instituted by packing the nose with 1/2-inch plain or vaseline gauze packing. The local anesthesia is then injected into the inside and outside of the nose, and into the septum. Some surgeons use liquid cocaine on pledgets to give topical anesthesia to the mucous membranes. Because of many people's sensitivity to cocaine and because of allergic reactions documented in the past, many surgeons are eliminating the use of cocaine and using the supplementary anesthesia instead to calm the patient while the local anesthesia is injected.

The concept of nasal surgery is to change the shape of the nose by changing the structures of the nose from within. No incision is made in the skin of the nose with one exception: the alar wedge resection discussed in **§ 11.7** to narrow the nostrils. All other nasal surgery is done through the nostrils. It is through the mucosa that the incision is made (see **Figure 11-1**). The two classical procedures for mucosal incisions are the *rim incision* made through the lower lateral cartilages, and the *intracartilaginous incision* made between the upper and lower lateral cartilages. Once this incision is made, scissors are used to separate the nose

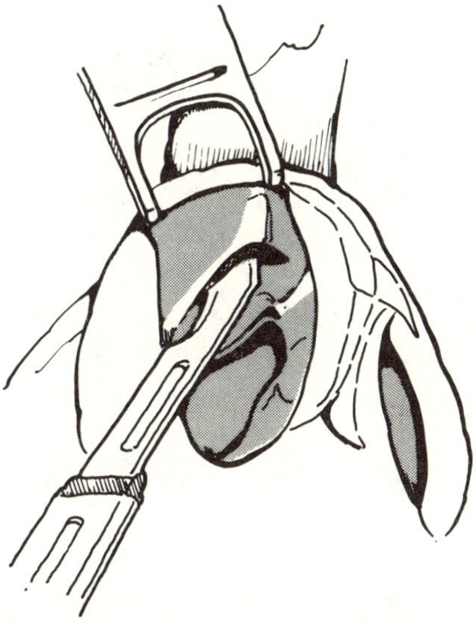

Figure 11–1. A number 11 blade is used to make a rim incision through the nasal mucosa of the right nostril. It is through this incision that the alterations in cartilage and bone are made.

from the underlined cartilage and mucosa. This undermining takes place from the point of incision up to the nasofrontal suture line at the top of the nose. This is done to separate the entire anatomy of the nose so one part is discernible from the other, and there will be no interference with the overlying skin. After the skin of the nose is separated, the upper and lower lateral cartilages are separated from the septum on both sides, leaving the septum free to alter and the cartilages free to reshape. The work is done under direct vision but can also be done tactically.

The revision of bone is usually done next; the dorsal hump of bone is removed with a guarded osteotome (see **Figure 11-2**) so that the skin will not be cut. A hammer is used to move the osteotome through the nasal hump, thereby cutting it, and a rasp is used to smooth out the edges (see **Figure 11-3**). Some surgeons prefer to use a saw to remove the hump of bone. When the dorsal hump has been removed and the nose is square in this area, the nasal processes of the maxilla must be severed at their base in order to move them in to form a new pyramid. The mucosa or the covering of the nasal bones must be cut at the base of the nasal bones, and a saw or chisel inserted next to the right and left nasal bones to cut them at their base. When this nasal fracture is done, an osteotome is placed perpendicular to the septum and moved out and in, effecting the in-and out-fractures. This allows the nasal bones to be mobilized and moved a millimeter or two toward the center of the nose, forming the new pyramid (see **Figure 11-4**). The reason that the nasal bone does not collapse is that the periosteum

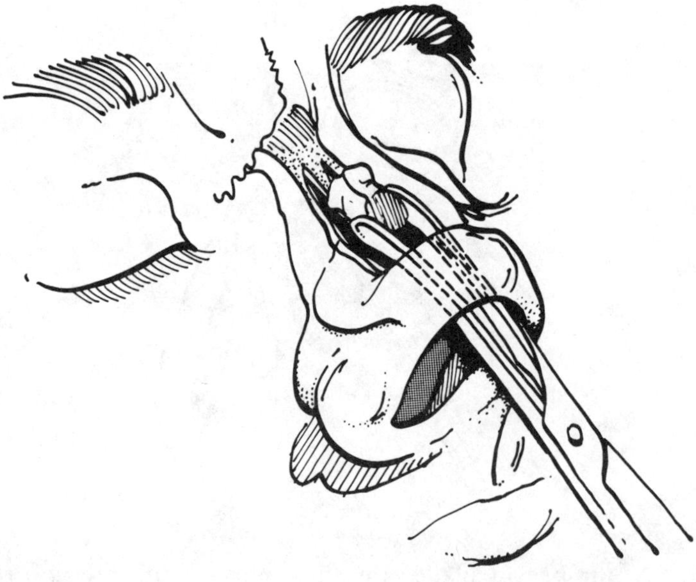

Figure 11–2. Forceps remove a piece of nasal bone (dorsal hump) after it has been cut with the osteotome (or in some cases, a saw).

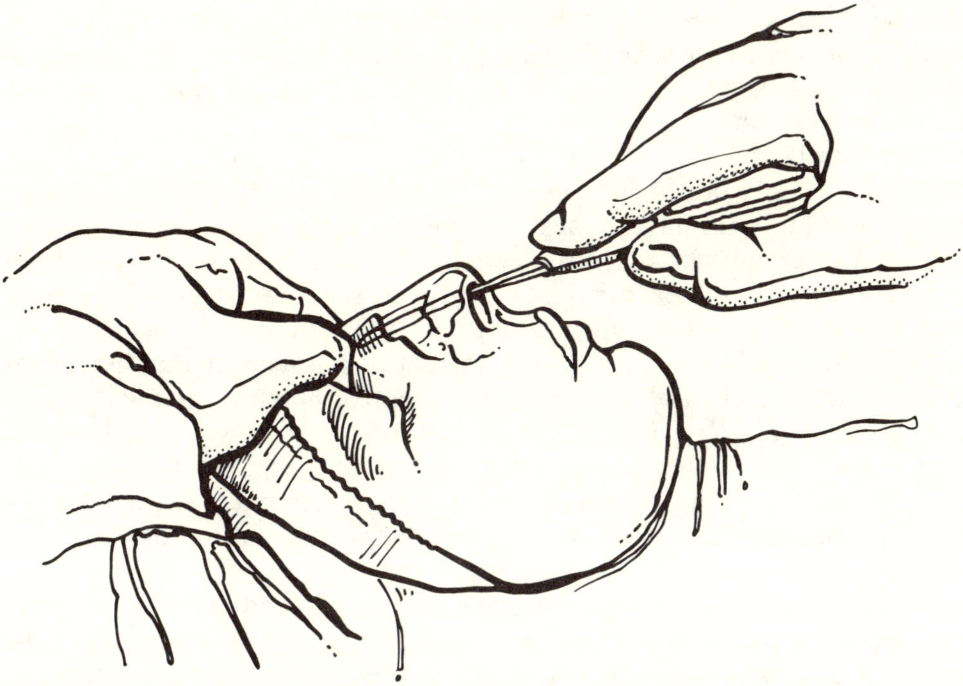

Figure 11–3. A rasp smooths the remaining dorsal nasal bones after being cut with the osteotome.

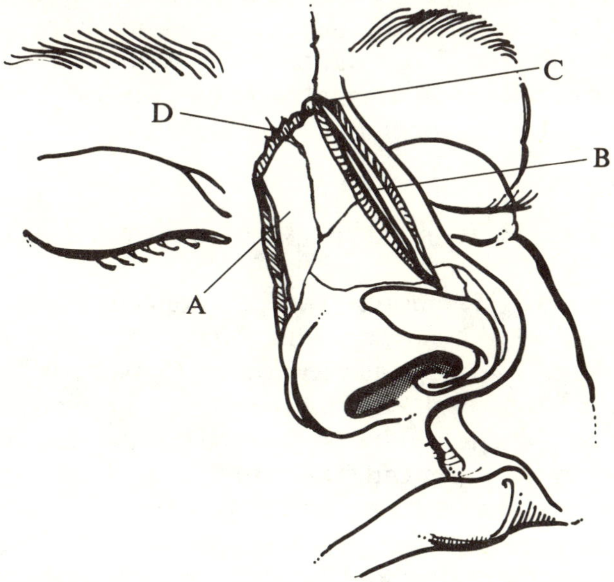

Figure 11–4. The new size, shape, and position of the nasal bones after the medial and lateral osteotomies. "A" is the site of lateral osteotomy with the nasal bone moved toward center. "B" is the site where the dorsal hump was removed. "C" is the site of the medial osteotomy. "D" is the nasofrontal suture.

that has been stripped only in the lower channel of it is still in place on most of the nasal bones, keeping it intact. The nasal bones are now manipulated into place and the dorsal hump is off and the top of the nose has a new height and shape.

The dorsal cartilage that remains has to be reduced to the new height of the nose. This is done with scissors or a knife and the dorsal cartilage is lowered to join the nasal bones. A portion of the upper lateral cartilage is removed to accommodate to the new height. The lower lateral cartilages are then reduced to accommodate the tip to the new height of the nose, and a smaller portion of mucosa is removed. If too much mucosa is removed, the nostrils will be notched. The mucosa is a contractal tissue that can pull the nostrils up, causing an unattractive notching and leaving the nostrils too high up so one can see into them.

It is easy to see that the judgment of the surgeon plays a large part in how much of each of these delicate tissues is removed. The determination for the reduction of most of the structures is done through a digital estimation.

When the operation is complete, one suture is placed between the anterior septum inside the nose and the columella or the skin portion of the nose that hangs between the two nostrils. The nasal packing that was put in before the operation and is now blood soaked is removed and replaced. Blood clots are suctioned out of the nose before the repacking. Tapes and malleable dental compound are used as a splint to keep the nose in place, reduce the edema, and, together with the packing on the inside, exert a counter pressure to keep the nasal bones in a fixed position. Ice is applied to the patient's eyelids in an attempt to reduce swelling and discoloration and the patient leaves the operating room.

§ 11.12 Complications and Undesirable Results

The complications of a rhinoplasty are different from the complications of other types of plastic surgery. The rhinoplasty is arguably the most difficult of all plastic surgical procedures to perform well and from which to get a good result, and is the most capricious in its healing. Many factors combine to produce a good result: the skills of the surgeon, the differences in the types and textures of the patient's skin, the healing of the cartilage and the mucosa, and the postoperative care that patients give themselves.

Again, although the patient looks well at approximately one month after surgery, it takes anywhere from six to 18 months for the nose to heal completely. Perhaps the most noticeable undesirable result from a rhinoplasty is an asymmetry or imbalance of one side of the nose to the other. Depending on how the cartilage and the mucosa heal, one side can be up one millimeter, one side can be more swollen than the other by one millimeter, a bone can be slightly more in on one side than the other, and symmetry is sacrificed.

The most important thing to realize about these early minor undesirable results in rhinoplasty is that most of them will correct themselves, or can be corrected after six months to one year with a small office procedure done under local anesthesia. If the surgeon has been conservative in doing the rhinoplasty and has not taken too much off, a little bit more can always be taken off or altered. The error that the surgeon sometimes commits in performing a rhinoplasty is that too much is removed and can only be replaced with great difficulty. Therefore, it is better to take off too little bone or cartilage than too much.

§ 11.13 —Hemorrhage or Epistaxis

Hemorrhage, or *epistaxis,* sometimes seen in rhinoplasty is, simply stated, a nosebleed. Sometimes, because of the disruption of the blood vessels of the nose during surgery, bleeding starts when the swelling recedes during the early postoperative stages. The bleeding can come from the anterior or posterior part of the nose. If the bleeding is anterior, it can often be cauterized under direct vision, or an anterior packing can be inserted into the nose. If the bleeding occurs posteriorly from a broken off blood vessel and the blood is going down into the nasopharynx, a posterior packing must be introduced to try to stop that bleeding.

Of course bleeding is more commonly seen in people who take aspirin or other blood-thinning medications. The patient should not take any drug with aspirin in it for at least two weeks prior to surgery. If the patient has any bleeding problems to begin with, this should be discovered on the preoperative blood testing. A bleeding and clotting time should be among those tests done before surgery.

§ 11.14 —Hematoma

Hematoma is a collection of blood that occurs beneath the skin or cartilage of the nose. If this occurs, it usually comes from intraoperative bleeding, and should be evacuated, as it will cause difficulty later on. Hematomas are not terribly common in the nose. An external splint and the packing within the nose exert an equalized pressure on the tissue and usually prevent hematoma.

One difficult area for a hematoma in the nose is in the area of the lateral osteotomy of the nasal portion of the maxilla. If there is a great amount of bleeding there the hematoma can cause the nasal bones to move and one or both bones can become malpositioned. Therefore, it is important when the splint comes off at the end of the first week that the surgeon exert a mild pressure on the nasal bones with his thumb and index finger, pushing them slightly together, forcing the hematoma out of the channel where the bones will heal.

§ 11.15 —Infection

Infection can come after any surgical procedure, but it is fairly rare in nasal surgery because of the rich blood supply to the nose. Antibiotics are often started, however, because of an abscess that can form at the top of the nose near the medial canthus of the eye. This abscess is often caused by contaminants from the nasal cavity seeping into the surrounding tissues. The symptoms include swelling outside the splint, pain in that side of the nose and eye, and heat in the tissue. The treatment is warm soaks and antibiotics. It takes two to three weeks for the abscess to subside completely, but the acute component of the infection is over in several days.

A rare but tragic complication to nasal surgery is *cavernous sinus thrombosis.* This is a blood clot in the sinus that can break off and move to the brain. If this happens, and if it is undiagnosed, it can lead to brain abscess and death. If diagnosed, it must be treated with massive doses of antibiotics and anticoagulants.

§ 11.16 —Edema and Ecchymosis

Edema and ecchymosis are not complications of nasal surgery, but rather natural sequelae. This means that they are expected and anticipated and it would be unusual for them not to occur. The *ecchymosis* (discoloration) goes away usually within 10 days. The *edema* (swelling) subsides for the most part after approximately two to three weeks. There is still, however, a certain amount of subclinical edema present. This swelling is seen around the patient's eyes and throughout the area of the nose. It recedes until it finally descends to the tip of the nose, which is the last area of the nose to regain sensation and to be free of edema. The thicker the skin, the greater the edema and the longer it will last. It must be impressed on the patient that it will be a full year before the nose is completely healed.

§ 11.17 —Injury to Lacrymal Apparatus

Because the tear duct is close to the lateral portion of the osteotomy at the site of the medial canthus, sometimes an injury occurs at the tear duct or lacrymal sac. This can be done by the needle during the injection of novocaine, or can be done with a chisel or a saw during the lateral osteotomy. When the problem with the tear duct is caused by pressure or swelling, this will subside spontaneously.

§ 11.18 —Septal Perforation

Septal perforations from surgery are less common today because of a different approach to submucous resection. Antibiotics cover a large degree of potential infections which could cause such perforations. Much more common today is a septal perforation, small or large, from repeated use of cocaine. These septal perforations must be closed by the use of mucosal flap or skin graft from the postauricular area. Closure is always difficult to achieve in a large septal perforation.

§ 11.19 —Nasal Obstruction

This is a late complication of rhinoplasty and most patients experience some degree of nasal obstruction from the edema of the mucosa, coagulated blood, or crusted mucosa within the nasal walls. This problem usually resolves itself spontaneously within a few weeks.

§ 11.20 —Anosmia

The olfactory area is high above the nasal cavity and should be out of the reach of the operating instruments. However, some patients have undergone at least temporarily a minor degree of altered sense of smell, or *anosmia.* This condition is sometimes permanent. It is usually a result of edema and when the edema subsides the sense of smell returns. However, the patient should be warned about this possibility at the outset, as there is no cure for the condition.

§ 11.21 —Callus Formation

Occasionally *callus,* the material laid down by the bone when it heals itself, can form on the junctions of the nasal bones at their fracture site. This can form several months after surgery as the bone heals. If it does occur and cannot be massaged away, then a small incision must be made in the mucosa and a rasp or other instrument introduced to level the callus formation.

In addition, because of edema or hematoma in the osteotomy canal, the nasal bone may spring out too far or fall in too much. If unevenness of the nasal bones is noted, it must be corrected and sometimes a second operation is required to refracture and realign the nasal bones.

§ 11.22 —Aberrant Cartilage

When the surgery is being done, the cartilage on both sides seems to line up with each other. As edema subsides, however, cartilage can shift before the nose is completely healed. It moves because of the healing of the mucosa, the introduction of scar tissue, and the redraping of the skin, which in some patients are beyond the control of the surgeon.

If the cartilage moves and the result is uneven, it can be corrected after six months by a minor secondary procedure in which novocaine is injected in the area and small scissors are inserted to remove the cartilage.

§ 11.23 —Notching

Notching of the nostrils is often seen in rhinoplasties done by inexperienced surgeons. The notching is caused by the removal of too much mucosa in the area of the lower lateral cartilage. When too much mucosa is removed, the mucosa will shrink and pull up in the area of the excessive incision. When the swelling disappears, the treatment for this problem is to open the mucosa and lengthen the inside of the nose, thereby allowing the outside to return to its natural position. This is done by means of a full-thickness skin graft taken from behind the ear.

§ 11.24 Summary

According to the American Board of Plastic and Reconstructive Surgery, rhinoplasty was the most commonly performed operation in the United States in 1986. This operation is sought by many patients because they are not happy with the shape of their nose. It does not depend on age as blepharoplasty and face-lifts do, and therefore it is sought by many more people than merely those who are aging. In addition, television and advertising tend to bring dissatisfaction to people who ordinarily would not seek an improvement in their looks. There is a certain percentage of patients who chose surgery to correct a breathing problem or a functional deformity. All in all nasal surgery is extremely popular.

It is certainly one of the most difficult of plastic and reconstruction surgeries from which to get a good result, and it should be done carefully and thoughtfully by a concerned and talented surgeon. Unfortunately, many people who perform nasal surgery are inadequately qualified and unexperienced.

Much of the abundant litigation in this area stems from the fact that patients who have had large noses since adolescence seek perfection. When this does not occur they sometimes want to strike out at the surgeon who performed the operation for them, often without giving the minor deformity a chance to be corrected. The massive litigation in nasal surgery often hinges on the lack of communication between patient and surgeon. If the patient is inarticulate when communicating to the surgeon the type of nose he wants, or if the surgeon is unable to understand the patient's needs and desires and does the operation in a routine fashion, the result is often litigation, resulting in everybody's unhappiness.

A young man with a large dorsal hump and a deviation of the septum into the left nostril came to a surgeon for correction. The operation was performed well, but after the surgery the septum swerved back into its original place in the left nostril, and there was an excess cartilage in the tip. The patient came back again for a second surgery for the minor corrections. The corrections did not work and the surgeon offered to correct the nose a third time. The patient, who was somewhat disturbed by the whole procedure, instead of having another correction, decided to sue the surgeon. Was the surgeon guilty of malpractice because the nose was not satisfactory to the patient? Possibly not. The patient's postoperative office visit record was sketchy and he admitted to the surgeon that he did not want to come back to see him because he was disheartened. It was during these early postoperative visits that a correction could have been made by the surgeon, had he had the opportunity to see the patient and treat him in that crucial early postoperative period. If there was negligence on the surgeon's part it would seem that there was contributory negligence on the part of the patient by not allowing the surgeon to continue a postoperative check-up of his work.

Misunderstanding and lack of communication are the greatest sources of litigation in nasal as well as any other surgery. It is crucial that the patient and the surgeon establish a good relationship.

§ 11.25 Illustrative Cases

There are some procedures in plastic surgery that are totally cosmetic in nature, both in the patient's motivation and in the actual performance of the surgery. Such procedures are face-lifts, breast augmentations, and otoplasties.

Other procedures are partially cosmetic and partially functional. This is true of abdominoplasties, in some cases blepharoplasties, and certainly in most cases the rhinoplasties. Because the nose is the primary organ of breathing, many irregularities in the construction of the nose that cause a cosmetic imperfection can also cause a functional impairment. Most patients have a deviation of the septum, however slight. The deviation of some patients' septums causes tremendous difficulty in breathing. The presence of swollen turbinates makes breathing even more difficult and a broken nose with the nasal bones out of the midline will cause difficulty in breathing, extra infections because of contamination of the mucous membranes, chronic sinusitis, and possible headaches. Therefore, many patients who seek nasal surgery are seeking it primarily for functional reasons and any cosmetic benefit that attaches is an extra added benefit.

See **Appendix B** for an example of a rhinoplasty complaint form.

Pasha v. Board of Medical Quality Assurance[1]

This disciplinary action was based upon two procedures performed by the defendant, Dr. Pasha.

In March 1980, Monique Brisson visited the defendant to inquire about cosmetic eyelid surgery. Dr. Pasha told Mrs. Brisson he would build up the bridge of her nose with ear cartilage. At the time of the consultation, Mrs. Brisson, a 26-year-old model and singer, had a low, wide bridge with a slight deviation, asymmetrical flaring nostrils, and a notch on her outer nostril.

Surgery was performed on March 18, 1980, and included an implant of a medium-sized *sclastic* (plastic-like implant over the bridge of the nose to build a bridge), a partial mucous resection to correct the deviation, and a bilateral resection of the *alae* (nostril) tissue at the base of the nose to decrease the notch of the right nostril. Antibiotics were prescribed postoperatively. Mrs. Brisson returned home that evening. Over the course of the next five days Mrs. Brisson's eyes became swollen and eventually infected. Although the patient's husband called Dr. Pasha repeatedly, the doctor failed to return any calls.

On March 25 the patient returned for a scheduled appointment. Dr. Pasha removed the dressings and prescribed medication for the eye infection. Brisson's nose continued to be swollen with the right nostril pointing up and the left nostril closed. On April 16 Mrs. Brisson became feverish, fainted, and was brought to the hospital. No diagnosis was made and she was released. Mrs. Brisson thereafter consulted another plastic surgeon, Dr. Hoefflin.

Dr. Hoefflin observed several "deformities" with Brisson's nose: (1) extrusion of two silastic implants from the right nasal rim and the

---

[1] 174 Cal. App. 3d 439, 219 Cal. Rptr. 778 (1985).

right intranasal area, (2) *stenosis* (contraction) of both nostrils and a corresponding difficulty in breathing, (3) a nasal infection, and (4) a 1 1/2 to 2 cm linear incision of the *dorsum* (bridge) of the nose which, according to Brisson, was not there before surgery.

In May Dr. Hoefflin surgically removed several silastic implants and a fibronous cotton-like material from Brisson's nose. He later performed several other surgeries on Brisson's nose as part of a multistage reconstruction program.

Dr. Hoefflin gave expert testimony on the standard of the appellant's care. His testimony supported the finding that the appellant was grossly negligent in failing to return Brisson's phone calls in the week following surgery. Specifically, a physician has an obligation to insure that the patient is properly cared for 24 hours a day. Given the facts as related by Dr. Hoefflin and Mrs. Brisson, it was "an extreme departure from the practice of medicine" not to "return the calls or to assure the patient is properly cared for."

Dr. Pasha's surgical technique similarly fell below acceptable professional standards. Dr. Hoefflin testified that, overall, the surgery "was one of the worst nasal operations" he had ever seen. He also had 20 "UCLA and world authorities on nasal surgeries" look at Brisson or her photographs who all agreed that the rhinoplasty was "an extremely poorly performed surgical operation."

Dr. Hoefflin went on to describe three specific problems with the surgery, each of which is reflected in the hearing officer's findings. First, the defendant drastically overresected (removed) nostril tissue, leaving an insufficient amount of soft tissue to cover the implant. As a direct result of this problem, there was stenosis of the nasal airways and lining, extrusion of silastic implants, and an infection. The "deformity" left by this overresection of tissue was evidence of incompetence. Dr. Hoefflin based this conclusion on photos taken of Brisson before and after the surgery, his own examination, and the patient's medical history.

Second, the appellant unnecessarily left a scar on the top of Brisson's nose. Dr. Hoefflin testified that the incision causing the scar must have been accidentally made because (1) it was not there prior to surgery, (2) there was no reason to make a purposeful incision there, and (3) he had seen this type of scar before when an instrument accidentally slipped. The scar was further evidence of an "incompetently performed rhinoplasty."

Finally, Dr. Pasha improperly used a silastic implant in the bridge of Brisson's nose. Dr. Hoefflin first noted that, although use of silastic in secondary or tertiary operations is not preferred, it is not evidence of incompetence. However, it is "an extreme departure from the standard of practice" to use a silastic implant when the patient was told that cartilage would be used.

The second procedure in this case involved a mammoplasty, mastopexy, and lipectomy.

Meretsky v. Ellenby[2]

The plaintiff brought an action against a physician for performing surgery on the nose beyond consent.

The plaintiff had sought treatment from the defendant for removal of a bump on the bridge of the nose. She signed a consent form which stated "rhinoplasty." During surgery the defendant performed procedures on both the protrusion on the bridge of the nose and on the tip of the nose. This resulted in a "turned up nose."

The plaintiff alleged that she instructed the defendant not to operate on the tip of her nose. The defendant claimed that the plaintiff's written consent to a "rhinoplasty" barred the suit based upon Florida's informed consent statute. The district court in reversing the trial court found that the informed consent provision did not apply because this was not a case alleging lack of informed consent but rather one alleging surgery beyond consent.

Folse v. Anderson[3]

The plaintiff alleged that the defendant was merely to perform surgery for the purpose of correcting a slight thickening of the skin on the end of plaintiff's nose and that he exceeded his authority by performing more extensive surgery on the nose, altering his appearance.

Additionally, the plaintiff alleged that the defendant had warranted that she would have an improved appearance and no breathing impairment.

The court found that the allegations of the plaintiff had no basis, pointing out the following relevant testimony: (1) Dr. Harold Cummings testified he had given the plaintiff a physical examination one year prior to the operative procedure in question and advised the plaintiff to see a psychiatrist; (2) Dr. James W. Burke performed a dermabrasion on the face a month prior to the rhinoplasty. The plaintiff complained of acne scars on the end of her nose and Dr. Burke indicated that dermabrasion would not help and referred him to Dr. Anderson; and (3) Dr. Anderson testified that the results of the rhinoplasty performed were well within accepted medical practice. He explained the steps performed: removing the nasal hump, narrowing the nose, shortening the nose, and working on the tip of the nose.

---

[2] 370 So. 2d 1222 (Fla. Dist. Ct. App. 1979).

[3] 202 So. 2d 404 (La. Ct. App. 1967).

Raschel v. Rish[4]

The plaintiff claimed her attending physician, Dr. Benito Rish, performed a submucous resection negligently at the defendant hospital. The plaintiff claimed the hospital was liable by not revoking Dr. Rish's privileges, liable for failing to obtain an informed consent, and derivatively liable for the acts of Dr. Rish. The court dismissed the derivative action finding that the plaintiff had directly engaged Dr. Rish as her physician and paid him directly.

The court did, however, find an issue of fact in the allegation that the hospital failed to adequately investigate Dr. Rish. Although a hospital is not responsible for the actual treatment of a patient by a private physician, when procedures for reviewing a physician's qualifications create a foreseeable risk of harm, an independent duty to such patients is established.[5]

To create this issue of fact the plaintiff showed that Dr. Rish had been sued at least three times.

§ 11.26 Bibliography

J.M. Converse, Plastic Reconstructive Surgery. (W.B. Saunders, 1977).

R.M. Goldwyn, The Patient and the Plastic Surgeon. (Little, Brown & Co., 1981).

R.M. Goldwyn, The Unfavorable Result in Plastic Surgery. (Little, Brown & Co., 2d ed. 1984).

W.C. Grabb, and J.W. Smith, Plastic Surgery. (Little, Brown & Co., 1984).

H. Gray, Anatomy of the Human Body. (Lea & Febiger, 30th ed. 1985).

Habal, Morain, Lewin, Parsona, & Woods, 5 Advances in Plastic and Reconstructive Surgery. (Year Book Medical Publishers, 1989).

S.H. Miller, Year Book of Plastic and Reconstructive Surgery. (Year Book Medical Publishers, 1989).

T.D. Rees, II Aesthetic Plastic Surgery. (W.B. Saunders, 1980).

J.H. Sheen, Aesthetic Rhinoplasty. (C.V. Mosby, 1976).

---

[4] 110 A.D.2d 1067, 488 N.Y.S.2d 923 (1985).

[5] Precedents include Bouhall v. Hanlon, 99 A.2d 857, 472 N.Y.S.2d 774 (1984); Elam v. College Park, 132 Cal. App. 3d 332, 183 Cal. Rptr. 156 (1982); Johnson v. Misercordia, 99 Wis. 2d 708 (1981).

CHAPTER 12

BREAST SURGERY

§ 12.1 Introduction

Many women are dissatisfied with the shape, the size, or the position of their breasts. If they are small, they may want them larger; if they are large, they may want them smaller. If they are hanging, they may like them picked up. After mastectomy as a result of breast cancer, they may like them rebuilt. This chapter discusses the four major operations that are used daily for breast transformation.

§ 12.2 Types of Breast Operations

Breast Reduction. If a woman feels her breast is too large or too large and pendulous, then the skin, fat, and breast tissue are reduced, and the breast is reshaped, reconstructed, or repositioned on the chest wall.

Dermal Mastopexy. If the breast hangs too low on the patient's chest wall, portions of skin are excised in much the same manner as for breast reduction, and the resulting breast is elevated to its former location.

Breast Augmentation. If the breast is too small or has lost volume due to pregnancy or breast-feeding, a silicone or saline implant (prosthesis) is inserted beneath either the breast tissue or the pectoralis muscle to enlarge, or augment, the breast.

Breast Reconstruction. A woman whose breast has been claimed by cancer may opt for the reconstruction of a new breast. There are exciting procedures to fashion a new breast for her, and several ways to accomplish this. The first is to borrow skin and muscle from the back utilizing a latissimus dorsi flap. Another is to use the abdominal muscle and its overlaying skin in a Tram flap. Thirdly, if there is enough skin left after the removal of the breast it can be mobilized and a prosthesis used to create the mound.

Surgery for Asymmetrical Breasts. In addition to these four conditions of the female breast, occasionally women seek treatment for noticeably asymmetrical breasts. A discussion of this treatment begins in § **12.37**.

Gynecomastia. Finally, the male breast sometimes suffers from a condition called *gynecomastia.* The name comes from two Greek words meaning "breasts of a woman." When, for hormonal reasons, men develop breasts that are too large, with either too much fat or too much breast tissue, or both, they can be reduced and reshaped by the plastic surgeon. This is discussed in § **12.49**.

§ 12.3 Consultation

The ideal candidate for a breast reduction is a woman of normal weight, stature, and height, with excellent health and emotional stability and breasts much larger than she desires.

During the first consultation, a thorough medical history and physical examination should be done. No patient considering surgery should be taking aspirin or aspirin-containing compounds nor should she be a smoker. A woman who does smoke should stop smoking two weeks prior to the surgery. Both aspirin and smoking can cause increased bleeding during the operation and add risk to the procedure.

The patient's *menarche* (beginning of her monthly periods) should be noted, and the physician should discern at what point in the cycle the breasts enlarge. One might consider discontinuing taking birth control pills prior to surgery because they are known to cause thrombophlebitis, an added danger to the surgical procedure. Does this ideal patient have children, has she been pregnant, did she breast-feed, when did her breasts become large, and does she have a family history of cancer of the breast? Any information that can be gleaned about her breasts and their development and change should be noted in her history.

The operation should be explained to the patient very carefully. Scarring is the greatest deterrent to this operation. For the most part, women seeking a breast reduction elect to have scars on smaller well-shaped breasts than to keep their unscarred large breasts. They find it easier to deal with the scars than they do with unwieldingly large breasts. However, many patients are much more concerned about the scarring after the surgery is done than they were before. Prior to the operation, they were expecting a new released freedom in the chest area, with breasts that do not weigh them down and cause them difficulty in dressing and movement. However, once this goal has been achieved, they start to concentrate on the unattractiveness of the scars. A diagram of the incisions should be drawn for the patient, and a copy given to her. An actual drawing with a felt-tip pen should be made on the skin of her breasts. It would be helpful to have a family member present. A Polaroid picture should be taken of these markings and entered into the chart.

What women seek breast reduction? Any woman from teenage to old age whose breasts are too large is a potential candidate. The complaints range from physical discomfort to psychological distress. The chief indication for breast reduction at any age is excessive weight and discomfort of the breasts. These patients complain of many symptoms: the weight of the breast pulling on the ligaments causing pain, cyst formation, fibrocystic disease, labored breathing, and difficulty dressing. Special bras have to be constructed for women with extremely large breasts, who may develop ridges in their shoulders caused by their weighty breasts. Some women go on to develop *intertrigo,* a rash underneath the breast, where the skin is contiguous. Postural changes develop, such as *lordosis* (arthritis of the cervical spine).

Peer pressure motivates some adolescents to have their breasts reduced. Some young full-breasted girls do not like to be stared at by high school boys. They are often the object of ridicule and derision. This is psychologically damaging to many girls, their self-image becomes a problem, and they yearn to look more like others. In addition, they would like to play sports, and run and jog with more ease than they can with large breasts. When their breasts become more pendulous because of aging, many women would like the comfort of smaller, more manageable breasts. It is for this reason that many women over 60 are having breast reductions.

As women age, a real fear is the development of cysts or fibrocystic disease within large breasts. These cysts can eventually turn into cancer, although much of breast cancer is linked to a strong family history of malignant breast disease. Some patients may never develop breast cancer, but are merely cancer-phobic.

§ 12.4 Informed Consent for Breast Reduction and Mastopexy

The informed consent must be part of the consultation for a breast reduction or a mastopexy. The problems of breast surgery must be clearly outlined for the patient. Perhaps the largest drawback to breast surgery is the postoperative scars. Some patients think that, if an operation is performed by a plastic surgeon, there will be no scars. This is not true. Every time a breast reduction or dermal mastopexy is done, there will be telltale scars around the areola, vertically underneath the breast, and in the submammary line. At this point in the development of plastic surgery techniques, there is no way to avoid these scars, and their healing is contingent upon the patient's skin chemistry and unknown until it takes place. In addition, the skills of the surgeon plus the care the patient gives herself postoperatively will contribute to the way the scars heal. The patient must be told that the scars will look good right after the operation, but will then start to mature after four to six weeks. They usually stay red and thickened for several months to one year, at which time most scars will lose their red ropy quality and develop into a scar which is acceptable to the patient.

Because the operation is usually done in the hospital, and always under general anesthesia, the possible complications of general anesthesia must be discussed with the patient. These are thrombophlebitis, pulmonary embolism, pneumonia, atelectasis, and even death. These complications occur very infrequently but they must be pointed out to the patient in the informed consent consultation. The patient should be advised that breastfeeding after the operation might be possible but may be impaired as a result of interference with the mammary ducts. Patients should be warned that nipple sensitivity is usually not impaired after surgery, but sometimes the degree of erotic sensation in the nipple-areola complex may be decreased postoperatively. In the older woman requiring free nipple-areolar grafting, it should be made clear that there will be no sensation in the breast because the nipple and areola are removed and replaced as a full thickness skin graft.

The patient should be aware that she cannot exercise for one month after the operation and should remain in a brassiere for that length of time.

§ 12.5 Anatomy of the Breast

The breast, or mammary gland, is an accessory of the reproductive system in function. Its internal glandular system secretes milk for nourishment of the infant, but it is more closely related to the skin by virtue of its structure and its development. It is found in the adult female emulating from the anterior chest wall between the second and sixth or seventh rib, and from the lateral border of the sternum medially into the anterior axillary line. It is a prominence about 3 to 5 cm away from the chest wall and it is approximately 10 to 12 cm in diameter in the normal female. Its average weight is 150 to 200 grams and it increases to twice that weight during lactation. On most females, the left breast is somewhat larger than the right. The gland is formed in lobes radiating around the nipple, and each lobe has its own duct. The gland consists of *adipose tissue* or fat cells which are between the lobes and the *stroma* or connective tissue of the gland. The connective tissue in certain areas is known as suspensory ligaments of the breast or *Cooper's ligaments.*

The nipple projects as a small, round body slightly below the center of each breast at about the fourth intercostal space. The tip is perforated by 15 or 20 minute ducts which lead to the milk ducts. It is surrounded by the pigmented areola. The color of the nipple-areola varies from individual to individual. Under the areola are large sebaceous glands that make small elevations. These are the *Montgomery glands* which secrete a lubricating material used to protect the nipple during nursing.

During adolescence, the breast develops and enlarges its glandular tissue, particularly the ducts depositing adipose tissue between them. After the menstrual cycle begins, there is enlargement in the breasts every month until they reach their full development, sometime around the age of 16 or 17. During pregnancy the gland enlarges visibly as the duct system develops to accommodate the milk and secretion of the gland during the last three months of pregnancy. It is during this period that the fat cells are almost completely replaced by the normal breast tissue.

After lactation is finished, the gland gradually regresses by losing portions of its glandular tissue and ducts. Adipose tissue returns and there is a decrease in the size of the breasts as a whole. They usually become more flabby and pendulous than before the pregnancy. The pigmentation of the nipple and the areola tends to decrease but does not go away entirely.

The arteries supplying the breast are the branches of the lateral thoracic artery, the intracostal arteries, and the internal mammary arteries. In addition, there is a blood supply from the subdermal plexus, which is why keeping the dermal layer of skin intact around the nipple-areola is so important in preserving its blood supply. The nerve supply to the breast and nipple comes from the anterior and lateral cutaneous branches of the fourth, fifth, and sixth thoracic nerves.

The difference in the size and shape of the breast is determined by skin texture, the time of the woman's cycle, hormonal secretions controlling the breast, the amount of exercise and stretching one does, and in general the condition of the patient's skin, with its inherent elasticity. Breast size changes throughout adult life and when a breast reduction or mastopexy is decided upon it is important to know if the woman plans another pregnancy and lactation. It is important for the surgeon to be aware of the nerve supply to the breast. It must be preserved during the development of the flaps to ensure sensation to the nipple. One must be careful not to put too much pressure or tension on the breast by cutting away too much skin and closing the breast too tightly. This pressure could stretch the arteries, decreasing the blood supply to the flap causing it to die.

§ 12.6 Breast Reduction Techniques

Some form of reduction of female breasts was done as early as 400 years ago. One popular method for breast reduction was described by Biesenberger in 1928, in which an "S" shaped excision was made through the breast itself. A rotation of the remaining portion of the breast was made, and attached to itself to form a new round-shaped breast. This early method was adequate for reduction of the breast, but many complications occurred, including lack of blood supply to both the nipple and the skin, causing sloughing. Other well-known surgeons in the next 20 years made significant contributions to breast reduction technique. In the fifties, a Swedish surgeon named Strombeck devised a key-hole pattern for breast reduction in which he utilized and embellished a previously described concept of a dermal bridge. This was primarily to insure the viability of the nipple by transposing it on a dermal pedicle. In the Strombeck procedure, the mammary gland is resected both below and above the dermal pedicle.

In 1960, a famous Brazilian surgeon, Dr. Pitanguy, devised a method of breast reduction employing a horizontal dermal dissection with a "keel-shaped" resection into the capsule of the gland (see **Figures 12–1** and **12–2**). In 1972, McKissock described a vertical dermal pedicle for nipple transposition. This technique is widely used today and is known as the *inferior pedicle* (see **Figure 12–3**). To some surgeons this technique seems quite safe, because the blood supply to the pedicle is more reliable. This method yields well-shaped breasts with less possibility of nipple loss.

Today the two operations most commonly done are the inferior pedicle of McKissock, or a superior pedicle, usually variations of the Pitanguy or a modification of the Strombeck operation.

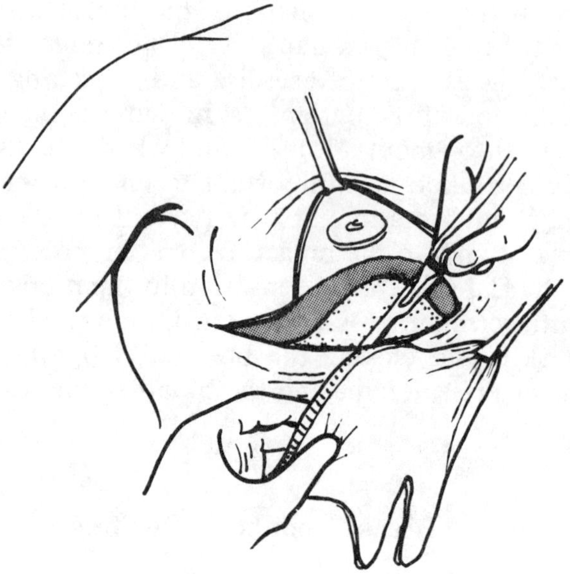

Figure 12–1. The dissection of the lower portion of the breast and at the submammary line in both the Strombeck and the Pitanguy procedures.

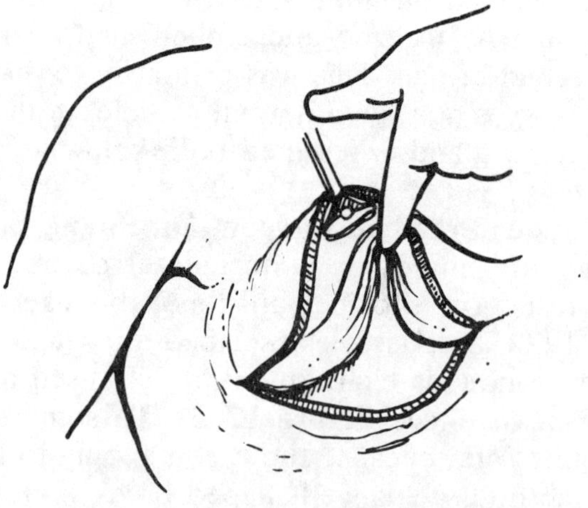

Figure 12–2. A finger is inserted underneath the dermal dissection and into the breast's capsule, which is the upper point of the dissection in the Pitanguy operation.

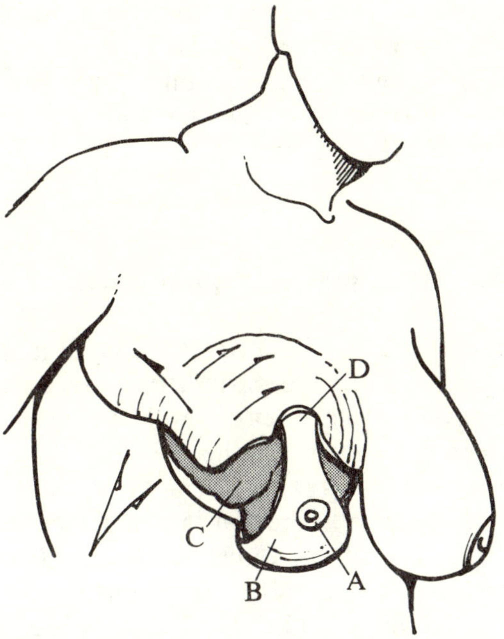

Figure 12–3. The inferior vertical dermal pedicle, or McKissock, operation. "A" is the nipple areolar complex left on the dermal dissection, "B" is the inferior pedicle, "C" is the part of the breast to be resected, and "D" is the future site of the nipple areolar complex.

§ 12.7 Anesthesia

Many patients ask if a breast reduction can be done under local anesthesia. It cannot, because there is too large an area to numb with the injections of local anesthesia. Furthermore, the incisions are too deep, with too much pulling and retraction on the breast to warrant local anesthesia. Total relaxation of the patient is needed.

Therefore, the operation is only done under general anesthesia. Some surgeons place the patient on her back with arms outstretched; others bring the patient to a sitting position on the operating table so that the breasts can hang in their normal configuration. Symmetry can be more easily achieved in this position, as well as a good shape for each breast while it is being operated on. The patient is intubated, and before extubation a supportive dressing is applied so that coughing or wretching during extubation will not disturb the stitches or cause any additional bleeding.

A well-administered general anesthesia is a safe and necessary component of this surgery. There are, however, risks involved in general anesthesia. These are discussed in § **12.11**.

It is important to know at this point that the time taken to perform a breast reduction varies from surgeon to surgeon depending on her speed, skills, and habits. Although the operation should not be performed in haste, it should be performed as efficiently and as expeditiously as possible in order to decrease the amount of time during which the patient is under general anesthesia.

§ 12.8 Description of a Standard Breast Reduction

Once the appropriate technique for a breast reduction has been selected to satisfy the particular needs of the patient (that is, according to the size, shape, and pendulousness of her breasts, and her age and general physical and emotional condition), she enters the hospital. Prior to surgery, a felt-tip pen is used to outline the areas of incision on the skin of the patient's breast (see **Figure 12–4**). The operation is performed under general anesthesia. The usual duration of the operation varies from surgeon to surgeon, anywhere from two-and-a-half to five hours.

The nipple-areolar complex is circumscribed with a blade and a dermal dissection is done on the skin around the areola. The blood supply to the nipple-areolar complex comes from the subdermal plexis, so great care must be taken to preserve this dermal layer.

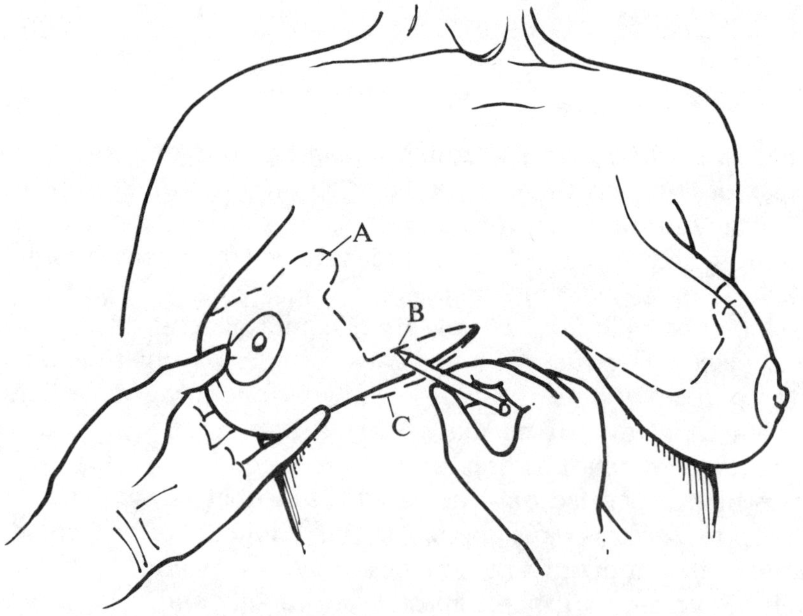

Figure 12–4. Breast markings prior to surgery. "A" is the new site for the nipple areolar complex, "B" is the medial line for dissection, and "C" is the lower limits of the dissection.

In doing the superior pedicle operation, three points are drawn in a triangular fashion around the nipple-areolar complex, and this skin is dissected within those points, leaving the dermis in place. Two other points on the lateral and medial portions beneath the breast are incised straight through the dermis to the subcutaneous tissue with one incision going from the lateral to the medial point in the submammary line. Then the amputation of the breast is done, excising large amounts of skin, subcutaneous tissue, fat, and mammary tissue itself. One procedure takes this dissection up to the capsule of the breast but experience, coupled with the desire of the patient for a smaller breast, must determine the amount of tissue to be removed. Bleeding, which can be copious, is usually quickly coagulated. The nipple is then elevated on its pedicle to its new position at point A, and the excess breast tissue removed. Points B and C are approximated with subcutaneous sutures (see **Figure 12–5**). The breast is then brought down to the submammary line and the vertical line (that line between the bottom of the areola and the submammary line) is approximated with several layers of sutures. An opening is made in the skin of point A, and the nipple-areolar complex is elevated on its pedicle to this point and sutured in place. A Penrose drain is used to relieve the dead space of any bleeding, and it exits from the breast laterally.

When the same procedure is accomplished on the other breast and when the nipple-areolar complexes are equal at the cone of each breast, the area is bandaged. The patient is then brought to the recovery room. When she awakes, she might experience some mild to moderate discomfort caused by the pressure of the dressing on her chest. This pressure dressing is applied tightly to avoid any postoperative bleeding.

The patient remains in this dressing for one to two days and then the dressing is removed and the Penrose drain is taken out. A brassiere is placed on the patient which she is asked to wear for three to four weeks.

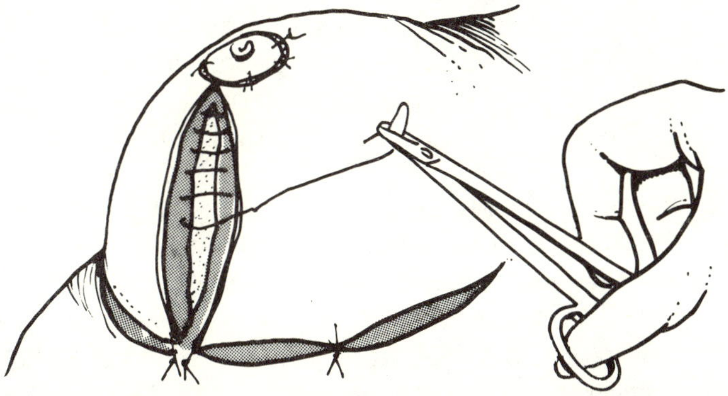

Figure 12–5. An absorbable suture is used for the subcutaneous layer. This layer is pulled from the areola to the submammary line, and the skin covers it.

Antibiotics are usually started intravenously during the operation and the patient is kept on oral antibiotics for the following week to avoid any chance of infection in this large dissected area.

§ 12.9 Postoperative Care

After a breast reduction, the patient must restrict her shoulder and arm movements. There are many stitches and a great deal of healing must take place in the breast area. When the arms are elevated or extended from the shoulders in any way, the pectoralis muscles come into play. The sutured breast tissue will move with the pectoralis muscles and so this activity must be limited. Patients should sleep on their backs, they should not carry packages, lift children, or reach for any articles on a high shelf. They should not drive for three weeks postoperatively. Any sexual activity involving the breast area is not permitted for at least one month. Showers should be restricted for at least one week until the initial healing occurs. Sutures are usually removed anywhere from 10 to 20 days depending on the procedure and the particular patient. Exercises should be avoided for one month. The patient should use common sense in determining her own postoperative limitations. Although the surgery for the breast is very important, it is equally important to have careful postoperative care to ensure the best results.

§ 12.10 Possible Complications and Unfavorable Results

The operation may be done well and a good result may be compromised because of bad postoperative care. When the patient sees an untoward result, such as infection, hematoma, skin slough, or excess scarring, she may think that it is a result of the surgeon's technique. But in fact her bad result may be brought about by her own postoperative care. It is very important for an attorney who is examining a plaintiff in this area to elicit a careful recounting of her activities from the time she left the hospital until a later date.

Unbeknown to her surgeon, one overweight young woman went on a liquid protein diet after a breast reduction. It was one year after surgery and, although the breast had healed well, there were large, ropy scars underneath the patient's breasts. A scar revision was done under local anesthesia by the surgeon to ameliorate the scars. The patient left the operating room and returned home to help her family move. On the night of surgery and for several days thereafter, the patient lifted heavy boxes from one house to a car and back from the car to a new home. Her stitches pulled apart and the scar areas became infected. Her lack of nutrition because of her protein diet caused further breakdown of the incisions. Certainly the surgeon was not at fault in this instance, because the patient performed activities that were well beyond the realm of normal good sense. In addition, she was specifically instructed by her surgeon to rest. A surgeon must carefully instruct the patient about her postoperative care, and she should follow those instructions. It is crucial for the attorney to elicit a meticulous, chronological sequence of activity in the postoperative period.

Another instance of skin slough occurred in a 48-year-old woman who had a breast reduction under general anesthesia. When developed, the skin flaps were too thin. Too much skin had been removed and the skin at the lower pole of the vertical incision was taut. Stretching of the blood vessels caused some necrosis of a triangular skin area at the inferior end of the vertical incision. The patient had been very careful postoperatively not to harm herself in any way. The area of skin was demarcated and was eventually debrided by the surgeon. The patient was unhappy with the resulting scar, although it did heal over with only the slightest discoloration, retaining a pinkish hue because of the granulation tissue. This was not a result of patient's postoperative care but was one of the complications that can occur. If the surgeon failed to warn the patient of this possibility,—that is, skin slough, which is one of the known possible complications of breast reduction—then he would be liable for performing an operation on her without her informed consent. In breast reduction, as in any other operation, the surgeon should warn the patient about any eventualities that could occur. The surgeon committed no negligence here. What occurred was a complication. What is at issue here is the informed consent.

§ 12.11 —General Anesthesia Complications

Breast reduction done by any accepted technique and under general anesthesia is a major surgical endeavor. Warnings must be clearly given regarding those complications which may ensue. Studies prove that the larger the breasts, the greater the possibility of complications.

In most breast reductions, there is approximately a 10 to 20 percent complication rate, depending on the skill of the surgeon and the patient's postoperative care plus her ability to heal. The common complications of general anesthesia are discussed below.

Thrombophlebitis

Thrombophlebitis can occur in heavy women who are immobilized under general anesthesia for long periods of time if there is any venous disease or stasis because of varicosities, congestive heart failure, or any other medical conditions. Taking the birth control pill can increase the possibility of thrombophlebitis. No patient should be put under general anesthesia unless they are wearing constrictive elastic stockings or pneumatic hose. *Thrombophlebitis* is a condition in which thrombus or blood clot forms in the vein and is attached to the vein wall. At a certain point, the thrombus breaks off from the vein wall, and travels back through the superior vena cava, through the pulmonary artery, to the lungs. This is then known as a pulmonary embolism.

Pulmonary Embolism

A *pulmonary embolism* is a broken-off blood clot traveling into the lungs causing necrosis over that portion of the lungs. This is a serious problem and a life-threatening situation. The treatment for this is anticoagulant therapy. This should be explained to the patient before general anesthesia is administrated.

Respiratory Complications

The respiratory complications following surgery are a major cause in 25 percent of postoperative deaths, and a major contributory factor in another 25 percent.

Acute respiratory failure is closely related to the oxygen level in the patient's blood. Proper ventilation during the surgery and maintenance of the oxygen level of the blood are crucial for good operative pulmonary status. The patient should be encouraged to breathe deeply and cough postoperatively so that mucus plugs do not invade the lungs and so that they expand properly to give the most efficient ventilation possible.

Atelectasis

Atelectasis comprises 90 percent of all pulmonary complications. It is a term derived from Greek meaning "incomplete expansion." In the postoperative patient, it means there are places in the alveoli of the lungs in which no air passes, generally because of the collapse of the alveoli in that portion of the lungs. The causes of atelectasis during general anesthesia are bronchial obstruction and hypoventilation. It is important that the anesthesiologist maintains the patient's respiratory status properly during the entire operation. Both atelectasis and pneumonia can occur usually during the first 24 to 48 hours after surgery, and the symptoms are sudden onset of fever and tachycardia, sometimes followed in severe cases by dyspnea and cyanosis.

Cardiac Complications

Dysrhythmias are irregular heart beats. They are frequently associated with general anesthesia and represent a potential complication of any surgical procedure. Sinus tachycardia is not by definition a dysrhythmia but is frequently found secondary to lack of oxygen, lack of circulating blood volume, and pain.

Other causes of sinus tachycardia are dehydration, hyperthyroidism, and congestive heart failure. Further complications include supraventricular tachycardia, atrial flutter, atelectasis, bradycardia, sinus arrhythmia, and atrial fibrillation, to name just a few.

There is a slight possibility that during the surgery the patient might have a myocardial infarction. This may be secondary to the trauma to the body, to the general anesthesia, or may be coincidental to both.

Cerebral Anoxia

Because of various situations caused during anesthesia, a lack of oxygen-carrying blood to the brain can occur and cause the serious complication of *cerebral anoxia.* If this dreadful eventually occurs, the anesthesia record must be carefully noted to insure the proper ventilation of the patient during the entire operation.

A Chicago case was recently decided during which a woman was having a plastic surgical procedure under general anesthesia. After the patient was prepared and draped in the usual manner, and the surgeon began to make the incision, he noted that the blood was dark. He mentioned this to the anesthesiologist who had stepped away from the operating table momentarily. Upon his return to the head of the table, it was noted that the endotrachial tube had become dislodged from the oxygen machine, and the patient was receiving no oxygen. Her respiratory muscles were paralyzed because of the anesthetic and she could not breathe. The plastic surgical procedure was discontinued. The patient was left virtually brain dead because of the lack of oxygen to her brain.

§ 12.12 —Hematoma

A hematoma can occur during a breast reduction or dermal mastopexy simply by virtue of the fact that there is a large area of dissection with many blood vessels appearing in the operative site. These are usually clamped, tied, or coagulated and, if one of them breaks open after the surgery is completed, pumping blood into that breast, a hematoma can occur. Although a Penrose drain is used as an exit pathway for the blood, sometimes this will not be sufficient. Even if a Jackson-Pratt drain is used, the breast may have to be reopened, the clot removed, and the bleeder coagulated. Because of pressure and careful coagulation before the closure of the breast, hematomas are not terribly common in breast reduction. However, the symptoms of pain tenderness and heat in the involved breast should be looked for. The patient should be warned that, if these symptoms appear, she should notify the nurse at once.

§ 12.13 —Infection

As with any surgical procedure, an infection can occur in this operation. It can be caused by a break in sterile technique or excess blood in the area which serves as a nidus for infection. It can also be caused by a patient's carelessness postoperatively, such as touching her breasts, applying dirty clothing to her breasts, or any trauma that could damage the tissue. Usually, patients are started on antibiotics during the surgery for breast reduction. Often 1 cc of Ancef is given intravenously and this is followed by Keflex postoperatively to prevent any infection that might take place.

§ 12.14 —Fat Necrosis

Because a large part of the breast is fat there can be some necrosis of the tissue. Fat necrosis can be caused by infection or will lead to infection if the area is under too much pressure. The treatment for fat necrosis is careful debridement, soaks, and antibiotics.

§ 12.15 —Skin Slough

If there is too much pressure on the skin, either from excessive excision of the skin in the vertical area or too much pressure and tension on the skin, there will be a slough or death of the skin. This is caused by stretching the arteries to the skin and lack of blood supply, which causes necrosis, and the death of the tissue in that area. It is usually seen at the point of greatest pressure, which is the inferior portion of the vertical scar where it attaches to the submammary line. If this happens, the stitches must be released in an attempt to save the skin, allowing granulation to take place.

§ 12.16 —Nipple Slough

The patient must be warned that in occasional but rare cases there could be a slough of the nipple. This is caused by developing too thin a skin flap, or by sacrificing the blood supply to the nipple by a bad dermal dissection. It can also be caused by too much external pressure on the nipple-areolar complex because of a tight dressing, interference by the patient, or infection. When this happens, the nipple will necrose and it must be debrided. Of course this is a terrible eventuality in the case of a young woman and, if it happens, the exact cause of the problem must be discovered to determine negligence. If the patient is duly warned about this possibility in advance, the informed consent has been given and this portion of the malpractice has been covered. If there is still negligent surgery on the part of the surgeon, this must be established. If the necrosis is caused by infection or other unforeseen causes, it would be a complication and not a negligent act. Furthermore, if the necrosis is caused by bad postoperative care by the patient, this is contributory negligence and alleviates the surgeon of any responsibility as long as the patient had been properly instructed.

In a recent case of a young girl who had a breast reduction, the left breast and nipple were in perfect condition, but the right breast and nipple, which was somewhat larger than the left, showed some nipple slough. The history of the right breast contained a cyst underneath the nipple, and this was noted. At the time of surgery the cyst was removed from the nipple-areolar complex, and this caused a partial compromise of circulation. The dressings were applied in the normal fashion and the nipple-areola was cyanotic for several days postoperatively. The stitches were released and the nipple continued to darken. Approximately 70 percent of the right nipple sloughed although careful antibiotic therapy, soaks, and meticulous attention by the surgeon was given for several weeks after the operation. The treatment for nipple slough is the reconstruction of the nipple-areola with full thickness groin skin as a graft. The patient began a suit against the physician claiming lack of informed consent and surgery not up to the standard of care in the community.

§ 12.17 —Malposition of the Nipples

After the amputation of the breast has taken place, a measurement should be made from the super sternal notch to each nipple to achieve symmetry when repositioning the nipples. The nipple should be 1 cm or so below the center cone of the breast because, as the swelling recedes, the breast will move slightly downward and the nipples will ride up. If they are placed high, when the swelling recedes and the breast takes its normal position, the nipple will ride up too high above center on the cone. Some allowance must be made for the decrease in swelling and the normal postoperative ptosis of the breast. It is important that both nipples be in exactly the same position.

Treatment for malposition of the nipples is to excise a portion of skin below the nipples and to reposition them at the cone of the breast.

§ 12.18 —Nipple Retraction

The nipples themselves can retract because of scar tissue underneath the breast and excess cutting in the area of the Cooper's ligaments. If nipple retraction is seen postoperatively, six months should be allowed to go by before the scar tissue is released and the nipple everted. This is not a usual occurrence after breast surgery, but it can happen, and it is quite disturbing to the patient.

§ 12.19 —Sensory Loss in the Nipples

Occasionally, because of the compromised blood supply to the nipple-areola complex or cutting of tissues causing trauma to some of the small sensory nerves, the patient experiences a decrease in sensation in the nipple-areola. Most patients demonstrate a temporary decreased sensory pattern for some months, or as long as one year after the operation. The larger the breasts, the greater the chance of decreased sensation because of the distance the nipples were moved. Sensation is not only the awareness of touch, but also a reaction of erectile tissue in the nipple. If this complication occurs, there is no way to correct it. It would be foolish for a surgeon to undertake this operation without warning the patient of the possibility of this happening.

§ 12.20 —Excessive Scarring

The patient should be aware of the possibility of unattractive scars on the breasts well in advance of surgery. Scarring of this kind is usually not because of the surgical technique, but depends on the skin's own chemistry and its ability to heal itself. Even after the reduction, the weight of the breast, although decreased, will still pull on the scars and stretch them. This is caused by gravitational pull during the postoperative period.

Immediately after surgery, the scars are usually of hairline quality, they have healed well, and the patient is satisfied. As they begin to mature, and the breasts begin to sag slightly as the edema diminishes, the scars become wider, especially in the lateral submammary lines and in the periareolar area. The vertical incisions between the areola and the submammary line usually heal the quickest and the best. From the second to the tenth month the scars are very red, thick, and wide. The application of vitamin E, cocoa butter, and steroid cream will sometimes decrease the width and improve the texture of the scars.

A minor scar revision can be done in these areas after one year to 18 months. No matter how bad the scars are, most patients feel that they are an improvement over the large breasts that they wanted to have reduced. It would seem that this operation makes most patients extremely happy postoperatively.

§ 12.21 —Dermal Mastopexy

There are patients who have breasts that may be a comfortable size, but whose position on the chest wall is not desirable. These patients suffer from ptosis or drooping of the breast; they have sagging skin with breast tissue that falls below the average site. Although these patients do not want their breasts made larger or smaller, they would like them raised. The procedure of choice for this deformity is called a *dermal mastopexy,* from Greek roots meaning "skin" (dermal), "breast" (masto), and "repositioning" (pexy).

The indications for a dermal mastopexy are breasts that have drooped because of pregnancy, weight loss, or just a change in the hormonal cycle. Of these drooping breasts,

1. The first is of adequate size and can be sometimes corrected by a prosthesis
2. Others are too large and this ptosis can be corrected by a breast reduction
3. Others are exactly the right volume but need a dermal mastopexy to raise the breasts by excising the skin envelope.

Ptosis of the breast beyond the aesthetically desirable limits can occur regardless of the existing breast size. When the breast size is small and the skin is not sagging too much, the insertion of a prosthesis may be able to correct the ptosis and at the same time bring the breasts up to a somewhat average position on the chest. The surgeon and the patient may consider themselves fortunate if they can solve the problem of ptosis with an implant. In some cases too large a breast implant would have to be used to correct the ptosis, and this would increase the volume of the breast too much.

Ptosis also can be associated with macromastia or large breasts, and this is corrected at the same time that the breast reduction is done.

The third category is that breast which is neither too large nor too small. The patient is happy with its size, but it droops below the desired limits on the chest wall. The skin envelope operation involved here is marked in much the same fashion as the reduction. Without changing the volume of the tissue, the breast can be raised by excising the amount of skin beneath it. The skin in this procedure is not undermined, but is rather removed and discarded.

The dermal mastopexy technique is much like the breast reduction technique. Depending on the selection of the technique (see **§ 12.6**), the markings are made prior to surgery and the dermal dissection is done from between a point above the breast and that below the breast. After the skin markings are made and the dermal dissection is done, rather than removing any breast tissue, the dermis-to-dermis suturing is done, thereby strengthening the wound and making the scar somewhat less noticeable than in the breast reduction. The nipple is then raised on its dermal pedicle and repositioned at the new site at the end of the cone. Some alterations may have to be made by extending the scars slightly in the submammary line, but these extensions are often less than the extensions of the breast reduction.

§ 12.22 Complications and Undesirable Results

Some of the complications of a dermal mastopexy are similar to those of the breast reduction, which are discussed in §§ **12.10** through **12.20**.

In the dermal mastopexy, the same general anesthetic complications obtain, although some surgeons prefer to do a dermal mastopexy under local anesthesia. This is possible because it is basically a skin operation and the breast is not entered surgically. A hematoma can occur with a dermal mastopexy, although it is less likely than with a reduction. Infection can always occur. There is no fat necrosis in a mastopexy. Some skin slough is possible, but the skin tension is usually less in this procedure than in a breast reduction. The nipples can be malpositioned even with a skin operation but do not retract in a dermal mastopexy. There can be some sensory loss in the nipples, although this too is less likely than in a breast reduction.

The main problems with mastopexies are the scarring, because of the patient's skin chemistry, and the continued sagging of the breast. In doing a dermal mastopexy, the breasts can be raised to a certain position on the chest wall and no higher. Patients with ptosis of the breasts have a lack of elasticity of the skin. After the mastopexy is done, more drooping may occur and a secondary operation may be required. The patient should be warned of this possibility prior to surgery.

§ 12.23 Introduction to Augmentation Mammoplasty

Augmentation mammoplasty means increasing the size of the breasts. This is a common operation in the United States today. Available data suggests that approximately 35,000 women undergo this procedure each year in this country. It is a simple and relatively uncomplicated procedure to both enlarge and elevate the breasts.

The type of patient seeking an augmentation is usually a well-adjusted woman in her mid-thirties, married with 2 or 3 children, who would like to be able to wear clothes better. Either she had small breasts from puberty or has developed small breasts after pregnancy and breast-feeding.

More often than not, these patients are psychologically stable, they are interested in getting on with their lives, and do not want to be concerned with their silhouette when buying clothes.

Contrary to popular opinion, and although augmentation mammoplasty or breast augmentation started with show girls and women who showed their breasts in public as a business, augmentation is very seldom done for sexual reasons.

Breast augmentation began approximately 40 years ago with the use of free dermal fat grafts from the buttocks. These procedures proved largely unsuccessful because of an unequal absorption of the tissue. Breast implants and breast augmentations became even more popular in the early sixties when silicone-filled breast prostheses were introduced on the market. Improvements have been made in this prosthesis until the present time (see **§ 12.26**).

§ 12.24 Areas of Incision

The incision for the insertion of the breast prosthesis is done from three different vantage points.

Submammary Incision

Perhaps the most popular incision, this was the first developed and seems to have endured with the fewest of complications. The incision is approximately 1.5 inches long and is placed in the submammary line, lateral to the midline to allow easy insertion of the breast prosthesis behind the breast tissue, on top of the pectoralis fascia, or even underneath the pectoralis muscle. With this incision, there is no interference with the breast tissue at all, nor is nipple sensation interfered with. The breast itself falls over the incision which, in a matter of six months to one year, will heal so that it can only be noticed by the most careful inspection.

Periareolar Incision

This is a semicircular incision on the lower half of the areola where the margin of skin reaches the pigmented portion of the areola. Once this incision is made, one can move the breast up and, dissecting around it, go down to the submammary area of the breast. Some surgeons even go underneath the pectoralis muscle from this incision. Other techniques involve splitting the breast itself and going through it, down to the point of insertion of the implant.

The advantage of this incision is that it shows very little scarring after the operation is completed because the incision site is at the margin of the pigmented area.

The disadvantage of this procedure is an occasional compromising of the sensitivity of the nipple by interference with the breast's nerve tissue.

Axillary or Underarm Approach

This type of incision has proven to be too difficult and has been discarded by many surgeons. Its advantage is that it too shows very little scarring but it is difficult to visualize the underlined tissue, and hematomas can develop.

§ 12.25 Position of Implants

The breast prostheses are most commonly placed between the breast tissue and the pectoralis fascia. This is an easy dissection and causes fewer hematomas than in other planes. Some surgeons advocate placing the prosthesis behind the pectoralis muscle. This is easily accomplished through the standard submammary incision. Some surgeons feel that a submuscular implant remains softer to palpation and has less chance of capsular formation. The chief disadvantage is upward movement of the prosthesis when the arm is raised, as well as a less natural look to the prosthesis in some patients.

One patient recently consulted a second surgeon because her implants were placed underneath the pectoralis muscle. Her breasts were large and the implant, which was of moderate size, did not fill out the skin envelope, resulting in a ridging of the breast in the lower portion. The breasts had a certain amount of ptosis and the insertion of the prosthesis under the pectoralis muscle did not correct this.

The second surgeon removed the prosthesis from the subpectoralis position and dissected another plane above the muscle and below the breast. The same prosthesis was inserted underneath the mammary gland and above the pectoralis muscle giving a nice contour to the breast, thereby correcting the patient's problem completely.

§ 12.26 Types of Prostheses

There are four types of prostheses popularly used today: the silicone gel prosthesis, the saline prosthesis, the double-lumen prosthesis, and the MEME prosthesis.

The *silicone gel prosthesis* is simply a high medical grade silicone gel which is self-contained in a polyethylene bag and inserted into the breast. In the past, silicone prostheses seemed to form a large scar contracture, which made them unpopular with some surgeons.

The *saline-filled prosthesis* was a deflatable polyethylene bag with a tube on it into which saline was injected once the implant was placed through a small incision beneath the breast tissue (see **Figure 12–6**). As

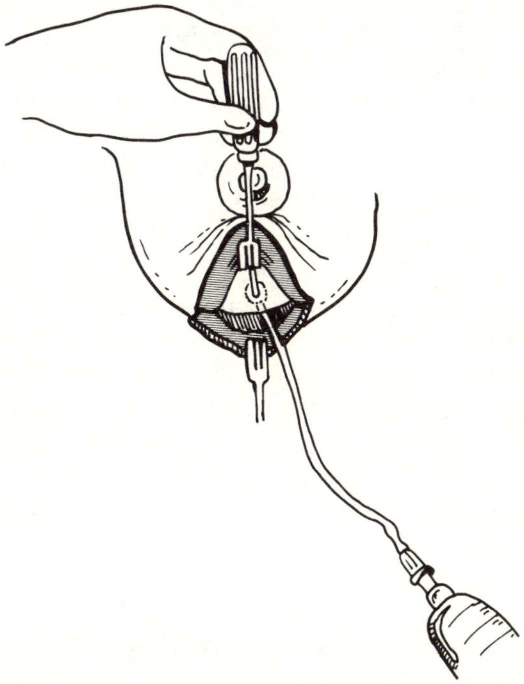

Figure 12–6. Injection of a saline-filled prosthesis after it has been inserted through a small incision beneath the breast tissue.

much saline could be injected into it as was desired, and the surgeon could watch the breast enlarge before her very eyes. The problem with the saline implant was that the saline often extruded from the implant, leaving a crinkly feeling to the implant at the periphery of the breast. Some surgeons even today use the saline prostheses, although more use the silicone prostheses.

A *double-lumen prosthesis* was developed, the inside of which was filled with silicone gel, and the outside was empty to be filled with saline after it was placed beneath the breast.

Recently, a new implant has been developed called the *MEME* implant, which is supposed to maintain a soft and natural breast. MEME is French for "the same." It prevents scar capsule contracture because of the dynamic relationship between the polyurethane covering of the prosthesis and the surrounding tissues. The scar capsule is attached to the surrounding tissues and the inner silicone portion of the prosthesis can move around freely within the scar capsule. The prosthesis itself does not feel firm.

The silicone and MEME prostheses are made in teardrop, oval, and round shapes. The teardrop implants are somewhat more difficult to position. The round prostheses seem to be the most useful on a general scale.

§ 12.27 Informed Consent for Augmentation

During the consultation the patient should be advised of the different incisions, the different types of prostheses, the different areas of implantation, what the limitations of activity are after surgery, and the complications. The main complication is capsular contraction, a phenomenon of scar formation that makes the breast feel hard.

A high percentage of patients have capsular contraction with the regular silicone implants. A conservative estimate would be about 30 percent. It is known that the capsule forms most noticeably on the same side as the hand the patient most frequently uses. A right-handed patient will have more capsule contractions on the right side, and the right breast will usually feel harder. This could be the result of friction caused by postoperative motion of the arm. It is obvious then that the patient must control her activities, wear a bra, and not carry, lift, or pull with her arms for at least two to three weeks after surgery.

§ 12.28 Anesthesia

The anesthesia for a breast augmentation can be either local, standby, or general. The determining factor is the emotional and mental status of the patient, whether the operation is done in the hospital or in an out-patient facility, and whether the surgeon feels that he can use a local anesthesia without too much pain to the patient. If the implant is going to be placed under the pectoralis muscle, at least a standby or a general anesthesia would be preferable.

The usual complications of general anesthesia can be present after an augmentation. However, the augmentation takes an hour or less in the hands of most surgeons, therefore the anesthesia time is decreased and the complications are fewer than with breast reduction surgery.

§ 12.29 Description of a Standard Operation

After the patient is prepared and draped in the usual manner on the operating table, with her arms at her sides, and either standby or general anesthesia has been administered, the incision that has been decided upon is made.

Submammary Incisions

If the incision is made underneath the breast in the submammary line, this incision is taken through the subcutaneous tissue and down to where the pectoralis fascia is located. Both sharp and blunt dissection can be done above the pectoralis fascia to accommodate the implant (see **Figure 12–7**). Once the plane has been dissected, the bleeding is carefully coagulated, because it is well known that blood can cause scar contraction. If

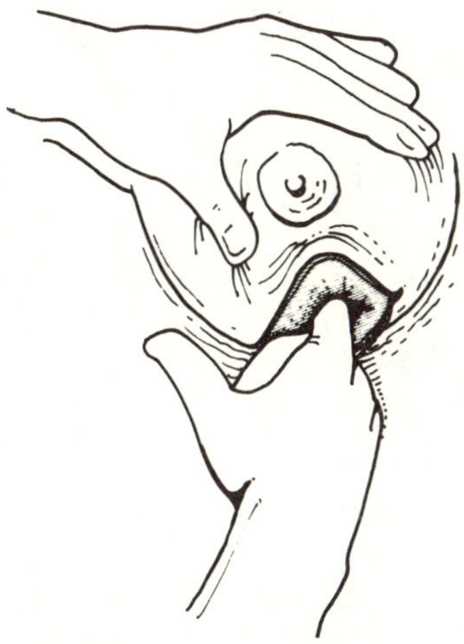

Figure 12–7. The breast tissue is separated from the underlying pectoralis fascia for the submammary insertion of the prosthesis.

the implant is placed underneath the pectoralis muscle, the corner of the pectoralis muscle is identified at the area of entrance through the skin in the submammary line. The pectoralis muscle is dissected away from the ribs and the implant is inserted within after the bleeding has been controlled (see **Figure 12–8**).

Periareolar Incisions

The breast is incised at the bottom of the areola and a blunt dissection is done to assure a large submammary space (see **Figure 12–9**). The wider dissection should be made at the base of the prosthesis to allow ample room for it to move about. A three-layer closure is made. Ace bandages

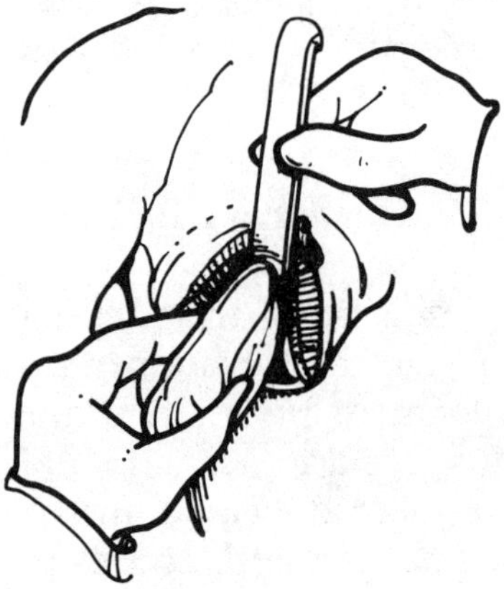

Figure 12–8. One hand holds the breast tissue up with a retractor while the other hand inserts the prosthesis into the submammary pocket previously developed above the pectoralis fascia.

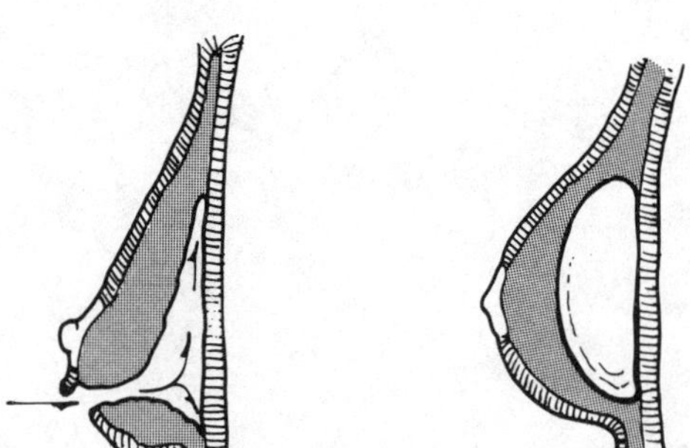

Figure 12–9. "A" shows the prosthesis being placed through the periareolar dissection into the dissected space below the breast tissue and above the pectoralis muscle. "B" shows the prosthesis in place.

are used after the surgery and the patient can go home either that evening or the following morning.

The patient should be fitted into a bra, which should be worn for several weeks after surgery to keep the breasts in place. She should be told at the same time to massage the breasts in several different directions, to try to decrease any capsular formation.

§ 12.30 Undesirable Results

The most common undesirable result of a breast augmentation is the possibility of the breast looking unnatural or "operated on." This can happen if the implant is too big, making the breasts appear taut and plastic, or is badly positioned, making them asymmetrical or uneven.

When patients decide to invest both financially and emotionally in an augmentation mammoplasty, they want the most they can get for their money. That sometimes means they would like the breasts to be made very large to compensate for years of having small breasts. The surgeon must try in these instances to convince the patient that moderation should be used in selecting the size of the implants. The patient might be excited about excessively large breasts for the first several weeks, but when she settled back into her life, she would probably find that her excessively large breasts are uncomfortable and unattractive, and she might then want them changed. It is the opinion of most plastic surgeons that the implant should be placed in the breast in such a way as to make it look natural and normal, not exaggerated and oversized.

Quizzing the patient psychologically in this instance is very important, and careful discussion before the surgery must take place. It is difficult to predict the size of the implant and the size of the breast before the operation because every woman's chest size is different, and the skin envelopes into which the prostheses are inserted look different on every woman.

§ 12.31 Complications—Hematoma

The incidence of hematoma following augmentation mammoplasty is very rare, less than 3 percent. A fiberoptic cautery facilitates the detection of bleeding vessels within the dissected area. If a good, clean dissection is done on the pectoralis muscles, there is minimal tissue destruction and not very much bleeding. Decreased bleeding seems to cause less capsule formation. A large vessel bleeding can cause a hematoma postoperatively, which will be detected by the patient's complaints of pain centered more on one side than the other, unless a bilateral hematoma is present.

Hematomas seem to be found more frequently with the periareolar and axillary approach because of the difficulty in visualizing the pectoralis muscle during the time of surgery.

A recent case to illustrate this point is that of a woman who went to an outpatient surgical clinic for an augmentation mammoplasty through the axillary approach. The incision was made in the axilla and the operation was done under local anesthesia with the patient tranquilized preoperatively. The right breast was operated on first and sewn up and, while the left breast was being operated on, a hematoma developed in the right breast. The surgeon completed the left breast and opened up the right breast in an attempt to find the bleeder. By the time the surgery ended, 300 cc of blood were removed from the right breast and, because of the difficulty with visualization, he could not see the bleeder within the fibers of the pectoralis muscle. Continued visualization failed to yield success in finding the bleeder and the patient was eventually packed and taken to a nearby hospital where another surgeon intervened. The implant had already been removed and only the bleeder needed to be found. The woman was in shock with a blood pressure of 80/60 when she arrived at the emergency room. She was taken to the operating room immediately and under general anesthesia a submammary incision was made and the breast tissue was lifted up. The bleeder was immediately identified and coagulated. The patient was transfused with two units of blood and the prosthesis was left out because of the problems with the dissection. The patient decided subsequently to have the other implant removed and did not want to deal with any surgery of her breasts again.

In this instance, was malpractice committed? The original operating surgeon did his best to insert the implants in the way which he and the patient had decided upon. He did not abandon the patient, nor was he negligent to her. The fact that he could not find the bleeder was not negligence on his part because he certainly tried to do it. If the patient had received the proper informed consent consultation—that is, that a hematoma could occur as is indicated in all these procedures—then she would have been aware of this possibility before the operation took place.

§ 12.32 —Infection

Infection is rarely found in a breast augmentation but sometimes it can follow a small hematoma, because clotted blood is a good medium for bacterial growth. Antibiotics can be given at the time of surgery to prevent any infection because foreign bodies are being introduced into the patient. Streptococcal infection is often found in the breast ducts and, if the approach to the augmentation is through the periareolar incision, the risk of infection is increased, possibly causing more capsular formation.

§ 12.33 —Decreased Sensation

Pressure from the implants or the disruption of the nerves in entering the breast with a periareolar incision could cause a decrease in nipple sensation. In addition, fibrous tissue caused by this incision through the superareolar area will cause a decrease in sensation quite frequently.

Periareolar and other scar formations usually heal well. Occasionally the scar will be thicker if the patient is prone to keloids. She should be warned of these possibilities in advance.

§ 12.34 —Malpositioning of the Implants

The malpositioning of the prosthesis is occasionally a problem at surgery but more often develops with scar formation postoperatively, when the prosthesis moves slightly upward or in another direction.

Severe malpositioning necessitates a second surgical intervention to break up the scar tissue and the adhesions within the dissected breast pocket. The prosthesis placed behind the pectoralis muscle is subject to displacement because of the movement of the arm pulling the pectoralis muscle up. The most common cause of a malposition and irregularity of the implants is thickened scar formation in that breast. This comes either from the use of the predominant arm or from excessive bleeding during the procedure.

A 34-year-old woman had had an augmentation mammoplasty by her gynecologist five years before she came to visit a plastic surgeon. She complained that the silicone implants were uneven and there was an uneven configuration of each implant with a ridging underneath the nipple. This was caused by scar tissue formation. The patient was extremely unhappy with both the scars and the look of her breasts. The surgeon suggested that she have a slightly smaller implant. The breast capsule was already formed, and a smaller implant would ride around in the pocket more easily. The amelioration of this situation could occur with an implant 22 cc less than the one already in place. The placement of the implant was submammary rather than subpectoral.

The operation was performed on this woman. The 200 cc implants were removed and 180 cc implants were reinserted. The thickened scar capsule formation was loosened up in the areas where it was felt necessary. The scar, which was placed in the submammary line, could not be made shorter but was refined. After the surgery, the patient had better-looking, symmetrical breasts without ridging. However, they were 20 cc smaller.

Eight weeks after surgery, there was more scar formation of the capsule. The patient became irate at the surgeon because a closed capsulotomy had to be performed. She sought the help of another surgeon, who reoperated on her putting a larger implant back in, and removed the scar tissue at surgery (opened capsulectomy). The breasts healed and more scar formation occurred. The patient sued the first plastic surgeon for malpractice, saying that he made the breasts smaller than she wanted them to be, but did not start suit against the gynecologist who had put the original prostheses in nor the second plastic surgeon, but sought the latter out as an expert witness.

The second plastic surgeon, feeling that the first plastic surgeon's work was satisfactory and that no malpractice had been involved, refused to testify on behalf of the plaintiff. Her attorney sought a plastic surgeon in the area who would say that the first doctor was negligent and at fault but none could be found. It was for this reason that the plaintiff dropped the case.

§ 12.35 —Deflation and Rupture of the Implants

Inflatable saline balloon implants have ruptured more frequently than the silicone gel type. Although easily inflated, the saline sometimes leaks out into the surrounding subcutaneous tissue through the polyethylene bag. There is no danger in this, but the implant deflates slightly and the prosthesis can be felt around the periphery of the breast. In these cases, the implant has to be reinflated or entirely replaced.

§ 12.36 —Seepage and Accusations of Silicone Causing Cancer

Although the saline implants can be deflated because of seepage of saline through the bag, it has been recently thought that some silicone could escape through the bag—minute amounts that could be carcinogenic. Recently, there has been a furor about this, so the drug companies and the FDA have sent out informative letters stating that this has been an experimental situation in laboratory animals, but that it does not happen in humans. Nonetheless, waves of fear went through the augmented community and queries were noted at offices of plastic surgeons throughout the country.

A recent study concludes that silicone prostheses do not cause cancer. Women who have had the operation should not be frightened, nor should it stop women from seeking the operation. If the silicone did seep in minute particles through the polyethylene bag it would stay within the scar capsule that had already been formed, and would not be disseminated through the body.

§ 12.37 Asymmetry and Atresia of the Breasts

Asymmetry usually appears at puberty when the breasts are developing. This is caused by genetic programming or some other retardation of the normal growth of the breast. Very often, both breasts will seem to be the same size and shape but one breast fails to develop (*atresia*). The other breast develops to a normal or greater than normal size.

This is a problem with young girls who are seen in locker rooms or in other situations where the discrepancy in the size of the breasts may be commented on by peers. This will often be an inducement for them to have the corrective surgery.

The treatment for this condition is usually to augment the smaller breast as this is a less-complicated procedure, although the larger breast can be reduced. Often a combination of reduction of the larger breast and augmentation of the smaller breast is done to achieve symmetry. This combined operation equalizes the breasts as much as possible and allows the patient to be much more content with her life.

§ 12.38 Introduction to Breast Reconstruction

Cancer of the breast is one of the most devastating and common diseases among women in the United States today.

Female breasts are considered a symbol of femininity as well as a secondary sex characteristic, and the loss of a breast can send a patient into panic, with feelings of loss, deprivation, and asymmetry. She simultaneously faces the threat of death and the psychic devastation accompanying the complete loss of a breast. She may feel unattractive. She may lose her self-image and self-esteem.

These feelings usually do not set in until after the patient is assured that she will not die and will not continue to have cancer. Once this happens, the normal reaction is to look toward some sort of reconstruction. Depression and panic can be reversed with the knowledge that reconstruction is a real possibility after a mastectomy.

Thousands of women undergo successful breast reconstructions every year. Nonetheless, the patient should be aware of the potential risks of surgery and the specific complications associated with a breast reconstruction. She should also be made aware that a postmastectomy reconstruction, while it improves her appearance and renews her self-confidence, can never perfectly mimic the other breast; it will be an improvement, but it will not be perfection.

Sometimes women are reluctant to undergo a reconstruction after a mastectomy because they have been overwhelmed by the loss of their own breast and the presence of cancer in their bodies. They have the feeling that a breast reconstruction will cause recurrence of the disease (it will not, nor does it interfere with treatment if disease should develop). Some women feel that, once the mastectomy is done, they have had enough surgery and want nothing more to do with an operating room.

Nothing was done about breast reconstruction until about 25 years ago. Starting with the early sixties, when breast augmentation was considered a safe and effective operation because of the advances of silicone chemistry, the silicone prosthesis was developed, which afforded a suitable breast mound. If not enough skin was left after a mastectomy, the prosthesis could not be adequately inserted, but it could be used when more distant tissue consisting of extra skin and sometimes covering was brought into the breast area.

The concept of flaps to cover the space where the breast was removed and the possibility of the insertion of a prosthesis under these flaps, has come about within the last ten to 15 years.

The philosophy of mastectomy has changed as well and the old Halsted-radical breast mastectomies are not being done today. Instead modified-radical mastectomies are being done, and sometimes a simple lumpectomy with a dissection of the axillary lymph nodes is recommended.

§ 12.39 Selection of Patients

The selection of patients for breast reconstruction is perhaps more demanding than for normal breast surgeries. Of course, the patient must be in the proper psychiatric state of mind to undergo this type of surgery. She should have a realistic approach to the result of the breast reconstruction; she should realize that the breast will not be perfect, but that it will improve her image by giving her symmetry. The patient should be cancer free when deciding to have a reconstruction. The other factors that are important are her age, her health, the size of the tumor, whether there were positive axillary lymph nodes, and the degree of tumor differentiation and blood vessel invasion. Patients with tumors of less than 2 cm in diameter and with uninvolved axillary nodes have the lowest risk of developing recurrent cancer.

If the remaining breast is pendulous, it may have to be reduced in order to approximate it to the other breast. This reduction is often done at the same time as the reconstruction on the opposite side.

§ 12.40 Timing of a Breast Reconstruction

Because the old radical mastectomy has been replaced by the modified-radical or even partial mastectomy, some plastic surgeons are inserting prostheses beneath the skin of the breast at the time of surgery, depending on the type of incision made by the general surgeon.

Although most women would like to have their breasts immediately restored to their original appearance, primary reconstruction in the opinion of many surgeons is probably not the best choice. There are many complications of mastectomy itself such as skin loss, hematoma, infection, and swelling, which make immediate reconstruction more difficult. It is also a good idea to redefine the stage of the tumor prior to the reconstruction.

If patients require chemotherapy or radiation therapy after a mastectomy, reconstruction is ill-advised, and should not be undertaken until all these modalities have been completed. Furthermore, if the patient has an immediate reconstruction and the reconstructed breast is not like the normal breast (which in most cases, it will not be), the patient may become dissatisfied. If, however, she lives for six months with no breast on one side, and then a man-made breast is done through reconstruction, she will appreciate it all the more, because she has already lived with her loss and her asymmetry.

§ 12.41 Options and Methods for Reconstruction

Depending on the type of incision and procedure used by the general surgeon to remove the breast in the first place, there are several options that the reconstructive surgeon has to create a new breast. The most popular ones are:

1. Insertion of a prosthesis when adequate skin coverage and pectoralis major muscle are present
2. Reconstruction with additional skin and muscle or myocutaneous skin flaps
   a. Latissimus dorsi flap
   b. Rectus abdominus (tram) flap
3. Use of a tissue expander.

Insertion of a Prosthesis

When the patient has had a partial mastectomy or a lumpectomy, and the pectoralis major muscle is left with a certain amount of skin coverage and subcutaneous tissue, it is fairly simple to insert a silicone prosthesis underneath the skin and/or pectoralis muscle to form a mound. Placement beneath the pectoralis muscle decreases capsular contraction and protects the implant from a thin skin cover. Approximately 200 to 300 cc of silicone or saline are used to give a satisfactory result.

In placing the implant in the subpectoral area, the most common problem is the high position of the implant.

Either of these implants can be inserted through the mastectomy scar if properly executed.

Reconstruction with Additional Skin Muscle (Myocutaneous Skin Flaps)

Patients who have tight, thin skin in the chest wall where the breast was amputated need extra tissue brought to the affected area. This tissue must be thicker than a skin graft and must have muscle underneath it for bulk. It is necessary to use a skin muscle flap rather than a skin graft because the skin on the chest wall is not thick enough to support a prosthesis and give the proper contour. The two myocutaneous flaps used are the latissimus dorsi flap and the rectus abdominus flap.

The difference between a skin graft to cover the breast and a flap to cover the breast is sometimes difficult to comprehend if it has not been witnessed in the operating room. A *skin graft* is a very thin piece of skin cut completely from another part of the body and applied over the muscles, subcutaneous tissues, or fat, providing skin coverage. The blood supply to the skin graft once it has been removed from its donor site is created by the blood vessels in the underlying tissues. It is able to assume this new blood supply because it is sufficiently thin to be nourished by the tissues beneath. However, when thicker portions of tissue are used, they must be brought around to the recipient site with their own blood supply intact. For these reasons, they are called *skin-muscle flaps,* and they are dependent on the artery that nourishes them in their original position. The definition of the flap then is the skin and/or muscle supported by its own nutrient blood supply and moved from its donor area to the area of need.

In reconstruction of the breast, one of the most used muscles is the wide muscle of the back or the *latissimus dorsi* muscle. This muscle is carried through the axilla with the skin and subcutaneous tissue and blood vessels intact above it. A portion of the muscle is detached and it is tunneled through the axilla with an elliptical pedicle of skin that is placed in the area of need on the mastectomy site. The back area or donor site is sutured, leaving a thin scar that usually presents no problems to the patient postoperatively. The muscle is attached to the surrounding muscles or their remnants. The skin is attached to the already available areas of skin, and the implant is placed underneath this mound of skin/muscle. Usually there is not enough muscle in this flap to form a mound itself, because the latissimus dorsi is a flat, thin muscle rather than a wide, thick one. It is for this reason that a breast prosthesis is inserted underneath the latissimus dorsi flap even though the muscle has been transferred.

This has been a very successful procedure and gives an excellent result for the most part, often mimicking the natural breast on the other side. If, however, the contralateral breast is large, it can be reduced. If it is small, it may be enlarged, thereby enabling both breasts to resemble each other fairly well.

Rectus Abdominus Flap

Recently another reconstructive technique has been used, employing the *rectus abdominus* muscle or strap muscle of the abdomen with a skin flap taken out at its inferior pole, turning the muscle on itself and tunneling it up through the bottom of the breast, setting the skin in place as in the latissimus dorsi flap. It allows the rectus abdominus muscle to act as a cushion for the implant. This procedure has attracted a lot of attention because inherent in it is an *abdominoplasty,* the decrease of the abdominal panniculus. This is good for women with generous abdomens but the procedure is fraught with complications because of the turning of the muscle on itself with possible subsequent kinking of the blood vessels. This muscle with its generous amount of fat and skin may form a mound large enough to eliminate the use of an implant. This of course will vary from patient to patient.

Tissue Expander

The last procedure used for breast reconstruction uses a tissue expander or balloonlike device made of synthetic material similar to the covering of the implants, and can be inflated once placed underneath the muscle. If the pectoralis muscle is left intact or partially intact, the tissue expander is placed underneath it and the overlying skin. It is filled from week to week or even day to day with a saline solution until the skin is stretched enough to allow the insertion of a regular prosthesis to create a better sound. Often a permanent tissue expander is used and it serves as a saline filled implant once the desired volume has been achieved. These tissue expanders are usually filled with anywhere from 350 to 550 cc of saline, and a large tissue expander can accommodate 700 cc.

The appropriate procedure for breast reconstruction is determined during the consultation, when the patient is interviewed and examined by the surgeon. She is usually shown pictures of the breasts of other patients who have had the operation. The pros and cons of the procedure are discussed by the surgeon and the patient, and the final determination is made.

§ 12.42 Nipple Reconstruction

After the creation of a mound with a successful flap transfer or the insertion of the implant, some patients decide they would like a nipple-areola reconstruction. Occasionally surgeons do this at the time of reconstruction, but it is generally thought that, by leaving the reconstructed breast and the reduced breast to equalize themselves by the alleviation of their swelling, after a few months they will come to rest in their normal position. This is important because the nipple-areola graft can be placed at the cone of the breast when the breast has reached its permanent location. Usually six months after the reconstruction is the advisable time to do this procedure.

The skin graft is taken from the vagina or the groin skin because of the deeper pigmentation of the skin in these areas. Full thickness skin grafts are used to reproduce the areola. Sometimes small pieces of diced cartilage from the concha of the ear are placed underneath the skin graft at the time of grafting to simulate Montgomery's glands, the small protrusions normally seen in an areola. A hole is cut in the middle of the skin graft and a mound taken from the earlobe or even from a toe is used to simulate the nipple. This central nipple portion is sutured into a skin bridge that is left when the skin is excised from the reconstructed breast. This simulates the nipple-areola complex. Although it is not a perfect match, it will be cosmetically pleasing for the patient, even when she is dressed in a T-shirt or a bathing suit.

§ 12.43 Complications and Undesirable Results of Reconstruction

These procedures, especially the myocutaneous flaps, are delicate and demanding and can have many complications. The common complications for breast flaps are:

1. Scarring
2. Hematoma
3. Infection
4. Skin loss
5. Loss of flap
6. Capsular formation
7. Asymmetry.

It seems that these complications are often seen in breast reconstruction because of the delicate nature of the operation and the difficult postoperative care. Some are of minor importance; some are of much greater importance. They will be examined one by one.

§ 12.44 —Scarring

The scars from these operations will be prominent but usually not a cause for concern. The scars of a reduced breast will be the same as those discussed in **§ 12.20**. In this situation, when the operation is not done for cosmetic purposes as much as to reconstruct an asymmetry, the scars will not be of so great of concern to the patient.

The scar on the reconstructed breast is usually an oblique scar from the upper medial portion of the breast down to the lower lateral portion depending on the method used to excise the breast originally. In the latissimus dorsi flap there is usually a large scar on the back going from the scapular downward toward the posterior iliac spine. The direction of this flap depends on the method used to reconstruct the breast, and which portion of the large muscle was taken.

These scars are often not hairline scars because of the movement of the arm pulling them apart during the postoperative period. This arm movement is usually unavoidable, and the patient should be warned that the scars will not be fine, hairline scars. Often the patient is asked to decide whether it is important to her lifestyle to wear a strapless gown or a bathing suit. If it is important then perhaps the scars could be placed lower.

The scar for the rectus abdominus flap is usually concealed by the patient's garments, but this can be a big scar or can be the normal suprapubic scar used in an abdominoplasty operation.

§ 12.45 —Hematoma

When a flap is brought around, bleeding can start inside the reconstructed area and any amount of excess fluid volume and any amount of blood inside the flap can exert tension and pressure on the flap, causing it to necrose by cutting off its blood supply.

Sometimes pain will not be detected in this area because of the decreased sensation of the tissues. It is important therefore to check the flap dressing every several hours during the first day of surgery to make sure that no hematoma is present. If one is present, stitches much be removed and the blood must be evacuated immediately. If there is a bleeder, it must be found, clamped, and coagulated.

Occasionally, a hematoma is found at the donor site, in the back or in the abdomen. When this happens, similarly the stitches are removed and the hematoma is expressed.

§ 12.46 —Infection

Infection can occur in any type of surgery, and especially in this type of surgery when two operative fields are present, the donor site and the graft site. Proper sterile technique is important during the surgery. Any breakdown in this technique could cause additional risks of infection, especially with the insertion of a foreign body prosthesis.

Prophylactic antibiotics are started intravenously at the time of surgery as long as the patient is receiving fluid through the veins. The patient should then receive prophylactic antibiotics for at least one week after the surgery.

§ 12.47 —Loss of Skin or Loss of Flap

Skin on a flap can be lost because of hematoma, infection, or excess tension on the flap. If the flap is pulled too tightly, and the blood vessel that supplies nutrition to it is stretched and goes into spasm, it will die, and a portion of the skin will necrose. If this happens, the remedy is to remove the stitches, thereby relieving as much of the tension on the flap as possible. A portion of the skin is lost; granulation tissue will come in secondarily. The skin is so delicate in this area after surgery that excess use of the arm, weight from clothing, or lying on the flap can cause loss of it during the postoperative period. The patient must be carefully warned about not doing this.

In the latissimus dorsi or the rectus abdominus flaps, the primary concern is the survival of the major artery on which the flap rotates. If too much pressure or tension is exerted on this artery, kinking occurs because of the rotation of the artery. The artery in addition may be cut during the dissection, and if a portion of the artery or one of the collateral branches is damaged, the flap may not receive adequate blood supply and will necrose. If this should happen, it would be advisable to remove the stitches and replace the flap in an attempt to save that portion of skin and muscle. Unfortunately, it is not often detectable as it is a slow but insidious process, and by the time it is noticed, cyanosis and anoxia have taken over to the point where the flap is no longer salvagable.

§ 12.48 —Capsular Formation

When the implant is used in a breast reconstruction, especially if it is next to the skin, a scar capsule is formed. The hardness or firmness felt is not the implant itself, but the scar tissue around it. This is treated the same as the capsule found in an augmentation mammoplasty. The capsule is broken up either by the application of external pressure with the hands or by surgical intervention.

The reconstructed breast may feel firmer and look rounder or flatter than the natural breast. Most likely it will not have the same contour as it did before the mastectomy, nor will it exactly match the opposite breast.

Reconstruction cannot restore normal sensation, but patients often feel a return of sensation to the breast area. If the nipple is reconstructed, there will be neither feeling nor erotic sensation, as these are simply skin grafts transferred to the breast for cosmetic purposes and do not function as nipples.

§ 12.49 Gynecomastia

Gynecomastia is the condition seen in males when hormonal influences cause them to develop femalelike breasts. It appears during adolescence; it may subside by the age of 18 or 20. Sometimes it is genetic, as in Klinefelter's syndrome, a hormonal imbalance associated with testicular atrophy. It can also be associated with thyroid disease, pituitary abnormality such as acromegaly, and benign and/or malignant adrenal or testicular tumors. If hypertrophy of either one or both breasts persists, surgery should be done to correct it, because it is a great embarrassment to young boys.

A thorough examination of the male with gynecomastia is essential, as is a consultation with an endocrinologist. If the problem is not hormonal, a surgical procedure is advisable. The condition is often caused by an excess of fat beneath the breast that protrudes, simulating the female breast. Both fat and breast tissue can be excised.

There are two methods for this correction. Without excess skin—when there is merely fat and breast tissue—a semilunar incision is made at the border of the areola. The breast tissue is removed through this buttonhole-type incision. The bleeding is coagulated, a drain is put into place, and the areolar incision is sutured. Especially in young men, the elasticity will allow the skin to go back more or less to its normal position. Using weights and exercising will develop the pectoralis muscle and will fill in any excess from the skin envelope.

A large amount of hanging skin in the area is a problem, as in a male who has been obese and then lost a large amount of weight. The reduction of skin cannot be done successfully in the circular areolar incision, and often a scar has to be made underneath the breast similar to that of a breast reduction scar, in order to remove the excess envelope of skin. Many males prefer the scar to having the appearance of a female breast.

The complications of a gynecomastia operation are the same as for other breast surgery—namely hematoma, infection, loss of skin tone, ridging in the area because of hematoma, and the lack of elasticity to bring the skin back to a normal position.

Careful postoperative care must be observed by the patient. An ace bandage should be worn around the chest at night for several months to allow the skin to retract back to its normal position. When this operation is successful, it is one of the most gratifying of all plastic surgery, because it alleviates the embarrassment that has plagued the patient for many years.

§ 12.50 Summary

Cosmetic and reconstructive breast surgery is among the most difficult surgery performed today. Women's feelings about their breasts go far beyond the skin, touching deep into their psyches. There are many reasons why patients have breast reductions or augmentations, other than pure physical comfort. Patients who come in for breast surgery should be evaluated very carefully psychologically because a bad result or bad scarring can cause them far-reaching problems that often extend all the way to the courtroom.

Surgeons must be very careful to give sufficient information for an informed consent to their patients. Without that, patients cannot properly decide to have an elective procedure. Most important to the patient's understanding when considering this type of surgery is the type of scarring and the way it forms. Most litigation involving breast surgery deals with bad scarring and/or sloughing of the nipple or the skin. These are serious complications and the patient should know that complications are possible before they embark on the operation.

There would be fewer lawsuits if there were better understanding between patients and surgeons.

§ 12.51 Illustrative Cases: Breast Reduction

Anderson v. Gorden[1]

The plaintiff, Kathleen Anderson, consulted with Dr. Howard Gorden to have a breast reduction. Dr. Gorden employed the Strombeck technique, which helps to maintain the patient's circulatory system in the breasts to reduce necrosis. He performed a two-and-one-half hour surgery removing more than 1500 grams of tissue.

Postoperatively the patient lost 30 percent additional breast tissue due to impaired circulation resulting in scarred, unevenly shaped breasts.

---

[1] 334 So. 2d 107 (Fla. Dist. Ct. App. 1976).

The jury returned a verdict in favor of the defendant finding that the evidence reflected that plaintiff's necroses was caused by blood circulation problems postoperatively and not related to the surgery itself.

Buckley v. Lovallo[2]

This case was an action to recover damages for negligence in the performance of a breast reduction.

The plaintiff prior to the surgery had lost over 70 pounds. However, her breasts still remained pendulous. She consulted a plastic surgeon who recommended surgery but advised the plaintiff that she should first obtain a medical consultation.

The plaintiff sought a consultation from the defendant, Frank Lovallo, upon the advice of her family physician. Dr. Lovallo was a general surgeon but he indicated to the plaintiff he had performed the surgery many times.

Lovallo used a Conway procedure. The plaintiff had bilateral scarring, misshapen breasts, and misplaced nipples postoperatively.

The plaintiff sued both the hospital and surgeon. The court dismissed the action against the hospital, finding that the plaintiff had failed to prove any violation of the hospital's standard of care based upon any theory of corporate negligence.

However, the jury did find against Dr. Lovallo.

At trial the plaintiff produced two experts. The first testified that he was unaware of any plastic surgeons performing breast reduction but, given the general standards in practice in Connecticut in 1977, thought that the defendant should have used a Weiss or Strombeck procedure with a McKissock procedure to transpose the nipple.

The second expert, the original plastic surgeon who was consulted, testified that although there are no new recognized procedures for breast reduction developed since 1923 the plaintiff did not fall within the category of patients who required a Conway-type operation.

Hillman v. Funderburk & Washington Hospital Center[3]

The court of appeals affirmed the jury verdict of the trial court awarding the plaintiff $20,000 on the issue of lack of informed consent.

This action arose out of a reduction mammoplasty in which the plaintiff brought three cases of action against Dr. Funderburk—namely, negligence, breach of warranty, and lack of informed consent.

On February 6, 1979, for functional and cosmetic reasons, the appellant underwent reduction mammoplasty (breast reduction) surgery. Dr.

---

[2] 2 Conn. App. 579, 481 A.2d 1286 (1984).

[3] 504 A.2d 596 (D.C. 1986).

Funderburk performed the surgery by following a modified McKissock procedure. After the reduction, assisted by three residents of the hospital, he used a combination of stitch types to close each breast, including interrupted vertical mattress sutures and simple sutures.

Following the operation, the appellant complained that her nipples had been placed too high and about the amount of scarring from the operation, specifically that she had "track mark" scars as a result of the interrupted vertical mattress sutures.

One day before trial began the appellees moved in limine to preclude the appellant from showing her breasts to the jury. The trial court granted the motion but permitted the appellant to get color photographs over the weekend for use at trial. The photographs the appellant obtained were later admitted into evidence.

The appellant's only medical expert witness was Dr. McKissock. He testified that Dr. Funderburk did not follow his McKissock procedure correctly, that the foreseeable result of Dr. Funderburk's modified procedure was to place appellant's nipples higher than they should be, and that her nipples were substantially higher than they should be as a result of the operation. Specifically, Dr. McKissock testified that the appellant's right nipple was approximately 4 to 4.5 cm (1.57 to 1.77 inches) too high and the left nipple was approximately 3 to 3.5 cm (1.18 to 1.37 inches) too high. Dr. McKissock also testified that the use of interrupted vertical mattress sutures in a reduction mammoplasty was beneath the standard of care because of the "unsightly scarring" that results, but that the appellant's scarring overall (that is, the scarring from stab wounds necessary for fluid drainage and from all the stitching) was within normal limits.

The appellant contended that the type of sutures used around her areolae were negligently put in and that, although her scarring overall was within normal limits, it was not as good as it would have been in the absence of negligence.

The defense called three medical expert witnesses, appellee Dr. Funderburk, Dr. Alfred Suraci, and Dr. Hugo Keunen. Dr. Funderburk testified that he modified the McKissock procedure to fit the patient population he normally worked with and that he had had good results in the past with the modified procedure. He testified that, according to the measurements he took after the operation, the appellant's right nipple was one centimeter higher than her left. He opined that from the photograph exhibits it appeared as if the nipples were "at most" 1 to 2 cm (less than an inch) higher than ideal positioning, but he added that it was difficult to tell from the photographs. He stated that when he last examined her in June of 1979 she had no visible scars as a result of the use of vertical mattress sutures and that he could not tell now from the photographs where she had any of the "track-mark" scarring characteristic when such sutures are left in too long or tied too tightly.

The jury restricted its verdict for the plaintiff to the claim of lack of informed consent, and awarded the plaintiff damages in the amount of $20,000. No verdict was returned against the Washington Hospital Center.

§ 12.52 Illustrative Cases: Breast Augmentation

Suria v. Shiffman[4]

In this action a transsexual testified that he requested the defendant to perform breast augmentation. The defendant injected silicone into both breasts in July and December 1974. In March 1975 the breasts became red and swollen.

The defendant Shiffman testified that he never saw the plaintiff until December 1975 and that the plaintiff sought treatment for her breast injury, not an augmentation. Shiffman said he treated the plaintiff without success. He subsequently found out that the plaintiff's friend had administered mineral oil injections into the breasts. Shiffman then said he referred the plaintiff to Dr. Dhaliwal, a plastic surgeon, for a mastectomy.

The trial court dismissed the claim against Shiffman finding contributory negligence was a bar. The appellant court reinstated this judgment. It found liability against Dr. Dhaliwal for lack of informed consent in the amount of $1,500,000. This was later reduced to $120,000 by the court of appeals.

Nacarati v. Garrett[5]

The plaintiff, Marion Nacarati, claimed that subsequent to the injection of breast implants, she developed extreme drooping, hardness, and bruises. The action was based on two causes of action, one for negligence and one for lack of informed consent.

The trial court returned a verdict in the defendant's favor for both claims.

Anderson v. Johns Hopkins[6]

Marie Anderson was born and reared in Beach Haven, New Jersey, where she still resided at the trial of this case in March of 1970. Married at age

---

[4] 67 N.Y.2d 87, 490 N.E.2d 832, 499 N.Y.S.2d 913 (1986).

[5] 351 Pa. Super. 437, 506 A.2d 428 (1986).

[6] 260 Md. 342, 272 A.2d 372 (1971).

19, she weighed 117 pounds and was endowed with a hypertrophy of the mammary glands requiring a size 40-C brassiere. After four children and several years, her breasts suffered, by her description, "complete collapse." She sought a corsetiere's help, to no avail. She supplemented her brassieres with adhesive tape.

She read about silicon-gel implants and in June of 1965 consulted Dr. Milton Edgerton, then employed by the Johns Hopkins Hospital. She told him she wanted relief from "being pendulous."

Dr. Edgerton scheduled the surgery for February of 1966. At Mrs. Anderson's urging, he advanced it to November 1965. He elevated the breasts, but judged he should not insert the implants at the same time; the skin would not be strong enough to support additional mass until it healed. Mrs. Anderson was disappointed. She had wanted the whole procedure, including implants, done in one operation.

In May 1966 Mrs. Anderson returned to Johns Hopkins Hospital. Dr. Edgerton and his assistant in surgery performed a "bilateral augmentation mammoplasty, silicone implants." Mrs. Anderson and her husband were still disappointed. In November 1967 they sued Dr. Edgerton and the hospital, alleging that the hospital was vicariously liable for the doctor's surgery, which he "performed in a careless and negligent manner" in both operations, and asked for sundry damages "as a result of the negligent and careless performance of the operations."

At trial, the Andersons introduced no expert opinion testimony of any kind. Upon the defendants' motion, the trial judge directed a verdict at the close of their case, observing: "There has been no evidence introduced in this case by the Plaintiffs, which showed the standard of skill ordinarily exercised by surgeons in similar cases and, further, that the Defendants failed to comply with those standards."

The plaintiffs, appellants now, asserted that the true and sole theory of their case is the appellees' failure to do the operation Mrs. Anderson consented to, and not negligence at all. They also urged that they were entitled to go to the jury without any evidence of what information a surgeon should give a patient contemplating the surgery here involved. The court held they never claimed lack of informed consent.

Skripek v. Bergamo[7]

The plaintiff instituted this medical malpractice action against the defendant, seeking to recover damages sustained as the result of a postoperative closed capsulotomy performed following breast augmentation surgery as well as negligence in performing the postoperative closed capsulotomy. Her principal claim and the sole theory upon which she pretried and tried

[7] 200 N.J. Super. 620, 491 A.2d 1336 (App. Div. 1985).

the case was lack of informed consent. Specifically, the plaintiff claimed that the defendant failed to advise her of the risks and the possible serious consequences attendant to the closed capsulotomy. The facts developed at trial are summarized generally as follows.

In November 1979 the plaintiff consulted the defendant for the purpose of eliciting information with regard to breast augmentation mammoplasty. The plaintiff, who was then 38 years old, in the process of obtaining a divorce, and the mother of two children, "believed that beautiful, firm breasts would improve her physical appearance." The plaintiff admitted that the defendant discussed the pros and cons of breast augmentation mammoplasty during the initial consultation. According to the plaintiff, the defendant told her that such surgery was "a marvel of science today that breasts can be returned to what you were born with. Many times they're even more beautiful." The defendant explained how prostheses would be used and that there was a possibility that the breasts would get hard. He also explained that scars would be "in the natural crevice of the breast line and that the scars would be tucked underneath and would not be visible." According to the defendant, he explained the risks of this type of surgery and did not make any guarantees regarding the success of the procedure, particularly because the plaintiff's breasts at the time of his examination were not symmetrical. It is clear from the proof that the defendant did not force or coerce the plaintiff to undergo the surgery and gave her the opportunity to discuss with whomever she wanted whether to have such an operation.

In early December 1979, after discussing the surgery and its implications with her husband, the plaintiff returned to the defendant's office and signed a consent form for the breast augmentation surgery and prepaid his fee. The plaintiff expressly authorized the defendant to perform the augmentation mammoplasty. In signing the form, she also acknowledged that "no guarantees have been made to me as to the results of the procedure to be performed . . . [and] that there are risks, consequences and complications associated with all surgery" and that she "understood," among other things, that "the procedure may not be successful" and that "there may develop a firmness of the breasts which may be due to excessive fibrous capsule forming around the implant, or for such other reasons, a malpositioning of the implants which may be due to the manner in which the implant becomes firmly secured." The proof at trial showed that, prior to signing the consent form, the defendant reviewed it carefully with the plaintiff to ensure that she understood its contents. According to the defendant, he had the plaintiff sign this special consent form because (1) there were discrepancies that existed in the plaintiff's breasts prior to surgery and he wanted to be sure that she understood that he was not promising her that they would be corrected, (2) she was married to an attorney and, perhaps more important, (3) she was in the process of a separation and a divorce. Although denied by the plaintiff, the defendant testified that he discussed other corrective procedures that would be performed, such as an excision of a mass of her right breast, a bilateral partial mastectomy, possible removal of her lower poles, excision of chronic granulation tissue, release of the contracture of the left mammary region, and excision of the multiple lesions of her face and body.

On December 6, 1979, the plaintiff entered Mountainside Hospital in Montclair, New Jersey, for the surgery. Before undergoing the surgery she executed the hospital's consent and operative permit that authorized the defendant to perform the requested surgery. This form recited that "[t]he nature and purpose of the operation, possible alternative methods of treatment, the risks involved and the possibility of complications have been explained to [plaintiff]." After the plaintiff signed the form, the defendant performed the surgery. The plaintiff was pleased with the results. She saw the defendant about a week later and felt that she looked fine. She returned to the defendant about a month later in mid-January 1980 at which time the defendant noticed that her right breast was a little hard, something she had not complained to him about. He told her to lie down and that he was going to give it a "little squeeze and it should soften it right up." The plaintiff permitted the defendant to squeeze her breast but, according to the plaintiff, her breast remained hard.

About a month later, in February 1980, the plaintiff returned to the defendant's office. She was still satisfied with her appearance, but the defendant noticed that her right breast was still hard. Although the plaintiff did not complain about her appearance nor was she unhappy with her right breast, defendant again told her to lie down, that he was going to give it another squeeze to soften it up. The defendant, however, did not explain to the plaintiff that anything would happen except "it may hurt a little bit." She acceded to his request. He told her to hold his arm while he performed the procedure. According to the plaintiff, the defendant cupped his hands beneath her breast and squeezed and pushed. At this time she screamed because it was painful. She further testified that she could almost feel the palms of his hands touching and heard a loud crunch. She was so sore that she could not move; she had a throbbing pain and was light-headed. The defendant told her that she would be all right in a few minutes. However, when the plaintiff arrived home she was extremely sore and her breast was "really red." The following day it discolored, turning black and blue. She called the defendant and told him that she was extremely sore. He told her to take a hot shower, put hot compresses on her breast, and massage it. After about a week the discoloration went away, but she noticed a bulge forming underneath the crease in her breast and that the scar was raising. She called the defendant who, in the plaintiff's words, responded "it's all in my [the plaintiff's] imagination."

In early April 1980 the plaintiff saw the defendant who examined her and told her that her right breast was the more natural looking of the two and that she ought to come back in six months. In July 1980, before the six months passed, the plaintiff fell and scraped her shoulder. She went to her gynecologist, who recommended that she seek plastic surgery because "there's a lot of gravel still in there." She immediately made an appointment with the defendant and saw him either July 7th or 11th. The defendant examined the plaintiff's shoulder and gave her a prescription to apply to prevent any scarring. He then examined her breasts and told her that he would like to do further surgery on her left breast. Although the plaintiff made an appointment for the surgery, she cancelled it. She decided she wanted the right breast corrected because that was the one that was painful and uncomfortable.

Eventually the plaintiff consulted Dr. Robbie Meyjer, a plastic surgeon, who performed several operations. Dr. Meyjer testified that when the plaintiff came to him she had an hour glass deformity of the right breast because the implant had slipped below the bra line. He performed an open capsulotomy on both breasts, releasing both implants: the left to soften the breast and the right to correct the deformity. Shortly after that operation the plaintiff told Dr. Meyjer that she was unhappy with the different levels of the folds underneath the breasts. Dr. Meyjer performed an open capsulotomy on the left breast but this time the result was that the fold of the left breast became lower than the right. Another operation was performed and the plaintiff was pleased with the result.

Dr. Charles Scher, a plastic surgeon who testified for the plaintiff, explained that a closed capsulotomy is a procedure in which the breasts are squeezed, causing a tear in the scar tissue which forms around the implants. Such a procedure allows the implants to be more mobile so that the breasts are less firm. An open capsulotomy is a procedure whereby an incision is made and the scar issue is released. According to Dr. Scher, the risks in a closed capsulotomy are bleeding, discoloration, rupture of the implant, displacement of the implant, and inability to actually perform the capsulotomy—that is, failure to rupture the scar tissue. He further testified that in February 1980 it was accepted practice to advise a patient of these risks before performing the procedure. The alternatives to the procedure were an open capsulotomy or no treatment at all and it was accepted practice for the doctor to inform a patient of those alternatives. Dr. Scher was of the opinion that the closed capsulotomy caused plaintiff's right breast to turn black and blue and the implant to drop and that this drop in turn caused the scar to become more visible. He was of the opinion that it would have been a deviation from accepted medical standards if the defendant did not inform the plaintiff of the risks and alternatives involved in the procedure.

Dr. Steven LaVerm, the defendant's expert, testified that the defendant had not deviated from the standard of care because he did not fail to advise the plaintiff of the risks and alternatives to the closed capsulotomy. According to Dr. LaVerm, the defendant's notes showed that he explained the capsulotomy procedure to plaintiff before performing it and he offered her the alternatives of doing nothing or doing an open capsulotomy. However, Dr. LaVerm acknowledged that if the defendant had not told the plaintiff of the alternatives and the risks of the procedures he would have deviated from accepted medical practice.

At the conclusion of the proofs, the trial court submitted the case to the jury on special interrogatories. The jury found that the defendant did not obtain the plaintiff's "informed consent before performing the procedure known as a closed capsulotomy." However, the jury also found that had the plaintiff been fully informed of the risks and alternative procedures before the closed capsulotomy was performed, a reasonably prudent person in her position would have consented and submitted to the procedure. The trial court thereupon molded the verdict and entered judgment in favor of the defendant of no cause for action.

The court rejected a claim for battery because it was never pleaded and addressed the informed consent issue as following:

> The leading medical malpractice case holding that a patient bears the burden of proving the causal relationship between the physician's failure to disclose the risks and alternatives and the injury to the patient is *Natason v. Kline,* 186 Kan. 393, 350 P.2d 1093 (Sup. Ct. 1960), *on motion for rehearing,* 187 Kan. 1986, 354 P.2d 670 (Sup. Ct. 1960). All the major informed consent cases in New Jersey cite this case, obviously recognizing its persuasiveness and authoritativeness in this area of the law.[8]

§ 12.53 Bibliography

J.M. Converse, Plastic Reconstructive Surgery. (W.B. Saunders, 1977).

R.M. Goldwyn, The Patient and the Plastic Surgeon. (Little, Brown & Co., 1981).

R.M. Goldwyn, The Unfavorable Result in Plastic Surgery. (Little, Brown & Co., 2d ed. 1984).

W.C. Grabb, & J.W. Smith, Plastic Surgery. (Little, Brown & Co., 1984).

H. Gray, Anatomy of the Human Body. (Lea & Febiger, 30th ed. 1985).

S.H. Miller, Year Book of Plastic and Reconstructive Surgery. (Year Book Medical Publishers, 1989).

T.D. Rees, II Aesthetic Plastic Surgery. (W.B. Saunders, 1980).

---

[8] *Id.* at 1344.

CHAPTER 13

THIGH-LIFTS AND LIPOSUCTION

§ 13.1 Introduction

Many women develop fat deposits in the buttocks, hip, and thigh area. Some patients consider these deposits unattractive and not in keeping with the streamline figure that they would like to present. The medical term for this condition is *trochanteric lipodystrophy,* which means an abnormal deposit of fat in the area of the greater trochanters, or bones in the hip area. This "riding breeches" condition is thought to be particularly correctable when the patient is slim or of normal size from the waist up and from the knees down, with only her buttocks, hips, and thighs disproportionately large. No matter how much these patients diet, the fat in these areas cannot be reduced.

§ 13.2 Thigh-Lifts

An operation for this condition was popularized in the seventies by a Brazilian plastic surgeon and called a "thigh-lift." For a while, this operation made many patients happy, because it corrected surgically in a matter of a few hours (plus several weeks of postoperative care) that which could not be corrected by diet in months or years. In the seventies people were flocking to plastic surgeons to have a thigh-lift done. At last they had found a solution to a problem that had confounded them for much of their adult lives.

The operation consists of an incision from the outer portion of the hips down into the subgluteal fold—that is, the fold underneath the buttocks—continued onto the medial aspect of the thighs adjacent to the vagina. Here large elipses of skin, subcutaneous tissue, and fat are removed on both sides and the incision is brought down to muscle and fascia. Portions of fat and skin are discarded bilaterally, and the lower portion of the thigh, especially posteriorly, is undermined and brought up to meet the dissected portion of the underbuttocks fold. This gives a wonderful silhouette for a short time.

Even though there is a long scar after this operation, people did not mind it at first, because the surgeons promised that it would be hidden within their "bikini line"—that area of the body that is covered by a bikini bathing suit. Later, however, gravity pulled the scars down below the bikini line and nothing could pull them up. As the tissues healed, they crept down below the satisfaction of the woman who wanted to have the operation, and below the expectations of the surgeons. Although the scars blended to a certain degree with the skin texture, they were scars nonetheless.

Scarring is the healing process that normal human tissue forms by virtue of *fibrosis* or scar tissue, which is laid down between adjacent areas of traumatically or surgically incised skin. The result is called a scar, and scars are permanent. The condition and the quality of the scar may change but the fact that it is there can never be erased even by the cleverest of plastic surgeons. It is a misconception that plastic surgeons can operate without a scar. The scars left after a thigh-lift proved to be unacceptable.

§ 13.3 Liposuction

Because of its resulting scars, the thigh-lift fell into disfavor as the seventies rolled into the eighties. It was replaced by a procedure called *liposuction,* or aspiration of fat, devised by a French plastic surgeon. This operation removes fatty tissue without leaving large scars. A small incision approximately half an inch in length is made in the subgluteal fold, or even on the hips, and will be undiscernible from the normal observer's eyes. Through this small incision a long cannula is inserted into the area underneath the skin. This cannula measures approximately 12 to 15 inches, is made of metal, and has a hole in one end of it. At the opposite end is a handle attached to a polyethylene tube, which is connected to a suction machine. The cannula is easily moved around in the area of the fat, breaking up the trabecular fibrous connections in the area. As it makes its sweep underneath the skin, the fat is sucked in through the hole and out through the tube to the suction machine. The deep pressure from the suction machine pulls the fat out and leaves the skin intact without causing a major scar. The size of the cannula used differs from one part of the body to the other and is either straight or curved at the end, depending on the geography of the area to be reduced.

This fat suction operation has replaced the thigh-lift. When the operation proved successful in the thigh, buttock, and hip area, other areas of the body were investigated, such as the abdomen, the medial portion of the knees, the back, and the breasts. A small cannula has been developed to use in facial suction in the cheek, neck, and chin area.

Until 1987, the most popular plastic surgical procedure throughout the country, as reported by the American Board of Plastic and Reconstructive Surgery, was the rhinoplasty or nose operation. In 1988, liposuction was the most popular operation performed.

Fat is a problem in the United States because of diet and lifestyle. Fad diets, protein diets and other means of losing weight quickly have been the rage among Americans for years because we do not want to sacrifice very much for very long to achieve the figure we desire. A recent television commercial shows a popular female star in a gymnasium saying that, if a beautiful body came in a bottle, everyone would have one. With the advent of liposuction, many people believe that maybe it does, and they are flocking to plastic surgeons and nonplastic surgeons alike throughout the country to have these bothersome areas of fat removed without dieting or sacrifice.

Problems have arisen, however, when the operation, which does not seem technically very challenging to perform, falls into the hands of unqualified and unethical surgeons, and even into the hands of physicians who were not surgeons. There are minor complications to the operation even when done in skilled hands, but major complications resulting in death have received notoriety through the news media.

The patients who died were usually operated on by people who were not trained plastic surgeons. The enthusiasm of the operating doctor, and sometimes the technician, would encourage them to take out more fat than was safe at one time. Several of the deaths were caused by fat embolism and fluid imbalance. Operations were being performed by gynecologists, dermatologists, ear, nose, and throat doctors, general surgeons, and general practitioners. The operation was being done in outpatient clinics and doctor offices alike, and—because it seemed so simple—the proper respect was not given to this procedure which, if done in the proper hands, is excellent.

The American Board of Plastic Surgery has tried to standardize this operation, and now has splinter groups concerned only with the correct performance of this very important and effective, but potentially dangerous, procedure.

§ 13.4 Patient Selection

In order to perform a liposuction properly, the patient must be in good health. She must have discrete areas of fat that need to be reduced, for instance on the thighs or buttocks, and should not be fat all over. A patient who weighs 300 pounds is not a good candidate for this operation. The same type of patient who was a candidate for a thigh-lift would be a good candidate for a fat suction in the buttocks or hips (see **§ 13.1**). Ideally, the patient should be below 40 years old, because of the degree of elasticity in the skin before that age. If a large amount of fat is removed from a certain area of the body, the skin must be elastic enough to allow it to retract and look good over the new, decreased proportion. If the operation is done in patients over 50 years old, the elasticity is decreased and the amount of retraction of the skin will be less. Thus such a patient would have decreased girth of the thighs and buttocks, but hanging skin. This should be carefully explained to the patient. If they are not bothered by the condition of their skin postoperatively, then the operation can be performed. Otherwise, they should be advised against having it.

§ 13.5 Complications

Death can result from a fat embolism or from a fluid imbalance that is caused by the removal of too much fat at one time. A safe amount of fat to be removed in one operation is between 1000 and 1500 cc. The patient should be under either a general or supplemental anesthetic and should have an electrocardiogram running in the operating room with an anesthetist present. An IV should be kept open for the entire procedure.

When death has occurred, the procedure has usually been done by unqualified people who have removed up to 5000 cc of fat, causing abrupt and severe physiological changes.

A fat embolism can occur in any patient, whether fat is removed from the body or whether a bone is broken. If everything is done properly, the occurrence of a fat embolism is a complication, not malpractice. This has been reported in several cases in which the procedure had been done properly, but this is very rare.

The more frequently seen complications are less serious and consist of mottling of the skin and slack or redundant skin over the areas. This is primarily seen in patients who are over 40 years old, but can be seen in younger patients if the cannulas is placed too close to the skin, not leaving an area of subcutaneous fat.

Some patients present with so-called "cellulite." If this exists preoperatively, then it will likely be present after the fat suctioning, because the procedure cannot change the configuration of the skin.

Swelling will naturally take place after the surgery and will usually go away in approximately six months, the major portion of it going away in two or three weeks. Elastic garments, especially in the buttock and thigh areas, are worn and will help the swelling recede evenly, leaving the configuration of the skin more normal and less mottled.

§ 13.6 Results

Fat suctioning in the heavy fat of the outer thigh, hip, and buttock area is more successful than in other areas of the body where the skin is not as thick and the fat is not as hard. For example, many patients who really need abdominoplasty seek liposuction of the abdomen. This gives a less pleasing result. The skin of the abdomen is more flaccid and the fat is of a different composition than it is in the thigh and buttock area. The soft fat in the abdomen can be aspirated on people with large abdominal panniculi, but for most patients who have a smaller amount of fat there will be unevenness and mottling of the skin of the abdomen simply because of the anatomical configuration in that area.

Patients who have heavy legs from the knees down usually have unsuccessful results from fat suctioning. The area in the medial portion of the knee can be reduced nicely. This area is so bothersome to many women that a small scar in the area of the knee is a small price to pay for the reduction of the knee's girth.

Older patients sometimes want the reduction of fat from the upper arms. This is tempting when there are fatty arms present, but the problem is that the skin will still hang, and may even look less attractive than it did with fat, because there will be nothing but hanging skin and no substance to the upper arm.

Liposuction is an excellent operation, and has been the source of great satisfaction to many, both patients and surgeons alike. Because it is a relatively new procedure and because it has become very popular, patients who seek it must be extremely careful to find a qualified plastic surgeon who will advise them conservatively about the amount of fat to be removed, the areas from which it should be removed, and the safest way of doing it.

§ 13.7 Bibliography

J.M. Converse, Plastic Reconstructive Surgery (W.B. Saunders Co., 1977).

R.M. Goldwyn, The Unfavorable Result in Plastic Surgery 821-90 (2d ed., Little, Brown & Co., 1984).

R.M. Goldwyn, The Patient and the Plastic Surgeon (Little, Brown & Co., 1981).

W.C. Grabb & J.W. Smith, Plastic Surgery (Little, Brown & Co., 1984).

G.P. Hetter, Lipoplasty (Little, Brown & Co., 1984).

S.H. Miller, Year Book of Plastic and Reconstructive Surgery (Year Book Medical Publishers, Inc., 1989).

CHAPTER 14

INJECTABLE AND INSERTABLE MATERIALS

§ 14.1 Introduction

In recent years, contouring of the face and body has risen to new heights. Although in the early days of plastic surgery, the primary method of changing contour and shape was reduction of tissue—such as excising facial skin, or removing breast tissue and fat to do a breast reduction—in recent years the approach has been upgraded. Contouring now involves the insertion of silastic or silicone implants of several varieties, or the injection of silicone, collagen, or fat.

The face and the breasts are the most common areas for the injection and insertion of these materials. Obviously breast implantation or augmentation has become one of the most popular operations in America today. The various types of breast prostheses and their uses, as well as their position in the chest wall, have been discussed in **Chapter 12**.

The face, however, is also frequently sculpted today. In addition to removing skin and aspirating fat from the face, removing bags from under the eyes, and reducing the hump of the nose, a very frequently used modality today, is the augmentation of various angles and the landmarks of the face.

For example, a silastic or silicone implant is used to heighten the nose in those patients whose noses are naturally low in the bridge area. It is also used if too much bone has been removed during previous surgery or after the loss of bone following an accident (see **§ 14.4**).

Very often, when a nose is large, the patient will seem to have a receding chin. If there is a congenital underbite, in which the mandible is pushed back beneath the maxilla, a simple chin augmentation will not suffice. In this case, a more complex pushing forward of the mandible is done to bring the entire jaw out, at the same time extending the chin. This is usually done by a maxillo-facial or dental surgeon. However, for a weak chin, or micrognathia of the lower jaw, a silicone or silastic chin implant is inserted (see § **14.2**). This may be inserted in the buccal mucosa, thereby avoiding a scar, or beneath the mental bones, leaving a very small submental scar.

Most recently, *malar implants* (implants to augment the cheekbones) are gaining popularity. Some patients want to have cheekbones like those of movie and TV personalities, in which the zygomatic bones are extended, leaving a sallow cheek, apparently a greater mark of beauty. These implants are made either of hard silicone with holes in them or of soft silicone gel in a polyethylene tubing. Malar implants come in several sizes and can be inserted through several approaches (see § **14.3**).

§ 14.2 Chin Implants

One chin implant is a small, carved piece of silastic material simulating the shape of the average chin. A second type of implant is the silicone gel implant encased in a polyethylene bag, which feels soft to the touch and, when inserted under the muscle, feels like normal tissue. Chin implants come in approximately five different sizes, depending on the size and shape of the chin to be augmented.

The implants can be inserted from two approaches. If there is going to be surgery or suction to remove fat from the submental area, a small incision is placed in the line underneath the chin. In this instance, the chin implant can be introduced into the chin area from below the neck with the scar measuring approximately 1.5 to 2 cm and usually placed in the normal line underneath the chin. The patient must be warned that the scar could be thick and noticeable, depending on the patient's healing. The subcutaneous tissue is dissected and a pocket is made above the mental bones for the chin implants to be placed. It is essential to center the implant. A common complication of chin augmentation is asymmetry. It is very important to coagulate the bleeding in this procedure because bleeding can cause a hematoma, which can dislodge the implant, moving it from one side to the other. If the dissection is too large, the capsule that forms around the chin implant, similar to the capsule that forms around a breast implant (see **Chapter 12**), will be formed on the wrong side, and another operation must be performed to stabilize it centrally.

Usually the procedure is done under local anesthesia separately or at the time of rhinoplasty. Once in place the chin implant is secured by approximating the subcutaneous tissues and skin edges around the implant. Taping the incision helps keep the implant in place while it heals and forms its capsule.

The complications of augmentation mentoplasty are asymmetry, hematoma, infection, and extrusion of the implant. Extrusion of the implant comes not from the body's rejecting the implant. Extrusion is often the result of too much tension or excessive bleeding. Possibly the patient's own postoperative care could cause the implant to extrude or come out by jarring, touching, rubbing, or lying on the chin. Extrusion can also occur after the incorrect placement of the implant because of negligence on the part of the surgeon.

If there is no surgery to remove fat from the submental area, the chin implant could be put into place through the *lower buccal mucosa*—that is, the mucous membrane below the lower mandibular teeth. In this case, the area is infiltrated with local anesthesia and a small incision is made in the buccal mucosa. The tissues are dissected off the malar bone from above. Ample space must be dissected to insert the chin implant if this is the method chosen, and suturing of the mucosa can usually only be done in one layer.

The advantage of the mucosal approach is the absence of an external scar. The disadvantages are the greater risk of infection and the limitation of the patient's oral intake during the immediate postoperative period. Furthermore, the patient's tongue tends to inadvertently touch the area where the stitches are, causing them to be disrupted and sometimes loosened, allowing the implant to escape.

An implant inserted through the buccal mucosa may cause insensitivity of the lower lip and gums. A patient who had extensive facial surgery—that is, on her upper and lower eyelids, and a face-lift, rhinoplasty, chin implant, breast reduction, and abdominoplasty—within a few weeks' time, and in several different operations, had an excellent result with all her surgery. Her chin implant had been inserted through the lower buccal mucosa. The patient's only complaint postoperatively was a 1 cm area of numbness on the inside of the lower lip. Although the rest of her surgery was completely to her satisfaction, she plagued the surgeon for months afterward to remove some of the numbed area inside her lip. The surgeon, realizing that the numbness was perhaps being caused by the pressure on the lip, removed the chin implant, thereby alleviating 75 percent of the numbness.

§ 14.3 Malar Implants

There are three approaches commonly used when inserting an implant on the malar bone. The first is a *subciliary* incision—that is, beneath the lower eyelids. The second is a *temporal* incision behind the hairline in the temporalis fascia. This is especially useful when a face-lift is being done at the same time. The third approach is called a *Caldwell-Luc* incision, and is made through the superior buccal mucosa. Each surgeon prefers her own method of entry based on the individual patient, the hair distribution, and the type of procedure being done.

Malar implants come in several different sizes. They are available as hard silastic implants and soft silicone implants encased in polyethylene gel. When inserting malar implants it is crucial not to use implants that are too large. The surgeon must make sure that the pockets are symmetrical and right at the angle of the malar bone. These implants have caused many problems with patients because of movement of the implant and also because of asymmetry. Many implants have had to be removed because the patients, thinking that they wanted large cheek bones, insisted that large ones be used. They often gave a very unnatural look to the face and the patients were not happy.

Malar implants have their place in facial sculpturing but should be used judiciously and should be put in by experienced surgeons.

§ 14.4 Implanting the Nose

The nasal septum that separates the nares begins at the top of the nose and continues down to the tip. The upper two-fifths is composed of bone, and the lower three-fifths is made of cartilage.

There are three occasions when synthetic material might be used to alter the nasal profile. Some patients with a naturally low bridge with underdeveloped cartilage want the surgeon to elevate the bridge and narrow the width of the nose.

Secondly, in cases of trauma, as in an accident in which the nose is broken or fragmented and portions of it are lost, the nose will have to be reconstructed. Often synthetic materials are used to recreate the nose.

Thirdly, sometimes too much cartilage and/or bone has been removed during a rhinoplasty. This can result if the surgeon does not understand how low the patient wants the nose. Sometimes an overzealous surgeon, in an attempt to remove a large hump, will take off too much bone and cartilage, thereby giving the nose an unnatural swoop or "ski-nose" appearance. In these instances, insertable materials such as silicone implants or silastic gel implants are used to reconstruct the nose.

Nasal implants are usually preformed in several different sizes, ranging from small to medium to large, with two intermediary sizes of medium-small and medium-large. They simulate the pyramidal sweep of the nasal bones, and are inserted through a hole in the mucosa after a pocket has been made in the area to accommodate this heightening device. Often a surgeon will custom carve an implant from a block of firm silastic. If the tip is involved in the reconstruction, a *cantilever implant* may be carved. This is an implant that is formed in a right angle, the longer limb going into the dorsal portion of the nose above the septum, the right angle forming the tip of the nose, and the smaller limb being inserted in the septo-columellar angle, giving the nose the proper tip and projection.

Many rhinoplasties are done too radically, with too much bone and cartilage being removed. In the early days of plastic surgery, too much tissue was often removed in an attempt to make a very large nose more average-sized. These noses look "operated on" 25 to 30 years later, having pinched tips because of removal of too much cartilage, a scooped dorsum because of the removal of too much bone, or an abnormal notching of the nostrils because of the excision of too much cartilage. More often than not, these noses have not been corrected because the patients have gotten used to them over the years and, at the time when they were done, they did not seem to be unattractive to the patients.

However, today a nose must be very natural looking after surgery. It is for this reason that the silastic and silicone implants are being used with greater frequency.

In addition to the silastic and silicone implants, many surgeons choose to use autogenous materials for reconstruction. Cartilage taken from the posterior aspect of the concha of the ear increases the height of the nose. Insertion of this cartilage properly tapered and trimmed is very effective. Although there is a certain amount of resorption of this autogenous cartilage graft, some surgeons prefer it to synthetic materials. Cartilage from the rib and a portion of bone from the superior iliac spine are also sites for harvesting the patient's own tissues for nasal reconstruction.

Infection is one complication of insertion of a synthetic material. The infection rate is greater with a nasal implant, because the nose itself is a bacteria-filled cavity and, during the insertion of the implant through the mucosa, these bacteria invade the area. It is a ready site for infection, increased by the presence of the synthetic material itself. The surgeon should use a prophylactic antibiotic when inserting a nasal prosthesis.

A second complication for nasal prostheses is excess movement. If the pocket is made too large, the implant will move. Some surgeons do not believe in securing the implant but merely just putting it in a snug pocket.

After the swelling recedes, the implant may have a discrete palpable periphery noticeable beyond the normal configuration of the nose. If this happens, perhaps the implant should be shaved and tailored to a smaller size to fit the area more effectively.

Contrary to popular opinion, rejection of the implant seldom takes place. Rejection is a phenomenon that occurs when organs are transplanted from one person to another, and when the autoimmune system is challenged. In the instance of prosthetic implants, rejection as as we know it is not a problem. Problems come from mechanical or bacterial difficulties.

The possible complications of implantation in the nose are much the same when raising the height of the bridge. They are diminished slightly, however, because when no previous surgery nor trauma has occurred, scar tissue is not a factor. Scar tissue grows at an indeterminate rate and can impugn the integrity of the prosthesis.

Possible complications must be discussed with the patient during the preoperative consultation. Patients must be made aware that, when a surgeon is attempting to recreate a nose that has been traumatized or previously operated on, the risks are increased because of the presence of scar tissue and the irregularity of the previously operated tissues. Such patients must be aware that the new nose will, hopefully, be an improvement over the one presented to the surgeon, but will never be perfect nor like a nose that had not been previously operated on.

§ 14.5 Injections of Silicone, Collagen, and Fat

The new concept in facial contouring in addition to normal face-lift and eyelid procedures started when the SMAS procedure became popular 10 years ago. See **Chapter 10** for a discussion of SMAS. Since that time the advent of liposuction, which is now popularized for the submental area and even in the cheek area, pushes toward more complexed facial sculpturing—namely changing the dimensions and the characteristics of the face.

As far back as 25 years ago, a group of plastic surgeons was selected by the Food and Drug Administration (FDA) for testing a then-new material that was being injected into the face. The material was silicone, and it was injected drop by drop through a large bored needle into the areas of depression in the face, namely the nasolabial lines and the glabellar lines. The FDA never went on to fully approve the use of injectable silicone into the face, although the same group of surgeons who used it then are still using it "experimentally." Certain complications have arisen which have distressed the physician and patient population at large.

These procedures are being done by as many dermatologists as plastic surgeons. The concept of silicone injections into the face is to plump out the lines and depressions of the face by putting drops of silicone in small amounts into an area to build up and plump out those lines. However, because of the weight of the silicone, if it is injected too heavily or too readily into an area, it will lump together and move to another area which then produces a projection of silicone unpleasant in its appearance and often painful to the patient. The only way the silicone can be removed is by incision in the skin over the area.

Also there is a chance of infection during the injection of silicone from contaminants from the skin. In addition, from time to time, a patient will develop an allergic reaction to the silicone.

Silicone has been used by some researchers for facial hemiatrophy, and this is a successful procedure for a condition that previously had no apparent solution. Silicone in this instance is injected in large amounts into the intradermal layer of a face, one side of which is atrophied either traumatically or physiologically. It gives an improvement to such patients, who want some relief from the large caverns and crevasses found in the affected side of their face.

Today, however, silicone is used less frequently than other modalities and still legally only by those physicians who have been approved by the FDA.

Several years ago, a drug company produced a substance called "collagen" which was manufactured as Zyderm and now Zyderm I or Zyplast. *Collagen* is an animal protein taken from natural bovine collagen and has been developed for injections into nasolabial and glabellar wrinkles. A wave of excitement swept over the plastic surgical community when collagen was first introduced because it had none of the side effects of silicone, was not considered dangerous, was considered a part of living tissue, and therefore was believed to be the solution to the problem of facial depressions and lines. Collagen was widely used throughout the country at that point. The syringe had a small amount of local anesthesia mixed with the collagen, so the procedure was less painful than one might expect. It was put in also in small amounts in the intradermal areas and it plumped out the lines. After a day or two of swelling, patients seemed happy and satisfied with their new face.

The problem with collagen, however, is that it is not inexpensive, and it is effective for only six to 18 months. Patients and doctors alike became discouraged when the collagen disappeared and these injections would have to be repeated once or twice a year to keep the deep lines from returning to their previous condition.

Patients suffering from collagen diseases such as rheumatoid arthritis, and periarteritis nodosa, lupus erythematosis, scleroderma, and the like are not candidates for collagen injections because it aggravates their already inherent sensitivity to the substance.

Recently, researchers have developed a method of injecting patients' own fat into their faces to decrease the nasolabial and the glabellar lines. The fat is taken in a sterile syringe from the outer thigh area, then washed in a solution and immediately injected, under local anesthesia, into the lines of the face. This procedure is less dangerous, as it uses the tissue of one's own body. The tissue must be injected judiciously to avoid lumping, and may have to be done two or three times. At this point it is not known what the final outcome of this procedure will be. There are no serious complications to this operation and hopefully it will prove a workable solution to a difficult problem.

§ 14.6 Bibliography

Habal, Morain, Lewin, Parsons, & Woods, 5 Advances in Plastic and Reconstructive Surgery, 57–79 (Year Book Medical Publishers Inc., 1989).

PART III

RECONSTRUCTIVE SURGERY

CHAPTER 15

RECONSTRUCTIVE SURGERY

Frederick Lukash, M.D.

§ 15.1 Introduction

Although it has many subspecialties, plastic surgery is basically divided into cosmetic and reconstructive categories. Both disciplines are ultimately concerned with appearance. Cosmetic surgery is done to change characteristics of age and ethnic origin. Reconstructive surgery's goal is to restore to normal parameters deformities caused by birth defects, defects from diseases such as cancer, and injuries from trauma.

Although there are clear documentations of reconstructive surgical procedures as far back as the fifteenth century, the modern era was ushered in with World War I and World War II. As weaponry sophistication grew, the extent of injury increased. From this was born a group of surgeons who dedicated themselves to the rebuilding of the injured parts—especially facial structures. What resulted were new operations that eventually led to a new specialty, created officially in 1945: plastic and reconstructive surgery.

The many subspecialties within reconstructive surgery include pediatric plastic surgery, hand surgery, craniomaxillofacial surgery, burn surgery, and microsurgery. Common problems seen include cleft lip and palate, ear deformities such as prominence or microtia (absence), postmastectomy breast deformities, dysfunction from hand surgery, and deformities resultant from burns.

The roles of the attorney in plastic surgery cases can be as different as the subspecialties. Usually in cosmetic surgery cases, because the patient starts off healthy and "normal" by many parameters, the legal implications are adversarial. Negligence, malpractice, and breach of contract are the plaintiff concerns. Expectations greater than reality and standard of care are the defense positions. With reconstructive plastic surgery the medical-legal roles are more collegial than adversarial. The deformity may be a birth defect without assignable blame, or the litigation may center on a physician other than the plastic surgeon, such as an obstetrician. The deformity may have resulted from trauma, in which case the role of the plastic surgeon is that of improver and advisor. The litigants are the victim and the initiator of the injury. Here the plastic surgeon will frequently render opinions regarding disability, costs for reconstruction, and permanency of scars.

It is often said that, with cosmetic surgery, patients start off healthy and become ill. With reconstructive surgery, the patients are disabled or injured from the outset and the goals are for functional, anatomic, psychologic, and social restoration.

Reconstructive plastic surgery is always moving in new and unchartered waters. With the advent of myocutaneous flaps and microsurgery, entire new vistas in reconstruction have been seen. These range from replantation of parts to complex reconstructions in which tissue from distant parts of the body are used. When the goal is normalization, the standards for success are often times far less elegant than those in cosmetic surgery. Cases must be evaluated on individual merit and judged against the presurgical deformity.

§ 15.2 Scars

The paramount role of a plastic surgeon with regard to scars is the understanding of the biology of tissue injury and wound repair. This enables the surgeon to inform patients of what their scars might be like following various types of surgical procedures, to revise bad scars, and to periodically bear the unfortunate news that existing scars are permanent.

All wounds, whether caused by accident or surgery, heal by the same basic mechanism—that of fibrous scar tissue. This applies to bones and internal organs as well as to skin. The basic ingredient in wound repair is a body product called *collagen.*

Following injury there are three phases of healing. The initial phase lasts only a few days and involves the body's signaling system to manufacture collagen to "glue" the wound together. From a surgical viewpoint this is the time when stitches are in the incision.

Phase two lasts about three weeks and is an intense period for wound healing. Here collagen is actually being manufactured and deposited into the wound. Scars during this period often appear red and thick, even though all sutures have long been removed. This is especially true for children and young adults who naturally possess good collagen mechanisms.

The third and final phase of wound healing is called the *maturation phase.* This period starts around the fourth week following injury and can last from many months to beyond a year. During this time, the body tries to remodel the scar close to the original tissue. It is in this time frame that scars soften and fade—but never totally disappear. Injured tissue, whether by accident or purposeful, never again becomes normal.

There are many factors that influence a scar's outcome. Foremost is the location. There are areas of the body such as the eyelids where the skin is thin and soft and hence incisions heal very well. There are other areas such as the thick skin of the extremities or back where scars traditionally widen because of the powerful muscles or joint motion beneath. Also, where normal skin is elastic and recoils, scars are inelastic and with constant stress can give way and spread. Another important factor is the direction of the scar. If a scar falls within a facial crease or in one of the body's relaxed skin tension lines it will be more favorable than if it crosses perpendicular to these lines. Genetics and age are also extremely important in scar residual. Fair complected individuals tend to have better scars than those of darker complexions and older skin scars more than younger skin, probably because of a decrease in collagen production.

The universal but false belief of the lay public is that a distinct scar is a keloid. A *keloid* is a metabolic disorder affecting collagen manufacturing and maturation. People affected with this problem experience very thick scars that blossom way beyond the area of injury. Keloids occur more frequently in black individuals and in locations such as the earlobes and chest skin. What most people are experiencing when they say they have "keloids" are either fresh scars that are immature and thick but within the confines of injury or scars that have widened over time.

A good plastic surgeon is skilled in solving wound problems but cannot perform the miracle of scar erasure. Often a fresh wound can be given its best chance by meticulous cleansing and freshening of skin edges followed by a precise layered closure with fine sutures that are removed early. Once the sutures are removed, splinting the incision line with tape can add additional support during the healing phases.

A bad scar can often be made better by camouflage techniques, such as altering its direction into a line of relaxed skin tension, breaking up a continuous scar line into smaller lines in different directions, or revising a scar when there appears to be discrepancies in the levels of the edges. A scar can also be improved by massage. The continued use of pressure appears to have a favorable effect on collagen maturation. It is not creams such as vitamin E but the pressure of massage on the wound that helps the softening and flattening.

The understanding of incision placement, wound healing, and scar permanency should impact greatly on any decision for plastic surgery.

§ 15.3 Burns

Burn injuries can range from the simple, requiring only first aid, to the complex, in which critical care is required for many months and reconstruction takes many years.

Burn injuries are commonly classified as first, second, or third degree, indicating the depth of involvement and type of expected healing. A *first degree* burn is an injury to the outermost layer of skin, the epidermis. The color is pink or red. There is no violation of the deeper surfaces and no blisters. Healing is spontaneous within days. A sunburn typifies this level of injury.

A *second degree,* or partial thickness, burn is an injury that effects the outer epidermis and a partial thickness of the underlying dermis. There is blistering and weeping and the skin surface can be a mottled red. These burns also usually heal spontaneously in two to six weeks with local cleansing care to the wound. If the injury was truly only to a partial thickness of the dermis then scarring should be minimal and the discoloration residual should fade and blend with time. Partial thickness burns are most often caused by spill scalds or flashes of flame. If a partial thickness burn becomes infected it can extend the depth of injury and become a full thickness, or third degree, burn.

Third degree burns—also known as full thickness injuries—involve the complete depths of the epidermis and dermis. The skin looks white and leathery and has no sensation. These wounds will not heal spontaneously and require skin grafting.

Hospitalization is required in large second degree and in most third degree burns. Care of the burn patient also involves care of the wound itself.

Evaluation of the extent of burn injury is done by the *rule of nines,* in which regions of the body are assigned a percentage value based upon their surface area. Burns that are second and third degree and exceed 20 percent of the body surface area require intravenous fluid replacement for the patient because of evaporation through the large open surface.

There are two other types of burn injuries that deserve attention. The first is the respiratory burn. This is usually caused by inhalation of carbonaceous materials in a closed space such as from being trapped in a room or having one's head under the hood of a car. Care here is directed towards decreasing the edema and inflammation in the tracheal and bronchial airway. The other type of injury is the electrical burn. This is a devastating injury in which the victim's tissues act as resistors of current as electrical energy tries to dissipate and escape to the ground. All other types of burns involve only the skin; electrical injuries can involve all tissues of the body. Late sequelae of significant electrical burns are cataracts, myocarditis, and spinal injury.

Rehabilitation from burn injury is very long and painful. Scars frequently thicken and joints can contract if scars cross them. Often many revisional surgeries are required to either functionally or cosmetically improve the involved area.

Because significant burn injury is so painful and deforming there can be overwhelming psychological problems that will require intensive attention. Also, once rehabilitated, many victims are not able to return to the same type of employment and therefore vocational rehabilitation may be required.

§ 15.4 Hand Surgery

There is a strong emotional bond between an individual and his hands. They are constantly and deftly performing tasks for work and activities of daily living, as well as expressing emotion either by gesturing or touching. Any injury to one's hands can significantly effect the way a person lives and interacts in the world.

Surgical problems with the hand are usually congenital, traumatic, or degenerative with age and disease. It is often the trauma cases that are seen in court.

Trauma to the hand can obviously injure any or all of the tissues, but most often problems center around the bones, nerves, and tendons. Fractures are probably the most common injuries seen in a hand practice. Treatment, depending upon the severity of the fracture, can range from simple manipulation and casting to operative intervention with plating or pinning. The nature of the injury results in inflammation and swelling and can lead to scarring and stiffness. Potential problems from treatment include failure to maintain the position of the reset bone. This definitely can limit function, cause pain, and may require further surgery.

Injuries to tendons are usually from lacerations. Repairs must be surgical. During the operation the tendon edges are reapproximated. Careful and prolonged rehabilitation follows. A critical balance must be established between early motion with the possibility of tendon rupture and prolonged immobilization and limitation of motion and function. Either rupture or limitation of function can lead to secondary surgical procedures for correction.

Nerves, like tendons, are most often injured by laceration. Whenever a nerve is cut in the hand there is numbness in that area. Repair is by surgery. To protect the surgical site casting is necessary. If healing is impaired it is either by rupture or scar formation, and correction requires additional surgery. In spite of the additional surgery sensory deficits may persist.

Following any operation there are obligate periods of immobilization to allow the repaired structures to heal. This frequently results in joint stiffness that requires therapy to improve. Full recovery after surgery can take many months. This impacts the patient's work and lifestyle. If an injury is job related or requires third-party reimbursement, the plastic surgeon is frequently involved as the evaluator for compensation, which places her before review boards and juries to aid in settling cases. Many times other surgeons skilled in this subspecialty will evaluate the initial surgery for second opinions or evaluate disability pre- and postsurgery. The surgeon must constantly be aware of people who lack motivation and desire monetary gain from limited hand function and sort them out from those whose injury truly justifies compensation.

If a hand is significantly injured it will most likely never be a totally normal hand again. The degree of deficit is related to severity of injury, success of correction, and rehabilitation therapy.

§ 15.5 Facial Fractures

Facial injuries may be simple problems such as a laceration or nasal fracture or may be complex soft tissue losses and massive bony damage or both. They may be isolated or be part of a constellation of body trauma.

The initial examination begins with palpation of the facial bones and observation for loss of symmetry. Evaluation of vision and jaw function is also performed. A complete set of x-rays and often CT scans are necessary to visualize the extent of injury. Treatment programs can then be formulated. The first priority when managing facial injuries is to protect and secure the respiratory airway and to stop all bleeding. Next is the repair of open soft tissue wounds. Once the patient is stable, structural bony surgery can be performed. Often there is a large window of opportunity in which to operate. Therefore swelling is allowed to diminish and most surgeries are deferred for 48 to 72 hours.

Types of Facial Fractures

Nasal. The nose is very vulnerable to trauma because of its protruding position in the center of the face. Fractures may involve the bones, cartilage, or both. They may be isolated or extend to the teeth and maxilla, the air sinuses of the midface. Reduction of the fracture may be simply performed by manipulation or casting with packing under local anesthesia, or may require formalized surgery under general anesthesia.

Mandible. This is the second most frequently fractured facial bone. Injury can influence chewing, speaking, and swallowing. A severe injury can block the airway. Fractures can involve any part of the mandible depending upon the direction and degree of force. The most common site of surgery is the alveolar ridge where the teeth are supported. Other frequently injured sites are the angle and the condyles. Sometimes multiple regions of the mandible can be fractured. Injuries may involve the skin and oral membranes as well.

Treatment goals are to place the mandible back into the preinjury original occlusion with the upper jaw and secure the position. This may be done on simple cases with braces or may require surgery with plate fixation of the segments.

Tripod or zygoma. This bone forms the cheek prominence. The axis of this tripod extends across the floor of the orbit and over to the top of the mandible. Therefore injury to the zygoma causing displacement can effect vision and/or jaw function. Correction is surgical and requires repositioning and then maintenance of the bony segments. If surgery is not performed, a permanent visual or masticatory defect is possible.

Midface. This region is like a giant air bag protecting the brain. With significant injury this area collapses in an effort to dissipate the force of injury and protect vital structures. To avoid permanent aesthetic defect these fractures must be reduced and secured. This is a complex surgical procedure that can take hours. Most of the injuries seen are a result of motor vehicle trauma. The surgeon becomes involved not only with the patient but also with the attorneys and insurance companies. Evaluations for changes in appearance, alterations in function, and time lost from work all become part of the equation.

§ 15.6 Breast Reconstruction after Mastectomy

Breast cancer affects more than one woman in 10; therefore, the possibilities of having to cope with the trauma of mastectomy are not remote. Reconstruction is performed to improve the quality of the patient's life; it has no influence on the ultimate outcome of the disease. It will not cause it to spread or hide a recurrence. There also has never been a case of cancer as a result of a silicone breast implant. The decision for reconstruction rests with the individual.

There are many methods and timing sequences for breast reconstruction. It is essential to choose an experienced plastic surgeon who can provide a treatment plan best suited to an individual's needs and not based upon his own limitations. Also important is to understand the realities of what can be accomplished.

Factors such as obesity and surgical scars on the chest and abdomen can influence the types of procedures used and their results. A patient's desire is another consideration. Some patients want only a mound to eliminate the need for an external prosthesis. Others will go to any length to achieve the most natural and symmetrical result possible.

The breast is a three-dimensional structure consisting of an outer skin envelope, an inner glandular filling, and a projecting nipple with a surrounding areola. Successful reconstruction provides for replacement of all these lost tissues. Although total breast reconstruction can be carried out in one procedure, most experienced plastic surgeons elect to perform it in stages to insure the best possible shape, size, and symmetry.

The first stage in a reconstruction is the creation of the breast mound. This is performed either with a silicone implant or with the patient's own body tissues. If an implant reconstruction is selected, the initial stage is designed to provide an adequate skin envelope. This is most often provided by the technique of tissue expansion in which a deflated balloon is surgically placed beneath the skin and muscle at the mastectomy site. Fluid is then periodically injected with a needle through a small valve beneath the skin. This serial filling results in a progressive stretching, like the abdomen during pregnancy. Once accomplished, the expander is removed and a permanent silicone prosthesis is replaced.

If an immediate reconstruction is planned, the expander is positioned at the time of the mastectomy. If delayed, the procedure can be performed on an ambulatory basis under local or general anesthesia. The exchange procedure is likewise an ambulatory one.

The other popular method for mound creation utilizes the skin and fat from the lower abdomen. This tissue, usually discarded in a "tummy tuck," is supported and transferred to the breast area by the rectus abdominis ("sit up") muscle. It can be shaped into a remarkable breast facsimile and eliminates the need for an implant. It is a major procedure lasting from four to six hours. Hospitalization averages five to seven days and ultimate recovery can be from three to six weeks. Because it is possible that a blood transfusion may be required, this procedure is often performed electively after the initial mastectomy so patients can donate and store their own blood.

Once the mound is made, attention is turned to the nipple and areola and to insuring that there is as much symmetry as possible with the opposite breast. Despite the best of efforts, it is rare that a reconstruction can reproduce an individual's opposite normal breast. The closest possible symmetry is achieved by a "matching" procedure using an uplift, a reduction, or even an augmentation.

The nipple areolar complex is fashioned to complete the reconstruction usually at the time of the matching procedure. This involves either a sharing of the normal nipple/areolar tissues if they are overly large, or by borrowing from hidden sites such as the upper inner thigh where color matches are remarkably close. Refinements in color can also be improved by tatooing pigment into the reconstructed nipple and areola.

The average total time commitment for a staged breast reconstruction is six months. Like any surgery, breast reconstruction has its own set of risks and complications. In addition to bleeding and infection, there is the possibility of hardening of the tissues around the implant and, in the case of abdominal tissue reconstruction, partial or complete flap loss. However, when procedures for reconstruction are carefully selected and appropriately performed, the results are excellent. Most women who have dedicated themselves to reconstruction feel they have a renewed sense of wholeness. See also §§ **12.38** to **12.48**.

§ 15.7 Cleft Lip and Palate

Clefts of the upper lip and *palate* (roof of the mouth) are among the most common of all birth defects. Approximately one in 750 newborns is affected with a lip and/or palate problem. It occurs equally in all races and ethnic backgrounds. Although the exact cause is unknown, it seems to be a result of parts of the middle third of the face failing to close during the fourth to seventh week of intrauterine life. Because the lip and palate close at different times during this period, it is possible to have only a cleft lip, a cleft palate, or both. Also, the severity can vary from small notches to complete splits.

Many parents of children with this condition experience guilt regarding the pregnancy. Others fear that their spouse has hidden some family history. Although there seems to be a hereditary factor, there is no genetic link, and there is no related factor to medicines or illnesses during pregnancy. Many parents with family histories of clefts give birth to normal children and many "normal" parents with no family histories experience cleft problems. Individuals with a cleft history should seek genetic counseling to better understand the problem and specifics as they may apply to their individual situation.

The types and severity of this condition may vary from child to child. A lip may have only a small notch in the *vermillion* (red part) or there may be a complete separation of the upper lip extending into the nose and involving the gum line. The deformity may be on one side (unilateral) or affect both sides (bilateral). A cleft of the palate is an opening in the roof of the mouth that may only involve the *uvula* (the part that hangs in the back of the throat), may extend through the soft muscular part of the palate, or may be complete through all hard and soft portions and extend to the gum line.

Nearly all parents desire immediate correction to erase the problem. However, although the condition can definitely be corrected, time and patience are required.

The timing of repair is arranged so as to minimally impact on future facial growth and allow for the least risk for surgery and anesthesia. The lip is usually repaired at three months of age. At this time the child is large enough to more safely undergo the two-hour procedure. The palate is usually closed shortly after the first birthday. This time is chosen because it is just prior to the onset of organized speech development for which an intact palate is necessary to help in formation of sounds. This procedure also takes about two hours.

The technical aspects of these procedures and the residual scarring are beyond the scope of this text but should be explained in detail to the families prior to any surgery on their child.

Following the closure of the palate the basics have been completed. However, the child should not be abandoned from care. Intensive speech therapy is required, as is careful evaluation of hearing. Also, as the child grows, attention must be given to the development and alignment of teeth. Eventually correction of any nasal deformities and refinement of lip scars will be performed.

The care of these children is complex. It is for this reason that regional cleft lip and palate centers have been established. The teams in these centers consist of pediatricians, social workers, psychologists, dentists, oral surgeons, speech and hearing specialists, and ear, nose, and throat specialists, as well as plastic surgeons. The team's role is to coordinate care and try to meet all the child's and family's needs.

At birth the obstetrician or pediatrician should recommend a plastic surgeon skilled in the area of clefts. She, in turn, will refer the child to a cleft center.

Another important service available to families with cleft children are parent support groups. These are common and easily located by a pediatrician or plastic surgeon.

§ 15.8 Microtia

The term *microtia* is used to describe an ear deformity of failed development. This problem occurs around the fifth to eighth week of intrauterine life. The severity can range from slight irregularity in contour to complete absence of the ear. Microtia occurs about once in 6,000 births; it affects males twice as often as females and occurs twice as often on the right side. Rarely the problem involves both ears. Microtia can occur as an isolated event or be part of a larger constellation of facial disorders. Often there is a correlation between the severity of the outer ear deformity and hearing disability. The exact cause of microtia is unknown and does not have a direct genetic link; however, there does appear to be a familial tendency.

Because the birth of a child with microtia can create psychological havoc in a family, early consultation with a plastic surgeon skilled in the art of ear reconstruction is recommended. The initial consultation is usually right after birth and parents want the deformity corrected immediately. Unfortunately this is not possible. The initial interview serves to explain the problem, provide a timetable for reconstruction, and give needed psychological support.

It should be carefully explained that if the problem is only one-sided, the child will hear very well through the opposite normal ear and it is not necessary to attempt to rebuild an abnormal middle ear. If the problem is bilateral, then surgery is performed as an attempt to allow the child to hear with hearing aids.

Reconstruction of the external ear starts at around age six. This is an ideal time for many reasons. Anatomically ears have achieved their adult size by this age so matching the reconstruction to the opposite normal ear requires no guesswork for future growth. Additionally, the rib cartilages used for the reconstruction are now of sufficient size to be an acceptable graft. Psychologically it is not until ages six to nine that peers tend to deride for the pure pleasure of insult; therefore, the reconstruction can be completed before significant social damage can occur.

The first stage of this reconstruction is the largest procedure and entails admission to the hospital with a four-hour surgery and a five-day recuperative period. This procedure involves taking cartilage from the ribs and carving it to make a framework for an ear that tries to simulate the opposite ear. The crumpled cartilage from the microtic ear is removed and the framework placed beneath the remnant ear skin in anatomical position. The most significant complications from this surgery include skin breakdown over the rib graft with exposure of the cartilage. This would require another procedure to attempt to patch this area.

Approximately three months after the first stage, the next phase is undertaken. This is a relatively minor procedure that can be performed on an ambulatory basis but requires general anesthesia because of the child's young age. Here the earlobe, which is typically vertical in direction, is rotated and spliced onto the new ear framework to match the opposite ear.

Three months later a small piece of skin and cartilage is borrowed from the depths of the opposite normal ear to make the *tragus* (the small projection in front of the ear canal). This helps to create an illusion of a canal. (In unilateral microtias ear canals are not opened because of the high complication rate and little gain in increasing hearing.) This procedure also helps to pin the normal ear back closer to the head to try to match the reconstructed side.

The final stage performed approximately three months later is an elevation of the auricular framework from the side of the head to give it further three-dimensional properties. This procedure requires a skin graft that can be taken either from the back of the opposite ear or the groin area. This procedure can also be done on an outpatient basis.

Costs for these procedures can be quite high. However, because the deformity is congenital in origin, it should be covered by most insurance carriers. Preauthorization is highly recommended.

There is no question that when these procedures are properly performed the results can be outstanding. There are two important requisites to a successful result. The first is to select a surgeon who possesses the skill, artistry, and dedication to perform these operations. Secondly, it is very important to understand that no matter how excellent the reconstruction, it will never be a normal ear. At best it is a good facsimile of an ear.

§ 15.9 Prominent Ear Deformity

Most protruding ears are cup shaped because of a lack of normal ear architecture: a vertical fold of cartilage near the curled edge is missing. By pressing the outer rim of a prominent ear back towards the skull, this fold—the *antihelical fold*—readily appears. Far and away the majority of abnormal ears seen in a plastic surgeons office are normal in size but missing this fold. The problem can affect one or both ears.

Studies reveal that children with this problem can be placed under significant psychological stress by the torment of other children. The uncanny ability of playmates to pick out an abnormal feature begins at the school age. Fortunately, this period, between five and seven years, is when the ear has achieved full growth and is considered ideal for surgical correction.

The prominent ear deformity can have profound effects on adults as well. Many feelings of self-consciousness and insecurity can be carried forward from the distress and sensitivities felt during childhood. Early surgery can eliminate many years of unhappiness.

The *otoplasty* is a relatively painless procedure that is designed to create the missing vertical antihelical cartilage fold. Under most circumstances, it can be performed on an outpatient basis. The anesthesia can either be a local that numbs the ears or a general in which sleep is induced.

Although there are several approaches to this problem, the most often employed involves an incision behind the ear. This places the scar in an inconspicuous position in the groove between the ear and the side of the head. Once the cartilage is exposed it is weakened along the location of the soon-to-be antihelical fold. The ear is then easily folded back into a normal anatomical position. Stitches are then placed into the cartilage itself to permanently maintain its new shape. If there is any excess skin behind the ear it is removed and the incision is closed. Following surgery the ears are covered with a bulky earmuff-type of bandage. Within a few days, this is removed and traded for a headband placed over the ears for additional protection. The headband is worn for three weeks. After this time the surgical sites have healed and no further protection is needed.

The surgery is remarkably painless, and any postoperative discomfort can easily be controlled by medication. Most people are up and about soon after surgery. Children can resume school within days. Physical education and sports are usually delayed for four to six weeks so as to insure full healing.

Like any surgical procedure there can be complications. These include *hematoma,* or a collection of blood at the surgical site, and infection. Also possible is a breaking of the cartilage stitches, resulting in a popping of the ear back out to its original position. This usually occurs before the wounds have totally healed and requires a second surgery for correction.

Otoplasty is an elective procedure and insurance companies have various viewpoints regarding it. Some accept that the prominent ear deformity is a congenital problem and provide payment. Others consider it cosmetic because there is no functional hearing disability related to it. The otoplasty procedure to correct the prominent ear is not a functional operation because hearing is not impaired. Yet it is more than a cosmetic operation. It is a quality of life procedure.

§ 15.10 Ambulatory Surgery

A unique feature of plastic surgery is that great numbers of procedures lend themselves very well to *ambulatory,* or outpatient, care. Statistics from the American Society of Plastic and Reconstructive Surgery reveal that over 90 percent of eyelid surgery and chin implants and over 50 percent of nasal surgery and face-lifts are performed on an ambulatory basis. Ambulatory surgery is cost-effective and there is clear evidence that patients benefit physically and psychologically when surgery is performed outside of a hospital. There is an inherent "good feeling" knowing that one is not "ill" and will not be caught up in a busy hospital setting, where there are many critically sick people requiring urgent care.

Ambulatory surgery encompasses procedures that do not require overnight hospitalization. Recuperation is at home. The surgery itself and the immediate postoperative recovery occurs in three types of facilities, described below.

Hospital Day Op Centers. Many hospitals have established outpatient surgical centers. These were primarily designed to afford patients a high quality of care while eliminating the "hotel" aspect of recuperation. Surgeons who work in these centers are also usually credentialed to work in the affiliated hospitals. One benefit of this type of facility is that, if discharge is not possible, then hospital admission can be easily arranged.

Free Standing Surgical Centers. These facilities are usually multispecialty oriented like hospital day op centers, but are not directly affiliated with hospitals. In order to operate, however, these surgery centers must be accredited and licensed by state boards. They are subject to constant review and must meet high standards of excellence and safety.

Office Surgical Facilities. The most popular setting for ambulatory plastic surgery is the operating room within the physician's office itself. Here the patient is afforded complete privacy, which can be very reassuring if the surgery is cosmetic. The staff is very attuned to plastic surgical needs. Because the office revolves around the individual doctor, scheduling of surgery can more easily be arranged than in other types of facilities.

Quality control of office plastic operations is maintained by the American Association of Accreditation of Ambulatory Plastic Surgery Facilities. Certification by this organization establishes that the facility provides the proper environment for performance of plastic surgery.

As with the free standing surgical center, if one is not able to be discharged home, then transportation and admission to the doctor's hospital needs to be arranged.

Factors entering into deciding which type of facility is most appropriate are medical, psychological, and economic. If the patient is having a purely elective cosmetic procedure and is in good health, the office facility is the most economical. Costs for services are generally lower, which can be important when not reimbursable by insurance.

If surgery is reconstructive and reimbursable by health insurance, the patient must check with the carrier as to the location for the surgery. Policies will sometimes reimburse only if carried out in a hospital-related facility. The most important criteria is health. If there are special medical needs that require extra monitoring such as diabetes, heart disease, high blood pressure, or seizure disorders, then hospital-related ambulatory facilities should be used. This is also the case when children are having surgery and might require pediatric services.

The type of anesthesia may also influence the location. Many offices prefer not to put patients totally asleep but rely on sedative and local anesthetic techniques.

All facilities carefully monitor care. Plastic surgery and ambulatory surgery is real surgery and, although convalescence is at home, the postoperative instructions must be strictly followed. There must also be responsible people around to assist with the patient's needs. Living alone often precludes many types of ambulatory surgery.

The office operatory is used for local anesthesia and sedation cases such as excision of lesions, brow and eyelid surgery, chin implants, and limited nasal, facial, and liposuction surgeries. The inpatient hospital setting is utilized for breast reductions, abdominal (tummy tuck) surgery, major reconstructive plastic surgery, and of course for any surgery if a medical need necessitates it.

§ 15.11 Bibliography

Introduction

J.M. Converse, Reconstructive Plastic Surgery (W.B. Saunders, 2d ed., 1977).

W.C. Grabb & J.W. Smith, Plastic Surgery (Little, Brown & Co., 1984).

Scars

T. Krizek & J. Hoopes, Symposium on Basic Science in Plastic Surgery (C.V. Mosby, 1976).

D. Kernahan & L. Vistnes, Biological Aspects of Reconstructive Surgery (Little, Brown & Co., 1977).

Clinics in Plastic Surgery 4:2 (W.B. Saunders, Apr. 1977).

Burns

Clinics in Plastic Surgery 1:4 (W.B. Saunders, Oct. 1974).

Hand Surgery

R. Chase, Atlas of Hand Surgery (W.B. Saunders, 1984).

D. Green, Operative Hand Surgery (Churchill Livingston, 1982).

Facial Fractures

R.C. Schultz, Facial Injuries (Yearbook Medical Publishers, Inc., 3d ed., 1988).

R.B. Dingman & P. Natvig, Surgery of Facial Fractures (W.B. Saunders, 1964).

Breast Reconstruction

J. Bostwick, Aesthetic and Reconstructive Breast Surgery (C.V. Mosby, 1983).

Advances in Breast Reconstruction II Clinics in Plastic Surgery (Apr. 1984).

Plastic and Reconstructive Breast Surgery 15 Clinics in Plastic Surgery (Oct. 1988).

Cleft Lip and Palate

D.R. Millard, Cleft Craft—The Evolution of Its Surgery (Little, Brown & Co., 1977).

J. Bardash & K. Salyer, Surgical Techniques in Cleft Lip and Palate (Yearbook Medical Publisher, 1987).

Microtia

Aesthetic Aspects of Reconstructive Surgery 8 Clinics in Plastic Surgery (Apr. 1981).

D. Serafin & N. Georgiade, Pediatric Plastic Surgery (C.V. Mosby, 1984).

Prominent Ear Deformity

Aesthetic Aspects of Reconstructive Surgery, 8 Clinics in Plastic Surgery (Apr. 1981).

D. Serafin & N. Georgiade, Pediatric Plastic Surgery (C.V. Mosby, 1984).

PART IV

TRIAL OF A PLASTIC SURGERY MALPRACTICE CASE

CHAPTER 16

TRIAL OF A RHINOPLASTY CASE

§ 16.1 Introduction

The following rhinoplasty case is included because it uniquely illustrates the trial aspects of both the vanity suit and a reconstructive surgery. The original purpose of the operation was to correct the patient's deviated septum to improve her breathing. However, she had also hoped it would improve the appearance of her nose.

This case involved a claim by the plaintiff that the defendants negligently performed nasal reconstructive surgery necessitating a second procedure leaving her with a saddle form depression in the nose. The plaintiff further claimed a lack of informed consent for the initial surgery.

The patient was a middle-aged, Hispanic woman with a medical history of difficulty breathing and dizziness. She had previously received conservative treatment with decongestants at the hospital. A diagnosis of a deviated nasal septum was made and nasal reconstruction to correct the deviated septum was recommended. During the nasal reconstruction, a saddle form depression occurred necessitating a graft. Subsequently, the graft became displaced and it was removed during a second surgical procedure.

The plaintiff claimed that the initial surgery to improve her breathing was unnecessary. The procedure itself created a defect of the nose (a saddle form depression) which made a graft necessary. The graft moved and resulted in an obvious deformity. She further claimed that the deformity was never properly corrected. She believed that she never looked the same or felt the same because she became depressed as a result of this experience and suffered a nervous breakdown.

Although the defense did not deny that a deformity was created during the initial surgery, they did claim that this deformity was a result of the plaintiff's multiple fractures of the nasal bones and cartilages. Furthermore, the deformity was completely corrected in a second operation. The defendants could not predict the need for a graft prior to the initial surgery and therefore did not advise the plaintiff of the risk and complication of a graft. The defense also claimed that the plaintiff requested multiple vanity cosmetic surgeries for the eyelids and the nose. The plaintiff also had a history of depression and emotional problems prior to the nasal reconstruction. The defense claimed that her current depression was a result of her prior problems when she lost a child and her husband deserted her. Prior to trial a malpractice panel, consisting of a judge, lawyer, and surgeon, found no liability on the part of the defendants.

Comment. Such a finding by this panel, arrived at by reviewing briefs submitted by each party and conducting an oral hearing, is reported to the jury and gives the winner a decided advantage.

§ 16.2 The Opening

The opening is the plaintiff's best opportunity to persuade the jury. In this case the plaintiff had to convince the jury that the doctors operated on this clinic patient for a nasal obstruction when it wasn't medically necessary and without warning her that she might suffer a cosmetic defect. Her most serious damage was what she perceived to be a "bump on the nose" and the concomitant emotional depression. However, she did have a prior psychiatric history that her counsel needed to disclose. Counsel addressed this issue but left much for the defense to exploit.

The plaintiff's counsel tried to educate the jury about the medical relationship between the hospital, chief surgeon, and resident surgeon defendants in order to hold the hospital and chief surgeon responsible. He had to establish that the hospital and surgeon were liable for the acts of the residents. The defense claimed that she actually wanted a nose job for vanity reasons, not medical ones, and that she only imagined it did not turn out right.

Counsel began in a rather disjointed and unorganized fashion but then scored some good points. He made constant use of verbal crutches like "I guess," "okay," and "basically." These words are bad form and distracting. The cast of characters is:

Mrs. P.—Plaintiff
Dr. M.—Resident surgeon, defendant
Dr. A.—Resident surgeon, defendant
Dr. S.—Chief surgeon, defendant
Eye, Ear, and Throat Hospital—Defendant hospital

§ 16.3 The Plaintiff's Opening: The Deviated Septum

As I indicated, this case, basically, started back in 1980 and, back at that time, Mrs. P. developed a problem with breathing through her nose. Okay. It had been built up but it got to such an extent that, in 1980, she sought medical treatment for that. And she went to her, I guess, family doctor, Dr. T., who then referred her to the hospital.

At the hospital, she was seen by a Dr. A. who was a resident of the hospital. She went through the clinic. She was a clinic patient at the hospital and her problem breathing was through the left side of her nose. She had what is known as a deviated septum. The septum is the part that goes down the center of the nose and that was deviated or over to one side. That was preventing her from breathing properly through the left side of her nose.

§ 16.4 —The Treatment Plan

Now, she was seen in the clinic several times and a plan of treatment was developed whereby they were going to do a rhinoplasty, subcutaneous resection which, basically, is an operation where they would go in from the inside of the nose and cure the blockage that was preventing her from breathing. It is an operation designed to make the airway sufficient so she wouldn't have trouble breathing. Okay.

So that was the plan that Dr. A. presented to Mrs. P. and that Dr. A. got approval from the physician who was supervising him who was Dr. S.

Now, we have photographs of what Mrs. P. looked like prior to the procedure being performed. We have slides which I will be showing you in a little while. She was admitted to the hospital on October 31, 1981—or October 30th, I'm sorry—and on the 31st, the surgery was performed. The surgery was performed by Dr. A., as you have heard, under the supervision of Dr. S., but instead of merely just doing a rhinoplasty and a resection, an additional procedure was done which was an augmentation of Mrs. P.'s nose.

Comment. The use of slides and photographs (before and after) is a great idea if they are dramatic and unequivocal. The plaintiff was never told of the possibility of an augmentation of the nose by use of a cartilage graft. The graft was only necessary because the original procedure was performed negligently, creating a defect in her nose. This was the heart of her case.

Now the first time there is any evidence in the hospital records of any discussion of an augmentation of the nose is during the surgery. Augmentation of the nose is where a graft, piece of material, in this case a piece of cartilage, is placed in the nose to build up the nose.

Prior to the surgery, there was no need to have that done. We will introduce expert testimony by a doctor who will indicate that her nose did not need augmentation and, indeed, if you look through the records, it is clear there was no discussion of augmentation of the nose.

Comment. It is good practice to refer to your expert. But the expert's credentials should be included as well as a synopsis of his opinion. Here counsel only alluded to evidence that 'indicates' malpractice. This is weak. It could have been a much stronger statement. "We will prove," he might have said, "by expert testimony of a board-certified surgeon that the defendants cut too much and then concealed their error from the patient." His reference to the records to prove there was no discussion of the risks was very effective.

So the question then becomes—Why was an augmentation of the nose done, which is not a simple procedure? And you are going to hear conflicting opinions on that. But the reason the augmentation was done is because the procedure that Dr. A. did was performed improperly and it created a defect in her nose that had to then be corrected by an augmentation of the nose.

So a defect was created that was not there before the operation, was created by the operation, and was created by the negligence of Dr. A. and Dr. S. supervising him.

Now, there will be evidence that will establish that.

Comment. Now is the time to spell out what that evidence will be but counsel didn't. The jury is waiting and susceptible now more than any other time.

Now the importance of that fact becomes evident when we look at what happened after the surgery. She was in the hospital for approximately five days and that graft implanted in her nose. Now there are several risks associated with having a graft used anywhere in the body and in the nose, certain accepted risks. One of the risks is that the graft will migrate, it will come out of place—that is what migration means, it will just come out of place.

Now that is a risk of graft.

And that is exactly what happened in this case.

Comment. Counsel finally capsulized the main point of his case. A malpractice case must be simplified to its essentials. He next referred to photographs, but conceded that they may not be big enough for the jury. It would have been better if he had prepared blowups or individual copies for maximum demonstrative jury effect.

The graft, after the surgery, came loose and it affected Mrs. P.'s cosmetic appearance. Now the easiest way you can see the effect of the graft is if we show you two photographs that will be introduced into evidence and they are not that big so I hope you can see them. The first one here is dated October 31, 1981, and it is before the first operation. Okay, before the first operation performed by Dr. A. You will get to handle this and look at them closely later on, and the second photograph is dated November 4, 1982, and it is after, the second is after the first surgery and you can see the difference and how the graft is displaced in her nose. You can see that, the graft is displaced.

And, as I said, you will get to look at these closer and you will get to see the slides of this. Okay. This condition was caused because the graft was needed and the only reason the graft was needed was because [of] what they did wrong during the surgery, which you will hear about from witnesses. If the surgery had been conducted properly, no graft would have been needed and this result that we see here in this picture would not have occurred.

Now, she continued going to the Eye, Ear, and Throat Hospital because, naturally, with an appearance like that, she was dissatisfied and anybody would be with the graft projecting off the tip of her nose.

Comment. Under the law, the jury, as the reasonable person, determines whether the patient would have undergone the procedure if she did know all the risks.

And the doctors examined her and what they decided to do was to remove the graft, because it had migrated out of place, so they would have to do a second surgery to remove the graft.

Now that surgery was performed in November 1982 by Dr. M., again supervised by Dr. S. It was a two-day operation in which they went in and they took out the graft which had migrated out of place. Okay. But although they took out the graft, they seemed to have no concern for the cosmetic results of her nose; nothing was done to replace the graft that originally was needed, they just merely removed the graft and did nothing about the cosmetic problem that existed at that time.

So Mrs. P., at the present time, is left with a cosmetic deformity of her nose.

§ 16.5 —The Damages

Comment. Depression, more than the physical deformity, was the main theme of the damage claim. The defense claimed that the patient had been depressed for years because her husband left her and she lost a child in a miscarriage. The plaintiff's counsel continually used words like "indicating" instead of "proving" damages. This is a poor way to convince anyone. He also claimed that she got over her prior depression instead of admitting that it was a chronic illness that was aggravated by her surgical ordeal.

Now, in this connection, we will have testimony indicating where the deformity is but, more importantly, you will be able to see and judge for yourself, you will have pictures and Mrs. P. to judge for yourself what the end result is but since, as you are all aware, appearances are very important to men and women, and our noses and our faces perhaps the most important part of our bodies in terms of appearance, this change in the appearance of her nose and the fact that she had to undergo a second surgery affected more of Mrs. P.

than merely her nose. She began to have depression, she began to have lowered self-worth, she thought people would be looking at her nose and she was not satisfied with the way she looked and it affected her in many ways which you will hear.

And eventually, in 1984, she sought psychiatric treatment which, I believe, she was under for about two years where she was seeing a psychiatrist and they would talk about the problems and we arranged to have that psychiatrist come in and he will testify as to what he discussed with Mrs. P. and the effect that this had on Mrs. P.

Comment. This was important evidence that should have been completely revealed now, not later. The plaintiff had prior psychiatric problems and counsel wisely informed the jury before his adversary revealed it. However, he failed to describe what the psychiatrist was going to testify about and why it was not related to her present depression.

Now you will also hear that Mrs. P. had certain problems in her life prior to this. In 1975, she had a miscarriage. Her husband had left her and she was all alone. Okay. You will hear all that and that, naturally, had an effect on her. Nobody is going to deny that this didn't have an effect on her. So what that created was a condition where she was greatly affected by this change in the condition of her nose more so than someone who would have the support system of her family, children, things like that.

So, in conclusion, I would just ask you, keep an open mind. I know you are all going to be fair and impartial in this case, as you indicated while we were selecting a jury, but I would just ask you to keep one thing in mind.

Comment. Counsel ended abruptly without fully developing the liability of each defendant or the full extent of the emotional damages. He handled the prior emotional problems well by indicating that it predisposed the plaintiff to develop depression because of the operation. She was like a fragile eggshell. Even if the average person would not have gone to pieces over this, it was reasonable to expect that she would. He ended his opening, however, without ever admitting that he lost the malpractice panel. This was a serious error. He appeared insincere and misleading to the jury. In summary, this was a poor opening that displayed a poor group of the medical and emotional issues in the case and a serious lack of candor about the case's weak points.

You are going to be hearing a lot of testimony from doctors. You are going to hear a lot of lawyers make arguments to you and doctors and lawyers tend to talk in technical terms and talk in a cold manner.

But I would just ask you to remember that what we are talking about in this entire trial is a human being and that is Mrs. P.

§ 16.6 The Defense Opening

Comment. This excellent opening by counsel Millie Matos for the supervising surgeon made the following convincing points: (1) the malpractice panel voted in favor of the defendant and the plaintiff failed to advise the jury of this fact; (2) the plaintiff's alleged disabling psychiatric depression was a result of the death of her child and divorce from her husband; (3) vanity, not malpractice, was the motivation for this suit; (4) the defendants cured her breathing problem; (5) the plaintiff had always disliked her nose; and (6) she just couldn't accept herself and the defect was now all in her mind. The opening had themes and took a positive approach in stressing how the patient was helped, not hurt.

Ladies and gentlemen. If a trial is a search for the truth, you should be told all the facts, not just the ones that plaintiff wants you to hear.

If a trial is a search for the truth, why weren't you told that everything plaintiff just said to you today was rejected by a court-appointed impartial panel of experts in this very courtroom one year ago. Under our law, a board-certified surgeon, an expert lawyer, and a supreme court justice deliberate, just as you will about this case. They are given X-rays, medical records, testimony and expert opinions, and a brief. The lawyers then argue their positions. We are asked questions.

And after all this, what was this esteemed panel's verdict? No liability! No malpractice! Each and every one of these impartial court-appointed "jurors" found no malpractice. But you were not told this! Where was the plaintiff's candor? The panel was one thing but you are [the] most important jury to us. And we need your unanimous verdict too—it's more important than the panel because you are the voice of our community. What did we tell the panel experts? We told them that Mrs. P., in 1980, had complaints of headaches, dizziness, [and] hyperventilation and [was] found to have a deviated septum of the nose. She couldn't breathe well. The clinic treated her conservatively at first, but when she still suffered, surgery was recommended to correct her nasal airway. But she had prior fractures of the nose she didn't tell us about. They were only discovered during surgery. The operation went well. We didn't hurt her. We helped her. Because of her internal nose structure and her prior injuries the doctors had to give her a graft. It moved, as it does in many cases, a simple complication—not an error. There was a temporary bump but no more. It only existed for a short time.

Then we corrected it. But she wanted to look beautiful. She never liked her nose. She wanted a new one. She can't see the correction because the bump is all in her mind.

She breathes better today because of us but believes she doesn't look right. You look at her. Her nose is no different now than before the operation except that she breathes better. The bump only lasted a short time. But in her head it's still there because she magnified it because of her prior depression. She imagines a defect that is not there. That's because years ago she lost a child in a miscarriage and a husband in divorce. She went to doctors and psychiatrists. They gave her tranquilizers and antidepressants. She has had chronic depression ever since. It is not due to our treatment. We are only the scapegoat or a means to an end—she wants money she doesn't deserve. There was no malpractice.

If a trial is a search for the truth, why didn't they tell you she was on antidepressive drugs and under treatment of a psychiatrist before the nose job and that it is the same depression today.

Now that you have heard the same arguments, the same evidence we presented to the panel of experts, you see that the only verdict in this case should be, is the one they rendered—no liability.

Comment. This was eloquently simple and to the point. It exploited the themes of vanity and prior psychiatric problems and the lack of candor on the part of plaintiff's counsel.

§ 16.7 The Plaintiff's Examination of the Defendant Resident

Comment. In most malpractice cases, the plaintiff's counsel calls the defendant to the stand as his first witness in an attempt to discredit him and establish departures before the defense has a chance to make its case.

The resident in otolaryngology performed most of the original procedure. He was the main target of the case. As an adverse witness, he can be led with "yes" and "no" questions that help establish the plaintiff's case. However, counsel allows him too much leeway to discuss his medical background and volunteer other information helpful to the defense.

Educational Background

Q. Good morning, Dr. A.
A. Good morning.
Q. Are you appearing here pursuant to a subpoena my office served on you?
A. Yes.
Q. And are you licensed to practice medicine in the State of New York at the present time?
A. Yes, I am.
Q. And when were you licensed?
A. In 1981—'82.
Q. And where did you go to medical school?
A. I went to medical school, Madras Medical School in India.
Q. When did you come to the United States?
A. 1967, January.
Q. And when you came to the United States, at any time after that point, did you begin a relationship with the Eye, Ear, and Throat Hospital?

A. In 1976, when I came, I was surgical resident in training.
Q. Where?
A. At Jewish Memorial Hospital in New York City.

Comment. Some attorneys feel that a jury will be biased against a foreign resident who graduated from a foreign medical school. Defense counsel should address this issue in the selection of the jury to expunge the prejudice.

§ 16.8 —Liability of the Supervising Surgeon

Comment. Counsel wanted to use the resident to introduce the theme that the supervising surgeon was liable for the resident's negligence. However, he never seemed to nail this concept down and he let the witness talk too much. He did try to make an initial impression that residents are inexperienced but this is dissipated by the witness' excellent answers.

Q. And as a resident, are you supervised by other physicians?
A. At all times. We are supervised by physicians, attending physician who is the preceptor, the teacher is present at all times when you are operating or trying to take care of patients in the clinic, you are under direct supervision at Eye and Ear.
Q. And was Dr. S. [also a defendant] one of the supervisors for you back at that time?
A. That is correct.

§ 16.9 —The First Visit

Q. Now, Doctor, when you were at that residency program in 1981, did you ever have a patient by the name of Mrs. P.?
A. Yes, I did.
THE COURT: He wants to know when you first had contact with the patient.
Q. When you first saw the patient, the date.
A. October 16, 1980, I saw her in the clinic.
Q. When was the next time you saw Mrs. P.?
A. Well, October 22, 1981, in the nose and throat clinic.
Q. What was the purpose of her seeing you on that occasion?
A. Nose and throat diagnostic clinic for evaluation of stuffiness of the nose for which she had been seen a couple of times in the past.
Q. So, on that occasion, did she make complaints of having stuffiness in her nose?
A. Yes, she did.

Comment. Counsel conducted this "cross-exam" of the defendant too much like a deposition with open-ended questions. He should have used leading questions and focused on the departures and lack of informed consent issues. Instead, he is letting the defendant take over.

Q. And can you be any more specific than stuffiness of the nose? Can you describe to us what her complaint was?
A. If I may, she was seen in the diagnostic clinic for the same condition in the past, on 16 of October 1981, and she had been treated by the medical treatment with no improvement and she was referred specifically for possible surgical evaluation and treatment, if she would be a candidate for surgery for the nose and throat.
Q. My question to you, Doctor, is do you recall anything more specific about the complaint of stuffiness of the nose?
A. She did complain of appearance of the nose, also.

Comment. This was a key issue in the case. The defense claimed that the patient had a vanity desire for a new nose all along. Even though he wasn't asked, the resident volunteered this answer.

§ 16.10 —No Cosmetic Complaint in the Record

Comment. The defense claimed that the patient was a vanity case with a large ego that could not be satisfied. The plaintiff's counsel tried to establish that there was no proof that it was the reason for the operation. The record was silent. This exploitation of the discrepancy between the record and the doctor's trial testimony is an excellent cross-examination strategy.

Q. Did you write anything about complaints that she made of cosmetic appearance?
A. No.
Q. But you represent that today, as you sit here today?
A. It says trauma.
Q. I am asking you complaints that she made.
A. No.
Q. Do you remember her specifically complaining about the appearance of her nose?
A. Yes, I do.
Q. And what was she complaining about?
A. Of the dorsal hump and widening of the nose.
Q. But you didn't write down that she was complaining of those things?
A. Not in the complaints.
THE COURT: Not in that note.

Comment. The doctor was being evasive but counsel and the court insisted on an answer to the specific question.

§ 16.11 —Deviated Septum

Q. Can you tell us what a deviated nasal septum is?

Comment. The doctor should not have been invited to lecture. He tried to but the court cut him off. Counsel should have been leading the doctor by means of "yes" and "no"-type questions.

A. The nasal septum is the wall which partitions the nasal cavity into the right and the left side. If I may, I would like to show a diagram which shows that.

THE COURT: It is not a very complicated concept.

A. The septum is partly made of cartilage which is a soft bone and partly made of flat bone which separates it in a bony compartment between the right and the left side and also the septum holds the nose in position and gives a little character onto the top of the nose and it is almost like a strut of a pyramid where the nasal bones are resting on top.

Comment. The doctor was well prepared to take advantage of open-ended questions and lecture and use demonstrative evidence. When the physician is called by the plaintiff he must be prepared to make his case on the first day. It is too late to convince the jury weeks later during the defense portion of the case.

§ 16.12 —The Prior Trauma

Comment. The plaintiff's counsel suggested that the operation was not necessary in the first place because her deviated septum was caused by a trauma 25 years ago and she has functioned adequately. The defense suggested that the trauma might have been from an assault by her husband. She had denied it. In the following section, the plaintiff's counsel forced the defendant to admit that the cause of the trauma was not medically relevant. The defense also claimed that the patient never informed any of the doctors about the trauma. Therefore, they could not have anticipated the possibility of having to do a graft until they actually operated.

Q. Can you tell us what trauma is?

A. It's hard to say what trauma is.

THE COURT: Trauma is injury. You can't tell the precise nature of the injury—is that correct?

THE WITNESS: That is correct.

Q. My question really is can you just define trauma?

THE COURT: He defined it. Go ahead.

Q. Did you question Mrs. P. about what type of trauma she had?

A. I am sure I did.

Q. Do you recall what she said?

A. I don't recall now at this time.

Q. Would it be important to know what type of trauma a person has in determining that treatment?

A. That would be pertinent if the patient had a scar on top of the nose or the patient had a penetrating wound. A blunt injury to the nose, I do not think is going to matter, if the patient had an injury by falling down or if she had an injury from an altercation. It is purely academic, it is not going to make any difference in the treatment protocol.

Q. It wouldn't matter what the force of the trauma was?

A. I wouldn't think so in this particular case.

Q. So if the force was extreme, it wouldn't make any difference to you if it was just a little bump on the nose?

A. If the force was extreme, the patient would have a completely depressed nose to start with and not have stuffiness, but have shortness of breath—

Q. Isn't it important for discerning the course of treatment for a physician to determine exactly what type of trauma caused the condition?

A. That is true. If you—if you find out if the patient had a penetrating trauma, did not have a scar on the nose, then you would know that symptoms do not—symptoms do not coincide with the patient's signs but if the patient claims that the injury was a blunt injury and complains of stuffiness of the nose, then it goes to prove the patient's injury was not penetrating.

Q. You didn't write anything down about what kind of trauma she had, did you?

A. That is correct.

Q. Now, is it important, Doctor, from a medical point of view, to know when a trauma occurred, how long prior to your seeing the patient?

A. In the pediatric and adolescent age group, it is important to find out when the trauma occurred. In the adult population of trauma, if the patient is seen immediately after the injury, it does have an impact but a patient who has no history of other signs of trauma in the face and who has been treated medically for this, for a prolonged period of time, the type of trauma and the duration of trauma really does not have any bearing to the treatment.

§ 16.13 —Patient Didn't Need Surgery

Q. You don't think that would have importance in determining whether the patient had been able to adapt to the injury or was unable to adapt to the injury?

A. I don't think that would be, the signs and the symptoms of this patient and the clinic findings substantiate that this patient was not acutely traumatized in the recent past and I don't think that kind of trauma duration has any bearing to this particular form of treatment.
Q. Well, if she had a trauma 20 or 25 years prior to your seeing her, wouldn't that indicate to you as a physician that she was able to live her life and breathe through her nose without any problems for that period of time?
A. That is true.
Q. And is it your opinion, Doctor, that stuffiness was due to whatever the trauma was?
A. Probably.
Q. Is there anything in the record there that indicates when the trauma occurred in her life?
A. The note that was written initially when she was seen says that there is a history of trauma at the age of 16. There is a positive history of trauma at the age of 16.
Q. Is that when she was 16? How old was she when she saw you in October?
A. October of '81 she was 41, 42.
Q. So for that 26-year period of time, as far as you know, she had no treatment for that injury; is that correct?
A. I do not recall her giving me an answer for that question.
Q. And for that 26-year period of time, she had been breathing through her nose without going for any treatment; isn't that correct?
A. Probably.
DEFENSE COUNSEL: Objection, your Honor.
THE COURT: Overruled.

Comment. This was good cross-examination. Defense counsel saw where this line of questioning was going and tried to stop it, but to no avail. The plaintiff's counsel established that this was unnecessary elective surgery and the doctor agreed. However, he insisted that there were good medical reasons to do it.

§ 16.14 —Failure to Take X-Rays

Comment. Was it a departure from good practice not to take x-rays to determine the extent of the previous fracture? The doctor denied it in view of the long passage of time since the trauma.

Q. So it is your opinion that, even after someone has trauma to their nose, passage of time eliminates the need for you to take x-rays?
A. That is correct.
Q. And the x-rays would have no diagnostic value to you in planning a procedure on a person's nose?
A. That is correct. In this particular case.

Comment. This was a good question, but an even better answer. The doctor was forced to admit that as a matter of routine procedure, x-rays should be taken, but he quickly adds that it was not necessary in "this particular case."

§ 16.15 —No Vanity in the Record

Q. Was the purpose of this proposed surgery, Doctor, to help her breathing?

Comment. The plaintiff was trying to stress the noncosmetic nature of the operation. But the witness tried to inject the cosmetic factor into the case again to suggest that Mrs. P. was a vanity case. But the plaintiff's counsel went to the record to prove that no cosmetic vanity complaint was ever recorded.

A. That's correct. Breathing and also to help her change the appearance of the nose to help her look a little better than what she was.
Q. Well, Doctor, I would like you to look at the patient's record for the first admission to the hospital. It's October 30, 1981 to November 3rd.
A. I have it.
Q. Does that have a section that indicates chief complaints?
A. That is correct.
Q. And that would be what the patient was complaining about?
A. That is correct.
Q. And what the patient is coming into the hospital for?
A. That is correct.
Q. And what's written in that area?
A. Stuffiness of nose.
Q. Is there anything in that area about changing the cosmetics of Mrs. P.'s nose?
A. No.

§ 16.16 —No Informed Consent Documented

Q. Would you agree with me, Doctor, that a patient should be told the risks of different procedures before a procedure is performed?
A. I would agree with you on that.
Q. Did you ever have any discussion with—withdraw that.
A. On the October date, the last visit in the clinic that we talked about, I don't recall the precise date—

Comment. The plaintiff scored a major victory here by getting the doctor to admit that he had no actual recollection of informing the patient of risks. He only assumed that she was told because it was his usual custom to inform.

THE COURT: October 22.

Q. 22d. Did you have any discussion with Mrs. P. at that time regarding any risks of what you were planning to do?

A. Yes, I did.

Q. And what discussion did you have?

A. It is standard practice when a patient's presented in the nose and throat conference with these symptoms that a detailed analysis of the nose will be carried out, that possible risks, complications, and the alternatives of treatment are explained. And we usually do it before the conference so that the patient is aware she will be or he will be examined by five or six more doctors in addition to me and then after the—

Q. I don't mean to cut you off. I just asked you what you explained to her. I just asked you that question.

A. Risks and complications of undergoing correctional septum and open reduction of the fractured nasal bones.

Q. Can you tell us what specifically you told her?

A. I do not have a notation to that effect about the specifics of the complications but since I know the standard practice, I am sure I went through all of them step by step, starting from risks of anesthesia to risks of surgery.

Q. Do you have any recollection as you sit here today as to what risks you told Mrs. P.?

A. I do not have—recall those specific requests now.

Q. Do you have any recollection as you sit here today of any specific risks that you told Mrs. P. prior to the surgery on October 31st?

A. No, I don't.

Comment. His answer highlighted the weakness of the defense's position. He did not document the informed consent discussions. The plaintiff claimed that nothing was ever explained to her. Thus, even if the negligence case was dismissed, she still had a strong case for lack of informed consent.

§ 16.17 —Augmentation Never Anticipated

Q. Well, I am asking you what you recall. Do you recall whether part of the plan was to do any augmentation of Mrs. P.'s nose?

A. That was one of the possibilities which could have been carried out at the time of surgery. We did not specifically plan on augmentation preoperatively. When you treat a patient with a fractured nose, you always tell them there is a possibility at the time of surgery and the decision will be made on the operating table during surgery.

Q. Well, Doctor, were you present when Mrs. P. signed a consent to this operation?

A. Correct, I was.

Q. Can you take out the consent form, please?
A. I have it here.
Q. Does that consent form say anything about possible augmentation of her nose?
A. It does not say directly because augmentation was not planned preoperatively. What it does say, if I feel—
THE COURT: Doesn't say it. That is the answer.
Q. It lists in there exactly what you were planning to do; isn't that true?
A. That is correct.
Q. What does that list?
A. Submucous resection of nasal septum and open reduction of fractured nasal bones.
Q. Now, Doctor, isn't it true that by examination of a patient's nose and by palpation of a patient's nose you can tell what the condition of that nose is?
A. To a reasonable degree, yes.
Q. And isn't it true, Doctor, that the usual rhinoplasty surgery does not include augmentation of the nose?
A. I don't understand your question.
Q. Isn't it true that the usual rhinoplasty surgery does not include augmentation of the nose?

Comment. Counsel struck at the heart of his case. Augmentation is not usually done in the absence of error. This was good cross-examination. He was in control with short, pointed questions.

§ 16.18 —Informed Consent

After asking what the risks of augmentation are, counsel followed with this question:

Q. Would you agree with me, Doctor, that those risks would be what a reasonable physician in 1981 would tell a patient about augmenting their nose?
A. That's correct.

Comment. This was a great question because it was couched in the same statutory language that the court charged to the jury. It established a prima facie case for informed consent if the jury believed that the patient was not informed.

§ 16.19 —Implicating Other Defendants

Q. Can you tell us what the roles of each of you were in the surgery?
A. During surgery, the surgical chief resident operates on the patient and is instructed step by step by the attending surgeon, a preceptor, on how to

do the surgery and the preceptor is convinced if the surgical resident is capable of performing the surgery on his own that he lets him do one step at a time and tells him what the next step is but not putting his hand on it directly.

Comment. The resident admitted he did most of the surgery and acknowledged the responsibility of the codefendant surgeon. But the plaintiff did not implicate the surgeon enough. He should have because, ultimately, the judge dismissed the suit against the supervising surgeon for lack of evidence.

Q. You were the one who had your hands on the patient, so to speak?
A. That is correct.
Q. Did you perform all the parts of the surgery?
A. Probably because Dr. S.—I don't recall exactly every step of the operation that I performed on that day but Dr. S. was also there, he also participated in the surgery.

§ 16.20 —Shaving Can Create Deformity

Q. And isn't it true, Doctor, when you are using an osteotome you have to be very careful when you shave the bone?
A. That's correct.
Q. Isn't it true, Doctor, that if you are not careful and you take off too much of the bone, you will create a deformity in the nose?
A. That is correct.
Q. And then that deformity would need augmentation?
A. That is correct.

Comment. This was the key question. The resident was admitting that the deformity could have been caused by too close a shave by the surgeons. However, the resident denied any bone shaving.

§ 16.21 —Use of Photographs

Q. Doctor, did you ever take any pictures of Mrs. P.?
A. Yes, I did.
Q. And did you bring them here with you?
A. It's right here on the slide.
Q. These are the slides we have in the canister?
A. Yes.
Q. And—

Comment. Photos can have great potential if they demonstrate a clear change in the before and after slides. But in this case they did not. The picture on the large screen looked no different than the plaintiff sitting in the stand. The jurors would be looking from the preop slides to the plaintiff in ping-pong fashion. However, the lack of any discernible difference actually scored points for the defense.

Q. Now, Doctor, does this picture indicate to you or show to you that the graft is starting to migrate?
A. No.
Q. So is it your testimony, Doctor, that up until the time you stopped seeing Mrs. P. the graft never migrated?

Comment. The plaintiff now forced the resident to admit through photos that part of the graft has migrated.

A. That's correct.
Q. Can you review the operative report for the second admission, please? What is the date of that surgery, Doctor?
A. 11/26/82.
Q. And who performed that surgery?
A. Dr. M. and Dr. S.
Q. And what was that surgery performed for, what was the purpose of that surgery?
A. It's for revision of the SMR and open reduction and removal of cartilaginous graft.
Q. Removal of the graft you had placed in the first operation?
A. That is correct.
Q. Isn't it true that that graft had to be removed because it migrated out of place?
A. Probably.
PLAINTIFF'S COUNSEL: At this time, your Honor, I would like to show the witness two photographs.
Q. Doctor, I just direct your attention to those photographs of Mrs. P. and ask you to look at them. Upon examining those photographs, do you have an opinion with a reasonable degree of medical certainty as to whether the graft that you had placed on October 31, 1981, had migrated out of place?
A. Part of the graft appears to have been migrated because there is a swelling on the top. It's hard to say unless you clinically feel it and examine the patient. From the photograph, it looks like it is a possibility.
Q. And does that migration, in your opinion, create a cosmetic deformity that Mrs. P. didn't have prior to the surgery on October 31st?
A. Well, if that is swelling that she's complaining of, that is quite obvious it is.
PLAINTIFF'S COUNSEL: I have no further questions.

Comment. In summary, on the positive side, the plaintiff established that there was no documentation that the patient was ever informed that she might need augmentation and that the graft migrated out of place, necessitating a second operation. However, he failed to pin this defendant down to any admission of a departure.

§ 16.22 Doctor's Attorney Rehabilitates Witness

Comment. Because the plaintiff had already "cross-examined" the resident, defense counsel did a direct and personalized his client by informing the jury of his medical background and the defense case. It was essential to present the defense case now instead of waiting to bring the doctor back during the defense case. Counsel started by eliciting the professional experience and education of the defendant.

Q. Good afternoon, Doctor. Counsel asked you if you were licensed to practice medicine in the State of New York. Can you tell us more about your educational and medical background?

A. I graduated in 1973 and I did a training for one year in general surgery from 1973 to 1974 [and] in ear and cardiovascular and thoracic surgery between 1974 and 1975.

And then, in 1976, January, came to this country as a general surgical resident and, in 1977, I continued as a senior surgical resident and then I was an ENT head and neck surgical resident between 1978 and 1979.

I graduated in 1982 as a chief resident and I did a year of fellowship in 1983 in Pennsylvania as a head and neck surgeon and I came back as the chairman of the residency program as a program director and I continued for one year.

Now I am [in] full-time private practice and an assistant professor and chief of one of the services.

Q. And, Doctor, did you earn any academic honors?

A. I am an outstanding graduate from Madras Medical College with honors in those as what you have like magna cum laude and a lot of prizes and publications and—

Q. Could you tell us about your publications?

A. I have publications in surgery of the nasal cavity, the sinuses, for reconstruction, cancers, and I have written books, chapters in books on reconstructive surgery of the sinuses, on the septum, and I teach courses on laser surgery and nasal cavity and in the head and neck region and also sinus surgery at the hospital twice a year and I have some newer publications and newer innovative techniques in handling sinus surgical complaints.

Q. Doctor, are you a member of any medical groups?

A. I am a member of the AMA. I'm a member of the American Academy of Facial, Plastic, and Reconstructive Surgery. I am a member of the American Head and Neck Surgery Society. I am a member of the Head and Neck College of Surgeons in this country—

Q. Are you board-certified?

A. Yes, I am board-certified.

Q. In what specialty?
A. Board-certified in otolaryngology and head and neck surgery.
Q. How does one become board-certified in that field?
A. One has to complete a training program for a period of three years in ear, nose, and throat and neck surgery. After completing at least a minimum of two years in general surgery, we have to do a residency and then you take an examination and you take an oral examination after a written examination to become board-certified.

§ 16.23 —The First Examination

Comment. Defense counsel tried to prove that there was a good medical reason for the first surgery—the patient had an 80 percent obstruction of the airway.

Q. Now, on October 22, 1981, at the nose and throat clinic, Doctor, did you do an examination of Mrs. P.?
A. Yes. The examination was done by me on [the] 22d and I saw her with the symptoms that we already went through in the chart.
Q. Now, did Mrs. P. make a complaint to you?
A. Yes, she was complaining of stuffiness of nose.
Q. Could you describe—and did you make a finding as to how much of a blockage in Mrs. P.'s nose there was?
A. Clinically, she appeared to have a deviated septum to the left and—
THE COURT: What extent was the blockage, that is the question.
THE WITNESS: I didn't put the percentage down in my notes. And the previous notes state it got 80 percent obstruction.
THE COURT: Go ahead.
Q. Somebody—
THE COURT: On the left, previous note was on the left.
THE WITNESS: That's correct.
Q. Now, somebody with an 80 percent obstruction, how would you characterize their breathing?
A. Very stuffy and breathing is usually profound with strenuous behavior and trying to gasp for breath through the nose and a lot of them usually breathe through the mouth also.
Q. Demonstrate for us somebody breathing through the nose.
A. Like that. [Demonstrating]
Q. Thank you, Doctor. Could you tell us what your findings were, Doctor, on that first visit at the nose and throat clinic?
A. She had a deviated septum to the left with turbinates which were enlarged. Dorsal bony hump and she had a widened dorsum of the nose which is from the old fracture. She had asymmetry of the upper left cartilage which are cartilages right above the tip of the nose, had a boxy tip or drooping, flat tip. Had a very short columnella, turning the nose down. In addition she had fat in the medial compartment of both eyes.

Comment. Defense counsel rebutted the charge that there was no medical reason for the original operation. His theme was "the doctors helped to alleviate her suffering." Every good defense in a malpractice case must have a possible theme and not just a defense position.

Q. What was the main problem that Mrs. P. presented to you on October 22, 1981?
A. Stuffiness of nose.
Q. And had she received treatment at Manhattan Eye and Ear for her possible—before she saw you for that condition?
A. She appears to have been seen in the clinic by other physicians, starting from October 7th of 1980, which is almost a year, with stuffiness of nose and she had been placed on decongestants, nasal sprays, and had been seen by a couple more physicians who felt she needed an operation and she was counseled so, even in October 16, 1981, and she was seen by Dr. Levine who said she had a deviated septum to the left and in the front and a vertical ethmoidal plate which is bony obstruction to the right side and she was sent from there to the nose and throat clinic and she was seen on the same day in the morning and she presented to the conference in the afternoon.

§ 16.24 —The Informed Consent Note

Comment. Defense counsel tried to prove that the patient was given a full explanation of the risks by a nurse's note that mentioned the defendant's discussion with the patient. However, the plaintiff was alert and reminded the court that this witness had previously testified that he could not recall any conversation. The court sustained the objection. The witness should have been asked if the nurse's note refreshed his recollection. Defense counsel instead tried the acceptable, but less probative, "usual standard practice" question to prove that an informed consent was given.

Q. Doctor, what is the date of that note?
A. October 22, 1981.
Q. Could you read that note to us, please?
A. Patient seen and presented to conference by Dr. A. Explanation given to patient by resident who will schedule surgery. Patient acknowledged understanding. Crandall.
Q. Crandall?
A. The nurse. She is the head nurse in the nose and throat clinic.
Q. And these notes, the nurse's notes, are a part of the hospital record?
A. Yes, they are.
Q. Could you tell us what sort of warnings or what sort of discussion you had with Mrs. P. in regards to this particular surgery?
PLAINTIFF'S COUNSEL: Objection, your Honor.

THE COURT: Sustained. Said he didn't recall what discussion he had.
Q. Doctor, during a conference such as this, what would have been discussed?
THE COURT: What was the practice?
THE WITNESS: Usual standard practice is to tell the patient what the conference opinion was and then you explain to the patient what the risks, complications—
THE COURT: What are the risks that are usually explained to the patient before the patient consents to this type of surgery?
THE WITNESS: The results of the surgery may not necessarily be what the patient may want to have. The results will be definitely better than what she has. She will have improvements in breathing if the septum has to be corrected and if there is for any reason an infection or an irritation to the surgical site, the wound healing may be delayed. The graft may get rejected. If there is a wound infection or an irritation, or a rejection from the body itself, if the body immunity mechanism does not accept the graft, then you explain the—you explain to the patient that the graft, if it is necessary, you will be able to get a consent to that before, if not, probably to remain at the time of the surgery, if the need arises.

§ 16.25 —Was There a Language Barrier?

Q. What language was the conference?
A. In English.

Comment. The plaintiff was Spanish-speaking but there was no real issue made in the pleadings about her inability to understand English. Her deposition was in English. If there was a genuine language barrier a good case could be made for failure to use an interpreter. However, because the plaintiff testified in English, without an interpreter, such tactics could only prejudice the plaintiff's case with insincerity.

Q. What language was the clinic visit of October 22, 1981, before the conference, what was that conducted in?
A. In English because I don't know any other language other than English. So, unfortunately, I cannot communicate with the patient in any other language and the patient fully understood what I spoke to her about.
Q. To your recollection, [the patient] understood what you were talking about?
A. I think so, yes.

§ 16.26 —The Hospital Consent Form

Q. All right, were any documents signed at that point?
A. Yes, I have a history and physical.

THE COURT: Any documents signed. I take it you are talking about the consent form?

COUNSEL: Yes, your Honor.

A. Yes, she did.

Q. Was it at this time that the consent form was signed?

A. Yes.

Q. Could you find that in the hospital record, please? Was that signed after a discussion with the patient about the operation?

A. Yes.

COUNSEL: Your Honor, I would like to ask the doctor to read—

THE COURT: He can read it. The whole thing?

COUNSEL: Not the whole thing, your Honor.

THE COURT: We will read any part you want. Let me have it. I will read it. What do you want read? Tell me the number to read and I will read it. There are eight paragraphs.

DEFENSE COUNSEL: If you could read, your Honor, number three.

Comment. A witness or counsel or the court can read anything in evidence to the jury. Apparently counsel thought it would be more impressive if the doctor read it. He got a surprise bonus when the court volunteered to read it to the jury, thus lending a measure of credibility and authority to the informed consent document. However, the document, obviously written by lawyers, was too legalistic. The jury may believe it was too confusing for a patient to comprehend. Counsel, having had the court read the document, should have reinforced his point that the patient read, understood, and signed the form.

§ 16.27 —The Operation

Q. Dr. A., did there come a time when you performed the operation on Mrs. P.?

THE COURT: You operated on her the next day?

THE WITNESS: Yes, I did.

Q. Could you get the operation description, summary? Could you tell us what happened, what procedure was done?

A. The patient was taken to the operating room on 10/31/81 and, under local anesthesia with sedation, she underwent a resection of a deviated septum and correction of the airway. And at that time, we noted depression of the right nasal bone and vestibular obstruction and reconstruction of the nasal bones was performed in a routine manner. I am just trying to summarize this as I am reading sentence by sentence.

And after making sure patient did not have any bleeding, the nasal bones were refractured into proper alignment and, when this was performed, it was noted that the right nasal bone [was] a little lower than the left and, hence, the need for augmentation which is really a functional reconstruction of the dorsum of the nose was carried out—

Q. Could you tell us, Doctor, using your own nose as an example, could you tell us what the position was of Mrs. P.'s nose before she had the operation, the position of the septum?

A. The nasal bones were quite wide apart and the septum was obstructing in the front to the left and in the left and in the right posteriorly back of the nose where it is in contact with the throat. And we corrected the septum and then once we corrected the septum, we narrowed the nose on the top and when we narrowed the nose, we found out the right nasal bone was smaller in size compared to the left because of the old-standing trauma and the reabsorption and recontouring of the bone, so we needed to put a graft in to give a proper character to the dorsum of the nose which is this part of the nose. And, hence, we used the septal cartilages from the vormer which is bony from the septum to reconstruct.

Q. So the graft—where did the graft come from?

A. From the septum.

Q. It was her own bone?

A. Yes. The chances of one's own bone healing are better than putting in a prosthesis or even a bone from the other part of the body and it has been statistically proven that one's own nasal cavity's septum heals better than any other part of the body.

Q. What was to happen if the operation had not been performed?

A. Probably more accentuated depression instead of the hump and probably what is called a saddle nose deformity which is the depression of the dorsum of the nose with no bony contouring of that area.

Q. How long would the depression would have been, using your—

A. It would have been lifetime.

Q. Pardon?

A. Lifetime.

THE COURT: No, the depression, not in time.

THE WITNESS: Dimension, kind of hard.

THE COURT: In centimeters.

THE WITNESS: About a centimeter. About a centimeter and a half in length and about less than a centimeter in depth or height.

Q. Are there different factors that affect the outcome of an operation like this?

Comment. Defense counsel did a good job in having the doctor act like a teacher to the jury. He lectured and explained the medicine in a clear noncondescending manner to the jury. He became an authority figure.

A. Yes, there are.

Q. What factors in this particular case?

A. This particular case had a broad nasal bone and asymmetry of the nasal bone, asymmetry of the upper left cartilages so the previous trauma that had taken place had already produced some scar tissue on the bones on the right side.

When we realigned the nasal bones in the proper alignment anatomically, as one should see the right nasal bone was found to be at a lower level or the size of the height of the right nasal bone was not comparatively the same as the left so she needed to have a graft put in there to reconstruct that area to give a straight nose and also to support the septum, instead of the septum drooping down and buckling in that area.

Q. As a result of the operation, was there a change in the appearance of the nose?

A. Yes.

THE COURT: We have seen photographs. We don't rely on this witness. We have photographs before and after and the jury can conclude for themselves what changes, if any, there were in the appearance of the nose.

DEFENSE COUNSEL: Could I just ask one or two questions on it?

THE COURT: Sure. But we have direct evidence the jury can look at.

DEFENSE COUNSEL: Perhaps the doctor could explain the change.

THE COURT: What change did you observe?

THE WITNESS: I think the nose was nice and straight. It was narrow here. We were able to correct the septum so she could breathe better. Had a little straighter septum. Inside the nose was symptom-free after surgery.

Comment. Notice how counsel led the witness through an articulate, professional, and impressive medical explanation of the procedures and reason for the operation. The impression was one of competence, not negligence. The doctor had also reiterated the theme—"we helped her to breathe better—we cured her and there is no deformity except in her mind."

Q. Doctor, why don't we do this another way? Could you look at the hospital record, printed record, and tell us did you do a physical examination, I think you said December 10th, whenever, the next time that you saw her?

THE COURT: Next time was November 5th.

DEFENSE COUNSEL: I'm sorry.

A. November 5th.

THE COURT: Did you conduct an examination on November 5th?

THE WITNESS: I am looking for that. Sorry about this. I am a little mixed up here. November 5th I examined her.

THE COURT: The answer is yes.

Q. And, Doctor, did you do an examination—would you tell us what your findings were?

A. Wound was healing well. The mouth and throat and back of the nose looked normal and condition on discharge was good and she was asked to come back in a week.

Q. When was the next time that you saw Mrs. P.?
A. On the 12th, 11/12. The note says that the wound was healing well.
THE COURT: This is November 12th?

Comment. All this attention to detail manifested great concern for the patient and highlighted the help given to her for her breathing problem. The fact that the graft migrated necessitating a second procedure seemed to be a small price to pay. Notice how the name of the patient was used rather than the cold clinical appellation "the patient." This made the doctor much more likable.

§ 16.28 —Concluding Questions

Comment. Defense counsel summed up his defense on informed consent—it was the doctor's routine practice to obtain it and there was no reasonable alternative for the patient.

THE COURT: He has already testified his general practice was at the conference and then once again when she signed the form.
Q. Doctor, what was the primary purpose of this operation?
A. To reconstruct the inside of the nose so that she can breathe better and, at the same time, improvement in the appearance of the nose.
THE COURT: Sorry?
THE WITNESS: Improvement in the appearance of the nose.
Q. For Mrs. P., was there an alternative to the surgery?
A. I don't think there is another alternative other than to just go on medication probably forever.
DEFENSE COUNSEL: Thank you, Doctor.

Comment. The defense ended on a good note. There was no other alternative but to stay on medications with only partial relief forever. This rebutted the informed consent claim because a jury can conclude that the reasonable patient would have opted for the surgery even if she knew all the risks.

§ 16.29 Examination by Counsel for the Codefendant Surgeon

Comment. Counsel tried to show that this was elective surgery and that the patient therefore knew the risks well in advance. She did it by having the doctor lecture the jury in a very authoritative but simple, direct manner.

Q. You were asked this morning, Doctor, whether Mrs. P. needed this surgery either as an emergency or was it an elective surgery.

Would you explain to the members of the jury the difference between these two types of surgery?

A. Elective surgery is a surgery which is planned ahead of time. Patient's counseled well and it is surgery which is planned well ahead in such a way that the patient and the surgeon, both of them, should feel comfortable and that the patient has exhausted other means of treatment before surgery then she submits herself to it and she may at the last minute, even on the day of surgery, cancel before she goes to the operating room.

Q. Normally, elective surgery in a patient would indicate to the doctor that he or she wants to proceed and go to the surgery; is that correct?

A. That's correct.

Q. And this is discussed with the patient at the time that you were discussing the symptomatology, diagnosis, and the surgery?

A. Yes.

Q. In this particular situation, Dr. A., you indicated that Mrs. P. had a complaint of stuffiness of her nose; is that correct?

A. That is correct.

Q. And you also indicated that this stuffiness was due to some type of trauma that she sustained?

A. That is correct.

Q. And, at the time that you examined her in October of 1981, was there any way to determine the cause of this trauma to this patient?

Comment. Counsel was alluding to the possibility that the patient's ex-husband beat her and that she didn't disclose this important medical fact to the defendants. If they knew they could have anticipated the need for grafting. The wife beating issue was also relevant to the defense claim that her psychological damages were a result of preexisting problems in her marriage and not the appearance of her nose.

A. I can only say it is a trauma. It is almost impossible, if a penetrating trauma or nonpenetrating trauma without a scar. Since she did not have a scar, I presumed she had a blunt trauma to the nose.

Q. What is a blunt trauma?

A. If someone trips and falls or hits against a wall and busts the nose, bleeding from inside the nose without any obvious external cut to the skin, it's a blunt trauma.

If you have a penetrating trauma, it is something like a sharp instrument or a knife or a sharp blade which cuts the skin in addition producing a deviated or a fractured septum or a fractured nose. That is called a penetrating trauma.

Q. If it's a blunt trauma, could that also be caused by a punch in the nose or a slap?

A. Yes.

Q. Of the face?
A. Yes.

Comment. This is a good example of suggesting wife beating without actually being able to prove it. The plaintiff's counsel should have objected long ago and stopped it. Notice the excellent form of the following questions. Counsel told the story of the defense through leading questions to the witness.

Q. Now, you indicated that the trauma resulted in the deviated nasal septum; is that correct?
A. That's correct.
Q. And, as a result of this deviated nasal septum, the patient had difficulties with her breathing; is that correct?
A. That is correct.
Q. And you indicated that this history of trauma referred back to when she was 16 years of age?
A. That's correct.
Q. So for 26 years the patient suffered with problems with her nose and breathing; is that correct?
A. That's correct.
Q. And, at that time when she came to see you, she requested something to be done about her condition; is that correct?
A. That's right.
Q. And that is the reason you decided at that point to proceed with the surgery to correct the deviated septum; is that correct?
A. That is correct.

§ 16.30 —The Mayan Nose

Comment. Counsel pointed out that this Colombian woman had ethnic Mayan nasal characteristics that are genetic and weren't caused by the surgery. The jury was not composed of Latino or South American people.

Q. Now you also described here the boxy tip.
A. Right.
Q. Would you explain to us what that means?
A. All things considered, there is a certain amount of ethnic variation in the type of nose, the Gaelic nose and the Italian nose is different and the Mayan Inca nose is different and different varieties of noses depending on religion and the characters and the previous generations. This is what is called an amorphous boxy tip because this area does not have any cartilage and that area has a lot of thick skin and a lot of fatty deposits under the skin and for refinement, it is not possible, that is what is called a boxy tip.

Q. And you indicated as you were describing this particular nose that it is related to your ethnic background. Is it genetic?
A. It is.
Q. And if you come from a particular group or ethnic background, is it possible that you would have this type of nose?
A. Yes, absolutely. It is well documented in the literature. Not my doing.
Q. Can you describe this?
A. Amorphous boxy tip, either of the Mayan Indian type of noses.

§ 16.31 Redirect Examination by the Plaintiff's Counsel

Q. I would just like to clarify, Doctor, you don't recall any conversation with Mrs. P. regarding any risks of any of the treatment you rendered to her; is that correct?
A. That is correct.
Q. And that form doesn't list on it anywhere the particular risks of the surgery, does it?

Comment. Counsel did a good job of reminding the jury that the consent form was incomplete and the plaintiff did not have a saddle deformity before the surgery.

A. No. Types of risks that I have explained are not on the form, no.
Q. Did Mrs. P. have a saddle deformity before this surgery?
A. No.
Q. Would you tell us what saddle deformity is?
A. When the dorsum of the nose has no bony support. It is very commonly seen in a boxer, the tip of the nose will be over-projected and there will be a depression beyond the tip of the nose from here to here.
THE COURT: Up from about the middle of the nose to a point between the eyes?
THE WITNESS: That is correct.
Q. And she didn't have that condition prior to the surgery, correct?
A. That is correct.
Q. But that condition developed during the surgery; isn't that correct?
A. That's correct.
Q. And it is for that reason that you had to place a graft on the nose?
A. That's correct.
Q. Doctor, you mentioned something to us before about scar tissue that you observed during the surgery and about the bones that you observed during the surgery.
A. Correct.
Q. Isn't it true that you don't have any recollection of the surgery?
A. Absolutely.

Q. Other than the report?
A. That's correct. The graft was made there to reconstruct the—according to the report.
Q. But is there any indication in the operative report there of any scar tissue?
A. I will take a look. There is no mention of scar tissue but—
THE COURT: All right, that is the answer. Next question.
Q. Doctor, you said that after the surgery that you performed, the dorsum of the nose was nice and straight, to use your term?
A. That is correct.
Q. And that's this part here on top of the nose?
A. That's correct.
Q. But that didn't stay nice and straight, did it?
A. During any postoperative visits?
THE COURT: No, at some point after that.
A. Till I saw her before I left, it was nice and straight and, after that, from the evidence that I see, it didn't stay like that.
Q. It didn't stay straight?
A. That is correct.
Q. And can you read for us your note of January 7th, for us, the clinic visit?
A. On examination, the septum was seen to be right inferiorly. The turbinates were plus, plus, plus, which is enlarged. Dorsal nasal tenderness. Small bony mass palpable. No polyps seen. Otolaryngology, as far as I can see, is normal. Return to clinic one week for follow-up.
Q. When you say there is a small, bony mass palpable—
A. That's correct.
Q. —and was that located on the dorsum of the nose?
A. That is correct.
Q. And would that create a bump on the dorsum of the nose?
A. No, the bony mass is the graft that I put there.
Q. That was on the—
A. Dorsum.
Q. Dorsum of the nose?
A. Right.
Q. And did the dorsal tip subsequently become depressed while you were still treating her?
A. I have to look at the chart. Yes.
Q. And when did that occur?
A. On February 25th.
Q. And can you tell us what that means, the dorsal tip depression?
A. Supratip tenderness is the area between the graft and the tip of the nose and not the dorsum, it's called dorsal supratip which is right beyond the lower lateral cartilage which is very commonly seen after you put in a graft.
Q. But that occurred while you were still examining her?
A. That is correct. That is not the area of the graft.
Q. And can you read your note from May 4, 1982?
A. Followup for external for the left ear and stuffiness of nose. On examination of the left tympanic membrane intact, with regard to auditory canal,

normal, right tympanic normal. Turbinates enlarged. No polyps seen. Return to clinic in two weeks. Suspension, two drops three times a day. Tablets, one tablet a day.

Q. What is the cartilage you are talking about?

A. Mild deviation or depression, it's really a depression of columnella that caused the depression.

Comment. This was a good, crisp cross-examination. In some respects it was better and more to the point than the rambling prolix direct examination. It hit the highlights in a leading yes-no format. But it is probably too late. The defense won this round already.

CHAPTER 17

TRIAL OF A RHINOPLASTY CASE: DIRECT AND CROSS OF DEFENDANT SURGEON

THE PLAINTIFF'S EXAMINATION

§ 17.1 The Plaintiff's Examination of the Defendant Surgeon

A plaintiff's counsel should always call a defendant as an adverse witness because, if well-prepared, she can "cross-examine" the defendant and present him in the worst light. This is a very effective strategy if the doctor is the first witness and gives the plaintiff a psychological edge. The defense's only hope is to thoroughly prepare the doctor for cross-examining and to present the defense's case through the doctor immediately after the plaintiff finishes questioning.

The plaintiff's strategy here was to establish that the supervising surgeon was negligent in permitting the resident to remove too much tissue. Because this defendant was older and more experienced than the young resident he was an appropriate target.

Counsel tried to establish that this defendant took full responsibility for the resident's actions as well as his own. Usually, the plaintiff does not ask the doctor questions about his background, because the answers may impress the jury. But here, for some reason, counsel did. It was a mistake, because this defendant was able to make a very impressive appearance.

§ 17.2 Hospital Responsibilities and the Resident's Role

Comment. The plaintiff qualified the target defendant as if he were his own expert. This was not good. He should have established the foundation for his departure questions, not let the witness impress the jury with his background. After eliciting information on the surgeon's hospital duties, counsel got to the resident program.

Q. Were there residents at the hospital at that time?
A. Yes.
Q. And can you tell us what a resident is?
A. A resident is a physician who has graduated from an accredited medical school and is licensed to practice medicine in the State of New York, medicine and surgery, and has undergone very intensive screening and has been selected to participate in a specialty of otolaryngology.
Q. Is a resident program in layman's terms called a training program?
A. Yes.
Q. And did you have anything to do with the training program at the hospital?
A. Yes.
Q. And what was your function in 1981?

A. I voluntarily attended the—in addition to what I mentioned before, I voluntarily attended [the] ear, nose, and throat specialty clinic.

Q. What was your duty with respect to the residents?

Comment. Finally, the plaintiff's counsel got to the residency connection. He should have started here. Note how the doctor slipped in the word "voluntarily" to ascribe altruistic values to his role.

A. We helped the patients with problems that they would have, particular patients that were difficult medical problems or surgical problems we brought to this clinic and they would be examined by a group of attending doctors.

And then we would all sit in a conference and discuss the patients and come to some consensus as to how we can help the patients, what we can do for them.

Comment. The doctor's comment that he voluntarily came to conference for clinic patients to "see how we can help them" was an excellent defense tactic. This witness was obviously well prepared for his interrogation. He had learned how to turn the question to his advantage.

Q. Would you, in essence, supervise the work of the residents?

A. I don't understand the question. Supervise, what way?

Q. Would you oversee what the residents were doing with the patients?

A. Yes. We would.

Q. Would you also oversee the residents when they were performing surgery on patients?

A. Yes.

Comment. These were the key points of the cross-examination but, by themselves, did not prove any departure from good practice. The plaintiff's strategy was to make this defendant responsible for any negligence during the original surgery and for the failure to obtain informed consent.

§ 17.3 Approval for Surgery

Q. And when a resident proposed a patient for surgery back in 1981 would the resident have to get the approval of somebody else before he could conduct the surgery?

A. Depended on the surgery. You mean in the clinic, we're talking about in our nose and throat clinic?

* * *

Q. Whose approval would the resident need?

A. The consensus of the attendings at the clinic.

Q. Were you one of these attendings in that clinic at that time?
A. Yes.
Q. Was one of your functions to approve or disapprove proposed surgery for patients?
A. Yes.

Comment. The intent of this line of questioning was to make the witness responsible for the decision to operate. The plaintiff contended that the surgery was unnecessary in the first place. There can be no malpractice without the condition precedent of a doctor-patient relationship. But there was no real issue here as to that relationship. However, if the patient was a service patient (no attending personal physician had admitted the patient) and not a private one, there may have been an issue as to whether the hospital's insurer was liable for the doctor. The hospital assigns an attending doctor from its staff of attending doctors.

§ 17.4 Reason for Surgery

Q. Was she being seen for a breathing problem at that time?
A. Yes.
Q. And what was the extent of her breathing problem at that time?
A. She had just about a total airway obstruction on the left side and a partial airway obstruction on the right side.
Q. So both sides were obstructed?
A. Yes, to some degree.
Q. What was causing the obstruction?
A. She had a severely deviated septum, a crooked septum and a nasal fracture, multiple.
Q. Now—
A. Means the nose had fractured multiple times.
Q. Do you know how long she had been complaining about the breathing problems?
Q. Would it be important for you in determining what course of treatment to give to a patient to determine how long the problem had existed?

Comment. Finally, plaintiff's counsel began his attack in earnest. He criticized the doctor for not taking a proper history, and suggested that she was treated poorly because she was only a clinic patient.

A. Might be.
Q. But you made no notation of that in the record?
A. It wasn't my function.
THE COURT: Who wrote that note?
THE WITNESS: I can't read the handwriting. I wouldn't know the handwriting.

THE COURT: Let me see. You can't tell who wrote it. All right, you didn't. I take it, generally speaking, on certain occasions, indeed, on private patients all or most of the notes are written by residents.

THE WITNESS: Well, we may be seeing 30 patients in one session. Yes, that is their responsibility.

Q. But as a physician, would you consider it good practice to inquire of the patient how long a breathing problem existed?

A. Yes.

Q. Did you question Mrs. P. when you saw her concerning whether she had any trauma?

A. I don't remember. It would be my usual practice to but I don't remember.

THE COURT: This is 7 1/2 years ago.

THE WITNESS: Yes, I don't recall.

Q. Who was the resident that is presenting Mrs. P. to the conference? Was that Dr. A?

A. It was either Dr. A. or Dr. S., I believe it was Dr. A.

Q. Have you ever had any conversation with Mrs. P. prior to the date of the conference?

A. No.

Q. And on the date of the conference, did you examine Mrs. P.?

A. Yes, I did.

Q. And did you have a conversation with Mrs. P.?

A. Yes, I did.

§ 17.5 Suited for Surgery?

Comment. The plaintiff's next strategy was to establish that this patient was not a good candidate for this surgery and should not have been cleared.

Q. Now, as part of your function at the conference, was it your job to see that the patient was suited for surgery?

A. Yes.

THE COURT: Can I interrupt for a moment? How many attendings were at the conference?

THE WITNESS: At this conference there were three I think.

THE COURT: Why were you the one who had apparently specific responsibility for this patient?

THE WITNESS: No, I didn't have specific responsibility. We collectively had specific responsibility.

THE COURT: But you supervised the surgery?

THE WITNESS: Yes, I did.

THE COURT: Why were you selected for that?

THE WITNESS: I was most able to do the procedure, the operation that was necessary. I'm a nasal specialist.

THE COURT: Oh, the other two attendings were not?

THE WITNESS: A nose and throat clinic and they do, one of the doctors is just—does just septum work. I do functional and reconstructive surgery.
THE COURT: Okay. And the third doctor?
THE WITNESS: Third doctor does both also but this was a difficult case for him so he—
THE COURT: Go ahead.

Comment. The court's question actually gave the witness a chance to enhance his reputation as an expert surgeon in this field.

Q. Is it one of your functions in conjunction with the other attending doctors to make sure that the patient is medically cleared for surgery?
A. I don't understand—
THE COURT: Well, the surgery involves certain risks.
THE WITNESS: Yes, the residents generally will clear the patient, call the medical doctor, get an evaluation.
THE COURT: That is not your function?
THE WITNESS: No, it's the resident's function, the resident instructor that works with them.

Comment. Was this defendant trying to shift the responsibility to the codefendant resident?

Q. Is it important that a patient be medically cleared prior to undergoing surgery?
A. Yes.
Q. So if a patient had a problem with the heart you would like to know that prior to putting the surgery through an operative procedure; isn't that correct?
A. Yes.

§ 17.6 Psychological Clearance

Comment. The plaintiff employed a clever ploy to blame the defendants for tampering with the nose of a very emotionally sensitive patient; they should have foreseen her strong emotional reaction. However, the danger of this approach was that it contradicted the claim that she had no emotional problems at the time of surgery. The plaintiff should have pled an aggravation of a preexisting but dormant psychological condition. In many vanity plastic surgery cases, the plaintiff can turn the tables on the defense by asking why a referral to a psychologist was not made before elective surgery.

Q. Now, is it also true that a patient must be psychologically cleared prior to surgery?

A. Are you asking me if every patient goes through a psychological examination before surgery, no.
Q. Is it important to assess the patient's psychological well-being prior to the surgery?
A. Yes, as best as we can do it.
Q. Isn't that something that should be done prior to the surgery?
A. We look at a patient and we evaluate whether there's anything overtly wrong with the patient. If they are asking for something that is out of the ordinary or something that is not practical, or we suspect any kind of psychological problems, we would call in a psychiatric consultation with the patient and seek a psychiatrist. Nowhere in the City of New York that I know of is it a routine practice to submit every patient that comes to the clinic for any—even a private doctor, my private patients, to undergo psychiatric examination when somebody is undergoing surgery.
Q. I am not asking you whether you should have evaluated by a psychiatrist. I am just asking you whether it is a good medical practice to yourself as a physician to assess whether the patient has any psychological problems?

Comment. If there is a genuine issue about the patient's ability to consent because of her mental state it may be advisable to have the patient consult with a psychiatrist.

A. As best as I can.
Q. I mean that is something that a resident should do also?

Comment. Counsel was now fishing to get the resident on the hook too.

A. No, we talk to the patient, talk to the patient.
Q. And based on your conversation and your examination of Mrs. P., prior to the surgery, was she in a depressed state at that time?
A. No, I didn't think she was but again—
THE COURT: All right.
Q. Was she suffering from any psychological problems?
A. Pardon?
Q. Was she suffering from any psychological problems at that time?
A. The resident asks the patient whether she has any medical—any past medical history.
THE COURT: Doctor, all counsel is asking you is, based on your recollection of your contact with this patient, did she impress you as having any psychological problems?
THE WITNESS: No.
THE COURT: Go ahead.

Comment. This was a very clever ploy because it contradicted the defense position that she was suffering from depression at the time of the surgery.

§ 17.7 Was It Cosmetic Surgery?

Q. Now, Doctor, on October 22d, 1981, did you come to some conclusion at the end of your examination and discussion with Mrs. P. as to whether the surgery that was proposed should go ahead?

A. What surgery?

THE COURT: The surgery proposed for this patient, what surgery was proposed for her?

THE WITNESS: Patient wanted cosmetic blepharoplasty and some other cosmetic surgery in addition to the nasal septum.

Comment. Here was the crux of the matter. The defense claimed that the patient wanted multiple cosmetic surgery for the eyelids and the nose as well as nasal reconstruction. The plaintiff claimed there were no vanity or cosmetic procedures involved.

THE COURT: Before the patient indicated what she wanted, what was proposed?

THE WITNESS: We proposed that she have the septum repaired and the bone straightened inside the nose.

THE COURT: Okay. Did you determine that that was appropriate surgery for her condition?

THE WITNESS: I thought it was necessary.

Comment. Notice how the court seemed to take over the proceedings.

Q. You just mentioned something about some cosmetic surgery that the patient wanted. Is there anything in the records there that indicated anything about proposed cosmetic surgery?

Comment. In any medical malpractice case the record is a powerful evidentiary tool to impeach the doctor. This surgeon claimed there was notice in the record of the cosmetic request by the patient. But he was impeached on this.

A. Yes.

Q. Where do you find that?

A. There is a note, I believe, by Dr. S., patient requested blepharoplasty and I have personally—

THE COURT: There is a note. What is the date of the note?

Comment. The question was, was there a note that indicated that the patient requested cosmetic surgery? The court was now helping the plaintiff by correctly pinning down the issue. Even if there was a note, did the note prove that the patient requested it? The court was really confining the defense and obviously defense counsel didn't want to challenge the court, or incur its wrath. However, the judge had left open the opportunity for the witness to explain his recollection later.

A. No note specifically saying patient requests anything.
THE COURT: Either on the 22d or another note?
THE WITNESS: To my recollection.

§ 17.8 No Consent for Augmentation

Comment. The plaintiff's counsel scored points with the following attack on the failure of the hospital to include the nasal augmentation in the consent form.

Q. What procedure does that consent form indicate is going to be performed on the patient?
A. Submucous resection of nasal septum and open reduction of nasal bones.
Q. Does that consent form say anything about augmentation of Mrs. P.'s nose?
A. Not specifically.
Q. Can you tell us what augmentation of someone's nose is, what the term augmentation means?
A. It means to add in or fill in, build up.
Q. Okay. Now, can you tell me your opinion with a reasonable degree of medical certainty as to whether there were any risks to augmentation of someone's nose?
A. Pardon me?
THE COURT: Are there any risks to augmentation? Were all the risks of graft displacement explained?
THE WITNESS: Yes.

Q. Can you tell me what the risks in your opinion are?
A. Depending on what you are augmenting with, if you are using the patient's own natural materials, bones and cartilages, there is a very small risk of infection.

There is a risk of the movement of the graft. It's a risk of dissolution—the graft dissolving and disappearing. There's a risk that the graft may come out, dislodge, come out inside the nose from the incision site.

That's about the most common risk that you would be facing with something like that.
Q. Doctor, do you have an opinion with a reasonable degree of medical certainty as to whether the good, accepted practice of medicine requires a physician to tell the patient the risks that you have just mentioned to us prior to augmenting a patient's nose?
A. If you know you are going to do an augmentation, yes.
Q. And failure to do that would be a departure in your opinion from accepted medical practice?

Comment. The plaintiff zeroed in on the million dollar departure question. But the doctor was ready for it. Counsel seemed intimidated by the answer and doesn't follow it up at all.

A. No, I don't think so.
Q. Now, prior to doing surgery on Mrs. P., were you planning to do an augmentation on her nose?
A. No.

§ 17.9 The Saddle Deformity

Q. Now, Doctor, can you tell us what a saddle deformity is?
A. Saddle deformity is a depression in the roof of the nose or the tip of the nose, generally between the tip and the roof of the nose between the eyes.
Q. That would be sloping down?
A. A sloping down or a divot.
Q. Did Mrs. P. have that condition prior to the surgery on October 31st, 1981?
A. No.
Q. Doctor, how would you repair a saddle deformity in a patient who had a saddle deformity back in 1981?
A. You would either make the nose smaller completely or fill it in with something.
Q. Augment it with something?
A. Fill it in with something. Augment is filling.
Q. What would you use to augment it?
A. Fill it in with cartilage or bone preferably from the patient's own tissues.
Q. Isn't it true, Doctor, that during this procedure on October 31st, 1981, a saddle deformity was created in Mrs. P.'s nose?
A. I would say a saddle deformity had developed in Mrs. P.'s nose.

Comment. This was the heart of the plaintiff's case. He scored points on this issue. He got the witness to admit that the first operation caused a saddle deformity in the patient's nose, which led to the necessity for a graft. But he still had to prove that it was the result of a departure from accepted medical care.

Q. It's for that reason, the development of the saddle deformity, that you had to put in that cartilage graft?
A. Not entirely.
THE COURT: Was that one of the reasons?
THE WITNESS: That was one of the reasons.
Q. Did you perform any parts of the surgery, Doctor?
A. I might have performed some small parts of it.
Q. Do you recall what parts you performed?

A. No.
Q. Do you recall who—
A. But they were minor parts.

Comment. This defendant wanted to minimize his role but counsel brought him back to earth by having him concede he "sometimes" told the resident what to do.

§ 17.10 Use of Deposition Testimony

Q. I am reading from page 10, starting on line 15:

> "Question: What part of your examination in particular led you to believe that was an old fracture?
>
> "Answer: The initial examination?
>
> "Question: Yes.
>
> "Answer: The septum itself was pretty solid. Even though it was broken and bent. The nasal bones were solid. There wasn't the swelling over the nasal bridge area, and the area around the nose was not significantly edematous. Everything had settled down."

Continuing on page 11, line 4:

> "Question: When you say mature, is that again more than one year?
>
> "Answer: I would say it was of operable time. It was adequate to operate on. There was no swelling around it. You could feel everything. The septal mucosa was—there was nothing moving in the septum. Everything was solid. There was no active bleeding. There was no sign of recent bleeding."

Do you remember testifying to that, Doctor?
A. Yes, I do.
Q. Doctor, isn't it true if the person's septum is broken into many pieces it cannot be used as a graft?
A. No, not true.
Q. Doctor, does a septum ever become unusable?
THE COURT: Are there any cases in which the septum cannot be used?
THE WITNESS: When you can't get it.
Q. Other than when you can't get it, are there any times when it could be broken into too many pieces and you couldn't use it?
A. No. Sometimes someone would crush the septum to use it—
THE COURT: The answer is no. Next question.
Q. So, the septum in your opinion is never unusable?
DEFENSE COUNSEL: Objection.
THE COURT: Overruled. Is that correct?
THE WITNESS: I can never say never on anything.

Comment. The plaintiff made a good point. If she had a prior trauma to the septum she would not be a good candidate for this surgery. In fact, there might have been an alternative of using the ear as a donor site. Counsel adroitly used prior deposition testimony to make this point dramatically.

* * *

Q. Again I will ask you about your prior testimony in this case under oath, in reading from page 35, line 9:

> "Question: What are the circumstances when you would want to use cartilage from the ear?
>
> "Answer: We would use cartilage on the ear if there was an absence of septum. If somebody already had a submucous resection. The cartilage was removed from the septum or if the cartilage was completely unusable."

Do you remember testifying to that, Doctor?

Comment. The doctor appeared to be impeached but there was an explanation and he made it immediately. A witness should always promptly explain or qualify an apparent contradiction. Perhaps the plaintiff's counsel should not have used the prior statement because it was ambiguous.

A. That's in the record, sure. Which means that we couldn't get access to the septum.
Q. Also it means if it wasn't usable—
A. Usable means that you cannot use that cartilage in that septum. There is no way that we can get at it. This implication with the submucous resection is the cartilage was so bad we would perforate the septum if we had to go after the cartilage.
Q. In this case, you used cartilage as a graft?
A. Yes.
Q. So, it wasn't broken into thousands of tiny pieces—
A. It was broken into multiple pieces. We were very careful and with painstaking effort we were able to harvest enough cartilage to put in a graft.

Comment. Obviously this doctor is an excellent witness. He takes every opportunity to promote his defense in a very positive way. The use of phrases like "we were very careful" and "painstaking effort" and "harvest" are colorful and positive image provoking words.

§ 17.11 Postoperative Changes

Comment. Counsel now came to the obvious issue in the case. The graft had migrated out of place and created a cosmetic deformity. But how did the defendant handle it? Did counsel get him to state that it could have only come from a departure from good practice? Or was it an unavoidable complication?

A. A small portion of the graft was visible or had moved and was visible just above the tip of the nose.
Q. Had the graft migrated out of place?
A. Pardon?
THE COURT: He said moved.
DEFENSE COUNSEL: Objection.
THE COURT: He said it moved.
THE WITNESS: I said might have moved.
THE COURT: You said a portion of the graft moved and was visible over the tip of the nose?
THE WITNESS: I can't say moved. It had moved obviously from where we put it—
THE COURT: So it had moved?
THE WITNESS: Yes.
Q. Did that create any cosmetic deformity in Mrs. P.'s appearance?
A. Yes.

* * *

Comment. The defense admitted that this was a visible deformity but that they corrected it totally in the next procedure.

A. Did I notice it?
Q. Yes. If she walked into the room, would you notice the deformity?
A. Yes, I would notice it.

Comment. The doctor handled this very well by candidly admitting that he would not deny deformity but he added that he recommended further surgery to correct it.

* * *

Q. Doctor, I'd like to refer your attention to the second hospital admission, particularly the patient assessments form. You can use my copy if that's all right.
Are there any indications of whether the patient made any complaints of problems with breathing?
A. Yes, she said, and there is a notation here about problems with breathing by the nurse.
Q. What does that indicate the extent of the problems with breathing were at the time of the second admission to the hospital?
A. This might have been an attempt for us to get her through the hospital bureaucracy—
THE COURT: What does the note say?

THE WITNESS: The note just says on here, "Difficulty on breathing and pains and headaches." Which she complained about prior to the first surgery. But every time—

Comment. The doctor's gratuitous remark about getting through the hospital bureaucracy was very dangerous. Did he mean he fudged a hospital record? Many cosmetic procedures are rewritten in medical terminology for insurance reasons. Although this was not the case here, lawyers and surgeons should be alert to this explosive issue in any cosmetic case. It is a crime to submit a false insurance form for both patient and doctor.

THE COURT: Next question.

Q. Doctor, I'd like again to ask you whether you remember being asked certain questions and giving certain answers, and referring to your deposition on page 52:

> "Question: Was there any functional problem with her nose at this time? This is around November, 1982?
>
> "Answer: She complained of tenderness over the area, I believe, and just from the records which were not mentioned to me, the only complaint she had was that there was tenderness over the tip of the nose. By and large, her airway was improved.
>
> "Question: Were there any complaints of stuffiness at this time?
>
> "Answer: Intermittently. I can say that one particular time she did. Sometimes she did and sometimes she didn't."

Do you remember giving those answers to those questions, Doctor?

A. Absolutely.

Q. So, Mrs. P. even one year after the first surgery was still complaining of problems with stuffiness in her nose, is that true?

Comment. The plaintiff finally fixed this important admission, about the patient's nasal problems, from the defendant. The examiner then let the defendant finish with an affirmance that what he did was good medical practice.

THE DEFENDANT'S CROSS-EXAMINATION

§ 17.12 Explaining Deposition Contradictions

Comment. This was really "direct" because the doctor was being questioned by his own counsel. Milagros Matos of Wilson, Elser, Moskowitz, Edelman, & Dicker was the counsel for the doctor.

Q. Dr. S., you are being asked by the plaintiff's attorney concerning questions and answers that you gave at your deposition and he read specifically from page 53 concerning stuffiness, complaints of stuffiness of the nose by the plaintiff.

I'm going to read also from page 53 and pick up where counsel was reading.

> "Question: Were there any complaints of stuffiness at this time?
>
> "Answer: Intermittently, I can't say at one particular time she did. Sometimes she did and sometimes she didn't.
>
> "Question: Did you attribute the stuffiness to any particular condition that she had?
>
> "Answer: She was a smoker. There may have been some allergic component to this. I'm not sure whether she was taking the Dimetap or the pills she was given. Sometimes sensitivity to weather change can produce that."

Comment. This is a good technique and makes it appear that the plaintiff's counsel was not totally candid when he didn't read this portion before.

Q. Do you remember being asked that question and giving that answer, Doctor?

A. Yes, I did and it still stands.

§ 17.13 Educational Background

Comment. Defense counsel should always bring out the impressive background of the doctor.

Q. Doctor, I am going to ask you to tell your Honor and the members of the jury a little bit more about your education background. Can you do that?

A. I graduated medical school in 1969. I was a resident in general surgery for three years at Mt. Sinai Hospital in New York.

Then I was a resident for two years in otorhinolaryngology, that is ear, nose, and throat in Mt. Sinai Hospital, and I was chief resident in otolaryngology at Mt. Sinai Hospital.

After graduation I taught surgery in Elmhurst Hospital and Mt. Sinai. Elmhurst is affiliated with Mt. Sinai. I specialized in nasal reconstruction and nasal surgery, airway problems.

I have also taught at—I teach at Eye and Ear Hospital and I taught at Lincoln Hospital, City Hospital in the Bronx where I also helped residents and taught nasal reconstructive and a functional surgery of the nose.

I have given lectures to the American Rhinological Society on badly fractured and deviated noses and also lectures on the teaching of residents by attending doctors and dealing in situations in the operating rooms that attendings deal with when they work in the operating room, resident managing cases.

And I have given various lectures at rounds in various hospitals such as Mt. Sinai, Eye and Ear, and Lenox Hill Hospitals.

Q. Do you have any teaching positions?

A. I don't teach anymore on a full-time basis. I am in full-time practice and I volunteered to teach residents.

Comment. Teaching is a great attribute because all jurors can relate to their high school teacher or college professor as authoritative figures.

Q. In 1981, did you have any teaching positions?

A. My teaching position at Eye & Ear was strictly a voluntary one and I volunteered to take over the role of teaching—of working in the nose and throat clinic with the residents.

Q. What was your title at Eye and Ear back in 1981?

A. Associate attending.

Q. What does that mean?

Comment. Qualifications should not be rushed through. They are the most important testimony that the defendant can ever make for himself. However, the doctor should not appear to be boasting or egotistical.

A. That means that I teach—entitled to admit patients into the hospital and entitled to—and considered a privilege to teach the resident, young doctors coming out, surgery and medicine in the field of otolaryngology.

Q. Are you board-certified?

A. Yes, I am.

Q. When were you board-certified?

A. 1976.

Q. Could you tell the members of the jury what board certification means?

Comment. This witness gave a wonderful explanation so that the designation "board-certified" took on its full glory.

A. Well, it's a two-day ordeal, a trial by fire, so to speak, where we are given about five hours of written examinations and interspersed with these written examinations we are given oral examinations by all the major professors of all the universities in the country on a two to one quizzing where we sit in the room opposite them on the table and are shown slides and given hypothetical problems and we have to try to solve them. And I have to talk about patient management but it's a very intensive two days, goes from eight in the morning to about five o'clock, six at night, two full days.

Q. What year were you board-certified?

A. 1976.

Q. What area?
A. Otorhinolaryngology.
Q. Ear, nose, and throat.
At the time in 1981 when—withdrawn.
In 1981, how many procedures had you performed on patients, surgical procedures involving deviated nasal septum?
A. Hundreds.

Comment. This was an important question. Jurors are often swayed by how many similar procedures the defendant has done.

§ 17.14 The Vanity Factor

Q. Now, what were the complaints that the patient was presenting on that particular day of the first conference?
A. Severe nasal obstruction. I mean, she couldn't breathe out of the nose and she was also unhappy about the way she looked.
She complained that she didn't like the nose but she had—her main problem was a severe, terrible breathing disorder.
She was mouth breathing and had no airway at all, minimal air was coming in her nose.

Comment. Notice that the defense has slipped in the revelation that the patient was unhappy with her nose even before the first surgery.

Q. Did you perform a physical examination on this patient?
A. On the nose I did, yes.
Q. And what were your findings, Doctor?
A. Her septum and I mentioned in the EBT—
THE COURT: Just answer the question, Doctor.
A. The septum was solid in the back but there was no septum in the front which, when I said the septum was solid, where it was cartilage it was solid, meaning it was not mobile, solid, stiff and scarred in, that meant there was an old fracture. Where it was mobile was the front, where no septum existed and the septum was like an accordion, like someone had hit her, and the septum had buckled and it looked like this, deep into the nose.

Comment. Another score—someone had hit her and she never told them and the septum was so bad they had to do an unanticipated graft.

THE COURT: Indicting that it was bent over.
A. Bent over, it's like this, kind of like that.
THE COURT: Like an accordion.

Comment. An excellent way to put it.

A. I mean like this, when you look into the nose.
THE COURT: That is the chart, Doctor.
A. And the edge was sticking into the left side of the nose while the back end was sticking into the right side.
Q. What would the effect of this condition be on the patient?
A. Severe, disruptive in breathing, valves were all closed, the nasal valves are right above the—when you go below the bond there is some pretty soft—the firm tissue right here and this is what they call the upper lateral cartilages and they come together and meet the septum in the middle. Like a tin post, they come together and they offer some resistance when you breathe in when the nose is badly deviated and broken. In her case the upper lateral part was scarred up against the septum valves, very narrow, made the situation even worse.

Comment. This answer defeated the claim that the first operation was unnecessary.

Q. Now, you indicated that there were some fractures also.
A. Yes, the nasal bones had multiple fractures in them.
Q. Do you recall making any inquiries or asking the patient concerning these old fractures?
A. I don't recall offhand, no.
Q. Were you able to determine how long the patient had these fractures?
A. They were multiple and they were pretty old. At least a year old and more than one.
Q. What would the significance of these multiple fractures of the nose be?
A. Well, the problem is the septum. We consider the septum like the foundation of the house and the nasal bones and all the other tissues are the outside of the house. When the septum is—when you have a multiple fracture in the septum it will—the septum breaks inside but it also strips the nasal bones as well, so the whole, the outside of the inside were—had multiple fractures in them. That answers the question.
Q. Now, as far as—did you come to any conclusion at the time of the conference as to what you were going to be doing with this particular patient?
A. Yes, we had hoped to reduce the nasal fracture and straighten the septum.

The primary purpose was to take the septum sitting this way and swing it over and to make it straight. It was like a gate post that was open in the pathway and you couldn't get through unless you opened it, so our purpose was to take the septum, rotate it over so it was sitting straight into the nose, and to remove any bone in the back of the septum that was sticking out.
Q. You also used the word, reduce the nasal fracture. Would you explain to us what that means?

Comment. It is always good form for the defendant to explain medical terminology to the jury.

A. Reducing a fracture means to put the bone into what we assume is its original position before any fracture took place.
Q. Now, Doctor, what was the purpose of the surgery on Mrs. P.?
A. To correct her breathing function.
Q. Was there any other or secondary purpose to this?
A. No.

Comment. The witness had forgotten about the cosmetic factor, but counsel adroitly led him back to it.

Q. Did you have an opinion, Doctor, at the time of the conference, including her cosmetic problems or her cosmetic appearance?
A. She had asked me about that at the conference. She asked me if I could please do something to correct her nose, to do something cosmetically with her nose, and I told her that it was an extremely difficult nose to operate on and I doubted if we could change—do any kind of major improvement in her nose at all.
Q. Why was this a difficult nose, Doctor, to operate on?

Comment. These were key defense points to make. She wanted a cosmetic change but the doctor told her it would be an extremely difficult operation and doubted that any cosmetic improvement could be obtained.

A. Because when the septum in the front which supports the tip of the nose was collapsed there was no septum there so there is no structural thing to hold the nose up.

Her skin was extremely thick. The nostrils were tethered down which is the skin between the tip of the nose and the lip comes down here, was very small, no way you could increase the—very few ways without doing radical surgery of increasing the distance between here and here.

And she had very little cartilages in the tip of the nose. They were nothing.

And so the best we would be able to do was perhaps smooth it out or something like—there wasn't a lot of—to tell the patient like this, that we have to tell her you couldn't do anything cosmetically with that nose at all.
Q. Did Mrs. P. acknowledge or understand what you told her at that time?
A. Yes, but then on the second time I saw her in the same day she asked me again and I told her again the same thing.

She was really desperate for some kind of cosmetic changes as well as the breathing and we explained to her there was no real good possibility of any kind of major change in her nose at all.

Comment. Counsel then elicited testimony about additional eyelid cosmetic surgery to underline the vanity aspects of the plaintiff's personality. She would never be satisfied (see **Chapter 2**).

§ 17.15 Experience with Procedure

Q. Now, what was the purpose of implanting a graft at the time of the surgery, her surgery?

A. We had multiple reasons for doing the grafting. We don't graft lightly. My philosophy is I never graft unless I absolutely have to, so what we did when we straightened out the septum we found that the upper lateral cartilages that were on this side of the nose were still collapsed downward and that the airway was still narrow.

In order to improve the airway so we could get a maximum breathing of the nose we took the cartilage and implanted it between the upper lateral cartilages so we were essentially separating and opening them up.

Also in the course of reducing the nasal fracture, a slight portion of the tip of one side on the bone—I don't recall exactly which—came off along with the septum so we were able to put the graft and lay it in from the very tip of the nasal bone down to the tip of the nose and spread the upper lateral cartilages as well as reduce a slight saddling over a depression that had occurred when we removed the diseased—the broken, smashed up septum and when we turned—when we turned the septum around to straighten it the forces in the nose were a little different.

The stresses on the nose were different so there was a little depression all the way down the front of the nose and that also worked in the same vein.

Q. Did the graft have any effect whatsoever with respect to her airway?

A. Yes.

Q. When was it determined, at what time was it determined that a graft would be necessary to put in place?

A. At the time we—after we finished doing the septum and after we had reduced the nasal fracture, we took out the fragments of bone that were implanted between the nasal bone that had been broken in and we had smoothed out the nasal bone as best we could and put it together.

We looked at the nose, we saw the upper lateral cartilages were collapsed and there was a slight depression in the tip of the nose.

Q. In your practice, Doctor, you testified earlier that you've done hundreds of these types of surgeries?

A. Now more.

Q. Have you done—how many surgeries have you done involving grafting?

A. I do—I've done hundreds of grafts in the nose as well.

Q. And in your practice?

A. Maybe more.

Comment. In any surgical case it is critical to advise the jury that the doctor is very experienced with the procedure. In this case, he proudly boasted that he has done hundreds.

§ 17.16 Informed Consent

Q. Now, have you had in your practice any patient refuse this type of surgery when told that a graft may be possible, there may be a necessity for a graft to be implanted?

Comment. This was an excellent question. Under the statute in New York the jury can still dismiss the informed consent case if they believe that a reasonable patient would have consented anyway.

Q. In your practice, Doctor, what kind of information do you give your patients when the grafting is necessary?
PLAINTIFF'S COUNSEL: Objection.
THE COURT: You mean what would you tell the patient?
DEFENSE COUNSEL: Yes, what would he tell them when he's going to regraft?
THE COURT: Overruled.
A. I tell the patients that there is a possibility the graft might move, might resolve, rarely gets infected, and I tell the patient that we generally take the graft in the septum of the nose when it is available.

And at that time, in 1981, that was our primary source of grafting unless we went into major grafts taken from limbs and ribs which is a major production when it comes to surgery.

But—
THE COURT: All right, you have answered the question.
THE WITNESS: Yes.
Q. Of all the surgeries that you have done, Doctor, how many patients have refused this type of surgery?
PLAINTIFF'S COUNSEL: Objection.
THE COURT: Sustained. You asked him that question three minutes ago or less. I didn't forget.
Q. In your opinion, Doctor, what was the result of this particular surgery?

Comment. The defense had to prove that the primary purpose of the surgery of clearing the airway was achieved. If the jury believed that the doctors cured the patient's suffering, her cosmetic complaints would seem almost frivolous.

A. I think the patient developed an excellent airway and after the surgery I was very happy with what we wanted to accomplish.

Unfortunately, some of the graft, small portion of the graft either dislodged or moved for some reason and necessitated that we go back and with a very simple procedure, remove it.

In my private practice I would do that right in my office but in our resident situation we don't—this is one situation where patients get really better care in some cases—we took the patient into the hospital to do it under very controlled circumstances.

Q. Did the patient's condition improve after the surgery?
THE COURT: Which one?
DEFENSE COUNSEL: The first surgery.
THE COURT: He said yes.
A. Definitely.
Q. How did it improve?
A. Breathing was markedly better. The crusting and dryness had improved significantly. She was able to get a good air passage on the left side as well as improvement on the right.
Q. After the second surgery, Doctor, how would you describe the patient's condition?
THE COURT: After the second surgery.
DEFENSE COUNSEL: After the second surgery.
A. I would say that she was functionally significantly improved over the condition she was in before and cosmetically about where she started from.
DEFENSE COUNSEL: No further questions. Thank you.

Comment. This was a good place to stop because the defense had ended on a high note. They had alleviated her suffering. Everything else including her damages paled by comparison.

THE REDIRECT EXAMINATION

§ 17.17 Confining Testimony

By Plaintiff:

Q. Now, Doctor, it is true, you don't recall ever telling Mrs. P. anything about the possibility of use of a graft or whether you were planning to use a graft; isn't that right?
A. Yes.
Q. And nothing on the consent form says anything about a graft?
A. Doesn't have to specifically say that.
Q. My question, Doctor, is there anything on the consent form that says you are going to be using a graft?
A. No. But it's the patient's own tissues.

Comment. The doctor, apparently conversant with the law, was trying to show that no foreign body was involved.

* * *

Q. Now, Doctor, before you saw Mrs. P. in the clinic on October 22nd, I believe, 1981, she was—she was seen by other doctors at the clinic; isn't that true?

A. Yes.
Q. And they examined her nose prior to your examining the nose; isn't that true?
A. Yes.
Q. And when the residents examine somebody, was it the practice at Eye and Ear Hospital for them to write down their findings in the medical records?
A. Yes.
Q. If they found something significant about somebody's condition, should they write it down in the records?
A. Yes, but not only—okay.
Q. Now, Doctor, you have testified that Mrs. P. had difficulty breathing both through the left and through the right, correct?
A. Yes.
Q. Now, I would like you to refer to the clinic records, if you would.
THE COURT: Give him a specific date.
Q. Right from the beginning. Start from July 3rd, 1976.
A. The problem is the clinic notes are arranged with two visits and they are not all together in one place.
Normally in the charts there would be but they have been divided some way. What date was that?
THE COURT: July 3, '76. You had asked the doctor about the note in July of 1976, is that correct?
COUNSEL: Yes.
Q. That was the first time she was seen at the hospital, in June of 1976?
A. The first note that I found was June 3rd, 1976. I wasn't there.
Q. What was the purpose of that visit at that time?
A. Headaches.
Q. Review that note, and are there any complaints there at all about breathing problems with the nose?
A. First of all,—
THE COURT: Just yes or no, Doctor.
THE WITNESS: It's an eye chart.
A. No.
THE COURT: The answer is no. Next question.

Comment. This was good cross. He led him and confined him to the point.

Q. If someone were to make a complaint of nasal stuffiness, is it good medical practice to inquire further to determine exactly the type of nasal stuffiness they have?
A. The tip?
THE COURT: How bad it is.
Q. How bad it is.
A. I am at a loss.
THE COURT: How severe.

THE WITNESS: Yes, it is a subjective complaint.
In a physical examination, it may vary from one day to the next.
Q. Didn't you indicate to us that it can become so bad that a person can only breathe through his mouth?
A. Yes.
Q. Is that something important to determine if a person is only breathing through his mouth?
A. Yes.
Q. I believe you mentioned some other problems that might develop because of a nasal obstruction?
A. Yes.
Q. Can you tell me one or two of them?
A. One of them is the complaint she complained about, vertigo, dizziness. Also complains of dizziness. That's one of them, yes.
Q. Any others that you mentioned? There were several others you mentioned before? Did you mention bad breath and things like that?
A. Yes.
Q. Would it be important to write all those things down?
A. That's a subjective complaint. To a smoker that might not mean anything.
Q. My question is, is it important to write down the different things that would indicate the extent of the problem?

Comment. Again counsel was doing an excellent job of proving that this complaint was never recorded, casting doubt on the credibility of the defendants.

A. I guess so.
Q. Is there any indication or anything to—withdrawn.
Is there anything written in the record indicating or that says that Mrs. P. only is breathing through her mouth?
THE COURT: At any time?
Q. Let's start at this point.
A. It's kind of hard to hyperventilate through her nose, so the term "probable hyperventilation" would imply she is a mouth-breather as well.
Q. Is that written down?
A. "Probable hyperventilation" would imply mouth-breathing at times.
Q. Isn't a "mouth-breather" a term that is well known and well used in your profession?
A. Yes.
Q. It's almost a term of art, isn't that true?
A. Pardon?

Comment. This "redirect cross" was actually sharper and more to the point than the original interrogation, which seemed to ramble.

* * *

Q. How long had her problem been a problem?
A. Her problem was chronic. She had a long-standing history of nasal stuffiness, years.
Q. Do you know what precipitated the problem, some trauma that started the problem?
A. Did the trauma start the problem?
Q. Was there some history of trauma that initiated the problem?
A. I don't recall offhand.
THE COURT: You have answered the question.
Q. Isn't it true, Doctor, that in the record there it indicates there was a history of trauma at the age of 16?
THE COURT: There is such a note.
A. Okay.
Q. Would that indicate to you that that's when her septum became deviated, at the age of 16?
A. Not necessarily. That might be one trauma.
Q. Assume that's the only trauma—
A. If this patient were a battered wife for instance, she might not tell us—
PLAINTIFF'S COUNSEL: I move to strike this nonsense.
THE COURT: Please. Please. Motion denied. He is giving an example. There is no proof in the record that the plaintiff is a battered wife.

§ 17.18 Final Questions

Q. Doctor, what is Mrs. P.'s condition with regard to her nose today?
THE COURT: He hasn't seen her today.
Q. In regard to the last time you saw her?
THE COURT: You examined following the second surgery?
THE WITNESS: Yes.
Q. How did you find her nose to be?
A. Significantly improved. The airway is significantly better on the left side where she was almost totally blocked off.
Q. No hyperventilation?
A. Not that I saw.
Q. And no stuffiness?
A. At the final time I saw her, there was no stuffiness.
Q. And she has a clear airway?
A. Yes.
Q. The breathing problem has been resolved?
A. Yes.

Comment. The defense got in the last word and hit its theme again. She did have complaints of breathing before the first surgery and she had been cured.

CHAPTER 18

TRIAL OF A RHINOPLASTY CASE: EXAMINATION OF THE PLAINTIFF

DIRECT EXAMINATION

§ 18.1 Personalized the Plaintiff

Counsel tried to personalize his client and portray her as a sympathetic figure. But his questions were somewhat disjointed and her answers were not particularly moving. The history of her child's death engendered sympathy but the defense claimed that was why she was so depressed. The pleadings did not claim an aggravation of her condition. Instead it was alleged that the nasal surgery and resultant deformity alone caused her depression. The defense tried to capitalize on her prior history of marital problems and the loss of her child as the real causes of her chronic depression. The plaintiff's counsel elected to have her explain that she was completely over any depression from her divorce or the loss of her child. However, her answers sounded somewhat improbable. Perhaps it would have been more plausible to admit that she was chronically depressed and that the nose deformity put her over the hill emotionally.

Q. How long have you lived at that address?
A. I lived there thirteen years.
Q. And do you live there with anyone at the present time?
A. By myself.
Q. Were you ever married?
A. Yes.
Q. And when were you married?
A. I marry in December 31st of 1970.
Q. And are you still married at the present time? Did you get divorced or separated?
A. Separated.
Q. When were you separated?
A. In 1978.
Q. And do you have any children?
A. No.
Q. Did you ever have any children?
A. I have a baby.
Q. What happened to your baby?
A. My baby die.
Q. When did that occur?
A. 1972.

Comment. These questions and the ones that followed were awkward. They should have been more conversational, leading, and in everyday language. "I refer your attention to a point in time" questions were too legalistic and tended to put distance between the lawyer and the jury.

Q. And now I would like to refer your attention to around 1980, okay? The year 1980. Did you at some time in 1980 go to the hospital?
A. Yes.
Q. And do you remember why you went to the hospital?
A. Because I have a problem with my ears.
Q. And what was that problem with your ears?
A. I have loss of equilibrium.

§ 18.2 Minimized Complaints

Q. Before this time, before this time, had you ever gone into any doctor for any problem with breathing with your nose?
A. No.
Q. So this was the first time you had consulted a doctor for the problem of breathing with your nose?

Comment. Counsel was trying to minimize her complaints to suggest that her first surgery to improve her breathing was probably unnecessary. It was during this procedure that an augmentation graft was necessary. It moved and resulted in an obvious deformity. However, the defense claimed they fully corrected it in a second operation. The patient claimed they didn't and she hadn't looked the same or felt the same since.

A. Yes.
Q. Now, did they make any recommendations—withdraw that.
Did they examine your nose when you went back to the hospital?
A. Yeah, they put something in my nose and they had told me that my—they want to help me—my breathing to drain out my septum.
Q. Who told you that they wanted to help you breathe by straightening out your septum?
A. Dr. A.
Q. Was that after he examined you?
A. Yes.
Q. I'd just like to show you some pictures.
DEFENSE COUNSEL: This is when, she looked like when, your Honor?
THE COURT: October 31st of '81. That is, I assume—before the operation. Nineteen is preop, full face, 20 is preop, left profile, and 21 is preop, right profile.
Do these photographs accurately—Mrs. P., take a look at these three pictures, 19, 20, and 21. Do those photographs accurately reflect your appearance immediately prior to the hospitalization in October of 1981? Is that what you looked like?
THE WITNESS: Yeah.
THE COURT: All right, I am going to show you two more photographs marked 17 and 18, dated November of '82. Is this what your appearance was in November of '82. Do those photographs show what you looked like at that time?

Comment. In plastic surgery cases, before and after photos provide dramatic demonstrative evidence. However, one must be sure that the alleged deformity is apparent in the after shots.

THE WITNESS: Yes, your Honor.

§ 18.3 Consent Issue

Q. And, Mrs. P., when you went to the hospital in October 1981 in the clinic where Dr. A. examined you, did he tell you what he was planning to do to you for your problem with breathing?
A. He said he want to help me.
THE COURT: He was going to help you?
THE WITNESS: Yes.
Q. Did he explain to you how he was going to help you?
A. Just straighten the septum.

Comment. Counsel tried to prove that there was no informed consent for this initial surgery and that it was negligently performed, leaving the patient with a saddle form depression in the nose. Because the defense claimed that the plaintiff asked for a cosmetic improvement of her nose, counsel asked her to emphatically deny any vanity motivation.

Q. Did you at any time when you were at the clinic ask to change the appearance of your nose?
A. No.
Q. Did you at any time make any complaints other than the problem you were having with stuffiness?
A. No.
Q. How did you feel about the appearance of your nose?
A. Fine.

* * *

Q. At any time before they did the operation, did anybody tell you that they were going to add a piece of graft, cartilage to your nose?
A. Oh, no. If they would tell me—
THE COURT: Please, you have answered the question. Next question.
Q. Do you remember when the surgery took place?
A. In the—in October 31st.

§ 18.4 Postoperative Complaints

Q. Okay. And, after the surgery, did you at some time learn that a graft had been placed in your nose?
A. A little bit later, I had felt that someone was—someone in my nose.

Comment. Note the simple but dramatic and effective explanation "someone in her nose." Counsel capitalized on the doctors' failure to inform their patient of the graft even after surgery. Was this a cover-up? If so, perhaps the jury would inflate the verdict with a punitive award.

Q. And after the operation, after about a month after the operation, did you notice any change in the way your nose looked from before the operation?

A. Yeah, yes.
Q. Can you tell me what you noticed about your nose?
A. I notice myself when I looked at a mirror I wasn't the same person. You know, my appearance has complete change and the other way that people been telling me—

Comment. The plaintiff again dramatically capsulized her predicament in simple, poignant words. However, to the jury the change was not apparent.

§ 18.5 "There's Something Wrong"

Comment. This was the major theme: the defendants admitted their mistake when they brought the patient back to correct the graft.

Q. Mrs. P., did there come a time when the doctors told you you needed another operation?
A. Yes.
Q. Who told you you needed a second operation?
A. Many, many doctors told me.
THE COURT: At the hospital?
THE WITNESS: At the hospital.
Q. Was one of those doctors Dr. M.?
A. Yes. Dr. M. and so many other doctors, I don't remember the name, but they belong to the hospital.
Q. Did they tell you why you needed a second operation?
A. They said there's something wrong, they have to removed.
Q. What did they tell you they had to remove?
A. The graft that I had in there.

§ 18.6 Plaintiff Very Depressed

Q. Now, during the time, say the seven months before that, before you went into the hospital to have the graft removed from your nose, can you tell me how you felt about your appearance at that time?
A. I been very miserable, very depressed about my appearance.
Q. And why was that?

Comment. This was the heart of the damage case, but it had to be convincing, and her explanation seemed exaggerated.

A. Many, many aspects. In the way I see I used to be before and the woman I'm now is complete different and that is what is depressing me every second of my life. I cannot see my favorite people daily. It keeping me very, very depressed.

Q. Did that continue after the second operation when they took out the graft?

Comment. The plaintiff's counsel had to fully bring out her prior psychiatric past, including treatment for depression with tranquilizers and antidepressants as a result of the breakup of her marriage and loss of her child. If he let the defense do it, she would lose credibility.

A. This be happening all this time.
Q. And how did that affect your life, your everyday life?
A. In every way.
Q. Can you tell me some of the ways?
A. That I used to be in the, like, how could I say, what do you want me to explain to you?
THE COURT: How did your depression affect your life?
THE WITNESS: In—I can't understand why this happened to me.
THE COURT: No, no. We understand that you were depressed. What effect did the depression have on your life? How was your life changed, if at all? Was your life changed by your depression?
THE WITNESS: Yes.
THE COURT: How was it changed?
Let the record indicate the witness has nodded yes.
THE WITNESS: Nervous breakdown.

Comment. This was not a very poignant or convincing way to sway the jury. The questions were too mechanical; the answer too conclusory and overly dramatic.

§ 18.7 Prior Depression: "I Can Handle It"

Q. Now, Mrs. P., I would like to go back again to before you went to the hospital, several years before, you told us at one time you had—you lost a baby?
A. Yes.
Q. And when did that occur?
THE COURT: 1972.
A. Yes.
Q. And how did you feel after that?
THE COURT: I take it that was, to say the least, an upsetting experience.
THE WITNESS: But I can handle it. It was an experience, you know, that upset anybody, any human.
THE COURT: Obviously.

Comment. What a terrible answer. She could handle the death of her baby but not a small bump on her nose. Was she prepared for this question?

Obviously not. She answered it the same way again and again. It's the kind of answer that jurors will take with them to the jury room.

THE WITNESS: But I can handle it on, you know.
DEFENSE COUNSEL: I object and move to strike the end.
THE COURT: Motion is denied.
Q. Mrs. P., when your husband left you, how—

Comment. Defense counsel moved to strike instinctively. But as she soon saw, the answer ridiculed the plaintiff. It wasn't believable and the defense counsel used it as her theme in cross-examination and summation.

THE COURT: When did your husband separate, '78?
THE WITNESS: Yes.
THE COURT: Sometimes it can be upsetting. Was it upsetting?
THE WITNESS: I was upset, but I can handle it also.

Comment. Again, she could "handle" her baby's death and her husband's desertion, but not a little bump on her nose.

THE COURT: Next question.
Q. By the time you were back, you went to the hospital in 1980, were you depressed at all from those two prior incidents that happened to you?
A. Not at all.

Comment. Counsel had cast the die. She was cured of the prior depression. But the proof and logic seemed to indicate that she was in remission but she was depressed and very suggestible to any problem when she had nose surgery.

Q. Mrs. P., can you tell us, me and the jury, please, how you feel about your appearance at the present time?
A. I feel very, very miserable.
THE COURT: Sorry?
THE WITNESS: Very miserable.
THE COURT: Okay.

§ 18.8 Mirror, Mirror on the Wall

Comment. Echoing the complaint of all vanity patients, she was devastated by the mirror.

Q. Can you tell us why you feel this way?
A. Because it's not me any more. I am not the same person I used to be.

Q. When you look at yourself in a mirror, do you see that your appearance is different from the way it used to be?
A. Yes.
Q. What do you see?
A. I see disfiguration in my face. And not only I see it but people been telling me daily that if anybody hit me, my husband beat me, if I play with a baseball and all the kind that I have to get from people since this happened to me. A miserable life that I am going through now since this happened.

Comment. This was only a bare bones recitation of her misery. How had it made a misery of her everyday life? What nightmares did she go through? How did she hide from men and women and from life? Where were the friends who could corroborate or document her suffering and change of appearance? We didn't get answers. The friends were never called during the trial as witnesses. Counsel also neglected or elected not to clarify the obvious cosmetic improvement after the corrective procedure. The defense conceded she had a deformity for a few months, but claimed they corrected it in the second procedure.

CROSS-EXAMINATION

§ 18.9 Medical Necessity

Comment. Defense counsel attempted to show that there was a medical necessity for the first operation. This witness, obviously not well prepared, denied completely that she had a breathing problem even though she admitted it in her deposition. She was, therefore, punished and impeached by her prior testimony.

Q. Mrs. P., before your operation on October 31, 1981, you had a problem with breathing; isn't that true?
A. Problem?
Q. Breathing.
A. Yes.
Q. Your breathing problem was so bad that it was affecting your sleep, wasn't it?
THE COURT: Was your breathing problem affecting your sleep?
THE WITNESS: My sleep?
THE COURT: Yes.
THE WITNESS: Not that I remember.
Q. Do you remember—
Your Honor, could you explain to the jury about an EBT?

THE COURT: Yes. In these cases, before the case is ready for trial, the parties, through their attorneys, have a right to question one another under oath very much the way a witness is questioned here in court. The reporter is present. The parties are represented by attorneys and questions are asked, the witness answers questions and they are all written down in a little booklet which counsel is apparently about to read from.

Q. When was this deposition?

A. The deposition was on May 31, 1985.

THE COURT: Mrs. P. testified on that day and answered questions put to her by an attorney for the defendant, perhaps by her own attorney as well.

Q. Do you remember being asked this question and giving this answer:

> "**Q.** Can you describe the difficulty?
>
> "**Q.** You said your problem progressed to include difficulty in breathing?
>
> "**A.** Okay. It became complicated because I couldn't breathe in my left nostril. I became worse and worse. I couldn't breathe. I even couldn't sleep. There was no air."

Do you remember being asked that question and do you remember giving that answer?

A. I don't remember.

§ 18.10 The Mystery Referral

Q. Mrs. P., you indicated on direct examination that you went to see a psychiatrist, Dr. R., in 1984; is that correct?

A. Yes.

Q. And you went to see him in 1984 because you had a nervous breakdown; is that correct?

A. Yes.

Q. And who referred you to Dr. R. then?

A. A friend of mine.

Q. Didn't your attorney send you to Dr. R.?

A. No.

Q. You were not sent by your attorney to the psychiatrist?

A. No.

Q. Who was your friend that referred you to Dr. R.?

A. Who was my friend?

Q. Yes.

A. I don't remember the name.

Q. Is this someone that you know right now?

THE COURT: Is this a friend that you still have contact with?

THE WITNESS: Yes.

Q. And when was the last time you saw this individual?

A. I don't remember exactly.

Q. And how often do you see this person?
THE COURT: You mean in the last year?

Comment. These answers were incredible. They suggested a lack of credibility on her part and lack of preparation for cross-examination. Defense counsel took full advantage of the circuitous answers. This is an excellent example of "ad lib" questioning to follow up unexpected answers.

Q. Let's say within the last year.
A. Once every six months, two months, one month, I just don't remember.
Q. And this person that you see once or twice or every six months, you don't recall what her name or his name is?
THE COURT: Is it a man or a woman?
THE WITNESS: It's a lady.
THE COURT: Okay.
Q. And you don't recall her name or you don't know her name?
A. I might recall the name but not right now.
THE COURT: All right, if you think of it between now and Tuesday, you can tell us on Tuesday. Try to think of it, okay? Go ahead.
Q. When was the last time you saw this individual, this woman?
A. I don't remember.

§ 18.11 Prior Depression

Comment. Counsel tried to establish the longstanding use of antidepressants since 1975, years before the plastic surgery. But, incredibly, the plaintiff claimed she can't remember using them.

Q. Now you indicated that you have been very depressed since your operation; is that correct?
A. Yes.
Q. And, as a result of that, you took some antidepressant medication?
A. Yes.
Q. And you took some medication for sleeping; is that correct?
A. Yes.
Q. Was this the first time that you had ever taken antidepressants?
A. No.
Q. You've taken antidepressants before; is that correct?
A. Yes.
Q. In fact, you have been taking antidepressants since 1975; isn't that correct?
A. I don't remember.
Q. Do you remember going to see Dr. G. sometime in 1972 or 1975—between 1972 and 1975?
A. Possible.
Q. And did Dr. G. give you any antidepressants?

A. You say 1972?
THE COURT: Sometime between '72 and '75.
A. It's possible.

§ 18.12 The Miscarriage

Comment. The defense claimed that her miscarriage was a cause for her chronic depression. But the witness attempted to downplay its effect on her mental state.

Q. Now, you had a miscarriage, isn't that correct, in 1972?
A. Yes.
Q. And how many months pregnant were you at that time?
A. Four months.
Q. And was this your first pregnancy, Ma'am?
A. Yes.
Q. You were never pregnant before that day; is that correct?
A. Never.
Q. And you have never become pregnant since then; is that correct?
A. Yes, that's correct.

Comment. Note the excellent use of leading questions here. Counsel had really taken over the examination and was in control.

Q. And you were very concerned over the fact that you had never been able to become pregnant; isn't that correct?
A. For a while, yes.
Q. And Dr. T. was—withdrawn.
And you saw Dr. T. because you wanted to get pregnant; isn't that so?
A. Yes.
Q. And Dr. T. prescribed some type of treatment for you in order for you to become pregnant?
A. I don't remember exactly, but he treat me for that.
Q. And the fact that you couldn't become pregnant, that made you very depressed, didn't it?
A. No, I come to the reality that if I don't become pregnant, it's up to God, so I went over.
Q. That is why you were going to the doctor, in order to help you get pregnant; isn't that true?
A. Just to, yeah, help myself and to the maternity, but since I cannot—since it was difficult, so I just leave it up to God. It was not in my hands to do it and I don't believe that he's going to do for anything such as that.
Q. That had some effect on you, didn't it?
A. For a while. And a mother, and in a human, I think it is normal, you know. But I handle it.

Q. You could handle it well. Didn't affect you at all?
A. It didn't affect me at all.
Q. And the fact your husband left you in 1976, that didn't affect you at all either; is that correct?

Comment. Remember this was the line during direct—"I can handle it"—that this lawyer objected to during direct testimony. But now she realized that it was the best cross-examination available.

A. I was kind of upset as any normal human. Kind of upset but it didn't affect me to discontrol my mind and hold me down and hide myself from people or something like that, no.
Q. So you went on with your life without any problems after your husband left you; is that right?
A. Yeah. And I made it.
Q. And you made it.
A. Yes.
Q. The fact that you had an operation on your nose, that made you depressed and that made you have a nervous breakdown? Not the fact that your husband left you and you lost your child?

Comment. This was a great follow-up question. It is the kind of "sound bite" television directors look for to advertise shows and news stories. It has staying power. It's the kind of question that jurors will take with them into deliberations.

§ 18.13 Reason for Surgery

Comment. Defense counsel's strategy was to prove that the plaintiff requested an operation to help her breathing and, more importantly, to improve her appearance cosmetically. She was always unhappy with her nose.

Q. Do you recall telling Dr. S. that you had a stuffy nose that day?
A. No. I saw him just passing by checking all the patients around. He didn't ask me that.
Q. Do you recall having any conversations whatsoever with Dr. S. on that date?
A. I asked him do I need an operation and he said yes. That's it. And then he walk out.
Q. Did you ask him why you needed an operation?
A. I don't remember, but I might so.
Q. Did he tell you you needed an operation to help you with your breathing?

A. Yes. That's what he said.
Q. Did you ask Dr. S. to do something to improve your nose so that it looked better?
A. No.

* * *

Comment. Because this witness was given to exaggeration, counsel asked her about her complaints, knowing that she was not under present treatment and that she also suffered from unrelated allergies.

Q. Are you having any difficulties with your breathing, Mrs. P.?
A. Still there.
Q. You have a stuffy nose today, your nose is still stuffy?
A. Want to feel it?
Q. When was the last time that you went to a doctor with complaints of stuffiness of your nose?
A. Last year, I don't remember exactly the day, but I went to see a doctor for stuffiness in my nose.
Q. Who was this?
A. He's [ ], I think.
Q. Is he an otolaryngologist?
A. Right.
Q. And when for the first time did you see him with complaints about your nose?
A. Maybe in May of '83.
Q. May of '83?
A. Of '83.
Q. You were complaining—
A. If I'm not mistaken, I'm not sure about that.
Q. This was after the second surgery; is that correct?
A. Yes.
Q. And at that time you complained to this doctor that you had difficulties with your breathing?
A. Difficult to my breathing and inflame my face.
Q. Your face was inflamed, swollen?
A. Swollen.

Comment. Counsel cleverly proved that the plaintiff's present complaints were the result of chronic allergies, not a result of an imperfect operation.

Q. Do you have any allergies, Mrs. P.?
A. Right now?
Q. In general.
A. In general, I wasn't having any allergies, but I don't know now, I guess so.
Q. Did you have any allergies before the operation, the first one?
A. No.

Q. Did you have any allergies between the first and second operation?
A. No.
Q. Are you presently having allergies?
A. Yes.
Q. And when did these allergies begin?
A. When the weather change.
Q. When did they begin, what year?
A. I don't remember. Maybe three years, '84.
Q. From '84?
A. Yes.
Q. To today.
A. Yeah.
Q. You've been having allergies?

Comment. Counsel set up the witness to prove that her present breathing problems were not the result of the operation, but of her unrelated allergy problems. Note the beauty of the following crisp questions as the very definition of an allergy.

A. Yes.
Q. And have you been treated for these allergies?
A. No.
Q. Are the symptoms of your allergy a stuffy nose?
A. Yes.
Q. And do you also get, like, teary eyes?
A. No, what I get is inflame my face, my nose.
Q. Your face gets swollen?
A. And there is days that I can hardly talk.
Q. So you have difficulties in speaking when you have your allergy, correct?
A. Sometimes.
Q. And you have difficulties breathing when you have your allergies?
A. Sometimes.
Q. And you also—your face also becomes swollen when you have your allergies; is that correct?
A. The allergies there daily. There's no way I can explain it, if it is correct or not, it is there.
Q. So you have allergies every day?
A. Mostly every day.
Q. And throughout the whole year?
A. Yes.

Comment. She finally admitted that the allergies and the attendant breathing problems were there every day throughout the year.

Q. And are you taking any medication for your allergies?
A. No.

Q. Have you seen any doctors for your allergy?
A. I saw Dr. C.
Q. And has Dr. C. given you any type of treatment for this allergy?
A. Cannot give me anything because it is not in his hand to give me anything. Immunization at all.
Q. Has he given you any medication to unstuff your nose?
A. He used to give me medication, yes.
Q. Have you ever taken any tests for allergies?
A. Yes, I did.
Q. And did you ever get the results of those tests?
A. Yes.
Q. And what were the results; do you recall?
A. I can't remember that.
Q. Were you told that you were allergic to anything in particular?
A. I wasn't allergic to anything, but he gave me a whole list on that of the allergies.
Q. He gave you a list of things you were allergic to?
A. Yes.

Comment. This cross was excellent. Her entire present physical damage issue has now been relegated to her allergy problem.

Q. And what did he suggest when he gave you that list that you do?
A. He told me that there is nothing he can do about it.
Q. There is nothing that he can do about your allergy?
A. No.
Q. And you have to learn to live with it?
A. That's what I understood.
Q. And that is what you are doing right now, isn't that so?
A. I am trying hard to survive.
DEFENSE COUNSEL: Your Honor, I have no other questions of this witness.

Comment. This was a good point at which to stop. Counsel had reduced the patient's problems to an allergy that she had to learn to live with. The plaintiff's lack of candor in exaggerating her breathing difficulty, blaming it on her nose job, and her reluctance to name the person who referred her to the psychiatrist severely damaged her credibility.

CHAPTER 19

TRIAL OF A RHINOPLASTY CASE: DAMAGES

§ 19.1 The Treating Psychiatrist—Direct Examination

The damages in this case were primarily emotional. As shown in this chapter, the plaintiff called the psychiatrist to the stand to establish that the defect in the nose led to a severe depression. The psychiatrist denied that her prior emotional problems were the cause of her depression and explained his treatment of supportive therapy and medication. However, on cross-examination he was attacked on his misuse of medications, diagnosis, and bias toward his patient. In §§ **19.11** and **19.12** the testimony of the defense psychiatrist is presented and analyzed.

PLAINTIFF'S COUNSEL: At this time I call Dr. F. to the stand.
Q. Good morning, Dr. F.
A. Good morning.

Q. Dr. F., have we ever met prior to this morning?
A. No, we haven't.

Comment. Some attorneys want to establish that there was no prior rehearsal with a witness, yet it is foolish not to meet and prepare your damage expert before trial. Counsel proceeded to establish his credentials; however, they were not particularly impressive. He went to foreign schools and had never been board-certified in psychiatry.

* * *

Q. And can you tell us how she became a patient of yours?
A. Mrs. P.—okay, I have a niece who works at a—how you call that—for another doctor, as a receptionist, and Mrs. P. was a patient of this general practitioner.
Q. What is the name of that general practitioner?
A. Dr. Tejeda. Mrs. P. was there one day. She was complaining of being depressed and feeling low, feeling bad. She was talking to my niece. She told her, "I have an uncle who is a psychiatrist." So she picked up the phone and one or two weeks later, she called.

Comment. This is an odd referral and would make a good cross-examination subject.

§ 19.2 —The First Visit

Q. And what was your understanding based on your conversation and the history that you took as to how she was functioning prior to the time she had surgery on her nose?
A. She had been functioning pretty well. She was involved in community affairs. She had some social life. She was active.

Comment. The plaintiff elected to prove that there was no psychiatric problem at the time of the surgery. Actually it is more likely that she was still suffering from depression but that she was under control. The defense made hay on this issue because she had previously been on antidepressant medication.

Q. In your opinion, was she able to deal with the separation from her husband?
DEFENSE COUNSEL: Objection.
THE COURT: Sustained. The jury will disregard the question and answer.

Comment. The court probably believed that this called for an opinion on another person's state of mind. Although this is usually objectionable, it should have been allowed here because a psychiatrist is qualified to give this exact kind of testimony.

Q. Now, did you conduct a psychiatric examination of her that day?
A. Yes.
Q. Can you tell the jury how you go about doing that?
A. Well, we talk to the patient. We ask questions, how she feels, how is she understanding her problems. We examine her behavior, her blood, we see the overall aspect of the patient. She was okay. She was properly dressed. She was talking. She was—her manner was appropriate. When she talked about anger, she felt it in a way—she was depressed, she was low and she was crying.
Q. How long did this session you had with Mrs. P. take?
A. I usually saw her 45 minutes.
Q. During that time, did you spend the time talking to her?
A. I do more listening than talking.
Q. And at this first visit in 1984, did you come to any diagnosis of what she was suffering from at that time?
A. Yes.
Q. And what was your diagnosis at that time?
A. The diagnosis was dysthymic disorder.

Comment. This is a chronic depressive disorder as compared to an acute reaction to a recent event. The term itself suggested she had been suffering for a long time and not just because of the surgery. The doctor didn't quite explain it that way, which might suggest he was biased in her behalf. This is not unusual in the typical psychiatrist-patient relationship, which is based on trust and a therapeutic alliance.

§ 19.3 —Medication Regimen

Q. And what medication did you prescribe for her?
A. I started her on Asendin.
Q. Is that an antidepressant?
A. This is an antidepressant.
Q. How often was she to take that?
A. Excuse me?
Q. How often was she supposed to take that?
A. Once a day, 25 milligrams.

Comment. This is a normal starting dose, but by itself not therapeutic. The range recommended by the manufacturer is 125 to 175 milligrams but the doctor never ordered that dosage. This suggests that he either used the drug as a placebo or was not really competent in the use of these drugs.

§ 19.4 —Supportive Talk Therapy

Q. What types of complaints would she make?
A. She usually complained about the nose. The plastic piece, the allergies, the pain in the nose. The difficulty in breathing.
Q. And did you make any note in your records of the complaints that she made regarding her nose?
A. Yes, sir.
Q. And can you refer me to one of those notes?
A. Okay. 12/10/84, this is the first time.
Q. Can you tell me what that note says?
A. Want me to read the whole note?
Q. Yes.
A. Okay. 12/10/84. Ventilating her anger against her exhusband.
THE COURT: Sorry, ventilating anger?
THE WITNESS: Against her exhusband.

Comment. This answer actually helped the defense. Her symptoms referred to her exhusband who left her. Counsel should have candidly dealt with this now rather than left it for the defense to cross-examine and capitalize on it.

A. And of all the problems she has been having on account of her present situation. Somatic complaints, pain in the right side of the face, et cetera.
Q. What kind of complaints did she make about the face at that time?
A. The usual pain, she complained the nose was dropped and she felt pain and she could not breathe.
Q. And based on your examination of Mrs. P., and your discussions with her, do you have an opinion as to whether these complaints were real to Mrs. P.?
THE WITNESS: Yes, I feel they were very real to her.

Comment. A therapist is ethically bound to believe and accept the word of the patient. He cannot, by definition, be neutral.

Q. Doctor, can you read for us your note on March 11th, 1985?
THE WITNESS: Okay. It says 3/11/85, in better spirits. "Medication is making me very angry." This is her quote.
THE COURT: Angry?
THE WITNESS: Angry. She was encouraged to express it, mostly about hate problems with "the plastic piece," in quotes, in her nose.
THE COURT: Okay.
THE WITNESS: Her medication was decreased at this point, medication had been increased gradually and she started getting angry. I slowed down the medication because this is an effect medication may have.

So I had that, ventilate her anger and the following week I increased the medication again.

Comment. It is highly unlikely that such a small amount of the medication could have made her angry and it was not at an effective therapeutic level yet.

Q. When was the next time you saw the patient after this visit?
A. 3/18. That was seven days later.
Q. Can you tell us what happened on that visit?
A. She was feeling low, low today, crying, that's my own note. Apparently very sensitive to medication changes. Then she said my face is deformed. I can feel the plastic piece here. At that point I increased the medication again.

Comment. He now increased despite her sensitivity to medication changes. There was no plastic piece in her nose. It was a cartilage graft, but the doctor believed whatever his patient said.

Q. Can you tell me at this time what, in your opinion, Mrs. P.'s view of herself was from a psychiatric point of view?
A. I think she was very upset because she felt her face was deformed.
Q. And what do you base that opinion on?
A. Her mood, her feelings, her nose, the way she had withdrawn from social activities. She was not involved in any more community affairs and she was crying.
Q. And what, if anything, did you do for Mrs. P. regarding treatment at that time?
A. Well, I usually allow them to ventilate, give them support and wait until next week.

* * *

Q. Can you tell us what you meant by her self-esteem was low?
A. Well, she was feeling low. She was feeling worthless. She was feeling ugly.
Q. And did you attribute those feelings to anything in particular?
A. The nose, the problems with the nose she had.

Comment. Although this depressed reaction was extreme, it does underscore the emotional component in many vanity plastic surgery cases.

* * *

Q. How was the problem affecting her life?
A. It was making her miserable.
Q. What do you base that statement on?
A. Because she was becoming a recluse in her apartment. She was not socializing. She was not participating in anything.
Q. Did you give her any treatment at that time?

Comment. He apparently didn't try a different type of medication or a combination of drugs, consider hospitalization or shock treatments, or refer her to another therapist.

§ 19.5 —Cause of Depression

Q. Now, doctor, can you tell me if you have an opinion again with a reasonable degree of medical certainty as to the cause of this depression that Mrs. P. was experiencing?
A. At this point I have no doubt it was because of the state of her nose.
Q. Excuse me?
A. The state of her nose.

Comment. This doctor was overreaching by ignoring her prior psychiatric history. It would be interesting to see if he took the same position in Medicaid Insurance reports.

* * *

§ 19.6 Cross-Examination—Prior Depression

Q. Isn't that a fact, doctor, that Mrs. P. had been on and off antidepressant medication at least since 1975?
THE COURT: Did you get a history of any prior antidepressant medication?
THE WITNESS: No.

Comment. Actually she had been under the care of another doctor and on antidepressants but apparently she didn't reveal this history of medication to the witness.

* * *

Q. And you found that in December of '84 that she had no thought disorder; isn't that true?
A. Yes.
Q. You also found, doctor, she had clear sensation; isn't that true?
A. Clear what?

Comment. Counsel was minimizing the damages by stressing the negatives in the doctor's report. However, there was no claim of a psychotic thought disorder.

Q. Clear sensation.
A. No.
Q. Doctor, could you look at—
A. Clear sensorium.
Q. Sensorium, okay. What is clear sensorium?
A. Her senses were clear.
Q. All right, thank you, doctor. You found that she was well-oriented in December of '84; isn't that true, doctor?
A. Yes, that's correct.

Q. And you also found that her memory was preserved in December of '84; isn't that true, doctor?
A. It was preserved.
Q. Now, doctor, could you look at the next—note for the next time that you saw Mrs. P., I believe that is December 10th, 1984.
A. Yes.
Q. December 10th of '84, she was still ventilating her anger against her ex-husband; isn't that true, doctor?
A. It is true.
Q. Doctor, could you look at your note for February 11, 1985.
A. Yes.
Q. All right. And at that point, you know she was talking about her past life.
A. I'm sorry?
THE COURT: Do you know she was talking about her past life?
THE WITNESS: What's the date again?
Q. February 11, 1985.
A. '85, yes.
Q. And at that point, she was talking about her past life.
A. Yes.
Q. And, doctor, that would include the problems she had had with her husband, prior to the divorce in '78 and her feelings that she had of her divorce ever since then, ever since—
A. Also her upbringing and her father and her mother and her siblings, this past life.
Q. These would all be factors in her mental condition; isn't that true?
A. No, usually patient talks about that.
Q. Doctor, could you look at, let's deal with the last period that you saw Mrs. P. If you could look at your note for May 5th, 1986.
A. Yes.
Q. All right.
Q. And at that point she had no depression; isn't that true, doctor?
THE WITNESS: No depression.

§ 19.7 —Summing Up Question

Q. When Mrs. P. came to see you, doctor, you indicated in your records, the first note, that the patient lived alone; isn't that correct?
A. Yes.
Q. You also indicated she had been divorced for about six years at the time she came to see you; is that correct?
A. Yes.
Q. You also indicated in your records that she had no children; is that correct? And are all these factors relevant to you or important to you in your evaluation of the patient?
A. Yes.
Q. And do all these factors go to her mental condition at the time that you see her?

A. In what way?
Q. Are these factors—her loneliness, her lack of family, her husband leaving her, her having no children—relevant to you in your evaluation of this patient?
A. Yes.

Comment. This was an excellent summary of the defense cross, put together in a nicely packaged question.

§ 19.8 —Menopause Can Cause Depression

* * *

Q. Was this [medication] for her menopausal symptoms?
A. Yes.
Q. Does menopause, in your experience, cause certain changes in personality in a patient?
A. Some women think they are losing something; some women are happy because they are losing something.
Q. So women who think they are losing something, this may cause a certain degree of feeling low and depression; isn't that correct?
A. There is a possibility.

Comment. This was another good point to raise in cross. Her prior problems and/or her menopausal condition could have been the culprits.

§ 19.9 —State Reports

Comment. Often insurance or state reports present a different diagnosis or impression of the patient than the psychiatrist testifies about. This is because the therapist sometimes tries to help the patient by minimizing symptoms in official reports to avoid embarrassment.

Q. I refer you to this psychiatric medical report in your records to the New York State Department of Social Services, and you indicate the present problem is, she had been suffering from crying spells?
A. Yes.
Q. Insomnia, palpitations, correct?
A. Yes.
Q. Feelings of loneliness.
A. Yes.
Q. And sadness, is that correct?
A. Yes.
Q. And then as far as a clinical course is concerned, she responded well; is that correct?

A. Correct.
Q. You describe her as pleasant, cooperative, and friendly?
A. She was so.
Q. Doctor, she had no thought disorder at that time, did she?
A. No, she never had.
Q. Her speech was logical?
A. Yes.
Q. Her effect was appropriate?
A. Yes.
Q. Her mood variable, frequently low?
A. That's right.
Q. So she had ups and downs?
A. Her mood at times was low, at times more low; at times stable.
Q. And her change of mood was probably affected by her everyday activities; is that correct?
A. Or by her lack of it.
Q. Or by her lack of activities?
A. Yes.
Q. And that's why you encouraged her to get more involved in her community?
A. That's correct.
Q. Her attention concentration okay?
A. Yes.
Q. Her orientation, you described also as okay. Her memory, okay.
A. Yes.
Q. Her information, which is what, doctor?
A. Fund of general information. What is the capital of New York? Albany.
Q. So she was able to give you, when you asked her questions, she was able to answer appropriately.
A. Yes.
Q. And that was okay?
A. Yes.
Q. Her ability to perform calculations, serial events, that was all okay?
A. Yes.

Comment. Counsel made great use of this report to minimize the doctor's testimony and made it appear that he had exaggerated the entire case to the jury.

§ 19.10 Recross-Examination by the Defense Counsel

* * *

Q. Doctor, are you familiar with the DSM-3, the diagnostic and statistical mental disorders?

THE COURT: Sustained. Not appropriate on recross-examination. Going on to something about DSM-3, you should have asked it on your cross-examination. The purpose of recross-examination is to cover something covered by the plaintiff on redirect.
DEFENSE COUNSEL: That was the idea.
Q. You stated the diagnosis of Mrs. P. was dysthymic disorder.
THE COURT: Sustained. That was not discussed at all on redirect.
A. Yes.
THE COURT: Next question.

Comment. The judge was technically correct but unduly harsh. Nevertheless, this is a good lesson for the trial lawyer: don't put off on cross today what you can't do on recross tomorrow.

§ 19.11 Direct Examination of the Defense Psychiatrist

Comment. Now it was the defense's turn. Their case was based, however, on prior psychiatric records that were not in evidence. Therefore, they had a hard time proving that the plaintiff's depression was chronic and predated the surgery. However, this expert could testify in his opinion that the nasal surgery did not precipitate her depression.

* * *

Q. Doctor, could you tell us all the records that you looked at?
THE COURT: Yes.
A. I looked at the records of Dr. T. from '75 to '85 approximately. That to me I understood I cannot testify.
THE COURT: That's right, that is not in evidence.
A. That to me was the most pertinent psychiatric record.
THE COURT: That's not in evidence so you can't base any of your opinions on that at all.

Comment. Unfortunately, under New York law, these records could not get into evidence and the defense did not call this doctor to the stand. However, under the Federal Rules, a witness could base his testimony on hearsay if these records were the type usually relied on by the psychiatrist.

§ 19.12 —What Caused Her Depression

Q. Doctor, can you tell us with a reasonable degree of scientific certainty what caused—

THE COURT: Well, we—

Q. —Mrs. P.'s conditions?

THE COURT: I said we don't know what caused it. Why not ask it in the negative?

Doctor, I take it from your testimony that it is your view that this depressive neurosis that this patient has is unrelated to her nasal surgery; is that correct?

THE WITNESS: I would say not significantly caused by. Whatever effect it has I don't know. I think there are many other more pertinent issues in this woman's life that I think are pertinent to understanding why she has this dysthymic disorder.

Q. Doctor, do you—

THE COURT: Please, please.

A. And I touched on some of them earlier, I touched on her—the family history, without parents, without both parents since she was a child, this kind of loss, again before 1980 we used to talk about reactive depressions, involutional depression, postpartum depression based on the concept that we knew that postpartum caused the depression. We don't talk about it any more because we know we don't know but we still have some understandings, which still have some theoretical basis, still have some research that tells us certain things and we still know essentially that when we're dealing with depression, for the most part we are dealing with loss, fundamental loss. In whatever form it takes, the loss of parenting, the loss of the nurturing of the childhood in her case, the loss of culture, the loss of country when she came here, the loss of a child in her miscarriage, the loss of a husband, the loss of a spouse, this is a woman who had virtually no relationships in her life and minimal capacity to form them and she gets married and he leaves her and still, still up in my office after all those years, talking about it, that is a loss.

These kinds of things are, again—I would view them as a pattern that helps me to understand why Mrs. P. suffers from this disorder but I cannot say that any of them or even that all of them with any degree of medical certainty caused her to suffer from this dysthymic disorder. Because the information, the scientific knowledge, the scientific knowledge does not allow me to do that.

Comment. Unfortunately for the defense, this answer was not clear and definitive enough. However, it would do, particularly because the doctor couldn't rely on the prior treating psychiatrist's records because they were not in evidence.

THE COURT: Doctor—

A. Maybe next year but not now.

THE COURT: Doctor, did you have an opinion as to what impact, if any, the nasal surgery and let's—actually the need for the second operation and whatever alternation and appearance was produced—what impact, if any, that had on the mood disorder.

THE WITNESS: Again, my assessment of that—there was no indication from my examination and assessment of the records and the overall, the complexity of this woman's complaints I felt that this was—this was another kind of medical incident in a long—in a life of 10 years of medical incidents and that there was no specific relationship particularly when we're dealing with the fact that the more acute depressive anxiety state began in the middle of 1984 and that all of this had gone on 1980, '81, 1982. That's a long time ago to even be trying to make a cause and effect but even if they happen the same day I couldn't say that one caused the other because again that's the information—the information, the science, what we know doesn't allow us to do that.

Comment. This opinion was honest, but still may not have been definite enough to convince a lay jury.

§ 19.13 The Verdict

So how did the case end? The court dismissed the case against the supervising surgeon for failure to prove a prima facie case. The jury returned a defense verdict for the hospital and its residents. It found that there were no departures. The evidence showed only a complication that was inevitable and corrected. As to the informed consent issue, the jury found in favor of the defendants, probably because the plaintiff's testimony was not credible and she denied most of her prior psychiatric history. Her vanity also hurt her. The fact that the defendants cured her breathing problems also hurt her chances.

If the plaintiff had been more forthcoming about her prior psychiatric history and pleaded only aggravation, she would have had a much better chance of prevailing.

APPENDIXES

A. Face-lift Complaint
B. Rhinoplasty Complaint
C. Face-lift and Liposuction Verified Bill of Particulars
D. Rhinoplasty Verified Bill of Particulars
E. Dermabrasion Complaint
F. Breast Reduction Complaint
G. Interrogatories

APPENDIX A

FACE-LIFT COMPLAINT

This complaint is fairly well drawn. It specifically contains the procedure of the surgery, the purpose of the surgery, and the malpractice that occurred.

RETURN DATE: [date] [name], Plaintiff v. [name], Defendant	SUPERIOR COURT JUDICIAL DISTRICT OF [name] [date]

COMPLAINT

1. On [date], [name], M.D., was and ever since has been a duly licensed physician and surgeon engaged in the practice of medicine in the State of [ ] and a specialist in the field of plastic surgery.

2. Prior to [date], the plaintiff [name] requested the defendant to render surgical care to minimize wrinkling in connection with her sagging skin about the face and neck, and the defendant [name] agreed for compensation to render such surgical care to the plaintiff and agreed that he would attend to the plaintiff throughout the time of her surgery and would render appropriate medical care in accordance with the appropriate standard of care of surgical patients such as the plaintiff [name].

3. Prior to [date], the defendant [name] recommended that the plaintiff undergo an operative procedure for excision of degenerative skin of her face and neck.

4. On [date], the plaintiff entered [name] Hospital for the purpose of having said operation performed.

5. On [date], the defendant [name] performed excision of degenerative skin about the face and neck.

6. During the operative procedure on [date], the defendant [name] negligently cut the skin flaps on both sides of the neck and/or negligently applied inappropriate tension to the skin flaps on both sides of the neck of the plaintiff [name].

7. As a result of the defendant [name]'s negligence during the operative procedure of [date], the defendant caused interference with blood circulation on both sides of the neck.

8. Following the operative procedure, the plaintiff was discharged on [date], to be followed up at the defendant's office for removal of sutures.

9. Before the removal of the sutures, the plaintiff experienced redness, pain, and swelling over the incisions of both sides of her face, especially over the right side of the ear to the right cheek.

10. The symptoms of redness, pain, swelling, and skin sloughing, all consistent with a decreased blood supply to the skin, persisted through [date], at which time the defendant [name] saw the patient in his office.

11. On [date], the plaintiff [name] again saw the defendant [name] in his office and was again experiencing redness and sloughing on the sides of her neck.

12. The plaintiff continued to treat with the defendant [name] until [date].

13. As a result of the defendant's negligence, the plaintiff has sustained extensive, permanent, and disfiguring scarring on both sides of her neck and face.

14. As a result of the defendant's negligence, the plaintiff has expended and will continue to expend monies for hospitalization, physical therapy, medication, and medical care and attention for possible reconstructive surgery.

15. As a consequence of the defendant's negligence, the plaintiff [name] has suffered and will continue to suffer physical and mental pain and anguish and embarrassment and will be severely sore and disabled for the rest of her life.

16. As a result of the defendant's negligence, the plaintiff [name]'s ability to enjoy life's activities has been permanently and severely impaired.

17. The plaintiff [name]'s injuries were caused by the negligence of the defendant [name] in one or more of the following respects:

a. in that he failed to properly perform the surgery of [date] in that he cut the skin flaps on both sides of the face in such a way as to interfere with blood supply to the tissues, causing necrosis (tissue death);

b. in that he failed to properly perform the surgery of [date] in that he applied inappropriate tension to the skin flaps on both sides of the face in such a manner as to interfere with blood supply to the tissues causing necrosis (tissue death);

c. in that he failed to disclose to and inform the plaintiff of all material elements of the risks involved in connection with the defendant [name]'s care and treatment, including the nature and possible consequences of the treatment, the prospects of success, the prognosis if the procedure were not performed, and alternative methods of treatment available;

d. in that he failed to provide the plaintiff with proper preoperative and postoperative instruction;

e. in that he failed to make a proper diagnosis of the plaintiff's condition;

f. in that he failed to provide adequate and appropriate postoperative treatment for the plaintiff;

g. in that he failed to provide proper treatment for the plaintiff;

h. in that he failed to exercise the degree of care, skill and/or diligence employed by a physician specializing in plastic surgery under similar circumstances.

THE PLAINTIFF

By ____________________________

[name and address of attorney]

APPENDIX B

RHINOPLASTY COMPLAINT

This complaint contains only the barebones necessities. It is vague, rambling, and provides little information. Although such a complaint may be the subject of a motion to dismiss, the courts are generally lenient and advise defendants to await a bill of particulars or interrogatories.

SUPREME COURT OF THE STATE OF NEW YORK
COUNTY OF [ ]

[name], Plaintiff, -against- [name], Defendant.	*PLAINTIFF'S VERIFIED COMPLAINT*

The plaintiff, as and for her verified complaint, by her attorneys, respectfully alleges as follows:

AS AND FOR A FIRST
CAUSE OF ACTION ON
BEHALF OF THE PLAINTIFF

FIRST: Upon information and belief, that at all times hereinafter mentioned, the defendant [name] was and is a physician duly licensed to practice medicine in the State of New York.

SECOND: Upon information and belief, that at all times hereinafter mentioned, the defendant [name] held himself out as being competent and qualified to render medical care, attention, and treatment to the general public.

THIRD: Upon information and belief, that at all times hereinafter mentioned, the defendant [name] maintained an office for the practice of medicine located on [address], City and State of New York.

FOURTH: That on or about [date] the plaintiff [name] presented to defendant [name] seeking medical care, attention, and treatment.

FIFTH: That in or about [date] the defendant [name] undertook to render medical care, attention, and treatment to the plaintiff.

SIXTH: That on or about [date] the defendant [name] did perform a surgical procedure on the plaintiff, [name].

SEVENTH: That the aforesaid surgical procedure performed by the defendant [name] on the plaintiff [name] was performed in the said defendant's medical office located on [address], City and State of New York.

EIGHTH: That by reason of the aforesaid medical treatment, this plaintiff sustained a worsening of her medical condition resulting in severe and lasting personal injuries to her body as well as shock to her nervous system.

NINTH: That the aforesaid occurrence was caused solely and wholly through and by reason of the negligence of the defendant and the plaintiff in no way contributed thereto.

TENTH: That the aforesaid occurrence was caused solely and wholly through and by reason of the negligence of the defendant: in failing and neglecting to treat the plaintiff in accordance with good and accepted medical customs, practices, and standards; in performing a surgical procedure in a careless, reckless, and negligent manner; in failing and neglecting to take a proper history; in failing and neglecting to take and/or properly interpret appropriate tests and/or x-rays and/or other diagnostic procedures prior to and during the aforesaid surgical procedure; in failing and neglecting to treat the plaintiff in accordance with that degree of medical competence and expertise that the defendant held himself out as possessing; and defendant was otherwise negligent herein.

ELEVENTH: That by reason of the aforesaid, this plaintiff has been rendered sick, sore, lame, and disabled; that she was required to expend various sums of money in an effort to see herself cured of her said injuries and may in the future be so required; that she was compelled to seek medical care, attention, and treatment in an effort to see herself cured of her said injuries and may in the future be so compelled; that she was confined to her home and bed for a period of time and may in the future be so confined; that she was disabled from attending to her usual duties and activities and may in the future be so disabled; and that she has otherwise been damaged herein.

TWELFTH: That by reason of the aforesaid, this plaintiff has been damaged in an amount that exceeds the jurisdictional limits of all lower courts that would otherwise have jurisdiction.

AS AND FOR A SECOND
CAUSE OF ACTION ON
BEHALF OF THE PLAINTIFF

THIRTEENTH: This plaintiff repeats, reiterates, and realleges each and every allegation contained in the first cause of action as if fully set forth herein at length.

FOURTEENTH: That the defendant failed and neglected to inform and/or advise the plaintiff of all of the medical and/or surgical risks associated with the treatment rendered by said defendant; that the said defendant failed to receive an informed consent therefor; and the defendant was otherwise negligent herein.

FIFTEENTH: That by reason of the aforesaid, this plaintiff has been damaged in an amount that exceeds the jurisdictional limits of all lower courts that would otherwise have jurisdiction.

WHEREFORE, the plaintiff demands judgment against the defendant on the first cause of action in an amount that exceeds the jurisdictional limits of all lower courts that would otherwise have jurisdiction; the plaintiff demands judgment against the defendant on the second cause of action in an amount that exceeds the jurisdictional limits of all lower courts that would otherwise have jurisdiction; together with the costs and disbursements of this action.

Yours, etc.,

____

[name and address of attorney]

APPENDIX C

FACE-LIFT AND LIPOSUCTION VERIFIED BILL OF PARTICULARS

This bill of particulars, although setting forth specific allegations, includes virtually any act or omission. The plaintiffs intentionally included everything. When faced with such interrogatories and bills of particulars, the defendant should request the court to limit vague language such as "or otherwise negligent" or "any and all other."

SUPREME COURT OF THE STATE OF NEW YORK
COUNTY OF [ ]

[name], Plaintiff, -against- [name] and [name], Defendants.	*VERIFIED BILL OF PARTICULARS* Index Nos.: [ ]

The plaintiff, as and for her Verified Bill of Particulars, by her attorneys, [names], pursuant to the demand of the defendant, [name] sets forth as follows upon information and belief:

1. The malpractice, negligence, and carelessness of the defendant, his agents, servants, and/or employees occurred between [date] and [date].
2. The malpractice, negligence, and carelessness occurred on the premises of [name] Hospital and in the defendant's private office.
3. The negligence, malpractice, and carelessness of the defendant, his agents, servants, and/or employees, consisted in the following:

In failing to exercise and use due care and diligence and caution with reference to the plaintiff's condition; in failing and neglecting to use reasonable care and diligence to safeguard and protect the plaintiff's health; in failing to provide that degree of care that the plaintiff rightfully anticipated and expected; in negligently and carelessly attending to and caring for the plaintiff when the defendant knew or should have known in the exercise of reasonable care and caution that he was unfit, inexperienced, incompetent, improperly skilled, and unqualified to render such treatment and care;

In causing the plaintiff to undergo further medical and plastic surgical treatment; in causing the plaintiff to undergo procedures that were known to the defendant to be serious and dangerous to a person in the plaintiff's condition; in causing the plaintiff to undergo a regimen of hospitalization and treatment for the injuries suffered;

In failing to perform proper and/or necessary tests and/or procedures to determine the nature and extent of the plaintiff's condition; in failing to heed the complaints of the plaintiff; in failing to recognize the various signs, symptoms, and manifestations of the plaintiff's condition;

In failing to comply with and adhere to the accepted and approved standards, practices, procedures, techniques, and common usage and with customs prevailing in the medical and surgical community; in failing and neglecting to insure that he possessed and employed that certain degree of skill, ability, competence, and experience commensurate with those performing these professional functions in the medical and surgical community; in deviating and departing from the aforesaid standards set forth as common knowledge to those engaged in medical and surgical care; in negligently failing to render that treatment and care that a reasonable prudent provider of medical services would consider to be the standard required under the existing facts and circumstances herein;

In failing to furnish timely and proper operative, preoperative and postoperative care and treatment; in failing to heed the complaints and symptoms of the plaintiff during and following the plastic surgical procedures performed upon her; in causing, creating, allowing, and permitting the irreversible complications and conditions that occurred; in causing the complications that occurred; in failing to guard against the causation of the complications and conditions; in improperly evaluating and treating the plaintiff's conditions that developed postoperatively; in abandoning the plaintiff by not rendering adequate postoperative care; in failing to record all relevant facts, findings, tests, test results, observations, recommendations, reports of consultations, physical findings, and the like, pertaining to the plaintiff;

In failing to advise the plaintiff of the risks incurred as a result of submitting herself to care and treatment by the defendant; in failing to advise the plaintiff of the risks and hazards involved in a right temporal muscle dynamics sling with static fascia lata sling procedure; in failing and neglecting to obtain the knowing, informed, and valid consent of the plaintiff to the procedure; in failing to allow the plaintiff an opportunity to give an informed consent by not explaining the extent of the risks involved; in failing to make the plaintiff aware of the alternatives to said procedure; in improperly evaluating the laboratory, x-ray, and other studies performed upon the plaintiff; in failing to abide by such rules, regulations, and protocols as were in effect in the plastic surgery department on the dates upon which the negligent acts occurred; in improperly and negligently performing the aforesaid operative procedure upon the plaintiff; in failing to make proper operative, preoperative, and postoperative tests and diagnoses to determine the extent of the damage done to the plaintiff during the aforesaid operative procedure;

In failing and neglecting to expect, anticipate, and foresee the dangers, risks, hazards, and injuries incident to and attendant upon the use and employment of the aforesaid surgical procedure in the plaintiff's body; in causing, creating, permitting, and/or allowing the creation and causation of unreasonable, serious, and severe complications and conditions; in failing and neglecting to guard against the creation and causation of the aforesaid complications;

In failing to use due care and diligence in performing the right temporal muscle dynamics sling with static fascia lata sling procedure; in improperly and negligently incising the plaintiff; in incising the plaintiff at an improper location on her body in light of her physical condition; in improperly suturing the aforesaid areas of the plaintiff's body; in failing to take a proper history prior to said surgical procedure; in performing an improper surgical procedure; in employing an improper surgical technique; in improperly employing a surgical technique; in failing to consult with appropriate specialists; in performing an unnecessary surgical procedure; in performing a contraindicated surgical procedure; in performing a surgical procedure that was unnecessary and/or contraindicated in this patient; in employing an improper suturing technique; in unnecessarily and/or improperly injuring nerves and nervous tissue in and about the surgical site; in failing to be aware of and act upon the plaintiff's complaints during and after performance of the aforesaid surgical procedure; in continuing the aforesaid surgical procedure after complications arose; in aggravating and exacerbating the plaintiff's preexisting condition or conditions; in causing, permitting, and/or allowing the plaintiff's condition to be, become, and remain worse; in causing iatrogenic injuries;

The defendant, [name], was further negligent in that he failed to use and follow accepted practices and procedures with respect to the plaintiff and was negligent in that he, his agents, servants, and/or employees, failed to exercise the proper standard of skill, care, knowledge, and diligence called for and required to treat the plaintiff, all of which was a deviation from and not in conformity with, the accepted standards of medical and surgical practice in the community, and was a direct and proximate cause of the occurrence herein.

4. Other than the parties hereto, the plaintiff is presently unaware of the names or designations of witnesses to the acts of malpractice.

5. The defendant undertook to perform surgery on the plaintiff's face. The balance of this question is improper in the Second Judicial Department pursuant to *Patterson v. Jewish Hospital,* 94 Misc. 2d 680, *aff'd,* 75 A.D.2d 553, *leave to appeal denied,* N.Y.L.J., at 13, col. 6 (Nov. 3, 1978).

6. Withdrawn.

7. Withdrawn.

8. It is not known at the present time whether a claim will be made for improper or defective equipment. If such a claim is to be made, the defendant will be advised thereof prior to the time of trial.

9 and 10. These questions are improper for inclusion in a Bill of Particulars in the Second Judicial Department, pursuant to *Patterson v. Jewish Hospital,* supra.

11. As a result of the negligence, malpractice, and carelessness of this defendant, his agents, servants, and/or employees, the plaintiff sustained the following personal injuries:

Serious, severe facial scarring, and disfigurement
Inability to open right eye
Total ptosis of the right upper eyelid
Palpebral fissure of 4 mm in right eye
Loss of levator function in the right upper eyelid
7 mm epicanthal fold extending along the right lower eyelid
Enophthalmos of the right eye
Severe uncorrectable loss of vision in right eye
Depression
Inability to attend to usual and customary business and social matters
Loss of binocular vision
Loss of depth perception
Necessity for extensive regimen of corrective surgery.

All of the foregoing injuries are believed to be permanent in nature.

12. Confinement:

a. Bed and home: approximately two (2) months
b. Hospital: [name] Hospital
Admissions: 7/13–9/22/82
7/24–7/28/83
12/19/84 (E.R.)

13. Special Damages:

a. Physicians: approximately $6,000.00 to date
b. Nurses: included in "d" below
c. Medical supplies: approximately $50.00
d. Hospital: approximately $20,000.00 to date
e. Loss of earnings: and of future earning capacity is claimed in an amount in excess of $250,000.00.

14. At the time here in question, the plaintiff was unemployed.

15. The plaintiff was born on [date]. Social Security numbers, being improper means of identification, are improper for inclusion in a Bill of Particulars.

16. Plaintiff resides at [address].

17. Withdrawn.

18. See paragraph "3" above. This defendant is, in addition, not entitled to particularization of any claims against his codefendant.

19.–26. Omit.

Dated: New York, N.Y.
[date]

Yours, etc.,

____

[name and address of attorney]

APPENDIX D

RHINOPLASTY VERIFIED BILL OF PARTICULARS

This bill of particulars is more narrowly drawn and puts the defendant on notice of the exact nature of the claims.

SUPREME COURT OF THE STATE OF NEW YORK
COUNTY OF [ ]

[name],

Plaintiff,

-against-

[name], M.D.,

Defendant.

VERIFIED BILL OF PARTICULARS

The plaintiff by his attorneys [names], Esqs., as and for a Verified Bill of Particulars respectfully states as follows:

1. a. The defendant's course of treatment occurred between 9/23/85 and 11/10/86.
   b. The defendant rendered medical treatment to the plaintiff at the following locations: [ ], and Hospital, [address] New York.

2. The plaintiff presented himself before the defendant to correct the following conditions: comminuted fractures of both nasal bones with a deviation of the septum and bones, with associated difficulty in breathing and marked distortion of the nasal bones and septums.

3. That the negligent acts, omissions, and malpractice of the defendant consisted of failing and omitting to adequately and properly examine, diagnose, and treat the plaintiff and by departing from accepted medical practices and standards adhered to and in use by other physicians in the community; failing to correct the deviated septum resulting in breathing being obstructed through the left airway with diminished air going through the right side; departing from accepted medical practices in failing to perform a submucous resection or if such procedure was attempted the failure to properly complete said procedure; failing and omitting to properly inform the plaintiff of the risk associated with an open reduction of nasal bones and nasal reconstruction and to obtain consent of the patient.

4. The plaintiff is unaware at this time of any defective equipment but reserves the right to amend the Bill of Particulars regarding this item after the completion of discovery.
5. See answer to Number 3.
6. See answer to Number 3.
7. See answer to Number 3.
8. The plaintiff is unaware at this time of any other individuals for whom the defendant is vicariously liable for, but reserves the right to amend the Bill of Particulars regarding this issue after the completion of discovery.
9. The plaintiff suffers from the following injuries:
   a. Depression of right lower alar cartilage with slight irregularity of the tip, the nasal tip being slanted to the right
   b. Hanging columella left nostril as opposed to its counterpart right side
   c. Depression of the right upper lateral cartilage
   d. Nasal bones are asymmetrical at the dorsum and separated with palpation of the left nasal bone along the dorsum revealing an irregularity of being higher than the right nasal bone
   e. A deviated septum superiorly with the convexity at the right airway and the opposite airway showing the concavity. Anteriorly and inferiorly a definite ridging adjacent to the vomer within the right airway.

That solely by reason of the negligence of the defendant as hereinbefore alleged, the said plaintiff was rendered sick, sore, lame, and disabled and suffered and still suffers great pain and anguish and sustained severe and serious injuries in and about his head, body, limbs, nerves, and nervous system and was obliged to and did seek medical treatment, aid, and assistance and was required to expend various sums of money for said medical treatment, aid, and assistance and his pattern of life was varied.

10. The plaintiff was confined to his bed for approximately one week after the surgery.
11. The plaintiff's special damages regarding medical expenses shall be provided.
12. The plaintiff at the time of the alleged malpractice was a plumber employed by [name]. As a result of having broken his nose and the resulting difficulties in breathing the plaintiff was unable to work for a period of three months. At the time of the occurrence the plaintiff was earning approximately $280.00 per week.
13. The plaintiff's date of birth is 6/28/62.
14. The plaintiff's social security number is [ ].
15. The plaintiff resides at [address].
16. See answer to Number 3.
17. See answer to Number 3.
18. Collateral sources are not applicable at this time.

19.–26. These questions, which relate to a wrongful death action, are not applicable.

Dated: [date]

APPENDIX E

DERMABRASION COMPLAINT

This complaint, although sufficient, fails to specify and particularize the allegations or injuries. There are three causes of action, one for pain and suffering, one for lack of informed consent, and one for loss of consortium.

SUPREME COURT OF THE STATE OF [ ]
COUNTY OF [ ]

[name], Plaintiffs, -against- [name], Defendant.	Index No.: *VERIFIED COMPLAINT*

The plaintiffs, by attorneys, [name], as and for their Verified Complaint herein, allege, upon information and belief, as follows:

AS AND FOR A FIRST CAUSE
OF ACTION, IT IS ALLEGED

1. That at all the times herein mentioned, the defendant [name], M.D., was and still is a physician duly licensed to practice medicine in the State of [ ].
2. That at all the times herein mentioned, the defendant [name] claimed to be a specialist in plastic surgery.
3. That at all the times hereinafter mentioned, the defendant [name] was a professional corporation, duly organized and existing under the laws of the State of New York.
4. That at all the times herein mentioned, the defendant [name] operated and maintained an office for the medical examination and treatment of patients, located at [address].
5. That between approximately [date] and [date] the plaintiff, [name], was under the medical care of the defendant, [name].

6. That heretofore from on or about [date] through approximately [date], the plaintiff, [name], engaged the defendant, [name], as a physician to diagnose and treat her condition, and said defendant undertook as such physician to attend and care for such patient and to use due, reasonable, and proper skill and care in the treatment of the patient.

7. That defendant, his agents, servants, and/or employees were negligent and careless with respect to the services rendered for and on behalf of the injured plaintiff; in negligently and carelessly failing and neglecting to use reasonable care in the services rendered for and on behalf of the injured plaintiff; in negligently and carelessly failing and neglecting to ascertain the said plaintiff's condition or to heed said condition; in negligently and carelessly departing from accepted procedures in the services rendered for and on behalf of the injured plaintiff; in failing to follow good and accepted practice under the circumstances there existing; in performing contraindicated procedures upon the injured plaintiff; in failing to perform indicated procedures or to render the necessary treatment; and in departing from good and proper medical practice with respect to the examination, evaluation, care, and treatment undertaken, with injury to the said plaintiff resulting thereby.

8. That the negligence of the defendant physician caused injury to the said patient and consisted of negligently, recklessly, and carelessly failing to treat and to care for the said patient in accordance with standards of care and treatment generally accepted in the community; in negligently and carelessly failing to use approved methods in general use in the care and treatment of the said plaintiff; in negligently and carelessly failing to use reasonable care and skill in the care and treatment of the plaintiff; in negligently and carelessly failing to use the said defendant's best judgment in the care and treatment of the said plaintiff; and said defendant was otherwise negligent, reckless, and careless with respect to undertaking to and affording to the said plaintiff the requisite medical care.

9. That as a result of the aforesaid occurrence, the injured plaintiff sustained severe physical injuries, a severe shock to the nervous system, and certain internal injuries, and has been caused to suffer and for a long time to come, will continue to suffer severe physical pain and mental anguish; that some of these injuries are of a permanent and lasting nature; that said plaintiff has been confined to a hospital bed and home as a result thereof and has been caused to abstain from vocational activities as well as avocations, with impairment of earning capacity, and has necessarily incurred expenses or obligations for medical care and attention and for medication, with similar expenses anticipated, all to the damage of the said plaintiff.

AS AND FOR A SECOND CAUSE OF ACTION,
PLAINTIFF, [name], ALLEGES:

10. That the plaintiff, [name], was entitled to be advised of the risks, complications, and alternatives to the medical care administered.

11. That the defendant, his agents, servants, and/or employees failed and neglected to inform the plaintiff, [name], of the risks and hazards attendant upon the performance of the said treatment, which they either knew or should

have known, including the risks of infection, disfigurement, and pain, the danger of extensive and cosmetically disfiguring scarring and deformity, the persistent sensitivity and pain, and the alternatives thereto, and that no informed consent was given.

12. That, had the defendant properly informed the plaintiff of the risks inherent in the performance of the procedures that were attempted upon her, neither this plaintiff nor any reasonably prudent person in her position would have undergone the said treatment.

13. That the said lack of informed consent was the proximate cause of the injuries or conditions from which the plaintiff, [name], has suffered, does suffer, and will continue to suffer as a result of said treatment, all to her damage.

AS AND FOR A THIRD CAUSE OF ACTION,
PLAINTIFF, [name], ALLEGES:

14. That at all the times herein mentioned, the plaintiff, [name], was the mother of the plaintiff, [name], who resided with her and enjoyed the services and society of said [name].

15. That as a result of the foregoing, the plaintiff [name] has been deprived of the services of the injured plaintiff, [name], and has incurred expenses for the medical care, attention, and medicines required, and has expended monies and incurred obligations, with further expenses of similar character anticipated.

16. That the amount of damages sought herein exceeds the jurisdictional limits of any lower court that would otherwise have jurisdiction.

WHEREFORE, the plaintiffs pray for judgment, seeking damages in the amount to be determined by the trier of fact, together with interest and the costs and disbursements of this action.

Dated: Brooklyn, New York
June 23, 1988

Yours, etc.

____

[name and address of attorney]

APPENDIX F

BREAST REDUCTION COMPLAINT

This complaint is based upon allegations of breach of warranty. The complaint is fairly well drawn as it specifically mentions the nature of the warranty made by the defendant.

[name and address]
Attorney for Plaintiff

[name],	THE SUPERIOR COURT OF [state]
Plaintiff,	LAW DIVISION
vs.	DOCKET NO.
[name],	CIVIL ACTION
Defendant	COMPLAINT

The plaintiff residing at [address] in the City of [name], County of [name], State of New Jersey, complaining of the defendant says:

FIRST COUNT

1. At all times herein mentioned the defendant was and is a corporation duly authorized, existing, and doing business pursuant to the laws of the State of New Jersey.
2. On or about, before and after [date] the defendant [name] was a practicing physician and employee, agent, servant, or otherwise of defendant [name] holding himself out to the public and to the plaintiff as being skilled, careful, and diligent in the practice of his profession.
3. On or about said date the plaintiff consulted the defendants concerning a breast reduction procedure (Gigantanera). The plaintiff engaged the services of said defendants and the procedure was subsequently performed.
4. During the course of said consultation the defendant through its agent, servant, employee, or otherwise Dr. [name] made certain express

warranties concerning the outcome of said procedure in relation to the results desired by the plaintiff, to wit:

1. That the size of the plaintiff's breasts would be reduced
2. That any scars left by the surgical procedure would be unnoticeable and beneath the breasts.

5. It was the duty of the defendants to exercise reasonable skill and judgment when informing the plaintiff about the procedure and the effect it would have cosmetically upon the plaintiff.
6. Notwithstanding the duty imposed on the defendant as aforementioned and well knowing his duty, the defendant [name] negligently informed the plaintiff as to the results said procedure would produce upon the plaintiff.
7. As a result of the defendant's breach of express warranty and negligence as aforesaid, the plaintiff has been caused to suffer extreme emotional distress and humiliation, will require extensive corrective surgery, expend large sums of monies for medical expenses, and has been presently and severely disfigured.

WHEREFORE THE PLAINTIFF DEMANDS JUDGMENT AGAINST THE DEFENDANT FOR

A. Damages together with interest and cost of suit on each cause of action.

JURY DEMAND

The plaintiff demands a jury trial on all issues.

____

[attorney's name]

DATED: [date]

APPENDIX G

INTERROGATORIES

These interrogatories request very specific information that causes a defendant to comprehend the full nature of the claim.

1. Set forth:

(a) the date and place of your birth

[ ]

(b) your present address and dates of residence

[ ]

(c) the names and ages of all persons with whom you reside at the present time

[ ]

(d) your address at the time of the incident alleged in the complaint and the dates of residence there

[ ]

(e) the name and date of birth of your spouse if married

[ ]

(f) the names and ages of your children, if any

[ ], ages 12 & 10

(g) the extent of your education, to include all schools, dates of attendance, subjects studied, and degrees received.

2. Set forth whether you have ever been involved as a plaintiff in another lawsuit. If so, set forth the nature of the lawsuit, the name of the court, the docket number of the case, the reason you were suing, the present status of the case (whether pending or resolved), and the outcome.

NONE

3. If you are making a claim for lost wages, or any other loss of income, profit, or earnings, set forth:

NO CLAIM FOR LOST WAGES.

(a) the amount of lost wages or other income, profit, or earnings

N/A

(b) the name and address of your employer

N/A

(c) the amount of time lost from work

N/A

(d) the method of computing such lost wages or other income, profit, or earnings

N/A

(e) whether you have received or are receiving any benefits from your employer, insurance carrier or any other source as a result of your disability and set forth the source, amount, and date of payment

N/A

(f) attach copies of your Federal and/or State income tax returns, and all schedules attached thereto, for the period three years prior to the incident alleged in the complaint to the present.

N/A because no lost wages claim is being made.

4. Set forth whether you, or anyone on your behalf, has received, will receive, or may receive any money from any person, whether a party to this litigation or not or whether ever sued or not, under any settlement, covenant not to sue, release, loan, or other agreement related in any way to any of the injuries for which you seek recovery in this lawsuit. If so, set forth:

(a) the name and address of the person from whom you have received, will receive, or may receive money

(b) the amount of money

(c) the terms under which you have received, will receive, or may receive money, and, if set forth in any writing, attach a copy of the writing hereto

No money has ever been received by anyone in relation to this lawsuit.

(d) the reason you have received, will receive, or may receive the money

N/A

(e) if you filed any type of claim or lawsuit against any person from whom you have received, will receive, or may receive money, set forth the title and number of the claim or lawsuit, and the person, court, or institution with whom filed

N/A

(f) if you, your attorney, or any person on your behalf signed any release, covenant not to sue, stipulation of dismissal, settlement agreement, loan agreement, or other agreement, attach a copy hereto.

N/A

5. If you are making a claim for loss of income as a result of early retirement, attach copies of all claims, forms, reports, records, letters, and other papers submitted to your employer or the insurance carrier or other company to effect the early retirement.

No such claim will be made.

6. If you claim you are disabled, and are receiving or have received disability benefits from any State or Federal government, bond or agency, or from any employer, insurance carrier, or other company, attach copies of all claims, forms, reports, records, letters, and other papers submitted to obtain disability benefits.

Not receiving any type of disability benefits from any state or federal agency, employer, etc.

7. Set forth the names and addresses of all your employers for the period three years prior to the incident alleged in the complaint to the present, and indicate:

(a) each position held with each employer, and the dates you held each position

(b) your wage or salary for each position

(c) the name and address of your supervisor or superior for each position.

Not employed 3 years prior to date of incident.

8. State whether you have ever been hospitalized in your life, and if so, indicate:

(a) the name and address of each hospital

(b) the dates of each admission and discharge

(c) the reason for each admission.

Hospitalization has only occurred for pregnancy 12 and 10 years ago. Children delivered at [ ], N.J.
1981–[ ], N.J. Appendectomy.

9. Set forth the names and addresses of all physicians who have treated you during the past 10 years or to whom you have gone for checkups or examinations and indicate the reason for which you saw each physician.

[names and addresses]
Both physicians have treated
for colds, flu, appendectomy, etc.

10. Set forth whether any x-rays or any diagnostic tests of any part of the injured plaintiff's body have ever been performed, and if so, indicate:

(a) the date and place performed

1/22/86 Dr. [name]

(b) the part of the body involved

BREASTS

(c) the reason performed

BREASTS

(d) the results

MEDICAL REDUCTION

(e) the name and address of the physician ordering the x-rays or tests.

[ ], N.J.

11. Set forth the date you first saw this defendant and indicate the reason you saw this defendant.

1/22/86 Plaintiff had back pains caused by size of breasts. Dr. [ ] advised breast reduction to alleviate back problems.

12. Set forth each and every other date you saw this defendant and indicate the reason you saw this defendant on each date.

1/22/86 Back pains

2/3/86 Breast reduction procedure

2/6/86 Remove bandages

1 other visit but date is unknown. Inquiry made as to why such gross results occurred and constant pain.

13. Set forth the nature of this defendant's treatments on each date you saw this defendant including the description of all medication prescribed for you.

1/22/86 Breast examination

2/3/86 Breast reduction surgery

2/6/86 Remove bandage

Last visit was solely an examination.

14. Set forth whether you had any conversations, whether in person or over the telephone, with this defendant, or anyone acting on this defendant's behalf and, if so, indicate:

(a) the date of each conversation

(b) the reason for each conversation

(c) the substance of each conversation

(d) the names and addresses of all persons present during each conversation.

Defendant's receptionist, identity and name unknown, advised at last visit that operation and results were different than what was promised. Reason for conversation was that the plaintiff complained of cosmetic disfigurement and constant pain in breasts. [Name] was present.

15. Set forth each impairment, injury, condition, or symptom from which you are now suffering.

1. Back pain 2. same size breasts 3. massive scars on breasts 4. brown part of breast is disfigured 5. nipples have decreased in size 6. nipples hurt with or without clothes 7. nipples do not harden during sex 8. breast scars do not even match 9. I feel like an incomplete woman who is disfigured.

16. Set forth each impairment, injury, condition, or symptom that you allege was caused or has been caused by an act or omission of this defendant, and indicate specifically the act or omission causing the same.

This question calls for same information asked in #15. Same is repeated. These were caused by negligence in performance of surgery at his office.

17. Set forth all facts in support of your allegation that this defendant deviated from accepted standards of care, or was negligent in his or her treatment of you, and indicate:

Plaintiff reserves right to amend this answer.

(a) what this defendant did that he or she should not have done

(b) what this defendant did not do that he or she should have done

(c) exactly what this defendant should have done to treat you properly.

A) Breast reduction at his office with representations that scars would be minimal and breasts would be reduced with no pain or disfigurement. Then he denied ever operating on me.
B) He did not reduce my breasts.
C) He should have reduced my breasts with minimal scars.

18. Set forth all damages, costs, and expenses for which you seek recovery, including but not limited to expenses for hospitals, physicians, nurses, medications, and lost wages, and indicate the names and addresses of all payees, and attach true copies of all bills and other documentation of said damages costs and expenses.

COSTS

$2300 payment for services
Dr. [name] - Defendant
1/22/86 $2000
2/3/86 $ 300

No other treatment received to date, no lost wages; the plaintiff demands judgment in the amount of $200,000.00. The plaintiff reserves the right to amend this question.

19. Set forth whether your lifestyle or manner of living has changed as a result of any act or omission of this defendant and, if so, indicate:

(a) the nature of such change

(b) what act or omission of this defendant caused such change, and how.

A) Negligent breast reduction has caused plaintiff to refrain from sexual conduct and refrain from physical activity. I feel like half a woman, incomplete, violated. Back pains keep hampering my activity.

20. Set forth the names and addresses of all persons having knowledge of relevant facts regarding this lawsuit. Identify those persons who are related to you by blood or by marriage.

All parties to this action, attorneys, receptionist for Dr. [name], [name] (sister)

21. Set forth whether any party to this lawsuit has made any admissions and, if so, indicate:

(a) the name and address of the person making each admission

(b) the substance of each admission

(c) the date and place of each admission

(d) the names and addresses of all persons present when each admission was made

(e) if any admission was written, or reduced to writing, attach a copy.

A) Dr. [name]'s receptionist

B) That doctor did not perform correct surgery and results were different from those promised

C) At my last visit to Dr. [name]

D) Myself and [name]

E) Oral.

22. Set forth all medications, whether prescription or nonprescription medication, taken by you for the past five years setting forth the reason for taking such medication and the name of the physician prescribing same if a prescription medication.

DYCILL 250mg- Dr. [ ]
TYLENOL 500mg- Dr. [ ]

23. Set forth the names and addresses of all pharmacies where all prescriptions have been filled for you in the past five years.

[ ] Pharmacy

[ ] N.J.

24. Set forth the names and addresses of all proposed expert witnesses, and indicate:

(a) the qualifications of each expert

(b) the issues to which each expert will testify.

This question cannot be answered until the defendant releases medical records.

25. Set forth the substance of the facts and opinions to which each proposed expert witness is expected to testify, together with a summary of the grounds for each opinion.

See #24.

26. Attach hereto copies of all written reports of all expert witnesses and treating physicians.

See #24.

27. If any reports of proposed expert witnesses or treating physicians have been oral, set forth:

(a) the substance of each report

(b) the date each report was received

(c) the name and address of the person receiving each report

(d) whether any report was recorded or transcribed and, if so, attach a copy.

See #24.

28. Set forth whether you intend to rely upon any text, journal, treatise, or other writing in any manner during the course of this litigation or the trial of this matter and, if so, set forth the title, edition, date of publication, and page and section references of the writing on which you intend to rely.

See #24.

29. State whether any motion picture or videotape has been made for purposes of use at trial and, if so, state:

(a) the date, time, and place made

(b) the name and address of the person making the same

(c) whether the same has been edited and, if so, the name and address of the person by whom edited and exactly what was edited

(d) the names and addresses of all persons present during the making of the same

(e) exactly what was taped, and who determined what would be taped

(f) attach hereto copies of any and all communications to and from the persons making the movie or videotape, outlines or agendas of what to include in the movie or videotape, and any and all transcripts or writings relating to the substance of the videotape

(g) identify the name and address of the person in possession of all copies, edited and unedited, of the movie or videotape.

No pictures or videos have been taken. The plaintiff reserves the right to amend.

30. Set forth whether you contend any of your medical records or any medical records of the patient on whose behalf you are suing have been changed, modified, or altered in any way by any person and, if so, set forth:

(a) each particular record changed, modified, or altered

We believe records have been changed. Dr. [name] telephoned our office claiming he never treated the plaintiff and had no records. This may be because of the fact that he was paid in cash and file was in a separate category. The defendant has refused to supply medical records to be examined by an expert physician.

(b) the name and address of the person you contend changed, modified, or altered such record

(c) the particular change, modification, or alteration

(d) the date on which each such record was changed, modified, or altered

(e) what you contend was the reason for each such change, modification, or alteration

(f) attach a copy of both what you contend are the original records and the changes, modified, or altered records.

A) Defendant

B) Payment being received

C) Unknown

D) Avoid income reporting

E) Copies are in defendant's possession.

31. Set forth the names and addresses of all persons who furnished information for these answers to Interrogatories.

32. Set forth the date on which these Interrogatories were answered.

See certification.

GLOSSARY

This glossary defines commonly used medical terms in the field of plastic surgery; however, if further assistance is necessary, please see *Dorland's Illustrated Medical Dictionary* (26th ed., W.B. Saunders Co. 1981) and *Taber's Cyclopedic Medical Dictionary* (15th ed., F.A. Davis Co. 1985).

Abdominoplasty: an operation which improves the abdomen cosmetically by reducing its girth and removing excess fat and skin, and functionally by repairing the rectus muscles.

Acromegaly: disease caused by overfunction of the anterior pituitary and characterized by enlargement of the bones of the hands, feet, and face.

Ala: a winglike process or structure.

Alveoli: air sac of the lungs formed by terminal dilations of a bronchiole.

Anosmia: absence of the sense of smell.

Anoxia: reduction of oxygen in body tissues below physiologic levels.

Aponeurosis: white, flattened, or ribbonlike tendinous expansion, serving mainly as an investment for muscle or connecting a muscle with the parts that it moves.

Areola: the pigmented ring surround the nipple of a woman's breast.

Areolar tissue: fat.

Arrhythmias: any variation from the normal rhythm of the heartbeat.

Atelectasis: incomplete expansion of the lungs at birth. Collapse of the adult lung, occurring spontaneously or after general anesthesia.

Atonic: lack of tone, flaccid.

Atresia: absence or closure of a normal body orifice.

Atrophic skin: skin that has lost its elasticity, that is sagging.

Auricle: the portion of the external ear not contained within the head.

Autogenous: self-generated; originated within the body.

Axillary: pertaining to the axilla; the small hollow beneath the arm.

Blepharochalasia: relaxation of the skin of the eyelid, because of the atrophy of the intercellular tissue.

Blepharoplasty: the cosmetic operation that improves the looks of the eyelids by removing excess skin from the upper lids and herniated fat from upper and lower lids.

Bradycardia: abnormal slowness of the heart beat.

Buccal: pertaining to the cheek.

Buccinator: muscle; buccinator ridge of mandible; compresses cheek and retracts angle of the mouth.

Canthi: the outer corners of the eyelids.

Canthus: the angle at either end of the slit between the eyelids.

Capsulectomy: excision of a capsule.

Capsulotomy: incision of a capsule.

Cartilaginous: consisting of or of the nature of cartilage.

Chondroblast: an embryonic cell of the tissue from which cartilage is developed.

Cicatricial: because of scar tissue.

Cilia: plural of cilium. An eyelid or its outer edge.

Ciliary margin: the area of the eyelids.

Colon: part of the large intestine. (Colonic enema removes matter all the way past the sigmoid colon to the transverse colon.)

Columella: a little column.

Component: a constituent element or part.

Conjunctiva: the clear mucosal covering of the eye and the surrounding eyelids.

Contracture: shrinkage of muscles or scars, shortening, or distortion.

Cornea: transparent structure forming the anterior part of the eye.

Corrugator: that which wrinkles; a muscle which wrinkles.

Costophrenic: the anterior medial border of the ribs.

Cyanosis: blueness of the skin, often resulting from cardiac malformation causing insufficient oxygenation of the blood.

Cyanotic: pertaining to or characterized by cyanosis.

Debridement: removal of all foreign matter and devitalized tissue in or about a traumatic or other lesion.

Dehiscense: breaking down of the wound.

Dermal: pertaining to the skin.

Dermatochalasia: abnormal relaxation or looseness of the skin.

Dermis: the lower layer of the skin.

Diastasis recti: separation of the rectus muscles due to weakening.

Digastric: having two bellies; a muscle having two fleshy bellies with a fibrous insertion between them.

Dorsum: part of the external surface of the nose formed by the junction of the lateral surfaces.

Dyscrasia: an abnormal and depraved state of the blood.

Dyspnea: difficult or labored breathing.

Ecchymosis: discoloration, black and blue.

Ectropion: the hanging down of the lower eyelid because of scar.

Edema: presence of large amounts of fluid in the intercellular tissue spaces of the body.

Electrocautery: an apparatus for cauterizing tissue, burning the ends of the blood vessels causing them not to bleed.

Epidermolysis: loosened state of the epidermis.

Epinephrine: adrenaline which is used in local anesthetic in combination with the anesthesia; portion of the drug to constrict the blood vessels and avoid bleeding potential.

Epiphora: excess tearing.

Epistaxis: nosebleed.

Epithelialize: making new epithelium; new growth of cells to cover an area where they are lacking.

Eschar: a scab.

Ethmoidal: pertaining to the ethmoid bone.

Extubation: the removal of a tube.

Fascial: pertaining to fascia; strong connecting tissue that covers some areas of the body, as in the peritoneal fascia or the abdominal fascia.

Fibroblast: a cell that produces scar tissue.

Fibrocystic: partly fibrous and partly cystic.

Follicles: the epithelial tube within which each hair grows.

Foramen: natural hole or passage, especially one into or through a bone.

Frontalis: the fleshy portion of the occipitofrontalis muscle overlying the frontal bone.

Gluteal: of the gluteal or the buttock area.

Hematoma: collection of blood, usually underneath the skin.

Hemostasis: the arrest of an escape of blood.

Herniated periorbital fat: when the fat pushes through the muscles surrounding the eye like a hernia in the groin.

Hypertrophic skin: morbid enlargement or overgrowth of the skin because of an increase in size of its constituent cells.

Hypertrophy: enlargement or overgrowth of an organ or part as a result of an increase in size of its constituent cells.

Ileus: condition of the bowel which causes it to be paralyzed or static; in this condition peristalsis—the normal movement of the bowel—is not present.

Iliac: one of the bones in the pelvic girdle.

Inguinal: pertaining to the groin.

Innervation: distribution or supply of nerves to a part.

Integument: skin.

Intertrigo: a chafed patch of the skin that occurs especially on opposed surfaces.

Intubation: insertion of a tube; especially the introduction of a tube into the larynx.

Keloid: new growth or tumor of skin, consisting of whitish ridges, nodules, and plates of dense tissue.

Lacrymal: pertaining to tears.

Lacrymal caruncle: the small, reddish brown mucosa in the inner corner of the eye.

Lagophtholmos: a condition in which the eye cannot be completely closed.

Levator: that which raises or lifts up, such as a muscle or instrument for raising an organ or part.

Levator palpebrae superioris muscle: muscle that is elevated by a portion of the seventh cranial nerve; it elevates the upper eyelid.

Lipectomy: excision of fatty tissue or a lesion of the subcutaneous fatty tissue.

Malar: pertaining to the cheek or cheekbone.

Mammoplasty: plastic surgery on the breast.

Masseter: muscle that raises mandible and closes jaws.

Mastopexy: the surgical fixation of a pendulous breast.

Milia: small whitish nodule in the skin, especially of the face.

Mucosa: a mucous membrane.

Mucous membrane: a thin layer of tissue composed of epithelium lining canals and cavities of the body which communicate with external air.

Musculofascial: area made up of muscle and fascia, the deep heavy connecting tissue.

Nasalis: relating to the nose.

Nasolabial: pertaining to the nose and lip.

Nasopharynx: the part of the pharynx that lies above the level of the soft palate.

Necrosis: death of a cell or of a group of cells in contact with nerve fibers.

Neuroma: tumor or new growth largely made up of nerve cells and nerve fibers.

Nidus: point of origin or focus of a morbid process.

Occipital: pertaining to the back part of the head.

Orbicularis hypertrophy: an increase or excess of the orbicularis oculi muscle (the muscle which surrounds the eye in a circular fashion).

Orbital septum: fibrous tissue surrounding the eye.

Orthostatic: pertaining to or caused by standing erect.

Osteotomy: surgical cutting of a bone.

Palatine: pertaining to the palate.

Palpebral fissure: space between the lids.

Panniculectomy: the removal of a panniculus or apron of fat from the abdomen.

Parenchyma: the essential or functional elements of an organ as distinguished from its stroma, or framework.

Paresthesia: a sensation of prickling, tingling, or creeping on the skin having no objective cause.

Parotid: gland situated near the ear.

Pectoralis: pertaining to the breast or chest.

Pedicle: the stem of a tumor or a flap.

Periorbital fat: fat situated around the eye which comes from the orbit.

Periosteum: the tough fibrous membrane surrounding a bone.

Peristaltic: the normal rhythmic movement of the intestines by which food and fecal matter are propelled from one end to another.

Peritoneal: pertaining to the peritoneum; peritoneal cavity is the closed cavity which contains the abdominal contents. It is open to the outside.

Platelet: circular or oval disk found in the blood of all mammals and is involved in coagulation of the blood.

Platysma: plate or platelike structure; muscle that wrinkles skin of neck, depresses jaw.

Plication: to sew, to take tucks, to approximate.

Procerus: skin over nose; draws down eyebrows.

Ptosis: prolapse of an organ or part; such as drooping of the breast or the excess hanging skin of the upper eyelids.

Ramus mandibularus: ramus of the jaw; branch, as of an artery, bone, nerve, or vein.

Reepithelialize: relining of vessels and other small cavities.

Retrobulbar hematoma: collection of blood behind the eyeball.

Rhinoplasty: a surgical procedure to repair or change the shape or size of the nose.

Rhytidectomy: face-lift.

Sclera: white part of the eye.

Sebaceous: pertaining to sebum or suet. Secreting a greasy lubricating substance.

Septum: a dividing wall or partition.

Sequela: any effect following or caused by an attack of disease.

SMAS: the superficial musculo-aponeurotic system.

Sphenopalatine: pertaining to or in relation with the sphenoid and palatine bones.

Stenosis: the narrowing of a duct or canal.

Sternomastoid: pertaining to the sternum and the mastoid process of the temporal bone: sternomastoid muscle, foramen, and so on.

Stroma: tissue that forms the ground substance, framework, or matrix of an organ.

Submammary: situated beneath the mammary gland.

Superciliary: pertaining to the region of the eyebrow.

Suspensory: serving to hold up a part.

Symphysis: the joining of two bones as in the symphysis pubis xiphoid.

Thrombophlebitis: a condition in which inflammation of the vein wall has preceded the formation of the thrombus.

Thrombus: a plug or clot in a blood vessel formed by coagulation of the blood and remaining at the point of its formation.

Tragus: the cartilaginous projection before the external meatus of the ear.

Transection: a section made across a long axis; a cross section.

Trigeminal: trigeminal nerve of fifth facial nerve.

Turbinate: a turbinated bone.

Vascular: pertaining to or full of vessels.

Vomer: the bone that forms the lower and posterior portion of the septum of the nose.

Xiphoid: the bone at the end of the sternum and the uppermost part of the abdomen which is the connection for the costophrenic angle.

Xylocaine and Lidocaine: types of local anesthesia used in the eyelid operation.

Z-plasty: plastic procedures to elongate a contracted scar.

TABLE OF CASES

Case	*Book §*
Karp v. Cooley, 493 F.2d 408 (5th Cir.), *cert. denied,* 419 U.S. 845, 94 S. Ct. 79 (1974)	§ 12.52
Kulak v. Nationwide Mut. Ins. Co., 40 N.Y.2d 140, 351 N.E.2d 735, 386 N.Y.S.2d 87 (1976)	§ 5.2
Marginian v. Allstate, 18 Ohio St. 3d 345, 481 N.E.2d 600 (1985)	§ 5.2
Meretsky v. Ellenby, 370 So. 2d 1222 (Fla. Dist. Ct. App. 1979)	§ 11.25
Merrit v. Reserve Ins. Co., 34 Cal. App. 3d 858, 110 Cal. Rptr. 511 (1973)	§ 5.2
Moser v. Stallings & Plastic Surgery Inst., 387 N.W.2d 599 (Iowa 1986)	§ 9.23
Nacarati v. Garrett, 351 Pa. Super. 437, 506 A.2d 428 (1986)	§ 12.52
Natason v. Kline, 186 Kan. 393, 350 P.2d 1093 (Sup. Ct. 1960), *on motion for rehearing,* 187 Kan. 1986, 354 P.2d 670 (Sup. Ct. 1960)	§ 12.52
Nelson v. F.W. Woolworth, Madison, WI, U.S. Dist. Ct. No. 81-6-643-5 (1984)	§ 1.1
Pasha v. Board of Medical Quality Assurance, 174 Cal. App. 3d 439, 219 Cal. Rptr. 778 (1985)	§ 11.25
Peter v. Travelers Ins. Co., 375 F. Supp. 1347 (C.D. Cal. 1974)	§ 5.2
Phelan v. State Farm Mutual, 114 Ill. App. 3d 96, 448 N.E.2d 579 (1983)	§ 5.2
Quadrini v. S. Korsky, 425 F. Supp. 81 (D. Conn. 1977)	§ 5.10
Raschel v. Rish, 110 A.D.2d 1067, 488 N.Y.S.2d 923 (1985)	§ 11.25
Schwartz v. Sar Corp., 19 Misc. 2d 660, 195 N.Y.S.2d 496, *rev'd on other grounds,* 9 A.D.2d 910, 195 N.Y.S.2d 819 (1959)	§ 5.2
Skripek v. Bergamo, 200 N.J. Super. 620, 491 A.2d 1336 (App. Div. 1985)	§ 12.52
Smoot v. State Farm Mut. Auto. Ins. Co., 299 F.2d 525 (5th Cir. 1962)	§ 5.2
Stiff v. Continental Casualty Co., No. 840402347 (Or. 1987)	§ 5.2
Suria v. Shiffman, 67 N.Y.S. 87, 490 N.E.2d 832, 499 N.Y.S.2d 913 (1986)	§ 12.52
Trader's & Gen. Ins. Co. v. Ridco Oil & Gas Co., 129 F.2d 621 (10th Cir. 1942)	§ 5.2
Wicker v. U.S. Fidelity, 211 So. 2d 420 (La. 1968)	§ 1.1

INDEX